POWER AND STATUS

20TH ANNIVERSARY VOLUME

ADVANCES IN GROUP PROCESSES

Series Editors: Edward J. Lawler and Shane R. Thye

ADVANCES IN GROUP PROCESSES   VOLUME 20

POWER AND STATUS

EDITED BY

SHANE R. THYE

Department of Sociology, University of South Carolina, USA

JOHN SKVORETZ

Department of Sociology, University of South Carolina, USA

2003

ELSEVIER
JAI

Amsterdam – Boston – Heidelberg – London – New York – Oxford
Paris – San Diego – San Francisco – Singapore – Sydney – Tokyo

ELSEVIER Ltd
The Boulevard, Langford Lane
Kidlington, Oxford OX5 1GB, UK

First edition 2003

A catalogue record from the British Library has been applied for.

ISBN: 0-7623-1030-8
ISSN: 0882-6145 (Series)

⊗ The paper used in this publication meets the requirements of ANSI/NISO Z39.48-1992 (Permanence of Paper).
Printed in The Netherlands.

CONTENTS

LIST OF CONTRIBUTORS

M. Hamit Fişek	Department of Psychology, Bogaziçi University, Istanbul, Turkey
Noah E. Friedkin	Department of Sociology, University of California, Santa Barbara, USA
Eugene C. Johnsen	Department of Mathematics, University of California, Santa Barbara, USA
Cathryn Johnson	Department of Sociology, Emory University, Atlanta, USA
Michael J. Lovaglia	Department of Sociology, University of Iowa, USA
Linda D. Molm	Department of Sociology, University of Arizona, Tucson, USA
Lisa Troyer	Department of Sociology, University of Iowa, USA
Marcel A. L. M. van Assen	Department of Methodology and Statistics, Tilburg University, The Netherlands
David G. Wagner	Department of Sociology, State University of New York at Albany, USA
Henry A. Walker	Department of Sociology, University of Arizona, Tucson, USA
Murray Webster, Jr.	Department of Sociology, University of North Carolina, Charlotte, USA
Robb Willer	Department of Sociology, Cornell University, USA
Morris Zelditch	Department of Sociology, Stanford University, USA

PREFACE

Last year we began a new trend in the *Advances in Group Processes* series. Our goal was to publish a set of five interrelated volumes that examine core issues or fundamental themes in the group processes arena. Each volume was to be organized around a particular problem, substantive area, or topic of study, broadly defined to include a range of methodological and theoretical orientations. Volume 20 represents the second volume of that series, addressing fundamental questions of *Power and Status*.

The volume begins with a paper by Friedkin and Johnsen. Its aim is to integrate their social influence network theory with affect control theory and expectation states theory. The latter two theories analyze situations in which the initial attitudes of group members are consensual – that is, all group members hold the same attitudes and beliefs at the onset of interaction. Friedkin and Johnsen relax this initial condition, asking what might happen if attitudes and beliefs are not consensually shared. They use social influence network theory to show how an influence network can alter initial beliefs in the direction of greater homogeneity. Their conceptualization brings principles of interpersonal influence, social network analysis, and affective organization to bear on the core ideas from affect control theory and the expectation states program.

The second paper addresses issues of influence and power from a different perspective. Linda Molm's "Power, Trust, and Fairness: Theoretical Comparisons of Forms of Exchange" examines how reciprocal forms of social exchange systematically differ from negotiated forms of social exchange. Her analysis shows that key dimensions of exchange (i.e. information regarding reciprocity, outcome contingencies, and timing of reward allocations) relate to perceptions of risk, exclusion or the withholding of rewards, and the salience of competitive interests. Based on these ideas, eight hypotheses are offered and tested with experimental data. The data are generally consistent with the hypotheses. Her work shows that different forms of exchange have different impacts on affective commitment, trust, and power use. The author concludes by discussing the broader implications of this work for general theories of exchange.

The next paper undertakes an unprecedented task in the negotiated exchange tradition. In "Exchange Networks: An Analysis of all Networks up to Size 9," Marcel A. L. M. van Assen considers the entire population of all unique exchange networks up to size nine, yielding 142,660 possible networks. Using the most parsimonious versions of Power-Dependence Theory and Network Resistance Theory, van Assen derives predictions for the entire population. He finds a tremendous amount of consensus between the two theories with respect to how networks are classified into strong, equal, or weak power types. The author also finds that, relative to their distribution in the overall population, empirically studied networks are disproportionately strong power types. This work promises to inspire tests of new and never before considered networks.

The next four papers address a compendium of issues related to status structuring in groups. First, in "Power, Status, and Collective Action: Developing Fundamental Theories to Address a Substantive Problem," Lovaglia, Willer and Troyer theorize connections between concepts at the heart of this volume: power and status. They assert that power is a fundamental basis for status when the negative emotional reactions emanating from power use are somehow blocked or mitigated. The authors propose a set of theoretical propositions to show how power and status are related. Several interesting implications are then derived, for instance, it follows from their theory that power users can increase their relative status through philanthropy. This insight suggests a solution to the classic free-rider problem in theories of collective action. Next, Fisek and Wagner offer a new test of Reward Expectations Theory in "Reward Expectations and Allocative Behaviors: A Mathematical Model." Here, the authors present a specific mathematical model to generate predictions in a setting where status differentiated individuals have the opportunity to allocate rewards to one another. Predictions from the model are then compared against two empirical studies conducted by Wagner. The data indicate a good fit at both the individual and aggregate level. This paper will undoubtedly draw substantial attention from those interested in status and justice processes because it expands reward expectations theory to incorporate new allocative behaviors and concrete settings.

The sixth paper represents a novel test of foundational ideas in the status literature. In "The Role of Social Identity Processes in Status Construction," Lisa Troyer presents an elaboration of Ridgeway's status construction theory that incorporates social identification processes as they relate to ingroup/outgroup bias. Specifically, she suggests that agents controlling resources will provide more rewards to those with whom they share a common social category than to others. This creates a kind of "double dissimilarity" known to trigger status construction processes. Troyer tests the new theoretical argument using data from thirty five dot-com organizations. This paper produces an interesting mix of ideas from theories of organizational culture, social identity, and status. The seventh paper entitled "Working on Status Puzzles" by Webster provides a comprehensive overview of the status literature. What differentiates this review from others of its kind is breadth of coverage and style of narration. In essence, Webster tracks different "puzzles" that emerged during each decade from the 1950s to today. The reader can see how theory construction and testing are intertwined, how the scientific brass rings of yesterday shape the ideas of today, and how the various branches of status theory came into existence. Overall, this paper is a wonderful review both for newcomers to the status literature and for seasoned veterans.

The final two chapters examine issues of power and status via legitimacy theory. In "The Legitimacy of Regimes," Zelditch and Walker review their research program, the aim of which is to understand the conditions under which social relationships (and accompanying rules) come to be viewed as normative or legitimate. They explicate a basic legitimation assumption that undergirds their cumulative research program, giving four necessary conditions for legitimation to occur. These authors have a history of publishing capstone pieces in *Advances* (see Zelditch & Walker, 1984, 2000) and the present paper is no exception. They review two dozen studies across twenty years, documenting their many successes and failures along the way. An important aspect of the paper is that is clarifies how theory and method connect, showing that knowledge evolves through a punctuated process of conjecture and refutation. Finally, in "Consideration of Legitimacy Processes in Teasing Out Two Puzzles in the Status Literature," Johnson analyzes two anomalies in the status tradition. She first asks how the salience of gender in a local task group is affected by the gender composition of larger organizational structures. Johnson suggests that when the gender composition of a group and organization are inconsistent (i.e. a female team leader of an all female team in a male dominated organization), gender salience will not necessarily be automatic. Rather, Johnson asserts that one way gender becomes salient is when an evaluation by a legitimate authority creates inconsistency in the group status structure. Her analysis sheds light on factors that trigger gender salience. Next, she addresses when status-versus identity-related behaviors are likely to be enacted. Again, Johnson theorizes that the key resides in the initial status structure of the group, and the legitimacy of such behaviors. Overall, this paper answers several important questions regarding gender activation in the modern organization.

Shane R. Thye
John Skvoretz
Volume Co-Editors

ATTITUDE CHANGE, AFFECT CONTROL, AND EXPECTATION STATES IN THE FORMATION OF INFLUENCE NETWORKS

Noah E. Friedkin and Eugene C. Johnsen

ABSTRACT

This paper works at the intersections of affect control theory, expectation states theory, and social influence network theory. First, we introduce social influence network theory into affect control theory. We show how an influence network may emerge from the pattern of interpersonal sentiments in a group and how the fundamental sentiments that are at the core of affect control theory (dealing with the evaluation, potency, and activity of self and others) may be modified by interpersonal influences. Second, we bring affect control theory and social influence network theory to bear on expectation states theory. In a task-oriented group, where persons' performance expectations may be a major basis of their interpersonal influence, we argue that persons' fundamental sentiments may mediate effects of status characteristics on group members' performance expectations. Based on the linkage of fundamental sentiments and interpersonal influence, we develop an account of the formation of influence networks in groups that is applicable to both status homogeneous and status heterogeneous groups of any size, whether or not they are completely connected, and that is not restricted in scope to task-oriented groups.

Power and Status
Advances in Group Processes, Volume 20, 1–29
Copyright © 2003 by Elsevier Ltd.
All rights of reproduction in any form reserved
ISSN: 0882-6145/doi:10.1016/S0882-6145(03)20001-1

1

INTRODUCTION

Recently, there have been efforts to develop linkages between some of the major lines of work in sociological social psychology – affect control theory (ACT), expectation states theory (EST), and social identity theory. Ridgeway and Smith-Lovin (1994) have described possible linkages between affect control theory and expectation states theory. Kalkoff and Barnum (2000) have described possible linkages between social identity theory and expectation states theory. These and other linking efforts (Skvoretz & Fararo, 1996) indicate points of intersection based on shared theoretical constructs and shed an integrative light on the domain of social psychology by joining different theoretical structures. Such efforts advance knowledge by developing links between extant theories, in contrast to advancements that are predicated on competition through elimination or subsumption of theories.[1]

Our present effort is exactly in this vein of establishing productive linkages. We believe that it is feasible and useful to link social influence network theory (a combinatorial theory of attitude change) with affect control theory and expectation states theory. Social influence network theory and affect control theory intersect on *sentiments*, which in affect control theory are attitudes about particular persons measured by semantic differential scales of evaluation, potency, and activity. Social influence network theory and expectation states theory intersect on *performance expectations*, which in expectation states theory are latent attitudes that affect interpersonal influence in task-oriented groups. As attitudes, sentiments and expectations are subject to endogenous interpersonal influences, so they may be influenced by the attitudes of others. A network of such endogenous interpersonal influences is often formed in social groups. However, neither affect control theory nor expectation states theory grapples directly with the implications of the presence of such networks. We currently do not have a good theoretical understanding of how the fundamental sentiments associated with persons' social identities or the performance expectations associated with persons' status positions are modified by the displayed attitudes of other group members, or how endogenous interpersonal influences in a group may generate equilibrium sentiments and expectations that are quite different from (and possibly more consensual than) the initial array of sentiments and expectations.

As we shall see, social influence network theory does not add anything further to the accounts of affect control theory and expectation states theory when the *initial* attitudes of group members are consensual, i.e. when they view the same object in the same way.[2] In affect control theory and expectation states theory, this is the typical situation analyzed. When there is an initial consensus, interpersonal influences are moot and equilibrium attitudes are the initial attitudes of each group member. However, matters become more complex and interesting when the attitudes of group members toward the same objects are heterogeneous and there is a network of interpersonal influence that connects the members of the group. A contribution of social influence network theory is to show how an influence network may operate to modify attitudes and how a more consensual set of attitudes can emerge from a sequence of interpersonal influences. As a prelude to our analysis, we briefly and roughly sketch the main features of affect control theory, expectation states theory, and social influence network theory, and we develop some of the possible links between them. Our main analytical emphasis will be on the linkage between affect control theory and social influence network theory. We will demonstrate how these theories, once joined, may bear on the account of the core constructs of expectation states theory (the performance expectations that are associated with persons' status positions and the influence networks in groups) and how an influence network may emerge from the process of attitude change about group members' interpersonal sentiments. We also will show how the standard prediction equation for persons' performance expectations in expectation states theory can be employed to predict influence networks in our social-influence-network-theory framework and how a relaxation of the EST assumption of consensual performance expectations is easily accommodated by our framework.

THREE THEORIES

Affect Control Theory

Affect control theory deals with mechanisms and associated behaviors and emotions that underlie the formation, maintenance, and transformation of persons' definitions of situations in the particular social settings in which they are interacting (Heise, 2002; Smith-Lovin & Heise, 1988). A detailed description of affect control theory, related computer software, and an extensive bibliography of the theoretical underpinnings and empirical supports for this theory may be found on David Heise's website (http://www.indiana.edu/~socpsy/ACT/).

Affect control theory posits that social situations entail a constellation of sentiments toward various objects, including the social setting (classroom, home, workplace), the social identity of the persons who are located in the setting (doctor, nurse, husband, child), the behaviors of the persons in the setting, and other salient characteristics of the persons (mood, gender, status) and their behaviors. Hence, for n persons with k-dimensional sentiments toward q objects, the social situation would be defined in terms of an $n \times k \times q$ matrix of scores that are indicative of persons' attitudes about the q objects. Prior to any interaction among the persons involved in a social situation, a set of *fundamental* sentiments are triggered by persons' identification or recognition of the objects in the situation. Affect control theory assumes that these fundamental sentiments are *normative* in the sense that the same matrix of sentiments would be expected for a different set of persons in identical situations. This homogeneity is assumed to be based on a cultural consensus in the population from which the persons involved in the situation are drawn. Affect-control investigators have obtained empirical estimates from surveys of the fundamental sentiments for a large number of objects, so that in applications of the theory a matrix of fundamental sentiments can be obtained a priori for an immense number of theoretically possible social situations.

Affect control theory posits that each person in a social situation will have a normative *expectation* about the likelihood of various events that might occur in that setting, based on the fundamental sentiments that are entailed in their initial definition of the situation.[3] The events that occur in a social setting do not necessarily conform to these expectations for a variety of reasons. Affect control theory posits that any such *deflection* (deviation) of actual events from expectation are *transitory* and that these deflections are diminished by homeostatic control or balancing mechanisms (involving actions or redefinitions) that bring experienced sentiments into closer conformity or fit with expected fundamental sentiments. Although perfect conformity with expectations may not be feasible, it is the movement toward greater conformity that is the fundamental social mechanism with which affect control theory is concerned. Events trigger felt and displayed emotions that signal the degree of deflection of events from expectations.

Persons may reduce deflections by altering their behavior (eventually bringing their behavior into closer accord with normative expectations) or by *redefining* the elements of the definition of the situation. If the social identities, setting, and other salient conditions of the situation are *fixed*, then a deflection can only be mitigated by new behaviors in subsequent events that bring the sentiments for these subsequent events closer to the fundamental sentiments for these fixed conditions. However, affect control theory also allows for *reidentifications* that involve a relabeling of the setting or the identities and characteristics of persons and other objects. In effect, a reidentification may reduce deflection by changing fundamental sentiments, so that now the experienced events in a setting are more consistent with normative expectation and do not produce as much stress.

The balancing mechanisms of affect control theory are grounded on consensual understandings in the culture or subculture of a population that a particular set of fundamental sentiments are appropriate or correct for the situation. Without discounting this explanation, we point out that when there is a lack of initial consensus on what is appropriate or correct, *interpersonal influences* in a group may produce the shared meanings and the strong normative foundations that underlie the equilibrating behaviors postulated by affect control theory. That is, in a group of persons who find themselves interacting in a situation, a consensual understanding about what is expected and correct may be *constructed* by them on the basis of a network of interpersonal influences that is being formed in the group.

Introducing Influence Networks into Affect Control Theory

Social influence network theory and affect control theory intersect on the fundamental sentiments that deal with persons' attitudes toward objects in a social situation. In affect control theory, a *semantic differential scale* is employed to describe persons' sentiments toward the objects that define a situation and the events that take place in it. Semantic differential scales are among the most widely employed attitudinal scales in social psychology (Osgood, May & Miron, 1975; Osgood, Suci & Tannenbaum, 1957). Such scales are constructed from pairs of antonyms (good or bad, wise or foolish, and so forth) that might describe an object. For each pair of antonyms, a scale consisting of five, seven, or nine possible positions or locations indicate the attitude of a person toward the object; for example, a scale with nine positions would be coded $-4, -3, -2, -1, 0, 1, 2, 3, 4$, and the middle position would indicate that one adjective is not better than other, or that both adjectives are irrelevant.

Semantic differential scales of attitudes are widely employed, in part, because they allow a standard or uniform set of antonym pairs to be applied to a large domain of different objects. The frequent and successful employment of this scaling approach to attitudes has suggested, in turn, that persons may be responding to a wide variety of different objects in terms of a common metric. From factor-analytic studies of semantic differential antonyms, it appears that the many possible word-items (pairs of antonyms) that have been employed in the construction of semantic differential scales are indicators of three underlying dimensions – *evaluation* (e.g. good vs. bad), *potency* (e.g. strong vs. weak), and *activity* (e.g. lively vs. quiet). A person's mean scores on the dimensions of evaluation, potency, and activity are referred to as the EPA profile for the target-object from the point of view of the source-person, who is the holder of the attitude. If the EPA profile is treated as a set of coordinates in three-dimensional space, then a spatial model of the distribution of persons' attitudes toward a common target-object is produced.

Social influence network theory is introduced into affect control theory by allowing persons' fundamental sentiments to be affected by other persons'

fundamental sentiments (cf. Robinson, 1996). Heterogeneous fundamental sentiments toward the same object may arise in various ways: different subcultures
(e.g. male vs. female subcultures) may have different sentiments towards the same
object, persons with similar identities (e.g. males) from different cultures may have
different sentiments toward the same object (e.g. females), or persons with similar
identities may identify the same object differently. Thus, endogenous interpersonal
influences – sentiments affecting sentiments – may modify persons' viewpoints
about the objects in their social environments. Leaving aside the particular formal
specification of this influence process, the proposition that such interpersonal
influences might be occurring is hardly startling. Indeed, Newcomb (1951)
suggested that the occurrence of endogenous interpersonal influence should be
taken as a basic postulate in social psychological theory: "Any observable behavior
[attitude, emotion, action] is not only a response (on the part of a subject) which is
to be treated as a dependent variable; it is also a stimulus to be perceived by others
with whom the subject interacts, and thus to be treated as an independent variable."
An influence network is the *structure* in which such endogenous interpersonal
responses occur.

Although affect control theory emphasizes that definitions of the situation
are constructed on the basis of widely shared orientations toward identities and
expected behaviors, the theory allows for within-group processes that modify
the identities that persons attribute to themselves and others in a particular
setting. We have previously noted that affect control theorists argue that such
reidentifications redefine the situation so that there is a closer correspondence
between the situated identities and their behaviors. We believe that there also may
be some reidentification based on endogenous interpersonal influence, that is,
as a direct response to the displayed sentiments of significant others toward the
objects that define a situation.[4] Therefore, we introduce a process of endogenous
interpersonal influence into the construction of a definition of a situation, based
on the assumption that persons may take into account (to varying degrees) the
fundamental sentiments of their significant others in refining their own fundamental sentiments about the salient objects involved in a social situation. Social
influence network theory is nuanced in that it allows for individual differences in
susceptibilities to interpersonal influence; hence, we do not stipulate that persons
necessarily modify their sentiments through a process of interpersonal influence
or that all persons involved in a situation will do so to the same extent.

Thus, our contribution to affect control theory is the idea that the fundamental
sentiments upon which deflections are based are not always strictly based on the
specification of the dyadic situation consisting of the identities of two persons,
their modifying characteristics, and setting. We are proposing that the normative
foundations of the fundamental sentiments are not entirely specified by the

fixed contextual conditions of the situation, but may to some extent be shaped by the interpersonal influences in the situation. Hence, the basis of deflections may not be the discrepancy between the *initial* fundamental sentiments and the transitory impressions that are associated with a particular behavior, but instead may involve a set of *influenced* fundamental sentiments that have been shaped by the interpersonal influences of significant others. When there are multiple persons involved in a situation who are simultaneously forming sentiments about the salient objects in the setting, and when at least some of these persons are susceptible to interpersonal influence, then the normative sentiments (and expected behaviors) for the situation may be "negotiated" within the group to some extent. Interpersonal influence among persons with heterogeneous identities may produce sentiments that are very different from the initial fundamental sentiments that are broadly associated with the identities in the population-level culture. Indeed, once endogenous interpersonal influences are introduced it becomes at least a theoretical possibility that a person may come to hold sentiments that are radically inconsistent with his or her initial fundamental sentiments toward some object. Whether such persons experience stress as a consequence of such a structural deflection from their initial sentiments is an open question.

Expectation States Theory

Expectation states theory is a family of models concerned with the formation of inequalities of individual behavior and interpersonal interaction in task-oriented groups (Balkwell, 1991; Berger, Conner & Fisek, 1974; Berger, Fisek, Norman & Zelditch Jr., 1977; Berger, Wagner & Zelditch Jr., 1985; Fisek, Berger & Norman, 1991; Fisek, Norman & Nelson-Kilger, 1992; Skvoretz, Webster & Whitmeyer, 1999; Wagner & Berger, 1993). Following Bales (1950), the initial emphasis of the theory was on an account of how inequalities of interpersonal influence emerge in status homogenous groups, where there are no differences among group members on certain socio-demographic characteristics; however, the theory was quickly extended to include an account of how the emergent inequalities of interpersonal influence in heterogeneous groups are shaped by members' socio-demographic characteristics.

In expectation states theory, the key construct in the explanation of influence inequalities is a latent attitude – a performance expectation – that a person forms about each group member, including him or her self, concerning the value of a person's task-relevant opinions and actions. In status *homogeneous* groups, expectation state theory posits that the main antecedents of a performance expectation are initial manifest differences in behavior (e.g. persons' self-assertion or quiescence).[5] In status *heterogeneous* groups, the main antecedents of a performance expectation include general socio-demographic characteristics of the group's members (e.g. the members' age, sex, skin color, height, weight, attractiveness, and social class) and more specific task-related characteristics that suggest some relevant expertise. A major accomplishment of expectation states theory is the development of a "graph-analytic" model that predicts persons' performance expectations based on socio-demographic characteristics. Expectation states theory posits that group members compare each other in terms of their expected levels of task-related performance and that these comparisons govern their behavior toward one another, including their resistance or acceptance of interpersonal influence from particular persons in the group (Festinger, 1954). The empirical focus in expectation states research has been on the dyad, where influence outcomes have been measured as the proportion of disagreements resolved in favor of one member of the dyad or the other. Because expectation states theory assumes that the effects of status characteristics on performance expectations and interpersonal influence are based on population-level consensual understandings about the meaning and relevance of particular status characteristics, the predicted pattern of interpersonal influence that emerges in these dyads should tend to reflect the broader cultural consensus concerning the value of these different status characteristics in the population.

In recent path-breaking theoretical work, Whitmeyer (2002) has demonstrated that the graph-analytic models of expectation states theory, that have been employed to predict performance expectations, may be represented more parsimoniously by algebraic equations of the following form:

$$\Phi = \exp\left[-a\sum_r n_r g(r)\right] - \exp\left[-a\sum_r p_r g(r)\right], \tag{1}$$

where Φ is the predicted performance expectation for a person with a given array of status characteristics, $r = \{1, 2, 3\}$ is the relevance level of a status condition, p_r is the number of status conditions of relevance r on which a person's status value is high (positive), n_r is the number of status conditions of relevance r on which a person's status value is low (negative), $a > 0$ is a constant, $g(r) > 0$ is one of the following functions

$$g(r) = \begin{cases} c^{3-r} + c^{2-r} & \text{Berger et al. (1977)} \\ c^{6-r} + c^{5-r} & \text{Balkwell (1991)} \\ c^{1-r} + c^{-r} & \text{Fisek et al. (1992)} \end{cases}$$

and c is an estimated constant ($c \approx 3$). In turn, the performance expectations of group members $\{\Phi_1, \Phi_2, \ldots, \Phi_n\}$ are linearly transformed into a measure (B) of influence behavior; for instance, $B_{12} = \beta_0 + \beta_1(\Phi_1 - \Phi_2)$ in the case of a dyad.

We note that an alternative expression for Eq. (1) is

$$\Phi = \exp\left[-\beta_0 \sum_r \beta_r n_r\right] - \exp\left[-\beta_0 \sum_r \beta_r p_r\right], \tag{2}$$

where the β coefficients are estimable constants.[6] This reformulation suggests that even simpler expressions may suffice. For example, if we take the two leading terms in the infinite series expansion of the exponential function $e^{-x} = 1 - (x/1!) + (x^2/2!) - (x^3/3!) + \cdots$, that is $1 - x$, performance expectations might be adequately predicted by a simple linear combination of status variables, i.e.

$$\Phi = \sum_k \beta_k X_k = \beta_0 \sum_{r=1}^{3} \beta_r p_r - \beta_0 \sum_{r=1}^{3} \beta_r n_r = \beta_0 \sum_{r=1}^{3} \beta_r (p_r - n_r), \tag{3}$$

where each status variable X_k involves a dichotomous coding (-1 for negative status, $+1$ for positive status) and there are only *three* homogeneous classes of these variables with three corresponding distinct effects (β_1, β_2, β_3). These, in turn, can be transformed into interpersonal influences according to a function that we shall specify. Whether such a reformulation captures all of the effects of the standard expectation states formulation is an open question that we believe is worth pursuing.[7]

Introducing Influence Networks into Expectation States Theory

We have mentioned that most of the empirical work in the expectation states tradition has been concentrated on an analysis of dyads, and this focus is for us a major limitation of the tradition; see the work on larger discussion groups (e.g. Robinson & Balkwell, 1995; Smith-Lovin, Skvoretz & Hawkins, 1986). We are interested in the analysis of systems of interpersonal influence of arbitrary size; moreover, we suspect that dyadic systems have certain unusual properties and that it may be misleading to concentrate analysis on them.[8] In the expectation states research tradition, there has been some work on the effects of persons' performance expectations on other persons' performance expectations; it is assumed that the influential expectations are *fixed* conditions that are affecting the performance expectations of some focal person (Fisek, Berger & Norman, 1995; Troyer & Younts, 1997; Webster & Sobieszek, 1974; Webster & Whitmeyer, 1999, 2002). However, unlike persons' status characteristics, influential performance expectations may not be fixed conditions. While the performance expectations of a person are being influenced by the performance expectations of others, others' performance expectations also may be influenced and undergoing modification. Hence, in natural groups, the grounds on which persons are forming attitudes about themselves and others may be shifting rather than fixed, especially when there is substantial initial *disagreement* on appropriate expectations. In its account of the emergence of stable influence structures in newly formed task-oriented groups, we believe that expectation states theory somewhat overstates the general extent of *initial* consensus on performance expectations (the theory assumes consensus as an initial condition), and that it does not adequately detail the *mechanism* by which interpersonal agreements are produced on performance expectations through the interactions of the group members. Thus, when there is a consensus on performance expectations in a group, we believe that it often has been produced *within the group*, through a process of endogenous interpersonal influence among its members. When an observed consensus is not based on the simple importation of a population-level agreement, then the intragroup process that has produced the consensus should be formally incorporated into expectation states theory.

The work on interpersonal influences on performance expectations has not described a mechanism by which the expectations of the sources of influence are also being influenced and has not shown how, in concrete mathematical terms and under what conditions, a consensus will arise as a result of a sequence of interpersonal influences among group members. The work that has been conducted on the diffusion of shared understandings of the performance value of different status characteristics has been motivated by the assumption (central to expectation states theory, but one that we question) that persons *enter into* groups with a substantial degree of consensus about the relevance and performance value of various status characteristics to task-oriented activities (Ridgeway, 1991; Ridgeway & Balkwell, 1997). For us, what is most fundamental about expectation states theory is *not* the assertion of an initial consensus of status beliefs (we think that this assertion can be discarded); it is the assertion that status characteristics affect persons' attitudes about each other (their performance expectations) and that, regardless of the degree of initial consensus on group members' attitudes, social processes operate within groups to generate such consensus and, in turn, a stable network of interpersonal influence that reflects the agreement that has been constructed in the group. Our theoretical focus is on the social process within a group that generates such consensus and stable patterns of influence, where they do not exist a priori.

Social Influence Network Theory

During the past decade, there has been a dramatic increase of work on how social networks are formed and change (Arrow, 1997; Carley, 1990, 1991; Doreian &

Stokman, 1997; Lazer, 2001; Stokman & Berveling, 1998). Our focus is on the *influence* networks in groups that shape group members' attitudes, and we develop a model of the evolution of such influence networks in which the set of attitudes that group members have about themselves and others (i.e. their sentiments) affect the network of interpersonal influences among them, the influence network in turn modifies persons' sentiments, and so on, until an equilibrium is reached. Thus, our theoretical orientation to network dynamics is distinctly social psychological, and our present effort is to link these dynamics to theoretical constructs that are the cornerstones of affect control theory (sentiments and identities) and expectation states theory (performance expectations and status characteristics).

In much of our previous work (Friedkin, 1991, 1998, 1999, 2001; Friedkin & Johnsen, 1990, 1997, 1999), we have assumed that an influence network is a stable social context in which the process of attitude change unfolds:

$$y_i^{(t+1)} = a_{ii}(w_{i1}y_1^{(t)} + w_{i2}y_2^{(t)} + \cdots + w_{in}y_n^{(t)}) + (1 - a_{ii})y_i^{(t)} \qquad (4)$$

for each of the n persons in the group, $i = 1, 2, \ldots, n$ and $t = 1, 2, \ldots, \infty$. The attitudes of the persons at time t are $y_1^{(t)}, y_2^{(t)}, \ldots, y_n^{(t)}$ and their initial attitudes are $y_i^{(1)}, y_2^{(1)}, \ldots, y_n^{(1)}$. The set of influences of the group members on person i is $\{w_{i1}, w_{i2}, \ldots, w_{in}\}$ where $0 \leq w_{ij} \leq 1$, and $\sum_j w_{ij} = 1$. The *susceptibility* of person i to the influence of others is a_{ii}, where $0 \leq a_{ii} \leq 1$ and $a_{ii} = 1 - w_{ii}$. The system of equations described by Eq. (4) can be represented as

$$\mathbf{y}^{(t+1)} = \mathbf{AWy}^{(t)} + (\mathbf{I} - \mathbf{A})\mathbf{y}^{(1)}, \qquad (5)$$

where $\mathbf{y}^{(t)}$ is an $n \times 1$ vector of persons' attitudes on an issue at time t, $\mathbf{W} = [w_{ij}]$ is an $n \times n$ matrix of interpersonal influences, and $\mathbf{A} = \text{diag}(a_{11}, a_{22}, \ldots, a_{nn})$ is an $n \times n$ diagonal matrix of the persons' susceptibilities to interpersonal influence on the issue. Simply stated, the process is one in which at each time period, every person in the group forms a revised attitude that is a *weighted average* of the attitudes of the members of the group in the immediately previous time period (including the person's own previous attitude) and the person's initial attitude.

A Dynamic Influence Network

We have always viewed Eq. (5) as a *special case* of a more general model in which persons' susceptibilities and interpersonal influences might change over time (Friedkin & Johnsen, 1990),

$$\mathbf{Y}^{(t+1)} = \mathbf{A}^{(t)}\mathbf{W}^{(t)}\mathbf{Y}^{(t)} + (\mathbf{I} - \mathbf{A}^{(t)})\mathbf{Y}^{(1)}, \qquad (6)$$

but we have not previously attempted to specify the functions that govern the changes in the influence network. We do so now by linking social influence network theory and affect control theory. We shall describe a process in which persons' initial sentiments determine a network of interpersonal influences that, in turn, modifies sentiments that, in turn, modifies interpersonal influences and so on, within the constraints of interpersonal visibility, so that an initial set of fundamental sentiments are modified by interpersonal influences to produce equilibrium sentiments and a stable influence network.

The linkage between our theory and affect control theory is an $n \times n \times 3$ matrix of sentiments, $Y^{(t)} = [y_{ijk}^{(t)}]$, where $\{y_{ij1}^{(t)}, y_{ij2}^{(t)}, y_{ij3}^{(t)}\}$ is the EPA profile for person j from the viewpoint of person i. For $t = 1$, $Y^{(t)} = [y_{ijk}^{(t)}]$ describes the *fundamental sentiments* of the group members towards themselves and each other. For $t > 1$, assuming that the fundamental sentiments are subject to interpersonal influence, $Y^{(t)} = [y_{ijk}^{(t)}]$ describes the revised sentiments of the group members that have been influenced by other members' sentiments. In our model of the evolution of the influence network that is detailed below, we assume that sentiments affect interpersonal influence via a latent construct – the *salience* of self and others – that is at the foundations of interpersonal influence.

Interpersonal influence depends on interpersonal visibility and salience. Person j's attitudes cannot directly influence person i's attitudes unless they are visible and salient for person i. Let $R^{(t)} = [r_{ij}^{(t)}]$ be the *visibility* matrix for the group

$$
R^{(t)} = \begin{bmatrix} 1 & r_{12}^{(t)} & \cdots & r_{1n}^{(t)} \\ r_{21}^{(t)} & 1 & \cdots & r_{2n}^{(t)} \\ \vdots & \vdots & \ddots & \vdots \\ r_{n1}^{(t)} & r_{n2}^{(t)} & \cdots & 1 \end{bmatrix}, \tag{7}
$$

where $r_{ij}^{(t)} = 1$ if person i is acquainted with person j and $r_{ij}^{(t)} = 0$ otherwise.[9] We restrict our analysis to those groups in which every person is acquainted with at least one other person in the group; hence, we stipulate that $\sum_{k \neq i}^{n} r_{ik}^{(t)} > 0$ for all i. Let $S^{(t)} = [s_{ij}^{(t)}]$ be the *salience* matrix for the group,

$$
S^{(t)} = \begin{bmatrix} s_{11}^{(t)} & s_{12}^{(t)} & \cdots & s_{1n}^{(t)} \\ s_{21}^{(t)} & s_{22}^{(t)} & \cdots & s_{2n}^{(t)} \\ \vdots & \vdots & \ddots & \vdots \\ s_{n1}^{(t)} & s_{n2}^{(t)} & \cdots & s_{nn}^{(t)} \end{bmatrix}, \tag{8}
$$

where $0 \le s_{ij}^{(t)} \le 1$ indicates the potential salience of person j's attitudes for person i. In terms of these constructs, the matrix of interpersonal influence, $\boldsymbol{W}^{(t)} = [w_{ij}^{(t)}]$

$$
\boldsymbol{W}^{(t)} =
\begin{bmatrix}
w_{11}^{(t)} & w_{12}^{(t)} & \cdots & w_{1n}^{(t)} \\
w_{21}^{(t)} & w_{22}^{(t)} & \cdots & w_{2n}^{(t)} \\
\vdots & \vdots & \ddots & \vdots \\
w_{n1}^{(t)} & w_{n2}^{(t)} & \cdots & w_{nn}^{(t)}
\end{bmatrix},
\tag{9}
$$

is specified as one in which the weight accorded to one's self *is* the perceived salience of one's self

$$
w_{ii}^{(t)} = s_{ii}^{(t)},
\tag{10}
$$

and the weight accorded to an acquaintance is a function of the *relative* salience of that acquaintance

$$
w_{ij}^{(t)} =
\begin{cases}
(1 - s_{ii}^{(t)}) \dfrac{r_{ij}^{(t)} s_{ij}^{(t)}}{\sum_{k \neq i}^{n} r_{ik}^{(t)} s_{ik}^{(t)}} & \text{for } \sum_{k \neq i}^{n} r_{ik}^{(t)} s_{ik}^{(t)} \neq 0 \\[2ex]
(1 - s_{ii}^{(t)}) \dfrac{r_{ij}^{(t)}}{\sum_{k \neq i}^{n} r_{ik}^{(t)}} & \text{for } \sum_{k \neq i}^{n} r_{ik}^{(t)} s_{ik}^{(t)} = 0
\end{cases}
\tag{11}
$$

Hence, $0 \le w_{ij}^{(t)} \le 1$ and $\sum_{j=1}^{n} w_{ij}^{(t)} = 1$ for all i and $t = 1, 2, \ldots, \infty$. In turn, we posit that salience is a function of a linear combination of conditions

$$
s_{ij}^{(t)} =
\begin{cases}
\dfrac{\exp\{\lambda z_{ij}^{(t)}\} - 1}{\exp\{\lambda z_{ij}^{(t)}\} + 1} & \text{for } z_{ij}^{(t)} \geq 0, \\[2ex]
0 & \text{for } z_{ij}^{(t)} < 0
\end{cases}
\tag{12}
$$

where

$$
z_{ij}^{(t)} = \beta_{ij0}^{(t)} + \beta_{ij1}^{(t)} x_{ij1}^{(t)} + \beta_{ij2}^{(t)} x_{ij2}^{(t)} + \cdots,
\tag{13}
$$

$\lambda > 0$ is a constant and $-\infty < z_{ij}^{(t)} < \infty$. Note that Eq. (13) is *very* general in allowing a heterogeneous set of coefficients. A simple special case of Eq. (13) is

$$
z_{ij}^{(t)} = \beta_0 + \beta_1^{(t)} x_{ij1}^{(t)} + \beta_2^{(t)} x_{ij2}^{(t)} + \cdots
\tag{14}
$$

or, if $z_{ii}^{(t)}$ and $z_{ij}^{(t)}$ respond to different conditions, or to the same conditions in different ways,

$$z_{ij}^{(t)} = \beta_0 + \beta_1 x_{ij1}^{(t)} + \beta_2 x_{ij2}^{(t)} + \cdots \qquad (15a)$$

and

$$z_{ii}^{(t)} = \tilde{\beta}_0 + \tilde{\beta}_1 x_{ii1}^{(t)} + \tilde{\beta}_2 x_{ii2}^{(t)} + \cdots \qquad (15b)$$

for $i \neq j$. It may make sense to disentangle and treat separately the conditions that affect persons' attitudes about themselves from the conditions that affect persons' attitudes about other group members, as we have done in Eqs (15a) and (15b), although this theoretical distinction is not made in either affect control theory or expectation states theory. Even for those variables that have noteworthy effects on both "self" and "other" attitudes, the effects may be different; for example, the effect of knowing that some other person j is an expert on an issue may not be the same as the effect of knowing that you (i) are an expert. Moreover, certain group-level conditions, such as a general demand or pressure for consensus, may have an important main effect in lowering self-salience, but have no bearing on the level of salience accorded to particular others.[10]

FORMAL LINKAGES AND ILLUSTRATIONS

Linking to Affect Control Theory

In line with affect control theory, we posit that interpersonal sentiments toward one's self and particular others, on the dimensions of evaluation, potency, and activity, are among the immediate (direct) determinants of salience:

$$z_{ij}^{(t)} = \beta_{ij0} + \beta_{ij1} y_{ij1}^{(t)} + \beta_{ij2} y_{ij2}^{(t)} + \beta_{ij3} y_{ij3}^{(t)}$$

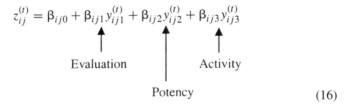

Evaluation   Activity

Potency   (16)

This equation may be easily elaborated to include other determinants of salience; for instance, bases of social power (French & Raven, 1959), status characteristics, and other conditions directly affecting persons' salience may be included. As we have illustrated in Fig. 1, we believe that many of these conditions are *antecedents* of the sentiments that are at the core of affect control theory (evaluation, potency,

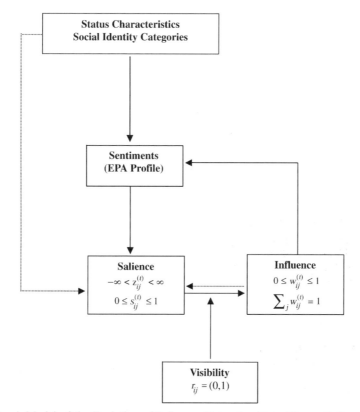

Fig. 1. A Model of the Evolution of Influence Networks. *Note:* The mediating role of
sentiments is an open empirical issue.

activity) and that these sentiments, in turn, affect salience. After controlling for
persons' sentiments, there may or may not be any noteworthy *direct* effects of
status characteristics and identity categories on salience. Our tentative theoretical
position is that persons' displayed sentiments towards themselves and others in a
group have a major role in the determination of interpersonal influence networks
and that alternative mechanisms may be discounted; specifically, in terms of the
path diagram shown in Fig. 1, we believe that two direct effects indicated by the
dotted arrows (⸺▶) may be negligible effects.

Hence, in this social influence process, the sentiments of group members
towards themselves and others are being shaped by interpersonal influences that,
in turn, are being affected by the sentiments of group members, and so on. The
displayed attitudes of influential others toward person *i* describe a viewpoint on

person i's identity that may change i's self-orientation depending on i's susceptibility to interpersonal influence. Person i's attitude toward self may be a *reflected
appraisal* of the attitudes of others, but this interpersonal determination of i's
self-orientation is governed by his or her susceptibility to influence. Interpersonal
influences on i may either support, lower, or heighten person i's self-orientation
depending on whose attitudes are influential. In this process, person i is not only
a potential recipient of influence, he or she is also a potential *source* of influence:
person i is simultaneously a recipient and an agent of influence and these "roles"
are determined, respectively, by i's susceptibility to influence and by the amount
of influence that is being accorded to i by others. Because person i may directly or
indirectly influence those persons who are having some influence on him or her,
person i may shape the social environment in which he or she is situated so that the
definition of the situation as construed by *others* more closely corresponds to person i's own *initial* definition. Hence, the agents of influence are in competition with
each other, whether or not they recognize it, in the determination of the definition of
the situation for each person. This competition is especially clear when a *consensual* definition of the situation emerges from the process, because in that case each
person's *initial* position (their initial fundamental sentiments) has a proportionate
contribution in determining the content of the consensual understanding of the
group as a whole.

   If this process, Eq. (6), attains an equilibrium, then

$$Y^{(\infty)} = A^{(\infty)} W^{(\infty)} Y^{(\infty)} + (I - A^{(\infty)})Y^{(1)} = V^{(\infty)} Y^{(1)} \tag{17}$$

where $V^{(\infty)} = [v_{ij}^{\infty}]$ is the matrix of reduced-form coefficients, $0 \leq v_{ij}^{(\infty)} \leq 1$ and
$\sum_j v_{ij}^{(\infty)} = 1$, that transforms the initial fundamental sentiments of the group members into their equilibrium sentiments, $Y^{(\infty)}$. These equilibrium sentiments are
the more or less *influenced* fundamental sentiments of the n group members about
each other on each of the three dimensions of evaluation, potency, and activity.
Group members' sentiments and the pattern of interpersonal visibility determines
persons' susceptibilities, $A^{(\infty)}$, and influences, $W^{(\infty)}$, so that the equilibrium
influence structure of the group also is completely determined by the initial fundamental sentiments among the group members about one another and themselves,
$Y^{(1)}$, and by the fixed pattern of interpersonal visibility in the group, R. The direct
or total influences, $W^{(\infty)}$ or $V^{(\infty)}$ respectively, may involve a consensual stratification of interpersonal influences or more complex patterns of heterogeneous
influences.

   If a group's equilibrium sentiments and influences are formed during the
discussion of a particular substantive issue, then the development of persons'
positions on the substantive issue may evolve in parallel with the process that is

forming the interpersonal sentiments and influences in the group. Once a stable influence network is formed, it may provide a fixed social context for a domain of subsequent issues that arise in the group

$$Y^{(t+1)} = A^{(\infty)}W^{(\infty)}Y^{(t)} + (I - A^{(\infty)})Y^{(1)} \qquad (18)$$

where now $Y^{(t)}$ represents any one of a number of other issues that may arise in the group. Equation (18) is simply the model described by Eq. (5), except that now we have provided for the evolution of the influence network that is observed in the group (i.e. $W^{(\infty)} = W$ and $A^{(\infty)} = A$).

To illustrate the application of this approach, consider the following matrix of EPA sentiments for a male husband and female wife:

Sentiments Held By	Sentiments About					
	Male Husband			Female Wife		
Male						
$t = 1$	1.18	1.59	0.62	2.31	1.17	1.06
$t = \infty$	1.39	1.55	0.68	2.19	1.12	1.04
Female						
$t = 1$	2.27	1.36	0.93	1.67	0.88	0.97
$t = \infty$	2.17	1.38	0.90	1.73	0.91	0.98

Each set of three numbers contains the evaluation, potency, and activity sentiments of the row person for the column person. The $t = 1$ sentiments were obtained from David Heise's INTERACT program. The $t = \infty$ sentiments are the equilibrium sentiments of the husband and wife that are predicted from the social influence network theory that we have described. We have based the salience of person j for person i on the raw score of the *evaluation* dimension of the EPA profile, on $\lambda = 1$ in Eq. (12) and on $z_{ij}^{(t)} = y_{ij1}^{(t)}$ in Eq. (16). The predicted equilibrium network of direct effects, $W^{(\infty)}$, is

$$\begin{matrix} 0.600 & 0.400 \\ 0.301 & 0.699 \end{matrix}$$

and the corresponding network of total effects, $V^{(\infty)}$, is

$$\begin{matrix} 0.810 & 0.190 \\ 0.093 & 0.907 \end{matrix}$$

Interpersonal influences have not strongly modified the fundamental sentiments of the husband and wife about themselves and each other, because the self-weight of each is high and, therefore, their susceptibilities to influence are low.

Linking to Expectation States Theory

It is possible to link social influence network theory with expectation states theory *without* the construct of persons' sentiments. In Fig. 1, simply replace the construct of sentiment with the construct of performance expectation. Hence, we might simply stipulate that

$$z_{ij}^{(t)} = \beta_{ij0} + \beta_{ij1} y_{ij1}^{(t)} \tag{19}$$

where $y_{ij1}^{(t)}$ is person i's *performance expectation* for person j, with the understanding that these performance expectations may not be measurable (expectation states theorists argue that they are not). An important special case of Eq. (19) is

$$z_{ij}^{(t)} = \beta_0 + \beta_1 y_{j1}^{(t)} \tag{20}$$

in which person j has the same salience at time t for all group members. In this special case, if the initial set of performance expectations are determined by Eq. (1), then the *initial* performance expectations are the predictions of the expectation states model, i.e. $y_{j1}^{(1)} = \Phi_j$. Given an initial consensus of expectations, the predicted equilibrium performance expectations are simply the initial performance expectations of the group, and the equilibrium influence structure of the group is determined directly (at $t = 2$) by these initial expectations. Thus, the constraints involved in the special case described by Eq. (20), i.e. consensual initial performance expectations, provide a straightforward dovetailing of expectation states theory and social influence network theory. From our perspective, it would be more interesting theoretically if *individual differences* were allowed and predicted in persons' performance expectations; that is, if Eq. (1) were modified so that different members of a group might have different performance expectations for the same target persons. But whether or not individual differences in performance expectations are allowed, if endogenous interpersonal influences are viewed as operating *directly* on persons' performance expectations, then an expectation states theorist may employ our approach to grapple with a larger domain of influence structures without incorporating into his or her theoretical account the *sentiments* that are the key constructs of affect control theory.

However, as Fig. 1 has illustrated, we believe that a more exciting line of theoretical development is to link expectation states theory and social influence network theory *through* the sentiments that are the focal constructs in affect control theory. In affect control theory, persons' fundamental sentiments are based on individual variables (identities and traits) and contextual conditions (situation, culture). The identities include a subset of the specific and diffuse status characteristics considered by expectation states theory as being determinants of persons' *performance expectations* for themselves and others in a particular task domain. Not all of these status characteristics are dealt with in the most recent implementation of affect control theory, but there is no theoretical limitation in affect control theory that would prohibit the inclusion of any specific or diffuse status characteristic. Moreover, a substantive application of affect control theory to *task-oriented* groups does not present any serious theoretical problems, because affect control theory is in principle applicable to such situations. Ridgeway and Smith-Lovin (1994, p. 225) suggest that task-specific status is "less easily handled by affect control theory" but this is not to say that fundamental sentiments cannot be formed that are the resultants of an interaction between status and task.

A key question is whether the performance expectations that are at the heart of expectation states theory have a theoretical status that is *independent* of the fundamental sentiments that are at the heart of affect control theory. Ridgeway and Smith-Lovin (1994, p. 225) state, "There is no simple translation between performance expectations and fundamental sentiments . . ." We are not convinced by Ridgeway and Smith-Lovin's negative appraisal of the possibility of a close relationship between these constructs; we suggest instead that this translation problem is an *open* theoretical issue (Driskell & Webster, 1997; Fisek & Berger, 1998; Lovaglia, 1997; Shelly, 1993). In task-oriented groups, persons' fundamental sentiments may determine a salience, i.e. each z_{ij} in Eq. (13), which is in substance a *performance expectation*.[11] If this is so, then the effects of status characteristics on performance expectations are *mediated* by persons' fundamental sentiments as in Fig. 1. Performance expectations may be high because of a positive *evaluation* of a person's competence, or because of the perceived *forcefulness* or capability of a person to achieve or foster group tasks, or because of the perceived *activity* or participation of the person with the task, or because of a combination of these dimensions (Kemper & Collins, 1990; Robinson, 1996; Skvoretz & Fararo, 1996).[12] If this general theoretical position has some merit, then it would establish a linkage between the three theories, and we think that this possibility is worth intensive investigation. It is premature in our view to dismiss the possibility of the existence of translation functions between persons' fundamental sentiments and performance expectations. For groups that are *not* task-oriented, the z_{ij} in Eq. (13) need not be a performance expectation, but instead a more general latent construct of the degree of a person's attitudinal respect, esteem, or admiration for themselves and particular other persons.

The following illustration shows how affect control theory incorporates status characteristics into its account of the definition of situations and how social influence network theory extends affect control theory to include an account of the emergence of an influence network. In this illustration, we again deal with a dyadic interaction between a male husband and female wife, but in this case the husband is educated and the wife is uneducated:

Sentiments Held By	Sentiments About					
	Educated-Male Husband			Uneducated-Female Wife		
Educated-Male						
$t = 1$	1.46	1.61	0.45	0.02	−0.73	0.51
$t = \infty$	1.46	1.61	0.45	0.02	−0.73	0.51
Uneducated-Female						
$t = 1$	1.88	1.77	0.93	−0.28	−0.94	0.04
$t = \infty$	1.46	1.61	0.46	0.02	−0.73	0.51

In this example, we have based the salience of person j for person i on the raw score of the *potency* dimension of the EPA profile: $\lambda = 1$ in Eq. (12) and $z_{ij}^{(t)} = y_{ij2}^{(t)}$ in Eq. (16). We shift the basis from evaluation to potency because the status differentiation of the husband and wife (educated vs. uneducated) is likely to make power the key foundation of salience.[13] Under these assumptions, the predicted equilibrium network of direct effects, $W^{(\infty)}$, is

$$0.623 \quad 0.377$$
$$0.992 \quad 0.008$$

and the corresponding network of total effects, $V^{(\infty)}$, is

$$0.998 \quad 0.002$$
$$0.990 \quad 0.010$$

The emergent influence network is highly stratified, with the influence of the educated male husband being much greater than the influence of the uneducated female wife. The total effects matrix indicates that the husband accords little weight to the wife (0.002) while the wife accords a substantial weight (0.990) to the husband. Note that while the fundamental sentiments of the husband have hardly changed, the wife's sentiments about her husband have come to more closely reflect his *own* initial sentiments about himself and the wife's sentiments about *herself* have come to more closely reflect the husband's initial sentiments about her. Her susceptibility to influence is large and his is not. Thus, issue outcomes should substantially reflect the initial preferences of the husband.

Expectation states theory also has been concerned with an account of the emergence of stratified influences in status *homogeneous* groups. The basic argument is that even when a group is homogeneous on various socio-demographic characteristics, there are individual differences that will generate unequal influence. Clearly, such an argument can be framed in terms of a translation of fundamental sentiments into salience. We believe that in most situations there will be some, more or less marked, degree of initial heterogeneity of sentiments (even among status peers). Hence, even in status homogeneous groups, variation among persons on the EPA sentiment dimensions may produce inequalities of interpersonal salience and influence.

To illustrate how individual differences among peers may generate a stable influence network consider the matrix of fundamental sentiments for four male engineers with different personality traits. Again, these sentiments are obtained from David Heise's INTERACT program.

	1	2	3	4
1	Confident (1.11, 1.50, 0.81)	Agreeable (1.19, 0.18, 0.36)	Indifferent (−0.12, −0.03, −0.18)	Stubborn (−0.61, 1.06, 0.44)
2	Intelligent (1.13, 1.28, 0.34)	Confused (−0.39, −0.32, 0.68)	Thoughtful (1.51, 0.74, 0)	Experienced (0.97, 1.01, −0.10)
3	Bossy (−1.12, 1.37, 0.64)	Stupid (−0.94, −0.44, 0.51)	Bored (−0.70, −0.30, −0.50)	Insecure (−0.61, −0.68, 0.32)
4	Reckless (−0.96, 0.72, 1.72)	Annoying (−1.10, 0.32, 1.21)	Apathetic (−0.57, −0.55, −0.25)	Cautious (0.82, 0.32, −0.36)

Engineer 1 is confident, engineer 2 is confused, engineer 3 is bored, and engineer 4 is cautious. Their sentiments are heterogeneous. For instance, the confident engineer views his confused peer as agreeable, his bored peer as indifferent, and his cautious peer as stubborn; the cautious engineer views his confident peer as reckless, his confused peer as annoying, and his bored peer as apathetic; and so on. If salience is determined by a magnified raw score of the *evaluation* dimension of these fundamental sentiments, i.e. $\lambda = 5$ in Eq. (12) and $z_{ij}^{(t)} = y_{ij1}^{(t)}$ in Eq. (16), then the emergent influence network of direct effects, $W^{(\infty)}$, is

$$
\begin{array}{cccc}
0.992 & 0.008 & 0.000 & 0.000 \\
0.000 & 0.000 & 0.000 & 1.000 \\
0.000 & 0.000 & 0.000 & 1.000 \\
0.011 & 0.011 & 0.011 & 0.967
\end{array}
$$

and the corresponding network of total effects, $V^{(\infty)}$, is

$$
\begin{array}{cccc}
1.000 & 0.000 & 0.000 & 0.000 \\
0.000 & 0.000 & 0.000 & 1.000 \\
0.000 & 0.000 & 0.000 & 1.000 \\
0.000 & 0.000 & 0.000 & 1.000
\end{array}
$$

The cautious engineer emerges as the dominant person of the group. Although the confident engineer is heavily self-weighted and is not susceptible to the influence of the cautious engineer, the two other engineers are influenced exclusively by the cautious engineer. Hence, if decisions are made by a majority rule, then the decisions of this group will reflect the initial preferences of the cautious engineer. The social process that has produced this stratified influence network also has produced a modified set of sentiments for engineers 2 and 3; their equilibrium sentiments are virtually identical to the *initial* fundamental sentiments of the cautious engineer. Hence, engineers 2 and 3 have *adopted* the viewpoints of the cautious engineer about the other group members. This illustration shows that the social process that we have described easily generalizes to an account of influence networks in groups larger than a dyad and that it is consistent with the emergence of complex forms of stratification in which not all members "agree" on the relative influence of each member.

In the three illustrations that we have presented, we note that the results may be sensitive to the parameterization of the function in Eq. (12) that transforms latent attitudes into saliences. In the two illustrations of the husband-wife dyad, the results do not appear especially sensitive to changes in $\lambda \geq 1$; however, in the case of the four engineers, the value of λ is consequential; e.g. for $\lambda = 1$, the confident engineer is dominant and the cautious engineer is not influential, which is just the opposite of our finding for higher values of λ. In the case of the dyads, we have set $\lambda = 1$ in order to apply a simple transformation of sentiments to salience; in the case of the engineers, we have set λ to the high value of 5 in order to operationalize a contextual condition of strong pressures toward consensus. In some situations, methodological and substantive criteria may be brought to bear *a priori* to constrain the values of λ. For example, if we require that an increase in the latent attitude ($z_{ij}^{(t)}$) should not result in an increase of the salience ($s_{ij}^{(t)}$) exceeding that of the latent attitude, then the value of λ is constrained to $0 < \lambda \leq 2$; and if we adopt the maximum sentiment value of $+4.3$ (given by affect control theory) as the value at which salience should be virtually 1, then the value of λ is further constrained to $\lambda \geq 1.77$; hence, we obtain the overall constraint $1.77 \leq \lambda \leq 2$.

DISCUSSION

We believe that three formal theories in sociological social psychology – social influence network theory, affect control theory, and expectation states theory – can be formally linked and that these linkages enhance the power and scope of each theory. Each of these theories represents an attempt to grapple with concrete social processes and structures of groups. Our focus has been on the discovery of fundamental and parsimonious mechanisms and on the formal integration of theory. As part of our effort to link these three theories, we have extended social influence network theory, so that the influence network is not only affecting, but also being affected by, the positions of group members on an issue – their sentiments about themselves and other group members. We have focused on persons' sentiments about themselves and others because of the importance of this construct in affect control theory and it's close bearing (in our view) on the performance expectations that, in expectation states theory, underlie the formation of influence structures in task-oriented groups.

Since the early work of Festinger (1954), Hovland et al. (1953) and Sherif, Sherif and Nebergall (1965) on opinion discrepancies, there has been considerable interest in how the distribution of persons' initial positions on issues affect their interpersonal influences. Various investigators have posited that the distance between persons' positions on an issue may affect the salience of the positions for others (Davis, 1996; Eagly & Chaiken, 1993; Turner, 1991). For example, a well known hypothesis is that interpersonal influence is a ∩-shaped function of the distance between persons' initial positions on an issue. This body of work on initial position discrepancies has not considered the possibility that issue-positions may include attitudes about *persons-as-objects*. If attitudes are being formed about persons during the course of interactions on other issues (or if such person-as-object attitudes *are* the issue), then an equilibrium influence network may be formed that reflects the outcomes of the interpersonal influences that have shaped group members' attitudes about each other. This is the basic idea that we have developed in the present paper.

There is an unresolved problem in our formal development of the theory and we want to draw our readers' attention to it. We presently do not know how the three dimensions of sentiment (evaluation, potency, and activity) combine to determine the salience of self and particular others; see Eq. (16) where the coefficients are unknown. Thus, in our illustrations of the theory, we have employed *single* dimensions of sentiment as the basis of salience. When data is available on both the initial and equilibrium sentiments of each member of a group, one could estimate the parameters for each sentiment dimension, as well as any other included variables. The problem of developing a more refined theoretical linkage between affect control theory and social influence network theory must entail dealing with the manner in which these sentiments combine to determine salience under different conditions. The present paper opens up this question as a line of inquiry. It is a problem that is analogous to the problem in expectation states theory concerning the way in which multiple status characteristics are combined to produce a performance expectation.

An additional point of ambiguity in our formal development is the specification of the pattern of interpersonal *visibility* that constrains the social process. In the present work, we have assumed that the pattern of visibility is stable and complete during the period in which the equilibrium influence network of the group is being formed: $R^{(1)} = R^{(2)} = \ldots = R^{(\infty)} = J$, the matrix of all 1's. In small groups, group members are often acquainted with each other, so that $R^{(t)} = J$ is plausible for all t. In large groups, visibility may be patterned and the pattern may be changing; for instance, if $R^{(t)}$ and $S^{(t)}$ become linked because persons are establishing ties with persons who are salient to them (Stokman & Berveling, 1998), then some function would have to be specified that describes this linkage in order to understand the evolution of the influence network $W^{(t)}$.

We also want to draw our readers' attention to the special theoretical importance of the *salience of self* in our theory. The salience of self constrains the relative weights of the interpersonal influences on a person. The susceptibility of person i to the influences of others is the converse of person i's self-weight, and it is equivalent to the *aggregate* relative interpersonal influences of others on person i, i.e.

$$a_{ii}^{(t)} = 1 - w_{ii}^{(t)} = \sum_{j \neq i}^{n} w_{ij}^{(t)} \tag{21}$$

High self-weight implies low susceptibility to interpersonal influence, regardless of the potential salience of others in the group. When all susceptibilities in a group are near their theoretical extreme values of 0 or 1, then (depending on the structure of the network of interpersonal influences in the group and the initial distribution of fundamental sentiments), a consensual set of sentiments may be formed. Otherwise, there will be some modification of sentiments that is short of consensual.

In conclusion, the cornerstone of our effort has been the analysis of sentiments that, in affect control theory, are the elementary foundations of persons' definition of a situation. Our theory introduces an influence network into affect control theory by allowing these fundamental sentiments to be modified by the sentiments of others. Thus, persons not only take into account the "macro-structural" normative information that is evoked by a given situation, but also the "micro-structural" individual differences of sentiment that are displayed by the persons who are involved in a particular situation. As a result of persons' interactions in a particular situation, endogenous interpersonal influences on sentiments can operate to form a set of within-group normative expectations that are conditional upon the particular social structure of a group and its setting.

NOTES

1. Joining theories sometimes requires raising the level of abstraction of their constructs so that a commonality and intersection can be established; it seems reasonable to believe that the less abstraction that is required, the more concrete and useful the linkage will be for those engaged in the empirical research program of each theoretical structure. When abstraction is required, the "stress" produced by the juxtaposition of the theoretical structures can be productive in stimulating the growth and revision of the structures so that they dovetail more seamlessly.

2. This statement applies to influence networks in which the influences are non-negative. If negative influences are allowed (e.g. boomerang effects), then an initial consensus may shift or break apart due to the reactance of individuals.

3. Behaviors of the person or the object (another person) conform more or less closely to the normative expectations associated with the particular social identities and other features of the setting and persons. For instance, persons would expect their friends to behave in particular ways toward them as a function of the setting, mood, and other attributes involved in the interaction. Thus, certain events (i.e. the nexus of a person-behavior-object) are expected and other events are not.

4. The sentiments may be communicated through behaviors, emotional expressions, gestures, or words.

5. We are not convinced that status differentiation on some dimensions is ever entirely absent in human encounters, because physical differences always provide a basis (however misguided) for attributions and imputations about the character and intelligence of others; hence, task-relevant meaning will be generated on whatever differentiating features are apparent to the persons involved in the interaction. Pure homogeneity may be a theoretical, but not a realistic, possibility in human groups.

6. Expectation states theorists argue that performance expectations are not observable. The estimation of these coefficients occurs in a reduced-form equation (predicting influence behavior as a function of status variables) in which performance expectations do not appear.

7. Although attenuation effects (i.e. diminishing marginal effects of additional status characteristics) on influence outcomes have been noted in various studies, there is no direct evidence that there are attenuation effects on performance expectations. It is important to recognize that performance expectations have not been subject to direct measurement in the expectation states research tradition. Additionally, direct indicators of performance expectations would allow an assessment of the degree to which group members actually do *agree* in their expectations at the start of the group interaction. If such consensus actually exists in a group, and we doubt that it does in most groups, then endogenous interpersonal influences may not have any effect in modifying these expectations. It is when such consensus is *absent* that social influence network theory becomes interesting theoretically for an expectation-states theorist.

8. See Friedkin and Johnsen (1999, pp. 11, 21–22). In dyads, unlike larger groups, there is a noteworthy chance that interpersonal influences will generate opinions that are outside the range of the group members' initial opinions on an issue.

9. Note that one might replace R with the matrix for a nonnegative valued network, including $\Pr(R)$ in which case one could develop an analysis that involves the *probability distribution* for alternative patterns of visibility.

10. This formulation addresses the issue of the relative versus absolute values of the variables that Ridgeway and Smith-Lovin (1994) discussed as a difference between expectation states theory and affect control theory. Fundamental sentiments enter as "absolute" values in the determination of salience. For self-weight these absolute values constrain the amount of interpersonal influence upon a person. For interpersonal weights, salience is relative.

11. In terms of Fig. 1, we are not *replacing* the construct of sentiment with the construct of performance expectation, as an expectation states theorist might be inclined to do, but we are suggesting that a performance expectation may be a *special case* of the general construct of salience.

12. We recognize that the simple linear combination described in Eq. (13) may not be sufficiently refined; for instance, a high level of activity may not substitute for low levels of evaluation or potency. This may or may not be the case for the status characteristics that affect performance expectations in Eq. (1).

13. We also shift the basis to reiterate an important theoretical problem pertaining to the application of Eq. (16); that is, the bases of salience may combine in different ways in particular groups and the dyads within a group. We presently do not have a good understanding of these rules of combination.

ACKNOWLEDGMENTS

This paper was presented at the 2002 Nags Head Conference on Research Agendas in Affect Control Theory, 17–20 May, 2002, in Highland Beach, FL. We are indebted to David Heise, Lynn Smith-Lovin, and Joseph Whitmeyer for their comments on an earlier draft of this paper. Direct correspondence to Professor Noah E. Friedkin, Department of Sociology, University of California, Santa Barbara, CA 93106 (friedkin@soc.ucsb.edu).

REFERENCES

Arrow, H. (1997). Stability, bistability, and instability in small group influence patterns. *Journal of Personality and Social Psychology, 72*, 75–85.

Bales, R. F. (1950). *Interaction process analysis*. New York: Addison-Wesley.

Balkwell, J. W. (1991). From expectations to behavior: An improved postulate for expectation states theory. *American Sociological Review, 56*, 355–369.

Berger, J., Conner, T. L., & Fisek, M. H. (Eds) (1974). *Expectation states theory: A theoretical research program*. Cambridge, MA: Winthrop Publishers.

Berger, J., Fisek, M. H., Norman, R. Z., & Zelditch, M., Jr. (1977). *Status characteristics and social interaction*. New York: Elsevier.

Berger, J., Wagner, D. G., & Zelditch, M., Jr. (1985). Expectation states theory: Review and assessment. In: J. Berger & M. J. Zelditch (Eds), *Status, Rewards and Influence* (pp. 1–72). San Francisco: Jossey-Bass.

Carley, K. (1990). Group stability: A socio-cognitive approach. *Advances in Group Processes, 7*, 1–44.

Carley, K. (1991). A theory of group stability. *American Sociological Review, 56*, 331–354.

Davis, J. H. (1996). Group decision making and quantitative judgments: A consensus model. In: E. H. Witte & J. H. Davis (Eds), *Understanding Group Behavior: Consensual Action by Small Groups* (pp. 35–59). Mahwah, NJ: Lawrence Erlbaum.

Doreian, P., & Stokman, F. N. (Eds) (1997). *Evolution of social networks*. Amsterdam: Gordon and Breach.

Driskell, J. E., & Webster, M. J. (1997). Status and sentiment in task groups. In: J. Szmatka et al. (Eds), *Status, Network, and Structure* (pp. 179–200). Stanford, CA: Stanford University Press.

Eagly, A. H., & Chaiken, S. (1993). *The psychology of attitudes*. Fort Worth, TX: Harcourt Brace & Company.

Festinger, L. (1954). A theory of social comparison processes. *Human Relations, 7*, 117–140.

Fisek, M. H., & Berger, J. (1998). Sentiment and task performance expectations. In: J. Skvoretz & J. Szmatka (Eds), *Advances in Group Processes* (pp. 23–40). Greenwich, CT: JAI Press.

Fisek, M. H., Berger, J., & Norman, R. Z. (1991). Participation in heterogeneous and homogeneous groups: A theoretical integration. *American Journal of Sociology, 97*, 114–142.

Fisek, M. H., Berger, J., & Norman, R. Z. (1995). Evaluations and the formation of expectations. *American Journal of Sociology, 101*, 721–746.

Fisek, M. H., Norman, R. Z., & Nelson-Kilger, M. (1992). Status characteristics and expectation states theory: A priori model parameters and test. *Journal of Mathematical Sociology, 16*, 285–303.

French, J. R. P., Jr., & Raven, B. (1959). The bases of social power. In: D. Cartwright (Ed.), *Studies of Social Power* (pp. 150–167). Ann Arbor, MI: Institute for Social Research.

Friedkin, N. E. (1991). Theoretical foundations for centrality measures. *American Journal of Sociology, 96*, 1478–1504.

Friedkin, N. E. (1998). *A structural theory of social influence*. Cambridge: Cambridge University Press.

Friedkin, N. E. (1999). Choice shift and group polarization. *American Sociological Review, 64*, 856–875.

Friedkin, N. E. (2001). Norm formation in social influence networks. *Social Networks, 23*, 167–189.

Friedkin, N. E., & Johnsen, E. C. (1990). Social influence and opinions. *Journal of Mathematical Sociology, 15*, 193–206.

Friedkin, N. E., & Johnsen, E. C. (1997). Social positions in influence networks. *Social Networks, 19*, 209–222.

Friedkin, N. E., & Johnsen, E. C. (1999). Social influence networks and opinion change. *Advances in Group Processes, 16,* 1–29.

Heise, D. R. (2002). Understanding social interaction with affect control theory. In: J. Berger & M. Zelditch (Eds), *New Directions in Sociological Theory* (Chap. 2). Boulder, CO: Rowman and Littlefield.

Hovland, C. I., Janis, I. L., & Kelley, H. H. (1953). *Communication and persuasion.* New Haven: Yale University Press.

Kalkoff, W., & Barnum, C. (2000). The effect of status-organizing and social identity processes on patterns of social influence. *Social Psychology Quarterly, 63,* 95–115.

Kemper, T. D., & Collins, R. (1990). Dimensions of microinteraction. *American Journal of Sociology, 96,* 32–68.

Lazer, D. (2001). The co-evolution of individual and network. *Journal of Mathematical Sociology, 25,* 69–108.

Lovaglia, M. J. (1997). Status, emotion, and structural power. In: J. Szmatka, J. Skvoretz & J. Berger (Eds), *Status, Network, and Structure: Theory Development in Group Processes.* Stanford, CA: Stanford University Press.

Newcomb, T. M. (1951). Social psychological theory: Integrating individual and social approaches. In: J. H. Rohrer & M. Sherif (Eds), *Social Psychology at the Crossroads* (pp. 31–49). New York: Harper.

Osgood, C. E., May, W. H., & Miron, M. S. (1975). *Cross-cultural universals of affective meaning.* Urbana: University of Illinois Press.

Osgood, C. E., Suci, G. J., & Tannenbaum, P. H. (1957). *The measurement of meaning.* Urbana: University of Illinois Press.

Ridgeway, C. L. (1991). The social construction of status-value: Gender and other nominal characteristics. *Social Forces, 70,* 367–386.

Ridgeway, C. L., & Balkwell, J. W. (1997). Group processes and the diffusion of status beliefs. *Social Psychology Quarterly, 60,* 14–31.

Ridgeway, C., & Smith-Lovin, L. (1994). Structure, culture, and interaction: Comparing two generative theories. *Advances in Group Processes, 11,* 213–239.

Robinson, D. T. (1996). Identity and friendship: Affective dynamics and network formation. *Advances in Group Processes, 13,* 91–111.

Robinson, D. T., & Balkwell, J. W. (1995). Density, transitivity, and diffuse status in task-oriented groups. *Social Psychology Quarterly, 58,* 241–254.

Shelly, R. K. (1993). How sentiments organize interaction. In: E. J. Lawler et al. (Eds), *Advances in Group Processes* (Vol. 10, pp. 113–132). Greenwich, CT: JAI Press.

Sherif, C. W., Sherif, M., & Nebergall, R. E. (1965). *Attitude and attitude change: The social judgment-involvement approach.* Philadelphia: W. B. Saunders.

Skvoretz, J., & Fararo, T. J. (1996). Status and participation in task groups: A dynamic network model. *American Journal of Sociology, 101,* 1366–1414.

Skvoretz, J., Webster, M. J., & Whitmeyer, J. (1999). Status orders in task discussion groups. *Advances in Group Processes, 16,* 199–218.

Smith-Lovin, L., & Heise, D. R. (1988). *Analyzing social interaction: Advances in affect control theory.* New York: Gordon and Breach.

Smith-Lovin, L., Skvoretz, J. V., & Hawkins, C. (1986). Social status and participation in six-person groups: A test of Skvoetz's comparative status model. *Social Forces, 64,* 992–1005.

Stokman, F. N., & Berveling, J. (1998). Dynamic modeling of policy networks in Amsterdam. *Journal of Theoretical Politics, 10,* 577–601.

Troyer, L., & Younts, C. W. (1997). Whose expectations matter? The relative power of first- and second-order expectations in determining social influence. *American Journal of Sociology, 103,* 692–732.

Turner, J. C. (1991). *Social influence.* Pacific Grove, CA: Brooks/Cole.

Wagner, D. G., & Berger, J. (1993). Status characteristics theory: Growth of a research program. In: J. Berger & M. J. Zelditch (Eds), *Theoretical Research Programs: Studies in the Growth of Theory* (pp. 23–63). Stanford, CA: Stanford University Press.

Webster, M., & Sobieszek, B. I. (1974). *Sources of self-evaluation.* New York: Wiley.

Webster, M., & Whitmeyer, J. M. (1999). A theory of second-order expectations and behavior. *Social Psychology Quarterly, 62,* 17–31.

Webster, M., & Whitmeyer, J. M. (2002). Modeling second-order expectations. *Sociological Theory, 20,* 306–327.

Whitmeyer, J. M. (2002). The mathematics of expectation states theory (unpublished manuscript).

POWER, TRUST, AND FAIRNESS: COMPARISONS OF NEGOTIATED AND RECIPROCAL EXCHANGE

Linda D. Molm

ABSTRACT

While classical exchange theorists excluded bargaining from the scope of their theories, most contemporary theorists have done the opposite, concentrating exclusively on negotiated exchanges with binding agreements. This chapter describes the theoretical logic and empirical results of a new program of research comparing the effects of reciprocal and negotiated forms of exchange. As the work shows, fundamental differences between the two forms of exchange affect many of the processes addressed by current theories. Reciprocal exchanges produce weaker power use, greater feelings of trust and affective commitment, and stronger perceptions of the partner's fairness than equivalent negotiated exchanges. I discuss the implications of this work for theories of exchange and social interaction, and outline future directions for the next phase of the research program.

INTRODUCTION

For the past 25 years, analyses of power have dominated research on social exchange (see Molm, 2000, for a review). Most of this work has concentrated on a particular form of exchange in which actors jointly *negotiate* the terms of strictly

Power and Status
Advances in Group Processes, Volume 20, 31–65
ISSN: 0882-6145/doi:10.1016/S0882-6145(03)20002-3

binding agreements. Classical theorists, in contrast, typically excluded bargaining and negotiation from the scope of their theories. Homans (1974 [1961]) observed that explicit bargaining is rarely part of enduring relationships, while Blau (1964) argued that the absence of negotiation is what distinguishes social from economic exchange. Only a few researchers have studied the non-negotiated, *reciprocal* exchanges of benefits that were the focus of these early exchange theorists (e.g. Burgess & Nielsen, 1974; Michaels & Wiggins, 1976; Molm, 1990, 1997).

For the past several years, my collaborators and I have conducted a series of experiments comparing how reciprocal and negotiated forms of direct exchange affect major exchange outcomes. This work comprises the initial phase of a larger research program, the first to systematically compare these two forms of exchange. In this chapter I describe the conceptual framework for the project, the theoretical mechanisms proposed to underlie the effects of the form of exchange on major exchange outcomes, and the first series of experiments that were conducted to test the initial predictions.

The results of this work have important implications for theories of exchange and for the wide use of negotiation in institutional settings. As they show, fundamental differences between the two forms of exchange affect many of the processes addressed by current theories: power use and inequality, the development of trust and commitment, and perceptions of fair exchange. More importantly, they *interact* with the structural effects that most theories have focused on. They also offer new insights into the logical underpinnings of social exchange, including such fundamental issues as how risk affects actors' willingness to engage in exchange and the strategies they employ; the tension between cooperative and competitive incentives in exchange, and the relative importance of reciprocity, value, reward maximization, and risk reduction in our assumptions about actors' motives.

Empirically, the prevalence of both forms of exchange in social life requires that we study both, in ways that allow systematic, controlled comparisons of their similarities and differences. Although Blau and Homans suggested, correctly, that negotiation is more typical of exchange in some settings (e.g. work) than in others (e.g. families), both forms of exchange are observed in a wide range of social contexts. Even in interactions among family and friends, some exchanges of favors, household work, and choices of activities are negotiated. Similarly, even in politics, business, and international affairs, unilateral initiatives are common and the expectation of future reciprocity is often left implicit (Keohane, 1986; Macaulay, 1963). Thus, questions addressed by this project are relevant for processes in organizations and institutions as well as micro-interactional settings. Many economic exchanges are embedded in ongoing social relationships, and the form of these relationships affects the social bonds that develop between individuals and the political, economic, and social commerce that they transact (DiMaggio & Louch, 1998; Granovetter, 1985).

I begin this chapter by reviewing the basic concepts and assumptions of social exchange and identifying the key features that distinguish negotiated and reciprocal forms of exchange. I then describe three causal mechanisms originally proposed to account for the effects of the form of exchange on power and related affective outcomes, the experiments that were conducted to test the predictions, and the findings and puzzles that resulted. I conclude by discussing the implications of this work for theories of exchange and interaction in natural settings, and outline several future directions that the next phase of this research program will take.

THEORETICAL BACKGROUND

Concepts and Assumptions of Social Exchange

All forms of exchange occur within structures of mutual dependence, in which actors control resources that others value. Following the basic tenets of power-dependence theory (Emerson, 1972a, b), I assume that actors are motivated to obtain more of the outcomes that they value and others control, that actors provide each other with these valued benefits through exchange, and that actors engage in recurring, mutually contingent exchanges with the same partners over time.

The mutual dependence of actors provides the structural basis for their power over each other. In an exchange relation between actors A and B, B's dependence on A increases with the *value* of benefits that A can provide for B and decreases with B's access to *alternative* sources of those benefits (e.g. alternative dating partners or alternative sources of expert advice). A's power over B derives from B's dependence on A, and vice versa. Unequal dependencies produce an imbalanced relation in which the *less* dependent actor has a structural power advantage.

When connected by a focal actor, exchange relations form larger *exchange networks* consisting of three or more actors (e.g. B_1-A-B_2). If B_1 and B_2 are alternative partners for A, then the B_1-A and A-B_2 relations are *negatively connected*: The more frequently A exchanges with B_1, the less frequently A exchanges with B_2 (Emerson, 1972b). In negatively connected networks, actors who have more or better alternatives have a *power advantage* over their partners that produces a corresponding inequality in exchange benefits in their favor. Thus, imbalances in actors' relative dependencies on one another create differences in structural power that, in turn, affect behavioral power use. I define power use as the inequality in benefits obtained by more and less powerful actors in a network.

Most exchange theories of network structure and power share power-dependence theory's emphasis on how the structure of alternatives in exchange networks affects actors opportunities to use power (Bonacich & Friedkin, 1998; Cook et al., 1983; Markovsky et al., 1988; Marsden, 1982; Skvoretz & Willer, 1993). Three dimensions of alternatives have been identified: number, value, and availability. Emerson's (1972a) original statement of power-dependence theory proposed that B's dependence on A varies inversely with the *number* and *degree* (i.e. value) of B's alternatives to exchange with A. Since Cook and Emerson's (1978) first report of a negotiated exchange experiment, however, the characteristic of alternative partners that has received the most attention is their *availability*. In negatively connected networks, the key determinant of "availability" is the alternative's own alternatives; that is, alternative partners whose own alternatives are poor or non-existent are more "available" than those whose alternatives are good or plentiful. The relation between these dimensions of alternatives and power use, however, may depend on the form of exchange.

Forms of Exchange

While all exchanges are characterized by reciprocal dependence between those who give and those who receive benefits, the form that reciprocal dependence takes can be either *direct* (A provides value to B and B to A) or *indirect* (the recipient does not return benefit directly to the giver, but to another actor in the social circle). The first phase of this program studied only direct forms of exchange; future extensions will examine indirect, or generalized exchange.

In direct exchange relations, the exchange of benefits can take one of two distinct forms: negotiated or reciprocal (Blau, 1964; Emerson, 1981; Lévi-Strauss, 1969). In *negotiated exchange*, actors engage in a joint decision process, such as explicit bargaining, in which they seek agreement on the terms of exchange. Both sides of the exchange are agreed upon at the same time, in a discrete transaction that gives each partner benefits of equal or unequal value. Most economic exchanges other than fixed-price trades fit in this category, as well as some social exchanges (e.g. agreements about the division of household labor). Research studying negotiated exchange includes the work of Cook and associates (Cook & Emerson, 1978; Cook et al., 1983), Friedkin (1993), Lawler and associates (Lawler, 1992; Lawler & Yoon, 1993, 1996); and Willer, Markovsky and Skvoretz (Markovsky et al., 1988; Skvoretz & Willer, 1993). In all of these programs, agreements are also strictly binding; i.e. they automatically produce the benefits agreed upon.

In *reciprocal exchange*, actors' contributions to the exchange are separately performed and non-negotiated. Actors initiate exchanges individually, by performing a beneficial act for another (such as giving assistance or advice), without knowing whether, when, or to what extent the other will reciprocate. Exchange relations evolve gradually, as beneficial acts prompt reciprocal benefit. Because the same act can complete one exchange and initiate another, discrete transactions are difficult to identify. Instead, the relation takes the form of a series of sequentially contingent acts; e.g. your neighbor cares for your house while you are gone, you invite him to dinner, he gives you advice on buying a car, and so forth. Reciprocal exchanges were the focus of my earlier research program comparing reward and coercive power (Molm, 1990, 1997), as well as much of the research on mixed-motive games (e.g. Axelrod, 1984).

The differences between the two forms of exchange comprise three dimensions of theoretical importance: The first dimension, the *contingency of actors' outcomes*, is the most fundamental. In reciprocal exchange, each actor's outcomes are contingent solely on another's *individual* actions; i.e. A's behavior individually produces rewards for B, and vice versa. Consequently, benefits can flow *unilaterally*: actors can initiate exchanges that are not reciprocated, and they can receive benefit from another – or from multiple others, *at the same time –* without giving in return. Popular teenagers, for example, often enjoy the attention of many peers with only minimal reciprocation. In contrast, when exchanges are negotiated, each actors' outcomes depend on the *joint* actions of self and another actor, and the flow of benefits within two-party relations is always *bilateral*: Neither actor can profit without an agreement that benefits both. In essence, the task of negotiation transforms the structure of exchange from one of mutual dependence to one of cooperation (Molm, 1994).

The second dimension, the *information* actors have about their partners' reciprocity, follows partly from the first. The joint task of negotiating agreements requires communication and exchanges of offers and counter-offers; consequently, actors know in advance what they are getting for what they are giving. But when actors individually give benefits to others without negotiation, they often do so without knowing what, if anything, they will receive in return. They may be able to infer the other's intentions once the relation is established, but their initial exchanges must take place without that knowledge. Even in established relations, exploitation is always possible.

The third dimension on which the two forms vary is the *timing* with which the equality or inequality of exchange emerges. In negotiated exchanges, each transaction produces an agreement that provides either equal or unequal outcomes for actors. In reciprocal exchanges, equality or inequality instead develops over time, and it is determined by differences in the *rates* with which actors reciprocate each other's giving, as well as the value of that reciprocity. Consequently, the nature of reciprocal exchange requires actors to take a longer time perspective than is required in negotiated exchanges. Because the relative benefits of alternative exchange relations may become apparent only over time, actors who respond too quickly to immediate benefits – or their absence – may fail to discover exchange patterns that would be more rewarding in the long run. This characteristic of reciprocal exchange is one reason why Blau (1964) and other theorists emphasized the importance of factors such as risk and trust in the emergence of reciprocal exchange relations.

The distinction between negotiated and reciprocated exchange is closely related to game theorists' distinction between *cooperative* and *non-cooperative* games. In cooperative games (and negotiated exchanges), strictly binding agreements are made jointly by players who can communicate; in non-cooperative games (and reciprocal exchanges), actors make choices independently, without knowledge of others' choices (Heckathorn, 1985).[1] The first phase of the research program, which I discuss in this chapter, compared these "pure" forms of negotiated and reciprocal exchange.[2]

Assumptions About Exchange Conditions

Apart from their defining characteristics, the two forms of exchange can vary on other dimensions that potentially affect behavior. The initial phase of this project assumed five additional conditions, consistent with most existing research on reciprocal and negotiated exchange. *First*, network relations are negatively connected. *Second*, negative actions are limited to the withholding of rewards. *Third*, exchange actions and agreements produce immediate benefits for actors (i.e. negotiated agreements are strictly binding), and all benefits obtained through exchange are "consumed" (i.e. they have no subsequent exchange value). *Fourth*, within exchange relations, potential joint benefit is constant, and exchange benefits have equal value for both actors. *Fifth*, the costs of exchange are proportional to the amount given. In negotiated exchange, the more A offers B, the less A obtains from an agreement; in reciprocal exchange, the more frequently A gives to B, the less A obtains from exchanges with other partners (i.e. A's "opportunity costs" are higher).[3]

The first two conditions are scope conditions that, in addition to the scope conditions of power-dependence theory, define the circumstances under which the theory applies. The last three conditions represent restrictions applied to the first phase of the project that will be relaxed and tested in subsequent phases of the work.

Exchange Outcomes

The first phase of the project examined how the key differences in negotiated and reciprocal exchange affect three important exchange outcomes: (1) power use and inequality, focusing particularly on the relations between dimensions of structural power and power use; (2) the development of trust and commitment; and (3) the perceived fairness of the partner's exchange.

The original focus of the work was on power and the relation between network structure and power, the topic that has dominated contemporary exchange work for several decades. Although the scope of the project subsequently expanded to include affective outcomes, power remains the structural force that underlies all of these processes. In this work I consider how the form of exchange affects the use of power, independent of structure, and how form influences the *relation* between network structure and power use. The latter has particularly important implications for theory, because virtually all of the theories that have been developed in the last two decades to predict the relation between structure and power use have assumed or studied negotiated exchanges.

The other exchange outcomes addressed in this project include some of the long-neglected concerns of the classical theorists, dealing with the more integrative aspects of exchange: the development of trust and commitment, the emergence of affective ties between exchange partners, and effects of "fair exchange" on perceptions of the partner. Recently, exchange theorists have begun to revisit these concerns (Hegtvedt & Killian, 1999; Kollock, 1994; Lawler & Yoon, 1993, 1996; Macy & Skvoretz, 1998; Yamagishi et al., 1998). Nearly all of this work, however has been conducted on negotiated exchange.

LINKING EXCHANGE FORM TO POWER AND AFFECTIVE OUTCOMES: THE CAUSAL MECHANISMS

The key dimensions on which the two forms of direct exchange differ – the contingency of outcomes, information about reciprocity, and the timing of inequality – influence three causal mechanisms predicted to underlie the relations between the form of exchange and exchange outcomes: how structural power is used, the risk and uncertainty of exchange, and the salience of competitive or cooperative incentives. The contingency of outcomes is the most fundamental dimension of form, and it affects all three causal mechanisms. Differences in information affect the risk and uncertainty of exchange, and the timing with which inequality emerges affects the salience of competition and cooperation in exchange. These mechanisms, in turn, affect exchange outcomes (see Fig. 1).

Fig. 1. The Causal Mechanisms Linking Key Dimensions of Exchange Form to
Exchange Outcomes.

Mechanisms of Power Use

In both negotiated and reciprocal exchange, B's dependence on A determines the
potential cost that A can impose on B; when A uses power, A transforms that
potential cost into actual cost (Emerson, 1972b). But *how* actors impose cost, and
how that action benefits them, varies for the two forms of exchange.

In negotiated exchange, powerful actors impose cost on some partners when
they make agreements with others, thus *excluding* some partners from valuable
transactions.[4] Exclusion induces actors to increase their offers in subsequent
negotiations, and consequently increases the inequality of those agreements (Cook
et al., 1983; Skvoretz & Willer, 1993). Inequality in exchange benefits arises from
both sources: unequal rates of exclusion from transactions, and unequal divisions
of profit within transactions. The former drives the latter. More powerful actors
benefit from a lower probability of exclusion *and* from the greater profit they
receive when they are included.

Inequality in reciprocal exchange is also produced by a form of exclusion: the
withholding of rewards from one partner while pursuing exchange with another
(Molm, 1990). But withholding rewards benefits powerful actors not by driving up
partners' offers, but by lowering actors' costs. Actors who can maintain one partner's exchange with only intermittent reciprocity have more opportunity to pursue
other exchange relations. And because benefits flow unilaterally, they can *receive*
benefits from multiple partners at the same time. Powerful actors benefit from
both their lower reciprocity and their consequent greater opportunity to pursue
other exchanges. Spouses who contribute less to household chores, for example,
not only do less work, but also have more time to devote to careers or leisure
activities. Disadvantaged actors, who must give more frequently to maintain
their powerful partner's intermittent reciprocity, must forgo more of the potential
rewards from these alternative activities (i.e. their opportunity costs are higher).

Neither reward-withholding nor exclusion requires any intentional or strategic tactics by powerful actors. Instead, both are *structurally* produced by differences in access to alternatives in negatively connected networks.

These mechanisms – exclusion and reward-withholding – should mediate the relation between network structure and power use for both forms of exchange, but with different consequences. The primary source of this difference is the contingency of actors' outcomes on joint or individual action. Whether benefits can flow unilaterally (as in reciprocal exchange) or only bilaterally (as in negotiated exchange) affects which exchange patterns will maximize powerful actors' benefits, the effect of those patterns on the costs imposed on the weaker partner, and the power use that results. Consequently, dimensions of network structure – the availability, number, and value of alternatives – should have different effects on power use for the two forms of exchange.

The differences are most marked for the relation between the *availability* of A's alternatives to exchange with B and A's power use over B. In negotiated exchanges, in which benefits are obtained only through bilateral agreements, actors should make agreements with those who offer the greatest rewards. More available (more dependent) partners will typically offer better deals than less available partners. Consequently, the more available A's alternative to B, the more likely A is to exchange with that alternative and to exclude B. That action increases B's offers to A and increases A's power use over B. In reciprocal exchanges, in which benefits flow unilaterally, advantaged actors can receive benefits from multiple partners at the same time. More available (more dependent) partners are more likely to give unilaterally to A, while A exchanges with another partner. Consequently, A will obtain more total benefit from *all* of A's partners by giving more frequently to a *less* available partner than to a more available one. The implication of this difference is that to the extent that actors follow these maximizing patterns, the relation between the availability of A's alternatives to B and A's power use over B should be reversed for the two forms of exchange: In negotiated exchange, the *more* available A's alternatives to B, the more frequent A's exclusion of B and the greater A's power use over B. In reciprocal exchange, the *less* available A's alternatives to B, the more frequent A's withholding of rewards from B and the greater A's power use over B. Thus, as numerous theories of negotiated exchange predict, A's power use over B should be greater in a network in which A's alternative to B is *more* available (e.g. C-A-B) than in a network in which A's alternative to B is *less* available (e.g. D-C-A-B). For reciprocal exchange, however, the opposite should be true.

Although power use in reciprocal exchange is not predicted to increase with the availability of alternatives for the powerful actor, it should increase with the *number* and *value* of alternatives, the variables in Emerson's (1972a) original formulation. Holding value and availability constant, a comparison of the two forms of exchange suggests that increasing the number of A's alternatives beyond a single alternative to B should have a stronger effect on A's power use over B when exchange is reciprocal than when it is negotiated. If A has n alternative partners to B, all equivalent in value and availability, then the frequency with which A excludes or withholds rewards from B will increase directly with n. Thus, for both negotiated and reciprocal exchange, B's benefits will decrease as a function of the decreasing probability of A's exchange with B. A's benefits, on the other hand, should increase with the number of A's alternatives in reciprocal exchanges, but be unaffected in negotiated exchanges. Both the equi-resistance solution of Willer and his associates (e.g. Skvoretz & Willer, 1993) and Cook and Yamagishi's (1992) equi-dependence solution predict that only an actor's "best" alternative, not the number of alternatives, affects the division of benefit in negotiated exchanges. The number of alternatives should increase the speed with which power use reaches its maximum, but the benefits that A receives from agreements with B at equilibrium should be unaffected. In reciprocal exchanges, in contrast, increasing the number of alternatives increases A's *opportunities* to obtain benefits, by definition, because A can obtain benefits from multiple partners at the same time. A's actual benefits depend on the extent to which A's partners decrease their rate of giving to A as A's rate of giving to each of them declines. As long as A's giving exceeds what A's alternatives could receive from their best alternative, however, A should be able to maintain their giving with a lower rate of reciprocity. If so, then the number of alternatives will have a stronger effect on power use in reciprocal than in negotiated exchange.

The prediction for the relative value of alternatives is simpler and more straight-forward: holding number and availability of alternatives constant, the relative value of alternatives should increase power use in *both* reciprocal and negotiated exchange. Unlike the other two dimensions of alternatives, the effects of value are not affected by the structural differences between the two forms of exchange. Instead, the basic mechanism that produces this effect is the same for both forms of exchange: More valuable alternatives for the powerful actor, A, increase the frequency of A's exchange with those alternatives. In negotiated exchanges, A's increased exchange with an alternative partner increases A's exclusion of B, drives up B's offers to A in subsequent negotiations, and increases the inequality of A's agreements with B, in A's favor. A benefits both from a lower probability of exclusion and from the greater profit A receives from agreements with B. In reciprocal exchanges, A's increased giving to a more valuable alternative partner decreases A's costs in the A-B relation while increasing A's opportunities for benefit from the alternative relation. If A is able to maintain B's giving with a lower rate of reciprocity, while giving more frequently to an alternative partner, C, then A can increase her benefits from *both* partners (again, because powerful actors in reciprocal exchanges can receive benefits from multiple partners at the same time).

This logic leads to the following three hypotheses:

Hypothesis 1. A's power use over B increases with the availability of A's alternatives to B in negotiated exchanges, and decreases with the availability of A's alternatives to B in reciprocal exchanges.

Hypothesis 2. The number of A's alternatives to B has a stronger positive effect on A's power use over B in reciprocal exchanges than in negotiated exchanges.

Hypothesis 3. In both negotiated and reciprocal exchanges A's power use over B increases with the magnitude of value offered by A's alternative to B, relative to the magnitude of value in the A-B relation.

Risk and Uncertainty

All forms of social exchange involve risk and uncertainty, but the amount and kind of risk vary. These variations in risk are produced by two of the key differences between negotiated and reciprocal exchange: the contingency of actors' outcomes on joint or individual action, and information about the partner's reciprocation.

In general, both the individual nature of the decision process and the lack of communication about terms make reciprocal exchange riskier than negotiated exchange (Molm, 1994). But the *source* of risk also differs for the two forms of exchange. In reciprocal exchange, actors must initiate exchange without knowing what they are getting in return, and with no guarantee of the other's reciprocity. Thus, their primary risk is the *risk of non-reciprocation* – of giving benefit without receiving benefit in return, an outcome comparable to the "sucker's pay-off" in the Prisoner's Dilemma.

In negotiated exchange, the bargaining process itself is a source of uncertainty; actors' choices of how hard to bargain, what tactics to use, and so forth all affect the terms of agreements and the likelihood of reaching an agreement. But once actors agree on the terms of an exchange, much of this uncertainty is eliminated: actors know what they are getting for what they are giving, and they can choose to engage in the exchange or not. The terms may be unequal and unsatisfactory to one or both parties, but unless both benefit more from the exchange than they would without it, it should not take place. If, in addition, the exchange is secured with conditions that make the agreement binding – conditions assumed in experimental research on negotiated exchange and characteristic of many negotiated exchanges in natural settings – then actors face no risk of non-reciprocation; both actors receive some benefit from the exchange. Instead, the primary risk in negotiated exchange is the risk of exclusion: of failing to make an agreement with a desired partner. Actors increase their chance of making a better agreement by bargaining harder and making fewer concessions, but by doing so, they decrease their chance of making *any* agreement.

These differences in risk are predicted to affect both the *use of power* and the *development of trust*. Power is influenced by actors' responses to risk. As previous research has shown, actors – particularly the disadvantaged, who face the greatest risk of exclusion or non-reciprocation – try to reduce both types of risk (Molm, 1994; Skvoretz & Zhang, 1997; Thye et al., 1997). However, their efforts to reduce the risk of exclusion or the risk of non-reciprocity should have *opposite* effects on power use. In negotiated exchanges, disadvantaged actors can reduce the probability of exclusion by *increasing the amount offered*; which *increases* power use by increasing the inequality of the negotiated agreement and increasing the powerful actor's benefits. In reciprocal exchange, disadvantaged actors can reduce the occurrence of non-reciprocity by *decreasing unilateral giving* (i.e. by limiting how often or how much they give to a partner without reciprocation), which *decreases* power use by decreasing the inequality in the rate of exchange and decreasing the powerful actor's benefits. If disadvantaged actors in both forms of exchange follow these risk reduction strategies, then, on average, power use will be greater when exchange is negotiated than when it is reciprocal. Because the risk of either non-reciprocity or exclusion increases with power imbalance for disadvantaged actors, this difference in power use should become greater as power imbalance increases:

Hypothesis 4. Holding constant network structure, power use will be greater when exchange is negotiated than when it is reciprocal; this difference will increase as power imbalance increases.

A long-standing (but rarely tested) proposition of social exchange theory also links risk to the development of trust. Numerous theorists have argued that risk is a necessary condition for trust, because attributions of a partner's trustworthiness can only be made in risky situations in which the partner has the opportunity to exploit or benefit the actor (Coleman, 1990; Hardin, 1991; Kelley & Thibaut, 1978; Kollock, 1994; Luhman, 1979; Yamagishi & Yamagishi, 1994). If, under these conditions, A behaves in a trustworthy manner, then B's trust in A should increase. A's untrustworthy behavior, on the other hand, should lead to B's distrust of A.

Based on this logic, the classical exchange theorists (Blau, 1964; Lévi-Strauss, 1969) proposed that trust is more likely to develop when exchange occurs without the explicit "quid pro quo" of negotiated transactions and without the assurance of binding agreements. Although, as we have seen, both forms of exchange involve risk, only reciprocal exchange involves the type of risk – the risk of non-reciprocation – that requires trusting another and that allows the demonstration of trustworthiness. In negotiated exchanges, known terms and binding agreements provide "assurance" that one will not be exploited, without enabling trust.[5] In reciprocal exchanges, the only form of assurance comes from the expectation of future interaction – the "shadow of the future" (Axelrod, 1984). This form of assurance is weaker than binding agreements with known terms, and it develops only over time. It should, however, make trustworthy behaviors at least as likely as untrustworthy ones under conditions of recurring exchange.[6]

This logic implies two main predictions: (1) that actors' trust in an exchange partner will be greater, on average, in reciprocal exchange relations than in structurally and behaviorally equivalent negotiated exchange relations, and (2) that the relation between behaviors signaling an exchange partner's trustworthiness – the partner's behavioral commitment to the actor, and the equality of their exchange – and the actor's trust in the partner will be stronger in reciprocal than in negotiated exchange.

Many discussions have linked risk not only to trust but to *commitment*. Both trust and commitment are emergent processes that arise in response to uncertainty and risk (Blau, 1964). The form of the relation between trust and commitment depends, however, on whether commitment is conceptualized as a purely *behavioral* pattern of repeated exchange between the same actors (Cook & Emerson, 1978; Kollock, 1994), or as an *affective* bond of attachment (Lawler & Yoon, 1996). Behavioral commitment – defined here as the extent to which an actor chooses repeatedly to exchange with one particular partner rather than with others – reduces uncertainty and contributes to the development of trust; it is one form of "trustworthy" behavior that should encourage the development of trust in a context of uncertainty and risk. Affective commitment – defined here as feelings of liking for, and attachment to, a specific exchange partner – should, on the other hand, emerge from the same processes that produce trust.[7] That is, in the absence of assurance structures that can explain a partner's positive behaviors, actors should be more likely to attribute the behaviors to the partner's personal traits and intentions. If so, then positive feelings of affect and commitment toward the partner will, like trust, tend to be stronger in reciprocal than in negotiated exchanges, and they will increase with the partner's behavioral commitment and with the equality of their exchanges. Behavioral commitment, on the other hand, is a means of reducing uncertainty in *both* reciprocal and negotiated exchange, and it should be no more common in one than in the other. Behavioral commitment should, however, be positively related to trust, particularly in reciprocal exchanges.

Hypothesis 5. An actor's trust and affective commitment for an exchange part-ner will be greater, on average, in reciprocal exchange relations than in equivalent (structurally and behaviorally) negotiated exchange relations.

Hypothesis 6. An actor's trust and affective commitment for a partner will increase with the partner's behavioral commitment to the actor and decrease with the inequality of their exchange; these relations will be stronger in reciprocal than in negotiated exchanges.

Salience of Cooperative or Competitive Interests

Objectively, the outcome structures of the two forms of exchange are equivalent. Both are "mixed-motive" structures in which actors' interests partially correspond and partially conflict. Because actors depend on one another for valued outcomes, exchange is mutually beneficial. But at the same time, each actor benefits in *inverse* proportion to what he gives the other. In negotiated exchange, the more A offers B, the less A obtains from an agreement; in reciprocal exchange, the more frequently A gives to B, the less A obtains from exchanges with other partners (i.e. A's "opportunity costs" are higher).

Despite their objective equivalence, the two forms of exchange can produce different *subjective* experiences of these two "faces" of exchange. Differences in both the timing with which inequality emerges, and the contingency of actors' outcomes, affect the process of exchange in ways that make the competitive aspects of exchange *more* pronounced for negotiated exchanges than for recip-rocal exchanges. Consequently, conflict should be more salient than cooperation for actors in negotiated exchanges, relative to those in reciprocal exchanges. A heightened sense of conflict can have important consequences for actors' perceptions of inequality and fairness in exchange.

First, because of differences in the timing with which inequality emerges, actors' outcomes are more easily compared in negotiated exchange than in reciprocal exchange. In negotiated exchanges, "success" or "failure" is more obvious because each transaction produces either equal or unequal outcomes for actors. In reciprocal exchanges, it is more difficult for actors to keep track of who fares better, or who owes whom, because the equality or inequality of the relation develops only over time.

Second, the relative costs of exchange are more transparent in negotiated than in reciprocal exchange, and the relation of one actor's gain to another's loss is more direct. In negotiated exchange, the more an agreement favors one actor, the less it favors another.[8] In reciprocal exchange, this "zero-sum" component is less evident because the costs incurred involve the loss of potential benefits from other relations, rather than reduced profit from the focal relation. That is, because disadvantaged actors must give more frequently to maintain their powerful partner's intermittent reciprocity, they must forgo more of the potential rewards from alternative activities.[9]

Third, inequality is more likely to be perceived as an intentional consequence of the partner's behavior in negotiated exchange. In the context of bargaining, acts of one party are, by definition, acts of commission, directed at the other party, with known consequences for self and other. In reciprocal exchanges, inequality results instead from acts of omission; i.e. from not acting, rather than from tough bargaining. Consequently, intent is more ambiguous: inequality may be the result of an actor's intentionally paying less for another's favors, or an unanticipated side effect of an actor's exchange with another partner.

This heightened awareness of the conflict between actors' interests can affect both cognitions and affect, influencing actors' judgments of the fairness of exchange as well as affective evaluations of their partners. Heightened conflict increases actors' tendencies to interpret exchange processes in a self-serving manner, leading actors to take credit for good outcomes while blaming the partner for poor outcomes (Hegtvedt & Killian, 1999; Thompson & Lowenstein, 1992). Self-serving attribution biases also make actors less likely to perceive the situational causes of others' behavior than of their own behavior (Nisbett & Ross, 1980; Ross, 1977). The more an actor attributes responsibility for inequality to the partner, and perceives the partner's behavior as intentional and dispositional, the more likely that the actor will perceive the partner's behavior as unfair (Cohen, 1982; Hassebrauck, 1987; Utne & Kidd, 1980).

Objectively, responsibility for inequality is shared by the actor to a greater extent in negotiated than in reciprocal exchanges; thus, an actor whose assessment of causality is veridical should be more likely to accept partial responsibility for unequal outcomes that favor the partner in negotiated exchanges, while attributing sole responsibility to the partner in reciprocal exchanges. Lawler (2001) has used this logic to argue that the greater jointness of the task in negotiated exchanges will produce a greater sense of shared responsibility and counteract the effects of self-serving biases. However, the give-and-take of bargaining is a double-edged sword: while it makes exchange more collaborative, it also brings into sharp relief actors' different interests and outcomes. Therefore, in contrast to Lawler, my colleagues and I have proposed that disadvantaged actors in negotiated exchanges will be more likely to blame the partner for unequal outcomes than disadvantaged actors in reciprocal exchanges, and more likely to perceive the partner's behavior as unfair – even when the two forms of exchange produce equivalent outcomes, in equivalent structures (Molm et al., 2003):[10]

Hypothesis 7. Independent of exchange outcomes and network structures, actors will perceive their partner's behavior as more fair in reciprocal than in negotiated exchanges.

In contrast to the distributive justice focus of most exchange work on power and fairness, this hypothesis addresses a question of *procedural* justice: it predicts that the form of exchange in which actors engage will affect their judgments of fairness, even when they receive identical outcomes, in identical network structures. The *direction* of effects predicted in Hypothesis 7, however, is contrary to that implied by most theories of procedural justice. Negotiated exchange – which incorporates collective decision-making, advance knowledge of terms, mutual assent, and binding agreements – clearly appears more fair than reciprocal exchange on most dimensions of procedural justice (Lind & Tyler, 1988; Thibaut & Walker, 1975; Tyler et al., 1996). Since fair procedures tend to enhance perceptions of others' fairness (Lind & Tyler, 1988; Tyler & Lind, 1992), these theories imply that negotiated exchange partners should be perceived as fairer than reciprocal exchange partners. Hypothesis 7 asserts the opposite, based on the logic that these effects may be undermined by the countervailing effects of the greater salience of conflict in negotiated exchange.

Previous research suggests that procedural issues primarily influence the perceived fairness of negative, or unsatisfactory, outcomes (Lind & Tyler, 1988). If so, then the effects of exchange process – in either direction – should be stronger for unequal exchanges, which disadvantage one party, than for equal exchanges. Similarly, both the salience of conflict and dissatisfaction with outcomes should be weaker when exchanges are equal, and actors should be less likely to engage in self-serving attributions. Consequently, the differences between reciprocal and negotiated exchanges should be greatest when outcomes are unequal.

Hypothesis 8. The relation in Hypothesis 7 should be stronger for unequal than for equal exchanges.

EMPIRICAL TESTS OF THE HYPOTHESES

My colleagues and I tested these predictions in a series of experiments that examined the effects of the form of exchange on power and inequality (Molm et al., 1999, 2001), the development of trust and affective commitment (Molm et al., 2000), and perceptions of fairness (Molm et al., 2003). All of the experiments were conducted in a standardized experimental setting in which undergraduate student subjects, who were randomly assigned to positions in exchange networks, engaged in either reciprocal or negotiated exchanges to earn money.

The Standardized Laboratory Setting

The Forms of Exchange

Two different exchange settings, one negotiated and one reciprocal, were created for the experiments. The settings were designed to be as comparable as possible on all dimensions other than their defining differences.

In the negotiated exchange setting, actors negotiate the division of a fixed amount of benefit within relations on a series of exchange opportunities. Each opportunity consists of up to five rounds of negotiation; on each round, all actors in the network simultaneously make offers to all alternative partners. After the first round, actors can accept another's offer, repeat their last offer, or make a counteroffer. Negotiations continue until all potential agreements are made or the five rounds are up. As soon as an agreement is reached, both actors receive the amounts they have agreed upon (thus, agreements are binding).

In the reciprocal exchange setting, each actor in the network gives points to one of his or her exchange partners on each exchange opportunity. Actors make these choices simultaneously and independently, without knowing whether or when the other will reciprocate; information about benefits gained is provided only after all actors have chosen. To hold constant the potential joint benefit of reciprocal and negotiated exchanges, the number of points that each actor could give to any partner on any single opportunity was fixed and equal to one-half the total points that actors in the negotiated exchange setting could divide on each opportunity. If, for example, subjects in a negotiated exchange relation could divide 16 points on an exchange opportunity, subjects in an equivalent reciprocal exchange relation could give each other eight points on an opportunity.

In all of the experiments except those specifically designed to study fairness judgments, information was restricted to control for equity effects. In the negotiated setting, subjects knew the range of points they could request from agreements and that, in general, the more they received the less the other person received. They did not know that a fixed amount of profit was divided, however, nor did they know how many points the other subject received from an agreement. Subjects made offers by *requesting* the number of points they wanted to receive from an agreement, and each subject's *request* for points was then converted, by the computer, into an *offer* of the remaining points for the other subject. In the reciprocal setting, subjects knew only the number of points they could receive from others, not the number of points they could give to others.[11]

The Exchange Structures

The experiments in the program studied variations of the two simple network structures shown in Fig. 2. In all of the networks, actors occupy one of two

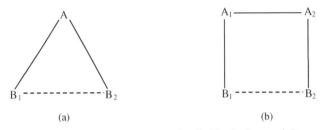

Fig. 2.   The Basic Network Structures Studied in the Research Program.
Note: Solid lines indicate potential relations with high exchange value, and dotted lines
indicate potential relations with low exchange value.

structural positions, A or B. Relations in the networks are negatively connected, and these connections are operationalized in the traditional way (Cook & Emerson, 1978): in negotiated exchanges, an agreement with one exchange partner precludes an agreement with another on that exchange opportunity, and in reciprocal exchanges, initiating exchange with one actor precludes initiating exchange with another on that opportunity. In both networks, A is more powerful than B, because B's only alternative to A is a low-value exchange with another B. In all experiments, the low-value B-B relations were worth four points, and the high-value A-B relations were worth 16 points.

The two networks shown in Fig. 2 vary the *availability* of A's alternatives to B: In Fig. 2a, B_1 and B_2 are both highly available partners for A (both Bs have only low-value alternatives – each other – to exchange with A), but in Fig. 2b, A's alternative to B (the other A) has a high-value alternative to exchange with A and is thus less dependent on A, and therefore less available to A, than is B. These two networks were compared in the first experiment on power (Molm et al., 1999). Subsequent experiments systematically varied the *value* of A's alternative to B and the *number* of A's alternatives to B. The value of A's alternatives was manipulated by varying the value of A's alternative to the A-B relation within each of the two networks in Fig. 2a and b, so that it was either six points less than, six points more than, or equal to the value of A's relation with B. The number of A's alternatives was varied by comparing the network in Fig. 2a with a similar network in which A had three (rather than two) Bs as alternative exchange partners, and each B had the option of exchange with another low-value B.

In most experiments, all actors in the networks were real subjects, interacting with one another. The one exception was the fairness experiments; to control for the objective equality or inequality of exchange in these experiments, subjects' exchange partners were computer-simulated. The fairness experiments also differed in one other respect: in these experiments, actors had full information about the shape of the network and the potential value of exchange with each partner;[12] in all of the other experiments discussed here, subjects' information about the network structure was restricted to knowledge of their own access to their own exchange partners and their potential benefits from these partners.[13]

Measures of Exchange Outcomes

In all experiments, power use was measured by the inequality in *total* benefits accrued over time by actors in the A and B positions.[14] This measure takes account of both the inequality of exchanges *within* the A-B relation and the *likelihood* of their exchanges with each other and with other actors in the network. In the experiment manipulating the relative value of alternatives, this measure is adjusted so that variations in total inequality across the different value conditions reflect only variations in the *proportion* of available points that A obtains relative to B, not variations in the absolute number of points available to A.

All evaluative measures are based on subjects' responses to a series of seven-point semantic differential scales administered at the conclusion of the experiment. These items measured subjects' evaluations of their exchange partners and relations. We measured trust with a single item asking subjects, "How much did you trust Person X during the experiment (very much/very little)?" We assessed affective commitment with two measures, one a single item asking subjects how committed/uncommitted they felt toward the partner, and the other a five-item scale measuring their affective evaluation of the partner.[15] We measured subjects' evaluations of their exchange partners' fairness with both a behavioral measure – the frequency with which the subject either made agreements with (negotiated exchange) or gave benefits to (reciprocal exchange) the partner – and with a scale comprised of responses to three items (fair/unfair, just/unjust, equitable/inequitable), with an alpha reliability of 0.91.

Experiments on Power and Inequality

The original focus of this project was on power and the relation between network structure and power, the topic that has dominated contemporary exchange work for several decades. Three experiments investigated how the form of exchange affects power use in exchange networks varying on three structural dimensions – the availability, number, and value of alternative partners for the most powerful actor(s). We predicted that the relation between each of these structural dimensions and power use would vary with the form of exchange (Hypotheses 1–3), and that across different network structures, average power use would be lower in reciprocal exchange than in negotiated exchange, with this difference increasing with power imbalance (Hypothesis 4).

In our first experiment, my associates and I tested Hypotheses 1 and 4 in an experiment that compared power use in the high- and low-availability networks shown in Fig. 2 in both the reciprocal and negotiated exchange settings (Molm et al., 1999). Recall that Hypothesis 1 predicted that power use would be greater in network (a) than network (b) for negotiated exchange, but that the opposite would be true for reciprocal exchange.

Experimental results confirmed Hypothesis 4's prediction of lower power use in reciprocal exchange (a mean of 0.61, compared with 0.70 when exchange is negotiated), and confirmed the logic on which Hypothesis 1 was based: powerful actors in negotiated exchanges earned more when they made agreements with *more* available partners, whereas powerful actors in reciprocal exchanges earned more when they exchanged primarily with *less* available partners. In addition, each of these patterns was strongly related to greater power use. But the predicted reversal in the direction of the relation between availability and power use did not occur: Although power use was significantly greater in the high-availability networks when exchange was negotiated (0.80) than when it was reciprocal (0.65), power use in the low-availability networks was no greater when exchange was reciprocal (0.57) than when it was negotiated (0.61). Powerful actors did not engage in the reciprocal exchange patterns that would have maximized their earnings and power use in these networks; instead, like powerful actors in negotiated exchanges, they exchanged primarily with more available partners. Consequently, power use increased with availability in both negotiated and reciprocal forms of exchange, although the strength of that relation was significantly weaker when exchange was reciprocal than when it was negotiated, as implied by Hypothesis 4.

Subsequent experiments varying the relative value of alternatives and the number of alternatives tested Hypotheses 2 and 3, respectively. Both hypotheses were supported. As Molm et al. (2001) show, A's power use over B increases significantly with the value of A's alternatives for both reciprocal and negotiated exchange, with no difference in the strength of this relation, supporting Hypothesis 3. A's power use over B also increases with the number of A's alternatives to B, but the increase is significant only for reciprocal, not negotiated, exchange, thus supporting Hypothesis 2.

Figure 3 provides a graphical display of the main results for all three experiments. Perhaps the most striking finding is the strong and consistent support for Hypothesis 4: in Experiments 2 and 3, as in Experiment 1, average power use is greater when exchange is negotiated rather than reciprocal. Across all three experiments, the two forms of exchange produce equal power use only in the

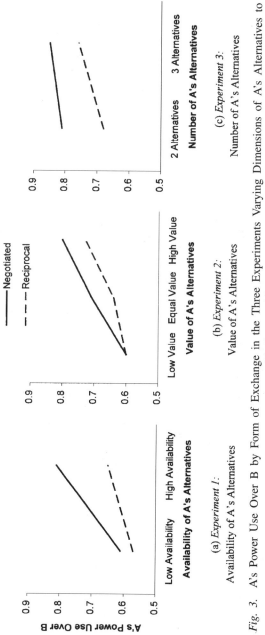

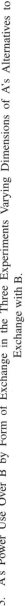

Fig. 3. A's Power Use Over B by Form of Exchange in the Three Experiments Varying Dimensions of A's Alternatives to Exchange with B.

two conditions in which power imbalance is very low (low availability or low value of A's alternatives). When power imbalance increases to either moderate or high levels in the first two experiments, the increase in power use is greater for negotiated than for reciprocal exchange. In the third experiment, the opposite is true, but the magnitude of increase is smaller (and power imbalance is high in both networks, with either two or three alternatives). Increasing the number of alternatives does not have a large effect on power use, even for reciprocal exchange, because the Bs decrease their rate of giving to A as A's giving to each of them declines (as the logic underlying Hypothesis 4 implies).

Thus, we find substantial support for the logic on which these first experiments were based, with one main exception – the failure to find support for the predicted reversal in the direction of the relation between availability and power use. One dominant pattern accounts for this deviant result: Actors in reciprocal exchange relations opted for reciprocity even when it did not maximize their outcomes. *Both* power-advantaged and power-disadvantaged actors – rather than only power-disadvantaged actors, as expected – tended to give to others to the extent that others gave to them. Although this pattern reduced risk and increased predictability for both A and B, the cost was far greater for powerful actors. Consequently, power use was lower for reciprocal exchange under virtually all unequal power structures, regardless of the source of the inequality, and the relation between power imbalance and power use was generally weaker.

Experiments on Trust and Commitment

Although our investigations of power show that reciprocal exchanges dampen the use of power, our investigations of actors' perceptions and evaluations of their exchange partners reveal that they are potent sources of positive affect – *independent* of power and power use. Holding constant network structure and partner's behavior, we found that actors in reciprocal exchanges evaluate their partners more positively than those in negotiated exchanges on a variety of dimensions: they trust them more, they like them more, they feel more committed to them, and they perceive their exchange behavior as fairer (Molm et al., 2000, 2003).

We first tested Hypotheses 5 and 6, on the development of trust and affective commitment, for actors in the two network structures shown in Fig. 1 (Molm et al., 2000). As predicted in Hypothesis 5, we found higher trust and related feelings of positive affect and commitment in reciprocal exchange relations than in negotiated exchange relations in both networks. This pattern holds for actors in both the A and B positions, but is much stronger for the disadvantaged Bs. Actors in negotiated exchange relations report average levels of trust *below* the neutral point on 7-pt. semantic differential scales, while those in reciprocal exchanges report average levels of trust *above* the neutral point. The form of exchange also has pronounced effects on affective commitment. Subjects report significantly stronger feelings of commitment, and evaluate their partners more positively, in reciprocal than in negotiated exchanges. All of these differences are still significant after controlling for the effects of the partner's behavioral commitment and the equality of exchange.[16]

We also found strong support for Hypothesis 6, which predicted that trust and affective commitment will increase with "trustworthy" behaviors (high behavioral commitment and low inequality), and that this relation will be stronger for reciprocal than for negotiated exchanges. The two networks shown in Fig. 1 produced the necessary variation in behavioral commitment and inequality to test this hypothesis; as expected, behavioral commitment was substantially higher, and inequality lower, for the A-B relations in network (b) than in network (a). All of the correlations between the partner's behaviors and the subject's feelings of trust, affect, and commitment are much stronger for reciprocal exchanges than for negotiated exchanges (an average correlation of 0.68 for reciprocal vs. 0.25 for negotiated). As expected, however, *behavioral* commitments occurred no more frequently in reciprocal than in negotiated exchanges; behavioral commitment is primarily influenced by power imbalance, not exchange form.[17] However, in the low-power networks (Fig. 1b) where behavioral commitment is highest, the two forms of exchange differed markedly in the *speed* with which actors formed commitments. In negotiated exchanges, committed relations formed early and changed little; in reciprocal exchanges, commitments formed gradually, in a step-by-step process that was similar to Blau's (1964) description of slowly evolving exchange relations as actors first test each other's trustworthiness and then gradually increase the frequency and regularity of their exchange. This condition produced particularly high levels of trust and affective commitment.

Extensions of these analyses to the data collected for the experiments on the value of alternatives and the number of alternatives provide further support for both hypotheses. These data also show that feelings of trust and affective commitment are greater in reciprocal than in negotiated exchanges, even after controlling for actors' behaviors (their behavioral commitment to each other and the equality of their exchange), and the correlations of these behaviors with trust and affect are higher for reciprocal exchanges than for negotiated exchanges. These patterns are stronger for the disadvantaged actors – the Bs – than for the advantaged As in all of these experiments, as the logic of risk would predict: exchange is riskiest for the Bs, and therefore reciprocal exchange provides a stronger test of their advantaged partners' trustworthiness.

Experiments on Fairness

Data from these first three experiments suggested that reciprocal exchanges not only increased feelings of trust, positive affect, and commitment, but perceptions that the partner behaved more fairly – even when their actual behavior was controlled. These results provided preliminary support for Hypothesis 7, that actors in reciprocal exchanges evaluate their partners as more fair than do those in negotiated exchanges.

A more rigorous test of this hypothesis required a different design than the one used in the power experiments, however – in order to *remove* potential equity effects, the power experiments restricted actors' information about the network structure and, most importantly, the partners' outcomes. To study fairness judgments, actors must have full information of the value of both their own and their partners' outcomes and of the exchange network within which those outcomes are obtained. Furthermore, physical rather than statistical control of the partners' behaviors is desirable: subjects should evaluate the fairness of partners who behave in equivalent ways, in equivalent structures, within the defining differences of the two forms of exchange.

Thus, three additional experiments were conducted in which subjects engaged in either reciprocal or negotiated exchanges with computer-simulated partners who were programmed to exchange either equally or unequally with the subject. This design allowed us to test both Hypothesis 7 and Hypothesis 8, which predicted stronger effects of the form of exchange on perceived fairness when exchanges are unequal rather than equal. The network shown in Fig. 1a was used in all conditions; the subject was always in one of the B positions, and the subject's interaction with actor A was the focus. In the negotiated exchanges, equal or unequal exchanges were created by manipulating A's initial requests/offers and subsequent concessions; in the reciprocal exchanges, equal or unequal exchanges were created by manipulating A's probability of reciprocating the subject's giving on the previous opportunity.[18] Thus, in the negotiated exchanges, equal or unequal trades occurred on discrete opportunities; in the reciprocal exchanges, equality or inequality emerged only over time. We also controlled, partly physically and partly statistically, for the frequency of exchange between the subject and A. An initial experiment compared equal and moderately unequal exchanges; subsequent experiments added a highly unequal condition and explored the effects of creating inequality in different ways within each form of exchange (Molm et al., 2003).

The results of these far more controlled experiments again support Hypothesis 7, clearly showing that actors regard their partners as *more* fair when exchanges are reciprocal rather than negotiated. Across three experiments, we consistently found that when all other aspects of exchange are constant, the form of exchange has strong and consistent effects on actors' perceptions of fairness. Exchanges that produce equivalent outcomes, in equivalent structures, are perceived as far more unfair when those outcomes are negotiated than when they are reciprocally exchanged, without negotiation, by partners making individual choices. This basic finding holds both for actors' reported perceptions of their partners' fairness and for their behavioral responses to inequality (i.e. the frequency with which subjects made agreements with or gave benefits to the focal partner).

Subjects' perceptions of fairness failed to support Hypothesis 8, however: the strength of the relation between the form of exchange and perceived fairness did not vary with the equality or inequality of exchange. Subjects perceived their exchange partners as significantly more fair when exchanges were reciprocal – about 1.5 points on a 7-pt scale – in *both* equal and unequal conditions. Furthermore, subjects engaged in *equal negotiated* exchanges viewed their partners' behavior as no more fair than subjects engaged in *unequal reciprocal* exchanges (means for both were slightly greater than the neutral point of 4.0). In *both* equal and unequal reciprocal exchange conditions, subjects rated their partner's behavior as "fair" – *above* the neutral point of 4.0.

Subjects' behavioral responses to inequality do support the predicted interaction, however. Subjects in either form of exchange were equally likely to exchange with A when terms were equal, but subjects in the negotiated conditions refused to agree to unequal terms more frequently than subjects in reciprocal conditions refused to give to partners who reciprocated unequally. Their resistance was greatest in the highly unequal exchange condition.

Two experiments that varied how inequality was created within each form of exchange provided new insights into their differences. While the general finding that reciprocal exchange is perceived as more fair than negotiated exchange was confirmed, these experiments indicated that what constitutes "fair exchange" in the two forms appears to be determined by quite different factors: by the *rate* of giving in reciprocal exchanges, and by the *value* given in negotiated exchanges. In the reciprocal exchanges, only variations in the rate of reciprocity affect actors' perceptions of their partner's fairness; the value of the benefits exchanged makes no difference. As long as partners consistently reciprocated the actors' giving, the subjects considered their partners' behavior to be very fair. For negotiated exchange, the opposite was true: the process of bargaining – whether initial offers were high or low, whether concessions were more or less gradual – made no difference; only the terms of the agreement eventually reached affected perceptions of the partner's fairness.

CONCLUSIONS, IMPLICATIONS, AND FUTURE DIRECTIONS

This research program has shown that fundamental differences between reciprocal and negotiated forms of exchange affect many of the processes addressed by current exchange theories. Reciprocal exchanges produce lower power use and inequality, higher levels of trust and feelings of affective commitment, and stronger perceptions of fairness than negotiated exchanges that are structurally equivalent. The lower inequality does not account for the more positive feelings; independent of behavioral inequality and behavioral commitment, actors in reciprocal exchange evaluate their partners more highly. Furthermore, the form of exchange *interacts* with the effects of both network structure and actors' behaviors in their effects on exchange outcomes. Key dimensions of network structures – particularly, the availability of actors' alternatives – have weaker effects on power use in reciprocal than in negotiated exchange, while exchange partners' behaviors have stronger effects on actors' evaluations of their partners in reciprocal than in negotiated exchange.

Three mechanisms were proposed to account for the different effects of the two forms of exchange: how power is used, the amount and type of risk, and the relative salience of the cooperative or competitive aspects of exchange. The results of these experiments provide substantial support for the predictions based on these mechanisms, but they also reveal patterns that were not predicted and that suggest other processes may be involved.

First, the predicted reversal in direction of the effect of availability of alternatives on power use was not supported for reciprocal exchange. In the low-availability networks, the powerful actors opted to exchange with their more available, more dependent partners rather than engaging in the pattern that would have maximized their outcomes: exchanging primarily with their less available partners. This was the only prediction whose support required actors to give *more* frequently to those who gave *less* frequently to them (when the value of benefits controlled by these exchange partners was equal), and it was the one prediction that was not supported.

Second, although both previous research and our theoretical logic implied that the form of exchange should have stronger effects on perceived fairness in unequal than in equal exchanges, both effects were of identical strength. Actors evaluated their partners as more fair, by the same amount, in reciprocal than in negotiated exchanges for both equal and unequal exchanges. Their behavioral responses offered some support for the predicted interaction, but their self-reports offered none.

Third, in reciprocal exchanges, actors' judgments of their partners' fairness were unaffected by the value of benefits received; only the rate with which the partner reciprocated an actor's giving mattered. Partners who consistently reciprocated others' giving were perceived as very fair, regardless of the value of their exchange. In negotiated exchanges, on other hand, only the terms of the agreement reached mattered; variations in the process of bargaining had no effect.

All of these discrepant findings show actors behaving in ways that imply they value the *act* of reciprocity, per se, *over and above the instrumental benefits of exchange.* Together, these results suggest that reciprocal forms of exchange may provide expressive benefits (feelings of group solidarity, of being valued by another) that are not acquired through negotiated exchange, and that may substitute for the value of other benefits foregone. Indeed, not only the act of reciprocity, but the *obligations* created by the unilateral giving that precedes reciprocity, may make reciprocal exchanges more valuable than negotiated exchange. As a form of social capital, outstanding obligations contribute to the continuity and stability of relationships (Coleman, 1988).

The implications of this research are important both for theories of social exchange and for interaction in natural settings. Theoretically, this work shows the limitations of theories developed exclusively for negotiated exchange and the need for greater understanding of the full range of exchange forms that characterize social life. Not only does the form of exchange affect a diversity of exchange outcomes – behavioral, cognitive, and affective – it affects the *relations* between network structures and outcomes. Our findings also raise questions about the core assumption underlying all contemporary exchange theories, that actors seek to maximize their benefits. Instead, the results suggest that reducing risk, or loss, may sometimes be a stronger motivation than increasing gain, and that the act of reciprocity may be more valuable than the particular benefits gained. Because most contemporary exchange theorists have focused exclusively on negotiated exchanges, these distinctions have been irrelevant. In negotiated exchanges, reciprocity is a trivial byproduct of a bilateral trade, and the same actions that reduce the risk of exclusion – raising offers – also increase gain and increase power use.

But in reciprocal exchange, reciprocity is not taken for granted, and it is likely that its significance extends beyond the return that it provides on one's investment. Reciprocal exchange may play a particularly valuable role in building and maintaining social relations, even those based primarily on economic exchanges. As Blau (1964) observed, the initial offer of a favor has special significance, because the person who makes the first overture risks not only the chance that the act will not be reciprocated, but rejection of the offer itself; i.e. the offer to enter into a relationship. Cultural anthropologists have long noted the symbolic importance, in traditional societies, of frequent reciprocal exchanges of resources with little economic value (e.g. Malinowski, 1922; Ziegler, 1990). And our research suggests that in modern societies, as well, reciprocal acts of small value may be more effective in building and maintaining social relations than a single exchange of large value. It is this capacity to form ongoing relations through a series of reciprocal, individual acts in which the distinction between completing one exchange and initiating another becomes blurred – and keeping accounts less relevant – that negotiation removes.

Although our conclusions are based on laboratory experiments, conducted in part with simulated actors, they also have important implications for interaction in natural settings. Ironically, they suggest that the very mechanisms that societies have created to reduce risk in transactions – joint decision-making, communication of offers and counteroffers, advance knowledge of terms, and strictly binding agreements that assure those terms are honored – have the unintended consequence of reducing trust and affective commitment in relationships. In addition, characteristics of negotiated exchange that are generally regarded as more procedurally fair, including greater voice, greater outcome control, and more information (Lind & Tyler, 1988; Thibaut & Walker, 1975), appear to diminish rather than enhance perceptions that the partner is behaving fairly. In exchanges between strangers, the loss of trust and sense of fairness may be a reasonable price to pay for protection against exploitation. But as negotiated exchange has acquired status from its use in important institutional settings (such as economic transactions and international relations), it has also become more common in exchanges between friends and intimates. In these settings, its advantages are more dubious.

These findings are particular relevant to current interests in the "social capital" that actors accumulate through their relationships to one another (Coleman, 1988; Paxton, 1999; Portes, 1998). Most of these discussions assume that the mechanism underlying the production of trust and positive affect in ongoing relationships is the *recurrence* of exchange between the same actors, the *closeness* of actors' personal ties through family or community, or the *length* of their relationship and prior history (e.g. Ben-Porath, 1980; Granovetter, 1985; Uzzi, 1996). But in natural settings, all of these characteristics tend to be confounded with the form of exchange; i.e. reciprocal exchanges are often associated with more intimate interactions with friends and family members that have occurred repeatedly for a long period of time. As our research shows, even when these characteristics are held constant, the form of exchange still has strong and predictable effects on trust, affective ties, and perceptions of fairness.

The next phase of this research program will pursue several important questions. First, as we have seen, a fourth causal mechanism – the value of reciprocity – may be contributing to the different effects of negotiated and reciprocal exchange, producing lower power use and greater feelings of trust, affective commitment, and fairness in reciprocal exchanges than can be explained by differences in risk or the salience of conflict. For most of the exchange outcomes studied, *at least two* of the four causal mechanisms identified – power use, risk, salience of conflict, and value of reciprocity – could potentially account for the observed results. Thus, identifying the independent (and, quite possibly, joint) effects of these mechanisms on the various exchange outcomes must be one of the primary goals for the next phase of the project. That objective requires independent manipulation of the key dimensions that distinguish the two forms of exchange – the contingency of outcomes, information, and the timing of inequality – and that, in turn, affect the intervening causal mechanisms.

A second objective for future work is to vary some of the conditions that were held constant in the first phase of the research, which was based on comparisons of relatively "pure" forms of negotiated and reciprocal exchange. The exchange settings compared in these experiments represented the features of each form of exchange that most researchers have studied; e.g. negotiated exchange agreements were binding, reciprocal exchanges were made without communication of intent, and potential joint benefit was held constant within relations. Studying variations *within* each form of exchange will allow us to test the robustness of effects under conditions that are more typical of these two forms of exchange in many natural settings, and to determine which characteristics are more theoretically important to their effects. Some of these features – e.g. whether agreements are binding – are central to tests of the causal mechanisms, and thus their manipulation can serve both purposes.

A third important objective for the next phase of research is the extension of the theoretical and empirical analysis to *indirect*, or *generalized, exchange*. Theorists have long argued that generalized exchange should promote particularly high levels of trust, commitment, and solidarity (Ekeh, 1974; Lévi-Strauss, 1969). A few empirical studies support this prediction (Bearman, 1997; O'Connell, 1984; Uehara, 1990), but no systematic comparisons of generalized, reciprocal, and negotiated exchange have been conducted. Furthermore, both theoretical (e.g. Ekeh, 1974) and empirical (Uehara, 1990) investigations have often confounded the direct or indirect structure of exchange with stipulation of the terms and timing of reciprocity, leaving the cause of any differences ambiguous.

For the causal mechanisms proposed to underlie the effects of different forms of exchange, chain-generalized exchange, which describes the structure observed in the Kula ring (e.g. Malinowski, 1922; Ziegler, 1990) and in matrilateral cross-cousin marriage (e.g. Bearman, 1997; Lévi-Strauss, 1969), would provide a particularly interesting comparison to reciprocal and negotiated direct exchange.[19] First, the risk of non-reciprocity is even greater in chain-generalized exchange than in reciprocal exchange, because the indirect dependence of actors on all others in the chain increases risk.[20] Consider the simplest form of chain-generalized exchange: a three-actor, circular chain in which A gives to B, B to C, and C back to A. If the probability of any actor's reciprocating exchange in this hypothetical three-actor network is 0.8, then the probability that A's giving to B is indirectly reciprocated by C drops to 0.64 (0.8 × 0.8). In addition, there is no opportunity for contingent action from the recipient; thus, no direct tit-for-tat strategies – including punishment for defection – are possible. Second, the salience of competing interests should be even less in generalized exchange than in reciprocal exchange, because actors do not give to the same actor from whom they receive benefits; thus, no direct comparison of benefits given and received by two actors is possible. Third, reciprocity – albeit indirect – should acquire even greater value under these conditions, because the consequences of either giving or not giving are so great: actors who give to others contribute to the maintenance of an entire network of exchange; those who defect can destroy the entire system (Yamagishi & Cook, 1993).

Each of these lines of work will contribute to the ultimate objective of this long-term project: the development of a new, more general theory of exchange that will address not only negotiated exchange but the reciprocal and generalized exchanges that characterize much of social life. The first phase of this project has laid the groundwork for that effort, by developing the conceptual framework for the theory, analyzing the key dimensions that theoretically distinguish among forms of exchange, and conducting a series of experiments that demonstrate the strong and consistent effects of the form of exchange on major exchange outcomes.

NOTES

1. Reciprocal exchanges constitute only one category of non-cooperative games, however. Actors make choices individually and without communication in all non-cooperative games, but the payoff structures of these games include relations that are not exchange relations.

2. In natural settings, these important analytical distinctions may become blurred. Negotiated agreements are not always binding, and over time, reciprocal exchanges may come to resemble negotiated exchanges as sequential dependencies develop between actors' behaviors and they acquire more information about each other (Molm, 1994; Thibaut & Kelley, 1959).

3. In negotiated exchanges (as they are operationalized in typical exchange experiments, and in these experiments), what A gives and what A obtains from an agreement are perfectly correlated in a zero-sum relation. In reciprocal exchanges, there is no *necessary* relation between the two in any particular set of exchanges; theoretically, A could give more or less frequently to B while still receiving the same amount from other partners. The contingency between A's giving and B's giving is one of the assumptions of power-dependence theory, however, and empirically, the reciprocal frequencies of actors' giving to one another are highly correlated. In the reciprocal exchange networks studied in this research program,

the average correlation is 0.76. Thus, for both negotiated and reciprocal exchanges, the costs of exchange are proportional to the amount given; in reciprocal exchanges, the more frequently A gives to B, the less frequently A gives to other partners, and the less those others give to A.

4. I use the term "exclusion" to refer to the behavioral outcome of failing to make an agreement with a desired partner because that partner made an agreement with someone else. How exclusion is produced – by a regulatory constraint (an exchange rule) or by decreased demand for one partner's resources after exchange with another – does not affect the analysis.

5. *Trust* refers to expectations based on inferences about another's personal traits and intentions, while *assurance* refers to expectations based on knowledge of an incentive structure that encourages benign behavior rather than exploitation (Yamagishi & Yamagishi, 1994).

6. Under other conditions, such as transient exchanges between strangers (Macy & Skvoretz, 1998), untrustworthy behavior might be the norm.

7. This conceptualization of commitment differs slightly from Lawler and Yoon's (1996). They define affective commitment as an attachment *to the relation or group*, characterized by positive emotions of pleasure and satisfaction, or interest and excitement. In contrast, our conceptualization is an attachment to a specific other, characterized by expressions of commitment to the partner and positive evaluations of the partner.

8. Integrative issues that offer the opportunity for agreements that provide greater total benefit for both actors through "logrolling" tactics are an exception (Lawler & Yoon, 1993).

9. Actors in both forms of exchange incur opportunity costs, but only in reciprocal exchange is the differential allocation of those costs a fundamental source of inequality.

10. This same logic should also extend to actors' evaluations of the partner along positive or negative dimensions, and to feelings of affective commitment to the partner. Thus, both differences in risk and uncertainty, and differences in the relative salience of competition or cooperation, lead to the same prediction (Hypothesis 5): that actors will express more positive affect for the partner in reciprocal than in negotiated exchanges.

11. Subjects in the reciprocal conditions exchanged for 400 opportunities; those in the negotiated conditions exchanged for 100 opportunities. Both sessions took roughly the same amount of time (two hours), and subjects were not informed of the number of opportunities in either. The monetary value of points was adjusted so that subjects in the reciprocal exchanges earned the same amount as subjects in the negotiated exchanges for comparable behaviors. More opportunities were run in the reciprocal exchange conditions to allow for the possibility that reciprocal exchange takes longer to stabilize than negotiated exchange, which consists of multiple behaviors – up to five rounds of offers – and more information on each opportunity. Trend analyses revealed no such differences, however; therefore, all behavioral means reported here are for the last half of the exchange period for both forms of exchange.

12. They did not know the potential or actual value of exchanges between their alternative partners (who were, of course, simulated actors who did not actually exchange); by omitting this information, both the equal and unequal exchanges between the subject and the focal partner were made plausible.

13. The first experiment varied structural information, giving subjects either full or restricted information about the network structure. In full information conditions, a drawing of the exchange network was displayed on subjects' screens, showing who could exchange with whom and which relations were high- or low-value. In restricted information conditions, no figure was displayed, and the screen informed subjects only of their own access to two partners and their potential benefits from those partners. Information had no effect on power use or any other measures, and subsequent experiments were conducted

with restricted information. For comparability, all analyses reported in this chapter – including those on the first experiment – are based on restricted information conditions.

14. Each position's power use (P) is measured by calculating the total reward (R) obtained by each actor in the position, averaging these measures of R across all N actors in the position, and dividing by e, the number of exchange opportunities. A's power use over B is then computed by taking the ratio of A's power use to the sum of both A's and B's power use, $P_A/(P_A + P_B)$.

15. The first four items of the scale asked subjects to evaluate their partner's behavior as good/bad, nice/awful, cooperative/uncooperative, and helpful/unhelpful; the fifth item asked subjects to describe their general feelings toward the partner as positive/negative. With responses to the five items averaged, the resulting scale has alpha reliabilities of 0.97 and 0.95 for A and B, respectively.

16. We measured A's behavioral commitment to B with a modified version of Cook and Emerson's (1978) measure of commitment, by computing how often A chose to exchange with B rather than with an alternative partner. We measured inequality within the A-B relation by dividing the difference between the value that A and B received from each other by the sum of the value that they received from each other.

17. When alternatives are limited and opportunity costs are low (as in Fig. 1b), commitments provide a means of reducing uncertainty at a reasonable cost; therefore, behavioral commitments vary inversely with power (Cook & Emerson, 1978; Lawler & Yoon, 1996; Tallman et al., 1991).

18. In the equal exchanges, both S and A received 12 points from each other; in the unequal exchanges, A received an average of 14 points for every 10 points that S received. In the negotiated exchanges, equal or unequal agreements were manipulated by varying A's initial requests/offers, which averaged 13 points in the equal and 15 points in the unequal exchange conditions. If S did not accept this initial offer, A decreased its request by one point on the second round and then held firm, behavior that produced equal 12-12 splits in the equal exchange conditions, and 14-10 splits in the unequal conditions. In the reciprocal exchanges, A responded to S's prior behavior with a modified tit-for-tat strategy in the equal conditions, reciprocating S's prior giving 90% of the time and initiating giving 10% of the time. In the unequal conditions, A reciprocated S's giving 10 out of 14 times.

19. Yamagishi and Cook (1993) refer to this structure as "network-generalized" exchange.

20. As Takahashi (2000) has noted, the existence of generalized exchange poses a particular challenge to assumptions of self-interested actors, because giving is not reciprocated by the recipient, there is no guarantee of reciprocity by a third party, and any member of a generalized exchange system can free ride.

ACKNOWLEDGMENTS

This research was supported by a grant from the National Science Foundation (No. SBR-9514911). I gratefully acknowledge their support and the work of my two collaborators on this project, Nobuyuki Takahashi and Gretchen Peterson. I thank the editors of this volume for helpful comments on the chapter.

REFERENCES

Axelrod, R. (1984). *The evolution of cooperation*. New York: Basic Books.

Bearman, P. (1997). Generalized exchange. *American Journal of Sociology, 102*, 1383–1415.

Ben-Porath, Y. (1980). The F-connection: Families, friends and firms in the organization of exchange. *Population and Development Review, 6*, 1–30.

Blau, P. M. (1964). *Exchange and power in social life*. New York: Wiley.

Bonacich, P., & Friedkin, N. E. (1998). Unequally valued exchange relations. *Social Psychology Quarterly, 16*, 160–171.

Burgess, R. L., & Nielsen, J. M. (1974). An experimental analysis of some structural determinants of equitable and inequitable exchange relations. *American Sociological Review, 39*, 427–443.

Cohen, R. L. (1982). Perceiving justice: An attributional perspective. In: J. Greenberg & R. L. Cohen (Eds), *Equity and Justice in Social Behavior* (pp. 119–160). New York: Academic Press.

Coleman, J. S. (1988). Social capital in the creation of human capital. *American Journal of Sociology, 94*, S95–S120.

Coleman, J. S. (1990). *Foundations of social theory*. Cambridge: Harvard University Press.

Cook, K. S., & Emerson, R. M. (1978). Power, equity and commitment in exchange networks. *American Sociological Review, 43*, 721–739.

Cook, K. S., Emerson, R. M., Gillmore, M. R., & Yamagishi, T. (1983). The distribution of power in exchange networks: Theory and experimental results. *American Journal of Sociology, 89*, 275–305.

Cook, K. S., & Yamagishi, T. (1992). Power in exchange networks: A power-dependence formulation. *Social Networks, 14*, 245–265.

DiMaggio, P., & Louch, H. (1998). Socially embedded consumer transactions: For what kinds of purchases do people most often use networks? *American Sociological Review, 63*, 619–637.

Ekeh, P. P. (1974). *Social exchange theory: The two traditions*. Cambridge, MA: Harvard University Press.

Emerson, R. M. (1972a). Exchange theory, Part I: A psychological basis for social exchange. In: J. Berger, M. Zelditch, Jr. & B. Anderson (Eds), *Sociological Theories in Progress* (Vol. 2, pp. 38–57). Boston: Houghton-Mifflin.

Emerson, R. M. (1972b). Exchange theory, Part II: Exchange relations and networks. In: J. Berger, M. Zelditch, Jr. & B. Anderson (Eds), *Sociological Theories in Progress* (Vol. 2, pp. 58–87). Boston: Houghton-Mifflin.

Emerson, R. M. (1981). Social exchange theory. In: M. Rosenberg & R. H. Turner (Eds), *Social Psychology: Sociological Perspectives* (pp. 30–65). New York: Basic Books.

Friedkin, N. (1993). An expected value model of social exchange outcomes. In: E. J. Lawler, B. Markovsky, K. Heimer & J. O'Brien (Eds), *Advances in Group Processes* (Vol. 10, pp. 163–193). Greenwich, CT: JAI Press.

Granovetter, M. (1985). Economic action and social structure: The problem of embeddedness. *American Journal of Sociology, 91*, 481–510.

Hardin, R. (1991). Trusting persons, trusting institutions. In: R. J. Zeckhauser (Ed.), *Strategy and Choice* (pp. 185–209). Cambridge, MA: MIT Press.

Hassebrauck, M. (1987). The influence of misattributions on reactions to inequity: Towards a further understanding of inequity. *European Journal of Social Psychology, 17*, 295–304.

Heckathorn, D. D. (1985). Power and trust in social exchange. In: E. J. Lawler (Ed.), *Advances in Group Processes* (Vol. 2, pp. 143–167). Greenwich, CT: JAI Press.

Hegtvedt, K. A., & Killian, C. (1999). Fairness and emotions: Reactions to the process and outcomes of negotiations. *Social Forces, 78*, 269–302.

Homans, G. C. (1974 [1961]). *Social behavior: Its elementary forms.* New York: Harcourt Brace & World.

Kelley, H. H., & Thibaut, J. W. (1978). *Interpersonal relations: A theory of interdependence.* New York: Wiley.

Keohane, R. O. (1986). Reciprocity in international relations. *International Organization, 40*, 1–27.

Kollock, P. (1994). The emergence of exchange structures: An experimental study of uncertainty, commitment, and trust. *American Journal of Sociology, 100*, 313–345.

Lawler, E. J. (1992). Power processes in bargaining. *The Sociological Quarterly, 33*, 17–34.

Lawler, E. J. (2001). An affect theory of social exchange. *American Journal of Sociology, 107*, 321–352.

Lawler, E. J., & Yoon, J. (1993). Power and the emergence of commitment behavior in negotiated exchange. *American Sociological Review, 58*, 465–481.

Lawler, E. J., & Yoon, J. (1996). Commitment in exchange relations: Test of a theory of relational cohesion. *American Sociological Review, 61*, 89–108.

Lévi-Strauss, C. (1969). *The elementary structures of kinship* (Rev. ed.). Boston: Beacon.

Lind, E. A., & Tyler, T. R. (1988). *The social psychology of procedural justice.* New York: Plenum.

Luhman, N. (1979). *Trust and power.* Chichester: Wiley.

Macaulay, S. (1963). Non-contractual relations in business: A preliminary study. *American Sociological Review, 28*, 55–67.

Macy, M. W., & Skvoretz, J. (1998). The evolution of trust and cooperation between strangers: A computational model. *American Sociological Review, 63*, 638–660.

Malinowski, B. (1922). *Argonauts of the western Pacific.* London: Routledge & Kegan Paul.

Markovsky, B., Willer, D., & Patton, T. (1988). Power relations in exchange networks. *American Sociological Review, 53*, 220–236.

Marsden, P. V. (1982). Brokerage behavior in restricted exchange networks. In: P. V. Marsden & N. Lin (Eds), *Social Structure and Network Analysis* (pp. 201–218). Beverly Hills, CA: Sage.

Michaels, J. W., & Wiggins, J. A. (1976). Effects of mutual dependency and dependency asymmetry on social exchange. *Sociometry, 39*, 368–376.

Molm, L. D. (1990). Structure, action and outcomes: The dynamics of power in exchange relations. *American Sociological Review, 55*, 427–447.

Molm, L. D. (1994). Dependence and risk: Transforming the structure of social exchange. *Social Psychology Quarterly, 57*, 163–176.

Molm, L. D. (1997). *Coercive power in social exchange.* Cambridge: Cambridge University Press.

Molm, L. D. (2000). Theories of social exchange and exchange networks. In: G. Ritzer & B. Smart (Eds), *The Handbook of Social Theory* (pp. 260–272). Sage Press.

Molm, L. D., Peterson, G., & Takahashi, N. (1999). Power in negotiated and reciprocal exchange. *American Sociological Review, 64*, 876–890.

Molm, L. D., Peterson, G., & Takahashi, N. (2001). The value of exchange. *Social Forces, 80*, 159–185.

Molm, L. D., Takahashi, N., & Peterson, G. (2000). Risk and trust in social exchange: An experimental test of a classical proposition. *American Journal of Sociology, 105*, 1396–1427.

Molm, L. D., Takahashi, N., & Peterson, G. (2003). In the eye of the beholder: Procedural justice in social exchange. *American Sociological Review, 68*, 128–152.

Nisbett, R. E., & Ross, L. (1980). *Human inference: Strategies and shortcomings of social judgment.* Englewood Cliffs, NJ: Prentice-Hall.

O'Connell, L. (1984). An exploration of exchange in three social relationships: Kinship, friendship and the marketplace. *Journal of Social and Personal Relationships, 1*, 333–345.

Paxton, P. (1999). Is social capital declining in the United States? A multiple indicator assessment. *American Journal of Sociology, 105,* 88–127.

Portes, A. (1998). Social capital: Its origins and applications in modern sociology. *Annual Review of Sociology, 22,* 1–24.

Ross, L. (1977). The intuitive psychologist and his shortcomings: Distortions in the attribution process. In: L. Berkowitz (Ed.), *Advances in Experimental Social Psychology* (Vol. 10, pp. 174–221). New York: Academic Press.

Skvoretz, J., & Willer, D. (1993). Exclusion and power: A test of four theories of power in exchange networks. *American Sociological Review, 58,* 801–818.

Skvoretz, J., & Zhang, P. (1997). Actors' responses to outcomes in exchange networks: The process of power development. *Sociological Perspectives, 40,* 181–197.

Takahashi, N. (2000). The emergence of generalized exchange. *American Journal of Sociology, 105,* 1105–1134.

Tallman, I., Gray, L., & Leik, R. (1991). Decisions, dependency, and commitment: An exchange-based theory of group development. In: E. J. Lawler, B. Markovsky, C. Ridgeway & H. Walker (Eds), *Advances in Group Processes* (Vol. 9, pp. 227–257). Greenwich, CT: JAI Press.

Thibaut, J. W., & Kelley, H. H. (1959). *The social psychology of groups.* New York: Wiley.

Thibaut, J. W., & Walker, L. (1975). *Procedural justice: A psychological analysis.* Hillsdale, NJ: Erlbaum.

Thompson, L., & Lowenstein, G. (1992). Egocentric interpretations of fairness and interpersonal conflict. *Organizational Behavior and Human Decision Processes, 51,* 176–197.

Thye, S. R., Lovaglia, M. J., & Markovsky, B. (1997). Responses to social exchange and social exclusion in networks. *Social Forces, 75,* 1031–1047.

Tyler, T. R., Degoey, P., & Smith, H. (1996). Understanding why the justice of group procedures matters: A test of the psychological dynamics of the group-value model. *Journal of Personality and Social Psychology, 70,* 913–930.

Tyler, T. R., & Lind, E. A. (1992). A relational model of authority in groups. *Advances in Experimental Social Psychology, 25,* 115–191.

Uehara, E. (1990). Dual exchange theory, social networks, and informal social support. *American Journal of Sociology, 96,* 521–557.

Utne, M. K., & Kidd, R. F. (1980). Equity and attribution. In: G. Mikula (Ed.), *Justice and Social Interaction* (pp. 63–93). New York: Springer-Verlag.

Uzzi, B. (1996). The sources and consequences of embeddedness for the economic performance of organizations: The network effect. *American Journal of Sociology, 61,* 674–698.

Yamagishi, T., & Cook, K. S. (1993). Generalized exchange and social dilemmas. *Social Psychology Quarterly, 56,* 235–248.

Yamagishi, T., Cook, K. S., & Watabe, M. (1998). Uncertainty, trust, and commitment formation in the United States and Japan. *American Journal of Sociology, 104,* 165–194.

Yamagishi, T., & Yamagishi, M. (1994). Trust and commitment in the United States and Japan. *Motivation and Emotion, 18,* 129–166.

Ziegler, R. (1990). The Kula: Social order, barter, and ceremonial exchange. In: M. Hechter, K. Opp & R. Wippler (Eds), *Social Institutions: Their Emergence, Maintenance, and Effects* (pp. 141–70). New York: Aldine de Gruyter.

EXCHANGE NETWORKS: AN ANALYSIS OF ALL NETWORKS UP TO SIZE 9

M. A. L. M. van Assen

ABSTRACT

In this study negotiated exchange under the 1-exchange rule is considered in the whole population of 142,660 exchange networks up to size 9. A review shows that 51 of these networks have been studied in the literature. Predictions for the whole population of networks are derived by parsimonious versions of power-dependence and exchange-resistance theory. All but 301 networks are classified similarly as equal, weak, or strong power networks by the power-dependence and exchange-resistance theory. Only 4% of the networks is classified as a strong power network, as opposed to the 43% of the networks studied in the literature.

INTRODUCTION

Homans (1958) was among the first social scientists to regard social behavior as exchange. More specifically, Homans (1958, p. 606) stated that "social behavior is an exchange of goods, material goods but also non-material ones, such as the symbols of approval and prestige." This approach to social behavior, called *social exchange theory*, was also used by other prominent researchers in the same time period, such as Thibaut and Kelley (1959) and Blau (1964).

Power and Status
Advances in Group Processes, Volume 20, 67–103
© 2003 Published by Elsevier Ltd.
ISSN: 0882-6145/doi:10.1016/S0882-6145(03)20003-5

It was Emerson (1962, 1972a, b) who introduced the network in social exchange theory. The network in social exchange theory represents the possible exchange relations that exist between actors in the network. If actors are directly connected they have an exchange relation; they are able to exchange, but do not have to exchange. If actors in the network are not directly connected to each other, they do not have an exchange relation and cannot exchange. Consider for example the T network in Fig. 1. The actors A and E are not directly connected and therefore cannot exchange. Actor A can exchange with B, but need not to, and A can also exchange with either C or D, or A does not exchange at all.

The branch of social exchange theory that is concerned with exchange in networks, called *network exchange theory*, focuses on outcome differentials that emerge when actors in a network exchange with one another.[1] Cook and Emerson (1978) first empirically tested some consequences of one network exchange theory, called power-dependence theory, formulated by Emerson (1972a, b). Soon other researchers joined the arena and an explosion of research on exchange networks occurred in sociology.

Research on exchange networks can be classified into research on generalized, productive, and direct exchange (Emerson, 1981; Molm, 1997). In *generalized exchange* or indirect exchange, the exchange occurs between three or more actors and cannot be reduced to exchanges between pairs of two actors. Generalized exchange is studied by Bearman (1997), Gillmore (1987), Takahashi (2000), and Yamagishi and Cook (1993). In *productive exchange* both actors in the exchange contribute to, and benefit from, a single produced event. If one actor fails to contribute, neither actor will benefit. Productive exchange is studied by Lawler et al. (2000). Finally, in *direct exchange*, two actors exchange benefits with each other. Of the three categories, direct exchange is by far the most studied category.

Another typology of exchange classifies exchange into negotiated exchange and reciprocal exchange. *Negotiated exchange* involves a joint decision process, such as bargaining, to determine the terms of exchange (Molm et al., 2000). The terms are agreed on at the same time, and the agreement is binding to both actors. The benefits of exchange enjoyed by the two exchange partners are easily identified as discrete transactions, in contrast to transactions in reciprocal exchange. In *reciprocal (non-negotiated) exchange* actors' contributions to the exchange are performed separately and are not the outcome of a joint decision process. An actor offers profit to another actor without knowing whether, when, or to what degree the other will reciprocate. In contemporary sociology there is a tradition of studying exchange networks with reciprocal exchange relations (see Molm, 1997). However, almost all research on network exchange deals with negotiated exchange. Negotiated exchange is also the focus of the present study.

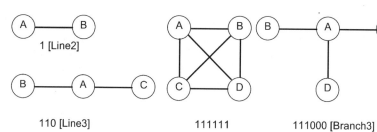

1 [Line2]

110 [Line3]

111111

111000 [Branch3]

110010 [Line4]

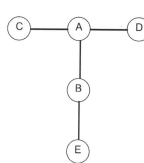

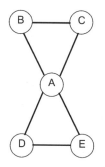

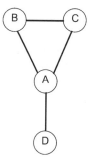

1110001000 [T]

1111100001 [Kite]

111100 [Stem]

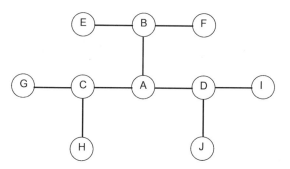

10-actor network

Fig. 1. Networks Often Considered in Studies on Network Exchange.

Research on negotiated exchange in networks, with the exception of some studies (see, e.g. Willer, 1987, 1999), represents a possible exchange relation by a split of a common pool of resources, usually, 24 points. Hence the outcome of an exchange between two actors is a division of 24 points among them, while these two actors obtain zero points in their relation when they do not come to an agreement on how to divide the 24 points. In experiments on network exchange the pool is discrete, instead of continuous. That is, it can only be split in two numbers of points of integer value, instead of real value. For simplicity it is here assumed that the pool is continuous.[2]

Another characteristic of most studies on negotiated exchange in networks is that they impose the 1-exchange rule. The *1-exchange-rule* entails that all actors in the exchange network can make either no or one exchange, but not more. For example, under the 1-exchange rule actor *A* in the *T* structure can exchange once, either with *B*, *C*, or *D*. If *A* exchanges with *B*, no other exchanges can occur. If *A* exchanges with *C*, still another exchange can occur, that is, an exchange between *B* and *E*.

To sum up, most research on network exchange focuses on the effect of the network structure on outcomes of negotiated splits of a common pool of resources in networks where all actors can make a maximum of one exchange. Negotiated exchange in networks under the 1-exchange rule is also the starting point of the present study.

A large number of theories and models have been developed that can predict outcome differentials in the exchange networks under consideration; power-dependence theory (e.g. Cook & Emerson, 1978; Cook & Yamagishi, 1992), exchange-resistance theory (e.g. Skvoretz & Willer, 1993), a graph-analytic theory using the graph-theoretic power index (GPI) (e.g. Markovsky et al., 1988), core theory (e.g. Bienenstock & Bonachich, 1992), optimal seek theory (Willer & Simpson, 1999), identity theory (Burke, 1997), Yamaguchi's (1996, 2000) rational choice model, expected value theory (Friedkin, 1992), and non-cooperative bargaining models (Berg & Panther, 1998; Braun & Gautschi, 2000). All aforementioned theories distinguish three different types of exchange relations. Firstly, equal power exchange relations. In *equal power exchange relations* actors obtain approximately half of the 24 profit points. Examples of equal power relations are the single exchange relation in the *Line2* structure and all relations in the completely connected four-actor network, both depicted in Fig. 1. Secondly, the theories identify strong power relations. In *strong power exchange relations* one actor obtains all or nearly all of the 24 profit points. For example, actor *A* in the *Line3* structure in Fig. 1 obtains almost all profit points in an exchange with either *B* or *C*. Finally, exchange relations can also be of weak power. In *weak power exchange relations* one actor consistently obtains more than half of the resource pool, but much less than the maximum number of points in the pool. It is the interaction between the network structure and the exchange conditions that determines whether an exchange relation is of equal, weak, or strong power (see, e.g. Markovsky et al., 1993; Skvoretz & Willer, 1993). In the present study we will not go into details of the factors that produce each of the three types of exchange relations. Here the types of exchange relations are merely operationally defined as equal power relations if both actors in the relation obtain 12 points, as strong power relations if one actor in the relation obtains 24 points, and as weak power relations if one actor in the relation obtains more than 12 but less than 24 points. Exchange networks themselves can and also will be classified using the same typology. An exchange network is defined as: (i) an *equal power exchange network* if all possible exchange relations are of equal power; (ii) a *weak power exchange network* if at least one exchange relation is of weak power; and (iii) a *strong power exchange network* if at least one exchange relation is of strong power and no relation is of weak power. Note that some relations in a weak power exchange network can be strong power exchange relations.

The predictions of the aforementioned theories are tested in empirical studies on network exchange by comparing the predicted exchange outcomes to the observed exchange outcomes. A first aim of present study is to provide a review of both empirical and theoretical studies on negotiated direct exchange networks. The review demonstrates that in total 23 different exchange networks have been used in experiments on negotiated exchange in the context of the 1-exchange rule. The networks used in these experiments never consisted more than seven actors. Additionally, the sample of 23 networks does not represent a random sample of the total number of 995 networks consisting of seven or fewer actors. More specifically, in general the density of the networks used in the experiments was small.[3] An additional number of 35 exchange networks have been referred to in discussing the exchange network theories and in deriving outcome predictions of these theories. Again, these networks are not representative of the complete sample space of possible exchange networks. Hence, the existing research on network exchange does not provide us with a general overview of the incidence of equal, weak, and strong power exchange relations and exchange networks.

The second and main goal of the present study is to obtain an overview of the incidence of the three types of exchange networks. For that reason a very large number of exchange networks is studied. More specifically, the study includes *all* networks, 142,660 in number, consisting of nine or fewer actors. To be able to classify an exchange network as belonging to one of the three types, predictions need to be derived on the basis of a network exchange theory. Here predictions are derived using versions of two of the most cited network exchange theories:

power-dependence theory (PD) and *exchange-resistance theory* (ER). There are
several reasons why precisely these two theories are selected. Firstly, the research
traditions in which PD and ER have developed exist for a longer time than any
of the other theories. Because of the long time span of these traditions a large
number of articles have been published in both traditions. Moreover, in many of
these articles researchers from one approach intensely criticized the research in
the other tradition. As a consequence, the two research traditions that led to PD
and ER largely shaped the other research on network exchange. Secondly, the
theories are based on comparable principles; PD is based on the *equidependence
principle*, ER on the *equiresistance principle*. In the present study PD and ER
are applied in their most parsimonious form such that the only difference between
the two theories is the principle on which they are based. Accordingly, PD and ER
resemble each other much more than they resemble any other network exchange
theory. Predictions of the other network exchange theories are not derived because
our main goal is to classify exchange networks, and not to distinguish and
compare the predictions of a large number of theories.

A third aim of the present study is to investigate the relations of the equidependence and the equiresistance principle with other possible principles or solutions.
The two principles are related to the Nash solution and another conception of the
equiresistance principle.

Finally, the fourth aim is to illustrate an analysis of a large number of networks
to compare classifications and point predictions of network exchange theories,
here versions of PD and ER. Two algorithms have been programmed, one for each
theory, which generate precise point predictions of the outcomes in exchange
relations for any exchange network under the 1-exchange rule. Comparing the
predictions of the two theories for all the networks is a significant task. For many
exchange networks the two (and other) theories make very similar predictions.
Therefore it is a relevant task to discover "critical" exchange networks for which
(if any) the theories yield different predictions. Only with these critical exchange
networks differential empirical evidence can be obtained for the different network
exchange theories. The critical networks can then be used in possible future
experiments to test the two and other network exchange theories.

In the second section, *Theories*, power-dependence and exchange-resistance
theory and their development are explained. Exchange-resistance theory is
reformulated such that it more closely resembles power-dependence theory, that
is, such that the difference between the two theories boils down to the use of two
different principles: the equidependence principle and the equiresistance principle.
The algorithms to generate the theories' predictions are also described. Finally, the
two principles are related to two other principles or solutions; another conception
of the exchange-resistance principle, and Nash's (1953) solution of two-person

cooperative game theory. In the third section, *The exchange networks*, a method of labeling exchange networks is described. In the fourth section, *Exchange networks considered in the literature*, a review is presented of empirical and theoretical research on exchange networks using the 1-exchange rule, with an emphasis on the exchange networks employed in the research. The *Goals of the analysis* section identifies the specific questions we attempt to answer in our analysis of the networks with the two network exchange theories. The *Results* section summarizes the outcomes of the analysis. Finally, the present study ends with a *Conclusions and discussion* section.

THEORIES

Power-Dependence Theory

In Emerson's (1962) original formulation of PD only dyadic exchange was considered. In subsequent work, Emerson and colleagues (Cook & Emerson, 1978; Cook et al., 1983, 1986; Cook & Gillmore, 1984; Cook & Yamagishi, 1992; Emerson, 1972b, 1976; Stolte & Emerson, 1977; Yamagishi et al., 1988) extended the logic of PD to apply also to exchange networks. Takahashi and Yamagishi (1993) adapted PD by incorporating additional assumptions on the probability that a particular exchange is carried out. In the present study the predictions are derived with a more parsimonious version of PD similar to the version described by Cook and Yamagishi (1992).

The logic of PD is based on the idea that the two actors in an exchange relation compare their possible profits in the exchange to the possible profits they can obtain in an exchange with another actor. Emerson and colleagues call the possible profit from an alternative exchange partner the *comparison level*, after Thibaut and Kelley (1959). In the present text the comparison level is called *conflict pay-off*, symbolized by C. PD's claim is that the actors' profits in their exchange relation, relative to their conflict pay-off, are equal. More formally, if actors j and k have the possibility to exchange then the exchange outcomes of $j(O_j)$ and $k(O_k)$ in relation jk are such that

$$O_j - C_j = O_k - C_k \tag{1}$$

The left hand of the equation is called the dependence of j on k, the right hand the dependence of k on j. The theory claims that the actors exchange at a rate at which their dependence on each other is equal. The theory's claim is also known as the *equidependence principle*.

To illustrate PD, consider the *Line4* structure in Fig. 1. An exchange between actors A and B is assumed to yield twelve points to each. These twelve points can be considered to be A's conflict pay-off in his exchange relation with C. Actor C has no alternative exchange partner hence C's conflict pay-off equals 0. Applying consequently the equidependence principle to determine the outcome of a possible exchange between A and C yields

$$O_A - 12 = O_C - 0 \tag{2}$$

Note that $O_A + O_C = 24$, therefore $O_C = 24 - O_A$ can be substituted in (2), which yields $O_A = 18$, and $O_C = 6$. Both actors' profit in the exchange relation relative to their conflict pay-off is equal to 6. Applying the equidependence principle to the two other exchange relations yields the following predictions: $O_B = 18$, $O_D = 6$ in exchange relation AD (relative profits of B and D equal to $18 - 12 = 6$), and $O_A = O_B = 12$ in exchange relation AB (relative profits of A and B equal to $12 - 18 = -6$).

PD's predictions of outcomes in exchange networks require that simultaneously in all relations the two actors in each relation are equidependent. Hence, for each possible exchange relation between actors j and k it holds that

$$O_j - C_j = O_k - C_k \tag{3}$$

Substituting $O_k = 24 - O_j$ in (3) results in the following prediction of O_j:

$$O_j = \frac{24 + C_j - C_k}{2} \tag{4}$$

The equidependence solution is equal to the kernel solution of cooperative game theory (see Bonacich & Friedkin, 1998). There always exists at least one solution of the kernel, hence there always exists a solution such that equidependence holds simultaneously in all exchange relations. An algorithm that is used in the analyses to obtain the predictions of PD in exchange networks is described later in this section.

The dependence of actors on each other can be negative in some exchange relations in a network, like for example the AB relation in the *Line4* structure. These exchange relations are called *suboptimal exchange relations* in the present paper. A suboptimal exchange relation is predicted to be used infrequently because both actors in the relation are predicted to gain more points in one of their other exchange possibilities. For example, in the *Line4* structure A and B are predicted to gain six more points in relations AC and BD respectively. The concept of a suboptimal relation is closely related to the concept of a *network break* (e.g. Markovsky et al., 1988; Willer, 1999). In the analysis of the exchange networks and of the predictions of PD and ER, the analysis is carried out separately in the case in which suboptimal exchange relations are taken into account and in the case in which they are disregarded.

Exchange-Resistance Theory

Of all studies on exchange networks, by far the most studies are based on or motivated by ER. It is to some extent problematic to describe ER because there are several different versions of the theory. Part of ER's diversity can be explained by the fact that different researchers, mainly Lovaglia, Markovsky, Skvoretz and Willer, have worked on its development. Below a brief description of the main ideas of ER is provided. See Willer (1999) for a detailed overview of the different formulations of ER.

Willer and Anderson (1981) developed one of the two foundations of current ER. That is, they introduced the concept of *resistance* into research on network exchange. They adopted the resistance concept from Heckathorn (1978, 1980), who developed a theory of the bargaining process in a bilateral bargaining situation, of which bilateral exchange is an example. Heckathorn's resistance theory identifies one outcome as the solution of the bargaining situation with the so-called *equiresistance principle*. In Heckathorn's theory the degree of resistance of actor $j(R_j)$ to the outcome O_j is given by

$$R_j = \frac{M_j - O_j}{M_j - C_j} \tag{5}$$

where M_j denotes the maximum profit actor j can obtain in the bargaining situation. Similarly, the degree of resistance of actor k to outcome $O_k = 24 - O_j$ can be formulated. The actors' resistances operate somewhat like opposing forces in the bargaining process. The theory assumes that the actor that is least resistant to O_j will make a concession. The concession making process is assumed to stop when the degree of resistance of both actors to the outcome is equal, that is, when the point of *equiresistance* is obtained:

$$R_j = \frac{M_j - O_j}{M_j - C_j} = \frac{M_k - O_k}{M_k - C_k} = R_k \tag{6}$$

These particular outcomes O_j and O_k are the solution of the bargaining situation.[4]

Willer and Anderson (1981), and later Heckathorn (1983) and Willer (1987) applied the resistance theory to exchange networks. Resistance theory was first applied to structures called branches, like for example the *Branch3* structure in Fig. 1. Resistance theory predicts 24 points for *A*, and zero points for the actor with whom A exchanges. In that case the degree of resistance of A and of his exchange partner is equal to 1 (0/0 for A, and 24/24 for the other actor).

The second and last part of the foundations of ER was created by Markovsky et al. (1988). They developed an index, called *Graph-theoretic Power Index (GPI)*, which enabled them together with a number of axioms and theorems on the process of seeking exchange to determine the relative profits for all positions in an exchange network. The GPI value of a position in the exchange network can be calculated as the sum of the position's non-intersecting odd-length paths minus the sum of the position's non-intersecting even-length paths. For example, the GPI value of A in the T structure equals 2 (3 − 1). The GPI value of C and D equal 1 (1 − 1 + 1); they have one path of length one, two paths of length two that intersect and therefore are counted as one path, and one path of length three. Similarly, it can be calculated that the GPI value of B and E are equal to 1. The original theory predicts that if in an exchange relation one of the actors has a higher GPI value than the other actor, then the first actor obtains more profits than the second actor. Markovsky et al.'s (1988) original theory making use of the GPI is revised, improved, and generalized several times (Lovaglia et al., 1995a, b; Markovsky et al., 1993; Skvoretz & Willer, 1993; Willer, 1999; Willer & Skvoretz, 1997a). In some of these revisions the GPI is combined with the concept of resistance into one theory, called exchange-resistance theory (ER) for the first time by Skvoretz and Willer (1993).

ER modifies the equiresistance principle in (6) by incorporating the GPI in the equiresistance equation. It assumes that the numerator of (6) is a function of the probability that an actor is included in an exchange. More precisely, Skvoretz and Willer (1993) modify (6) into

$$R_j = \frac{(M_j - O_j)^{P_j}}{M_j - C_j} = \frac{(M_k - O_k)^{P_k}}{M_k - C_k} = R_k \qquad (7)$$

where the probabilities of being included in an exchange (P_j and P_k) depend on the relative GPI values of j and k.

Other researchers of network exchange criticize the GPI and ER, in particular power-dependence theorists. The criticisms are not particularly focused on the accuracy of ER's predictions, but mainly on the theory and its assumptions. According to Cook and Yamagishi (1992, p. 262) the predictions of Markovsky et al. (1988) seem to be based on a "fairly arbitrary set of assumptions." Cook and Yamagishi (1992, p. 262, footnote 7) furthermore argue, "In the case of GPI (see Markovsky et al., 1988) no clear theoretical explanation is offered for the relationship between the graph-theoretic measure they develop and actual power processes." One can discuss whether the GPI is based on arbitrary assumptions or not, but we will not have that discussion in the present study. Here ER and the GPI are criticized for another reason. Comparing PD and ER it is evident that PD is simpler in the sense that it is based on fewer assumptions than ER. We wonder to what extent the two theories yield different predictions if the equidependence principle of PD is replaced by the equiresistance principle, with omitting the GPI such that both theories are based on a similar number of assumptions.[5]

Reformulating ER by replacing the equidependence by the equiresistance principle results in predictions of outcomes in exchange networks such that simultaneously in all relations the two actors are equiresistant. That is, for each possible exchange relation between actors j and k, it holds that

$$\frac{24 - O_j}{24 - C_j} = \frac{O_j}{24 - C_k} \tag{8}$$

Equation (8) is obtained from (6) by substituting 24 for M_A and M_B, and $24 - O_j$ for O_B. Solving for O_j yields the following prediction of O_j:[6]

$$O_j = \frac{24(24 - C_k)}{48 - C_j - C_k} \tag{9}$$

In all networks examined one solution was found such that equiresistance holds simultaneously in all exchange relations.

To illustrate the reformulation of exchange-resistance theory using (9), consider again the *Line4* structure. Assume first that the theory predicts an equal split of resources between A and B in exchange relation AB. Applying the equiresistance principle to AC and BD then yields $O_A = O_B = 16$ and $O_C = O_D = 8$ ($R_A = R_C = 2/3$). It can now be shown that the degrees of resistance of A and B in the suboptimal exchange relation are also equal: $R_A = R_B = (24 - 12)/(24 - 16) = 12/(24 - 16) = 1.5$.

The predictions of PD and ER are different for the exchange relations AC and BD of the *Line4* structure; PD predicts a larger profit for actors A and B (18 points) than ER (16 points). Note that the difference is entirely the result of the difference in the equidependence and the equiresistance principles, because the conflict pay-offs of the actors involved in the *Line4* structure are identical under both principles. In Table 1 the predictions of both theories, calculated with (4) and (9), are presented and compared as a function of the conflict pay-offs of both actors in the exchange relation. Four general conclusions can be drawn from the table. Firstly, if the conflict pay-offs of both actors in the relation are equal, both theories predict the same exchange outcome. Secondly, if the exchange relation is suboptimal ($C_j + C_k > 24$, with $C_j \neq C_k$), ER predicts a larger outcome for the actor with the higher conflict pay-off than power-dependence theory. Thirdly, if the exchange

Table 1. Predictions of Power-Dependence Theory (Third Column, PD) and
Exchange-Resistance Theory (Fourth Column, ER) of O_j in Exchange
Relation jk as a Function of C_j and C_k.

C_k	C_j	PD	ER	PD − ER
0	0	12.00	12.00	0.00
0	4	14.00	13.09	0.91
0	8	16.00	14.40	1.60
0	12	18.00	16.00	2.00
0	16	20.00	18.00	2.00
0	20	22.00	20.57	1.43
0	24	24.00	24.00	0.00
4	4	12.00	12.00	0.00
4	8	14.00	13.33	0.67
4	12	16.00	15.00	1.00
4	16	18.00	17.14	0.86
4	20	20.00	20.00	0.00
4	24	22.00	24.00	−2.00
8	8	12.00	12.00	0.00
8	12	14.00	13.71	0.29
8	16	16.00	16.00	0.00
8	20	18.00	19.20	−1.20
8	24	20.00	24.00	−4.00
12	12	12.00	12.00	0.00
12	16	14.00	14.40	−0.40
12	20	16.00	18.00	−2.00
12	24	18.00	24.00	−6.00
16	16	12.00	12.00	0.00
16	20	14.00	16.00	−2.00
16	24	16.00	24.00	−8.00
20	20	12.00	12.00	0.00
20	24	14.00	24.00	−10.00
24	24	12.00	12.00	0.00

Note: The last column presents the difference between the theories' predictions (PD − ER).

relation is not suboptimal ($C_j + C_k > 24$, with $C_j \neq C_k$), PD predicts a larger
outcome for the actor with the higher conflict pay-off than ER. Finally, note the
peculiar characteristic of ER's predictions of O_j in the case of $C_j = 24$. In these
cases the theory always predicts $O_j = 24$. This result can be proved directly by
substituting $C_j = 24$ in (9). The largest difference between the predictions of the
theories arises in one of these cases, if C_k is just smaller than 24 points while
C_j equals 24 points. The difference in predictions then reaches a theoretical
maximum equal to 12 points.[7] However, note that all differences in Table 1 assume
that the conflict pay-offs of the actors in the exchange relation are identical.

Differences in the predictions can also occur in exchange networks where the theories predict different outcomes in other exchange relations and hence other conflict pay-offs in the relation under examination.

The Algorithms

Simultaneously solving for equidependence and equiresistance in exchange networks is not carried out analytically, but numerically in a number of iterations. The algorithm used in the analyses to find the two solutions is similar but not identical to the algorithm reported in Cook and Yamagishi (1992).[8] Two matrices are central in the algorithm: Matrix C with elements C_{jk} that specify the conflict pay-off of j in exchange relation jk, and matrix O with elements O_{jk} that specify the exchange outcome of j in jk. In the case of no exchange relation jk the values of O_{jk} and C_{jk} are set equal to zero. Denote the m-th iterative approximation of O and C by O^m and C^m respectively. The m-th iterative step of the algorithm consists of two stages. In the first stage C^m is calculated on the basis of O^{m-1}. That is, each element C_{jk}^m is calculated as the maximum of O_{jk*}^{m-1} where $k*$ can be any actor other than k. In the second stage O^m is calculated on the basis of C^m. That is, if a relation between j and k exists, each element O_{jk}^m is calculated using C_{jk}^m with (4) to derive PD predictions, and with (9) to derive ER predictions. The iterative procedure stops when the differences between all corresponding elements in O^m and O^{m-1} between two subsequent iterations are negligibly small. In the first step of the algorithm all elements of C^1 are set equal to zero.

To illustrate the algorithm, consider again the *Line4* structure. The algorithm requires three iterations to converge and to yield a solution of PD. The results of the three iterations are presented in Table 2. The values in C^1 are all equal to zero. Therefore the profits of all actors in all relations in the first iteration are equal to 12 points (see O^1). The conflict pay-offs in C^2 are equal to 12 if the actor has at least two exchange relations, like A and B, and are zero otherwise. The predicted outcomes O^2 in the second iteration are either 12 if both actors in the relation have the same conflict pay-offs, or 18 if the row actor has a conflict pay-off equal to 12 and the column actor has a conflict pay-off equal to 0. In the third iteration the conflict pay-offs of A and B both increase from 12 to 18, but because the increase is the same for both actors the increase has no consequence for the predicted outcome: $O^3 = O^2$. The algorithm using the equiresistance principle also results in three iterations with the same results as reported in Table 2, with the only difference that the values equal to 18 are replaced by values equal to 16.

Table 2. Results of the Iterations of the Algorithm Applied to the *Line4*
Structure Using PD Theory.

	A	B	C	D	A	B	C	D
			C^1				O^1	
A	0	0	0	0	0	12	12	0
B	0	0	0	0	12	0	0	12
C	0	0	0	0	12	0	0	0
D	0	0	0	0	0	12	0	0
			C^2				O^2	
A	0	12	12	0	0	12	18	0
B	12	0	0	12	12	0	0	18
C	0	0	0	0	6	0	0	0
D	0	0	0	0	0	6	0	0
			C^3				O^3	
A	0	18	12	0	0	12	18	0
B	18	0	0	12	12	0	0	18
C	0	0	0	0	6	0	0	0
D	0	0	0	0	0	6	0	0

The algorithms not always converge in the same number of iterations. In the case of strong power networks the algorithm requires a much larger number of iterations, in particular when it uses the equiresistance principle. To speed up convergence in strong power networks a conflict pay-off is set to a value just below 24 (23.9999) if the conflict pay-off exceeds 21, and to a value just above 0 (0.0001) if the conflict pay-off is less than 3. To make sure that the predictions have converged for a specific exchange network, three more iterations were completed. The results of these iterations were never different from the originally generated predictions.

It was mentioned before that there always exists a solution that satisfies the equidependence principle, and a solution that satisfies the equiresistance principle. However, in a small number of networks an infinite number of solutions exist. Consider for example a structure sometimes called *Box*. The structure is like the *Line4* but with also a connection or exchange relation between C and D. The solutions for this network are characterized by divisions $(x, 24 - x)$ in relations AB, AC, DB, and DC, where x can be any number of profit points for A and D in the interval $[0, 24]$. For the reason that the predicted outcomes in the first iteration are all equal to 12, the algorithm selects the "equal power solution" from the set of solutions.

Other Solutions

The algorithm uses two different rules to generate predictions, equidependence of PD (4) and equiresistance of ER (9). Of course, in principle, an infinite number of other rules can be used to generate predictions of outcomes in exchange networks. At least two other rules have a theoretical foundation. One rule is another interpretation of ER, the other rule is based on the Nash (1953) solution of two-person cooperative games.

The equiresistance equation contains a conflict pay-off and a maximum pay-off for both actors. The conflict pay-off of an actor is equal to the profit he can obtain in another exchange relation. The maximum pay-off is equal to 24, the absolute number of points in the exchange relation. However, why not interpret the maximum pay-off correspondingly to the conflict pay-off? That is, why not interpret the maximum pay-off as the value the actor can obtain taking into account the conflict pay-off of the other actor? It can be argued that j cannot obtain more than $24 - C_k$, because k would never agree to an exchange if he receives less than C_k. Sometimes exchange-resistance theorists interpret the maximum pay-off in the equiresistance equation in this way, for example Willer (1999, pp. 58–59), Lovaglia et al. (1995b), and Willer and Skvoretz (1997a). This interpretation has consequences for the predictions of the exchange outcome. Taking (6) and substituting $O_k = 24 - O_j$, $M_k = 24 - C_j$, and $M_j = 24 - C_k$ results in

$$\frac{24 - C_k - O_j}{24 - C_k - C_j} = \frac{24 - C_j - 24 + O_j}{24 - C_j - C_k} \tag{10}$$

Simplifying (10) yields (4), hence the solution of this other interpretation of ER yields the same predictions as PD.

The Nash (1953) solution of two-person cooperative games applied to bilateral exchange yields a predicted exchange that maximizes the product of profits of the actors in the exchange relation. That is, the Nash solution is the value of O_j that maximizes the product

$$(O_j - C_j)(24 - O_j - C_k) \tag{11}$$

The maximum of the product is obtained at the value of O_j that is also identified by PD as described in (4). Hence two other principles that also have a theoretical foundation yield the same predictions as PD and need not be considered in the subsequent analysis.

THE EXCHANGE NETWORKS

In the present study the predictions of PD and ER are compared with respect to all exchange networks up to size 9. All these exchange networks are generated with the algorithm specified by Skvoretz (1996).[9] The algorithm results in an ordered list of exchange networks, where each exchange network is identified by a binary integer. The binary integer contains as many bits as the number of entries in the upper right triangle of the adjacency matrix that represents the exchange network, that is, $n(n - 1)/2$, where n is the number of nodes in the network. The bit corresponding to the entry jk of the adjacency matrix obtains the value 1 if there is an exchange relation jk, and the value 0 if there is no exchange relation jk. The whole binary integer is constructed by concatenating the values of all these bits, starting with the first row of the upper half triangle of the adjacency matrix, followed by the second, and so on. For example, binary integer 110010 identifies the *Line4* structure. However, the *Line4* structure can also be identified by many other binary integers, for example 100011. The result of the algorithm is that each exchange network is identified by the largest binary integer of all binary integers that correspond to the exchange networks that belong to the same isomorphic class. The largest binary integer of the structures that belong to the isomorphic class of the *Line4* structure is 110010. The total number of different isomorphic classes of exchange networks that exist up to size 9 is 142,660. The number of different isomorphic classes is presented in Table 4 as a function of the size of the exchange network.

In the literature, exchange networks are identified by names that describe the shape of the network, like for example the *Line4*, *T*, and *Branch3* structures. However, this procedure to identify exchange networks is in general not satisfying. Sometimes there exists more than one verbal description of the shape of a network (for example, the *Branch3* structure might also be called "*Star3*"). Or no verbal description might exist, which is the case for most more complex networks. Alternatively, the binary integers provide a standardized taxonomy of all exchange networks. Therefore a taxonomy based on binary integers is recommended, and is used in the remainder of the text.[10] When the structure has a common and a well-known verbal description, this name is mentioned as well.

THE EXCHANGE NETWORKS CONSIDERED IN THE LITERATURE

An overview of the studies on exchange networks is presented in Table 3.[11] All exchange networks up to size 9 investigated are enumerated in the table with the studies that investigate them. Note that the bilateral exchange network

Table 3. Overview of the Exchange Networks (1st Column) Considered in Empirical Studies (2nd Column) and in Theoretical or Simulation Studies (3rd Column).

Identifier of Network	Empirical Studies	Theoretical or Simulation Studies	Density of Network	Classification Network
110 [Branch2 or Line3]	3, 13, 18, 36, 48, 62	4, 6, 8, 9, 14, 15, 17, 20, 21, 27, 27[a], 30, 33, 37, 60, 68, 69, 70, 75	0.67	S
111 [Triangle]	3, 13, 18, 24, 24[a], 43[a], 44[a], 45[a], 58	6, 14, 27[a]	1.00	E
111000 [Branch3]	1, 18, 19, 32, 49, 50, 51, 52, 53, 54, 56, 68, 72, 73, 78	2, 7, 9, 17, 27, 28, 29, 33, 38, 47, 60, 63, 65, 66, 68, 69, 70	0.50	S
110010 [Line4]	1, 3, 11[b], 16[a], 18, 19, 25, 35, 36, 48, 49, 50, 51, 52, 56, 59, 72, 78	2, 8, 9, 10, 12, 14, 15, 17, 27, 29, 30, 38, 47, 60, 62, 65, 66, 70, 75	0.50	W
111100 [Stem]	1, 18, 19, 32, 35, 40, 48, 50, 52, 53, 54, 59, 78	2, 9, 14, 15, 17, 27, 29, 30, 33, 38, 47, 60, 66, 68, 75, 76	0.67	W
110011 [Box]	13, 15, 43[a], 44[a], 45[a]	12, 14	0.67	E
111110 [Box-Diagonal]	11[b], 13, 16[a], 53, 54	7, 15, 33, 68, 75	0.83	E
111111	22, 22[a], 53, 54, 55, 55[a]	10, 12, 20, 20[a], 21, 21[a], 23, 23[a], 24, 24[a], 28, 66, 68, 70, 70[a], 71, 71[a]	1.00	E
1111000000 [Branch4]	11[a], 68	9, 66, 69, 70	0.40	S
1110001000 [T]	1, 3, 11[b], 16[a], 19, 30, 41, 48, 59, 74, 77	2, 4, 7, 9, 12, 15, 17, 18, 27, 29, 33, 38, 39, 47, 64, 65, 66, 70, 75	0.40	(W, S)
1100010010 [Line5]	11[b], 18, 36, 59, 77	8, 10, 15, 17, 20, 30, 60, 61, 62, 65, 66, 69, 70, 75, 78	0.40	S
1111100000		18, 33	0.50	S
1110101000 [A]		15, 33	0.50	S
1110100001	48, 59	8, 10, 14, 15, 32, 33, 61	0.50	W
1110001010 [Box-Tail]	11[b]	33	0.50	S
1000010011 [Pentagon]	5[a], 15, 23[a]	61, 64[a], 70[a], 71[a]	0.50	E
1111110000 [Box-Diagonal-Tail]		34	0.60	S

Table 3. (Continued)

Identifier of Network	Empirical Studies	Theoretical or Simulation Studies	Density of Network	Classification Network
1111100001 [Kite or Hourglass]	3, 11[b], 13, 16[a], 18, 19, 31, 35, 40, 48, 50, 52, 78	2, 4, 7, 8, 9, 12, 14, 15, 17, 27, 29, 32, 38, 47, 61, 62, 66, 75, 76	0.60	E
1110001011		8	0.60	E
1111110010		12	0.70	E
1110110011		71[a]	0.70	E
1111100000000000 [Branch5]	68	9, 63, 66, 69, 70	0.33	S
1110000110000000 [H]	11[b], 18	35, 65, 69, 70	0.33	S
1100000100001000		2, 17, 19, 27, 29, 30, 38, 47, 66	0.33	W
1100001000010010 [Line6]	36	30	0.33	W
1100100000010010		2, 17, 19, 27, 29, 38, 47, 66	0.40	W
1100100000000110		18	0.40	S
110100101100000 [Hat]		9	0.40	W
1000001000010011 [Hexagon]	15	6, 9, 14	0.40	E
1111010001000100 [Kite-Tail]	13	2, 15, 17, 19, 27, 29, 38, 47, 66	0.47	W
1111111000010010		12	0.60	E
1111011101011000		12	0.60	E
1111010010001110		9	0.60	E
1111111000000000000000000 [Branch6]		17	0.29	S
1111000001000010001000000		65	0.29	(W, S)
1100000010000010001000	1, 18, 19, 30, 41	2, 9, 17, 27, 29, 38, 66, 69, 78	0.29	S
1100000100000000000110		30	0.29	S
1100000100000100010010 [Line7]	36, 59		0.29	S
1111001001000100000000		18	0.33	W
1111000001001000000001		18	0.33	S
1111000001000001000001		18	0.33	W

Network	Study	Density	Class
1110000010001000100001	36	0.33	S
1110000010001000000110	34	0.33	S
1110000010001000001111	5[a], 23[a]	0.43	E
1110000010000000000100110	30	0.25	S
1110000010000000000100101	26, 77	0.25	S
1110001010000010010010011	64[a], 71[a]	0.39	E
1110000011000101001001011	12	0.43	E
1111000001000000000000100110	30	0.22	E
1111000111000000100000101011	64	0.36	E

Notes: The studies, presented in the last row of the table, are identified by numbers. The density of the networks is presented in the 4th column. The classification of the exchange networks as equal (E), weak (W), or strong (S) power network is presented in the last column. If PD classifies the network as W and ER as S, the classification is represented by (W, S).

1: Berg and Panther (1998); 2: Bienenstock and Bonacich (1992); 3: Bienenstock and Bonacich (1993); 4: Bienenstock and Bonacich (1997); 5: Bonacich (1987); 6: Bonacich (1995); 7: Bonacich (1998a); 8: Bonacich (1998b); 9: Bonacich (1999a); 10: Bonacich (1999b); 11: Bonacich (2000); 12: Bonacich and Bienenstock (1993); 13: Bonacich and Bienenstock (1995); 14: Bonacich and Bienenstock (1997a); 15: Bonacich and Bienenstock (1997b); 16: Bonacich and Friedkin (1998); 17: Borgatti and Everett (1992); 18: Braun and Gautschi (2000); 19: Burke (1997); 20: Cook (1982); 21: Cook (1995); 22: Cook and Emerson (1978); 23: Cook et al. (1983); 24: Cook and Gillmore (1984); 25: Cook et al. (1986); 26: Cook et al. (1993); 27: Cook and Yamagishi (1992); 28: Emerson (1981); 29: Friedkin (1992); 30: Friedkin (1993); 31: Friedkin (1995); 32: Lawler and Yoon (1998); 33: Leik (1992); 34: Lovaglia et al. (1995a); 35: Lovaglia et al. (1995b); 36: Lucas et al. (2001); 37: Markovsky (1987); 38: Markovsky (1992); 39: Markovsky (1995); 40: Markovsky et al. (1993); 41: Markovsky et al. (1988); 42: Marsden (1987); 43: Molm et al. (1999); 44: Molm et al. (2001); 45: Molm et al. (2000); 46: Skvoretz and Burkett (1994); 47: Skvoretz and Fararo (1992); 48: Skvoretz and Lovaglia (1995); 49: Skvoretz and Willer (1991); 50: Skvoretz and Willer (1993); 51: Skvoretz, Willer and Fararo (1993); 52: Skvoretz and Zhang (1997); 53: Stolte (1988); 54: Stolte (1990); 55: Stolte and Emerson (1977); 56: Szmatka et al. (1998); 57: Szmatka and Willer (1995); 58: Thye (2000); 59: Thye et al. (1997); 60: Whitmeyer (1997); 61: Whitmeyer (1999a); 62: Whitmeyer (1999b); 63: Willer (1984); 64: Willer (1986); 65: Willer (1987); 66: Willer (1992); 67: Willer and Anderson (1981); 68: Willer et al. (1997); 69: Willer and Markovsky (1993); 70: Willer et al. (1989); 71: Willer and Patton (1987); 72: Willer et al. (1997); 73: Willer and Skvoretz (1997b); 74: Willer and Szmatka (1993); 75: Willer and Willer (2000); 76: Yamagishi and Cook (1990); 77: Yamagishi et al. (1988); 78: Yamaguchi (1996).

[a] Exchange relations vary with respect to number of points in their resource pool.
[b] Other experimental paradigm to study coalition formation.

is not included in the table. The table only enumerates the studies that focus on negotiated exchange with the 1-exchange rule. In some cases the exchange network investigated has unequally valued exchange relations. Studies that consider networks with unequally valued exchange relation are labeled with superscript a.

The second column of Table 3 contains the studies that empirically investigate exchange networks, that is, the studies analyze empirical results on exchange networks. That does not necessarily mean these studies have run experiments, it can also mean that they analyze data obtained in other empirical studies. Note that in particular the small sized exchange networks have been popular in empirical studies. In fact, an exchange network larger than size 7 was never investigated. Of the 23 empirically investigated networks, the most popular networks are the *Branch3*, *Line4*, *Stem*, *T*, and *Kite* structures (see Fig. 1), which are all investigated in at least 10 studies.

The third column mentions the studies that simulate actor behavior in exchange networks, predict analytically outcomes in exchange outcomes, or discuss properties of exchange networks. Fifty-eight exchange networks have been investigated in this way. Fifty of them are of size 9 or smaller and are included in the table, eight others consist of 10 to 13 actors. For a description of the large networks, see Braun and Gautschi (2000, p. 32), Cook (1982, p. 186), Cook and Emerson (1978, p. 726), Cook et al. (1983, p. 280), Bonacich and Bienenstock (1997b, p. 5), Borgatti and Everett (1992, p. 292), and Willer (1986, p. 444). One of the large exchange networks deserves specific attention because it played a significant role in the development of research on network exchange. It is the 10-actor structure in Fig. 1. The structure, introduced by Marsden and Laumann (1977), is used by Cook (1982) to demonstrate that in general an actor's exchange outcome is not an increasing function of the actor's centrality. *A* is the central actor in the structure but is expected to gain a smaller outcome than actors *B*, *C*, and *D*. The structure appears in a number of other studies on exchange networks (Emerson, 1981; Friedkin, 1993; Marsden, 1987; Willer, 1992; Willer & Markovsky, 1993; Yamaguchi, 1996).

Inspecting the third column of Table 3 leads to the conclusion that the same networks that are many times empirically investigated, are also most popular in simulation or theoretical studies. The exchange networks 111111 and the *Line5* structure have also received considerable attention in non-empirical studies.

GOALS OF THE ANALYSES

After having discussed PD and ER, and the exchange networks considered in the literature, the goals of the analysis in the present paper are briefly summarized before analyzing the exchange networks with both theories.

Initially, the incidence of equal, weak, and strong power networks is analyzed using both theories. The results of the analysis are compared to the classifications of the exchange networks that are considered in the literature. Thereby an indication is obtained whether the networks in Table 3 are representative of the whole population of exchange networks up to size 9.

Subsequently, the theories' classifications into equal, weak, and strong power networks are compared. The comparison is carried out for the cases where suboptimal exchange relations are incorporated in the analyses, and where they are not. The emphasis is on the latter analysis because the suboptimal exchange relations are used only infrequently. Finally, the theories are compared with respect to their point predictions of the exchange outcomes. Both the maximum absolute difference and average difference of all outcomes in a network are inspected. The goal of these analyses is to discover the exchange networks for which theories' classifications and point predictions are different, and to determine the characteristics of the networks that cause the theories' different predictions.

ANALYSES

Prior to the presentation of the results of the analyses, a comment must be made on the role of statistics in the analyses. Inferential statistics, that is, the use of statistics to make generalizations about a population by studying a sample from that population, is not required, because our sample coincides with the whole population of exchange networks up to size 9. Therefore, only descriptive statistics, that is, the use of statistics to classify and summarize numerical data, is all that is required in the analyses.

Classification of Networks

The classification of exchange networks into equal (E), weak (W), and strong (S) power networks is presented in Table 4 in the case where suboptimal exchange relations are not incorporated in the analysis, and in Table 5 where they are incorporated. In each table a cross-tabulation is made for the classifications by PD and ER, for each size of the exchange network. The rows at the bottom of Table 5 (Table 4) point out that around 75.0% (75.0%) of the networks is classified as an equal power network, 21.2% (23.0%) as a weak power network, and 3.8% (2.0%) as a strong power network. Clearly, equal power networks predominate the population of exchange networks up to size 9.

Comparing the characteristics of the classifications for the exchange networks in the sample of networks that are considered in the literature to the population of

Table 4. Classifications of Exchange Networks by PD and ER; the Case Where Suboptimal Exchange Relations are Included in the Analysis.

Size	Class. ER	Class. PD			Total	%
		E	W	S		
2	E	1	0	0	1	100.0
	W	0	0	0	0	0.00
	S	0	0	0	0	0.00
	Total	1	0	0	1	
3	E	1	0	0	1	50.00
	W	0	0	0	0	0.00
	S	0	0	1	1	50.00
	Total	1	0	1	2	
4	E	3	0	0	3	50.00
	W	0	2	0	2	33.33
	S	0	0	1	1	16.67
	Total	3	2	1	6	
5	E	11	0	0	11	52.38
	W	0	3	0	3	14.29
	S	0	2	5	7	33.33
	Total	11	5	5	21	
6	E	61	0	0	61	54.46
	W	0	36	0	36	32.14
	S	0	5	10	15	13.39
	Total	61	41	10	112	
7	E	506	0	0	506	59.32
	W	0	215	31	246	28.84
	S	0	55	46	101	11.84
	Total	506	270	77	853	
8	E	7,442	0	0	7,442	66.94
	W	0	3,084	36	3,120	28.07
	S	0	308	247	555	4.99
	Total	7,442	3,392	283	11,117	
9	E	99,006	0	0	99,006	75.84
	W	0	27,245	1,847	29,092	22.28
	S	0	1,951	499	2,450	1.88
	Total	99,006	29,196	2,346	130,548	
	Total	107,031	32,906	2,723	142,660	
	PD%	75.025	23.066	1.909		
	ER%	75.025	22.781	2.194		

Note: For each network size the classifications by PD and ER size are cross-tabulated.

Table 5. Classifications of Exchange Networks by PD and ER; the Case where Suboptimal Exchange Relations are not Included in the Analysis.

Size	Class. ER	Class. PD			Total	%	Av. Density
		E	W	S			
2	E	1	0	0	1	100.0	1.000
	W	0	0	0	0	0.00	
	S	0	0	0	0	0.00	
	Total	1	0	0	1		
3	E	1	0	0	1	50.00	1.000
	W	0	0	0	0	0	
	S	0	0	1	1	50.00	0.667
	Total	1	0	1	2		0.833
4	E	3	0	0	3	50.00	0.833
	W	0	2	0	2	33.33	0.583
	S	0	0	1	1	16.67	0.500
	Total	3	2	1	6		0.694
5	E	11	0	0	11	52.38	0.718
	W	0	3	0	3	14.29	0.600
	S	0	1	6	7	33.33	0.471
	Total	11	4	6	21		0.619
6	E	61	0	0	61	54.46	0.642
	W	0	36	0	36	32.14	0.500
	S	0	1	14	15	13.39	0.418
	Total	61	37	14	112		0.566
7	E	506	0	0	506	59.32	0.586
	W	0	215	0	215	25.21	0.484
	S	0	13	119	132	15.47	0.410
	Total	506	228	119	853		0.533
8	E	7,442	0	0	7,442	66.94	0.551
	W	0	3,084	0	3,084	27.74	0.453
	S	0	31	560	591	5.32	0.381
	Total	7,442	3,115	560	11,117		0.515
9	E	99,006	0	0	99,006	75.84	0.529
	W	0	26,741	0	26,741	20.48	0.445
	S	0	255	4,546	4,801	3.68	0.378
	Total	99,006	26,996	4,546	130,548		0.506
	Total	107,031	30,382	5,247	142,660		0.507
	PD%	75.025	21.297	3.678			
	ER%	75.025	21.086	3.889			

Note: For each network size the classifications by PD and ER are cross-tabulated. The average density of the exchange networks per classification by ER is presented in the last column.

networks reveals large and striking differences between the classifications in the sample and the population. Of the 51 exchange networks considered in the literature, including the bilateral exchange situation, 19 are classified as equal power networks, 10 (or 12 in the case of PD) as weak power networks, and 22 (20 in the case of PD) as strong power networks. That is, 43.1% (39.3%) of the exchange networks are classified as strong power networks by ER (PD) without incorporating the suboptimal relations, as opposed to the 3.889% (3.678%) in the whole population of networks.

Why does the large bias in the sample in favor of strong power networks occur? One cause of the bias is the selection of small-sized exchange networks in the sample. In the sample all 3 and 4 actor networks and a considerable number of 5 actor networks are included, but the larger sized networks are under-represented. As is evident from Table 5, the proportion of strong power networks in general decreases as the size of the network increases.

Another cause of the bias is the selection of networks with a low density. It is also evident from Table 5 that there is a relation between the density of the network and its classification; strong power networks on average have a lower density than the other two types of exchange networks. Analyzing the densities of the networks in the sample of networks considered in the literature reveals that for all sizes of 5 and larger, the average density of the networks in the sample is indeed smaller than the average density in the population. For sizes 5 to 9 the average densities in the sample are 0.531, 0.433, 0.320, 0.330, and 0.292, compared to the average densities in the population 0.619, 0.566, 0.533, 0.515, and 0.506, respectively.

Differences in Classification of Networks by PD and by ER

Exchange networks are most of the times similarly classified by PD and ER, as can be seen from the bottom rows of Tables 4 and 5. However, for a small percentage of networks the classification is different. Tables 4 and 5 show that ER and PD always agree upon an equal power classification, but sometimes do not agree upon whether a network is of strong or weak power. Consider first Table 4, which presents the results of the analysis where suboptimal relations are included in the analyses. Adding the number of exchange networks that are differently classified by the two theories yields a total number of 4,235 (2.969%) disagreements. In 2,321 cases PD classified the network as a weak power network and ER as a strong network, in the other 1,914 cases ER classified the network as a weak power network and PD as a strong network. Hence in total ER classifies more exchange networks as strong power networks than PD (2.194% vs. 1.909%, bottom rows of Table 4).

Consider now Table 5, the results of the analysis excluding suboptimal relations. The number of disagreements between the two theories has become considerably smaller, 301 (0.211%) instead of the 4,235 in Table 4. It can therefore be concluded that the suboptimal relations are the major cause of the different classifications in Table 4. That is, in 3,934 cases a suboptimal exchange relation that is a weak power relation according to one theory, is an equal or strong power relation according to the other theory. Consider for example the exchange network 1111100000, one of the networks considered in the literature and therefore included in Table 3. The network and the predictions of both theories are depicted in Fig. 2. Because *A* has strong power relations with *D* and *E*, and *B* and *C* have an equal power relation, the relations *AB* and *AC* are suboptimal. PD predicts an 18-6 division, and ER predicts a 24-0 division (see also Table 1) for these suboptimal exchange relations. Hence, as opposed to ER, PD classifies relations *AB* and *AC*, and therefore also the exchange network, as of weak power. However, if these suboptimal exchange relations are not considered, both theories classify the exchange network as a strong power network.

In all of the 301 cases that are classified differently in Table 5 ER classifies the network as a strong power network, while PD classifies the networks as a weak power network. This results in slightly more strong power classifications by ER than by PD (3.889% vs. 3.678%, bottom rows of Table 5). Inspecting these 301 cases yields to the conclusion that the different classifications are, like in the cases in Table 4, caused by different predictions for one or more suboptimal relations. However, in the 301 cases these different predictions for suboptimal relation(s) also result in another prediction in one or more optimal relations that are adjacent to this suboptimal relation(s). The list of exchange networks considered in the literature contains two exchange networks that are differently classified. Consider first the *T* network. The *T* network and the theories' predictions are depicted in Fig. 2.[12] Relation *AB* is suboptimal and affects the predictions in *BE*; PD predicts that *B* obtains 16 points, four more than is predicted by ER. The other network, 111100000100001000000, is also depicted together with the predictions in Fig. 2. In this network PD predicts that *B* and *C* obtain 16 points in their optimal relations, again four more than is predicted by ER. Finally, the only six-actor exchange network that is differently classified by the two theories is also depicted in Fig. 2. Note that the network, 111100001000000, closely resembles the *T* network, with one additional exchange relation for the *A* actor compared to the *A* actor in the *T* network. Also in this network PD predicts a 16-8 division where ER predicts a 12-12 division. The latter observable fact is not limited to these three networks; in *all* 301 cases, PD predicts a 16-8 division in an optimal relation, where ER predicts a 12-12 division. Note that this conclusion implies that on the level of optimal exchange relations, PD and ER always agreed upon

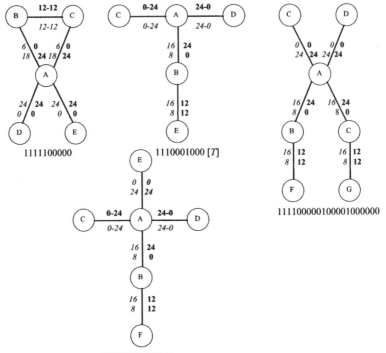

Fig. 2. Predictions of ER and PD for Four Exchange Networks. *Note:* Classifications of networks by PD and ER are identical for network 1111100000, but different for the three other networks. Except for network 111100001000000, the networks are considered in studies on network exchange. ER predictions are shown in bold above or to the right of each relation, PD predictions are shown in italics below or to the left of each relation.

strong power classifications, but sometimes disagreed upon whether a relation was equal or weak power.

Differences in Point Predictions of PD and by ER

To distinguish between PD and ER in an experiment, point predictions of both theories need to be derived for each exchange relation. The larger the difference between the point predictions, the higher the statistical power to distinguish the two theories, that is, the easier to obtain support for one theory over the other. The focus is here on uncovering the exchange networks with the largest maximum

Table 6. Maximum Differences in Point Predictions by PD and ER for each Exchange Network.

Maximum Difference		Size							Total
		2 or 3	4	5	6	7	8	9	
0	I	3	4	17	75	634	8,043	104,235	113,011
	II	3	4	16	71	556	7,689	99,537	107,876
1	I						232	807	1,039
	II						22	332	354
2	I		2	3	36	202	2,798	25,108	28,149
	II		2	3	36	209	2,910	25,734	28,894
3	I					4	13	136	153
	II					14	111	972	1,097
4	I					13	31	262	308
	II					1	1	217	219
5	I					0	0	0	0
	II					1	1	103	105
6	I			0	0	0	0	0	0
	II			1	4	46	307	2,501	2,859
7	I					0	0	0	0
	II					1	1	33	35
8	I			0	0	0	0	0	0
	II			1	1	15	33	435	485
9	I					0	0	0	0
	II					5	21	325	351
10	I					0	0	0	0
	II					5	21	328	354
11	I							0	0
	II							31	31

Note: The numbers of exchange networks with a particular maximum difference (rounded to the nearest integer) are presented in the cases where suboptimal relations are deleted (denoted by I), and where they are not (denoted by II). Cells are left empty if both numbers are zero.

(absolute) difference in point predictions of the complete set of exchange relations in the network.

The numbers of exchange networks with a particular maximum difference in point predictions are presented in Table 6. The numbers are presented separately for the case where suboptimal relations are not considered (rows indicated by I), and for the case where they are (rows indicated by II). The exchange networks are sorted in classes by rounding a network's maximum difference to the nearest integer. For the networks in case (I) that are sorted in the class with a maximum difference equal to zero, it holds that the maximum difference is *exactly* equal to zero. Hence, the theories' point predictions in all the optimal exchange relations are identical in 79.217% of the exchange networks up to size 9. Note that this percentage is much smaller than the 99.789% agreement between the theories' classifications that was found in the previous subsection. Apparently, most maximum differences larger than zero do not affect the agreement between the classifications. Considering also the suboptimal exchange relations, the theories predictions are identical in 75.582% (107,876 – 51 cases) of the exchange networks.

Differences in point predictions for an exchange relation can occur in four different ways: (a) at least one of the predicted conflict pay-offs is different, and the resulting different pay-off predictions point to a different network classification by the two theories; (b) at least one of the predicted conflict pay-offs is different, but the resulting different pay-off predictions do not point to a different network classification; (c) the predicted conflict pay-offs are identical, the predicted pay-offs are different and pointing to a different network classification; and (d) the predicted conflict pay-offs are identical, the predicted pay-offs are different but point to the same network classification. The analysis in the previous subsection demonstrates that different network classifications only occur in combination with different predictions of conflict pay-offs for adjacent suboptimal relations. Hence there are instances of class (a), but not of class (c).

Firstly, let us consider the case where the suboptimal relations are ignored. The 301 exchange networks that were classified differently by the two theories are all of class (a), because these networks contain relations with different predicted conflict pay-offs. The maximum difference in point prediction is equal to four. Note from Table 6 that no exchange network exists with a larger maximum difference. In fact, only seven exchange networks that are similarly classified have the same maximum difference. Therefore it can be concluded that the networks that are classified differently in general are also the exchange networks that are most suitable to provide divergent empirical evidence for PD and ER.

Exchange networks that are classified similarly but contain exchange relations with different conflict pay-offs (class (b)) are not abundant. In fact, none of the exchange networks in Table 3 belongs to class (b). Of the 29,649 networks for which the theories' point predictions are different, exchange networks belonging to class (d) are most common. That is, exchange networks with identically predicted conflict pay-offs that are similarly classified. Ten networks in Table 3 belong to this class, like for example the *Line4* and *Stem* structures, both depicted in Fig. 1. Different predictions in exchange relations in these networks must be entirely ascribed to differences in functions (4) and (9). From the fact that the maximum difference is never larger than four it can be derived that there are no exchange networks with an exchange relation in which one actor has a maximum conflict pay-off and the other actor a conflict pay-off larger than eight but smaller than 24 (see Table 2).

Finally, the suboptimal relations are also considered in the analysis. Two conclusions can be inferred from Table 6. First, the theories' predictions are different in more exchange networks (4,186) when also suboptimal relations are considered. Second, differences in predictions can be much larger when suboptimal relations are considered. The difference in predictions for at least one suboptimal relation is at least five points, with a maximum of 10.8, for 4,220 exchange networks. The maximum difference in predictions is equal to eight in the 301 exchange networks that are classified differently in case (I). Consider for example three of these networks in Fig. 2, for which PD predicts a 16-8 division in suboptimal relations as opposed to ER theory that predicts a 24-0 division.

CONCLUSIONS AND DISCUSSION

The present study focused on network exchange under the 1-exchange rule, where exchange is negotiated and represented by a split of a common resource pool. Although these conditions are quite restrictive, most research on network exchange is concerned with this special case. In fact, the literature review carried out here reveals that at least 78 studies were concerned with this special case. In total 58 networks have been considered in these studies, 51 of these networks consist up to nine actors.

In the present study all 142,660 different exchange networks up to size 9 were analyzed by two of the most influential network exchange theories; power-dependence theory (PD) and exchange-resistance theory (ER). Both theories were simplified as much as possible such that differences between the two theories boil down to the different principles on which the theories are based; the equidependence principle and the equiresistance principle. Two other principles with a theoretical foundation, the Nash (1953) solution and another conception of the equiresistance principle, were shown to yield the same predictions as the equidependence principle.

The incidence of equal, weak, and strong power networks in the population was examined by deriving point predictions of outcomes of exchange relations in all networks up to size 9 with PD and ER. ER and PD similarly classified 99.789% of all networks when suboptimal relations were not considered. In the 301 networks that were classified differently, the difference in the theories' predictions in optimal relations was also at a maximum, which was equal to four. Hence these 301 networks in general are also the exchange networks that are most suitable to provide divergent empirical evidence for the parsimonious versions of PD and

ER. Differences in theories' predictions were larger, up to 10.8 points, if also suboptimal relations were considered. However, for the reason that suboptimal relations are used only infrequently, suboptimal relations are not that appropriate to provide divergent empirical evidence for PD and ER.

Examining the incidence of strong power networks in the sample of 51 networks studied in the literature revealed that 43% of these networks were classified as strong power networks. This percentage is a huge overestimation of the percentage of strong power networks in the whole population of networks up to size 9. In the population three quarter of the networks were classified as equal power networks, while little less than 4% was classified as strong power networks. The large bias in the sample was explained by the decrease in the proportion of strong power networks as (i) the size of the network increases, and (ii) the density in the network increases. The networks in the sample were in general of small size and had a low density.

In the analysis the focus was on exchange networks up to size 9. The reasons for this choice were that larger networks are hardly ever considered, and that all networks up to this size can be taken into account in an analysis with the algorithm. However, characteristics of the population of exchange networks of a larger size can also be studied by generating predictions of PD and RD for a random sample of networks of this larger size. This analysis seems useful to examine if the trend of a decreasing proportion of strong power networks for larger sized networks also holds for larger sizes. It would also be useful to examine if differences in the predictions of exchange theories occur more often for large sized networks than for small sized networks.

Until now the spotlight was on deriving and comparing predictions of ER and PD, as opposed to real data. Of course, a comparison of the predictions to empirical data is relevant as well. The exchange networks that are examined in experiments are not critical, with the exception of the T structure. Inspecting the results of the empirical studies that examine the T structure clearly favors the equiresistance principle; in all studies mentioned in Table 3 actor B obtains on average number of points around 12 in his relation with E. However, the principles need to be compared in more critical networks to draw a more definite conclusion with respect to their relative predictive successes. Predictions of the theories can also be compared in networks that are not critical. For example, consider the *Line4* structure. Most empirical studies report an average profit equal to around 14 for A and B. The theories' predictions are considerably more extreme; PD predicts 18, ER predicts 16. This case shows that both theories' predictions can be somewhat off target. Both theories' predictions are most off target in the case of strong networks. Average profits near the extreme (23 or 24) or almost never obtained. However, the cause for this difference might be that in experiments subjects play only a small number of rounds in a strong power network. It can be suspected that if this number of rounds is increased the division of points approaches a 23-1 division in the last rounds.

The focus of the present study was more on classifying exchange networks than on comparing predictions of different network exchange theories. The classifications of the networks by the two parsimonious versions of PD and ER in general turned out to be highly similar. However, predictions and classifications of other network exchange theories as mentioned in the introduction might differ more from each other than PD and ER in the present study. For example, Skvoretz[13] created a program that allows the comparison of predictions of Friedkin's Expected Value theory, ER theory as specified in the present paper, and of Optimal Seek theory (Willer & Simpson, 1999). These comparison of predictions and classifications of other theories will result in the detection of critical networks, other than for example the *T* network, that distinguish these theories. These critical exchange networks can then be incorporated in experiments to test these theories.

Network exchange is more than negotiated exchange under the 1-exchange rule in a network with only equally valued exchange relations. More attention should be attributed to other types of network exchange, like network exchange with unequally valued exchange relations (e.g. Bonacich & Friedkin, 1998), exchange under other rules than the 1-exchange rule (the 2- or 3-exchange rule, e.g. Skvoretz & Willer, 1993), or exchange in inclusionary networks (e.g. Szmatka et al., 1995), etc. The algorithm described in the present study can be adapted to generate predictions of PD and ER in all these cases. Again, the predictions of both theories can be compared in a large population of networks to examine the critical networks for which both theories yield different predictions.

NOTES

1. Markovsky (1997, p. 68) uses the label "Network Exchange Theory," or NET, to refer to the specific theory and research program in which he is involved. In the present study the label "network exchange theory" refers to all theories of network exchange.

2. Assuming a continuous resource pool only has minor consequences for the subsequent analysis. The predicted outcomes in the analysis reported here can be transformed directly to predictions in the case of a discrete resource pool. Let x be the predicted outcome in the case of a continuous recourse pool. Then the predicted outcome in the case of a discrete resource pool is equal to $1 + 22x/24$.

3. The density of a network is defined as the number or links or exchange relations divided by $n(n - 1)/2$. The latter number is the maximum number of relations that can possibly exist in the network, i.e. when all actors have a relation with all other actors.

4. At least two other formulations of the equiresistance principle or solution exist in the literature that are equivalent to the formulation used in the present study. The formulation of equiresistance that is used most frequently in the literature (e.g. Willer & Anderson, 1981) identifies the equiresistance solution as the value of the outcomes O_j and O_k for which $(M_j - O_j)/(O_j - C_j) = (M_k - O_k)/(O_k - C_k)$.

5. Cook and Yamagishi (1992, p. 249, footnote 3) already mention that supposedly the equidependence principle can be replaced by the equiresistance principle in their theory and algorithm.

6. If either C_j or C_k is equal to 24, (8) does not exist and (9) cannot be derived. However, it is argued here that if one of the conflict pay-offs is equal to 24, Eq. (9) can still be used. Assume that $C_j = 24$ and $C_k = x < 24$. Take $C_j = 24 - \delta$, where δ is a small positive real. Substituting $C_j = 24 - \delta$ in (8) results in solution $O_j = 24((24 - x)/(24 - x + \delta))$, at which both actor's resistance equals $24/(24 - x + \delta) > 1$. By letting δ approach 0 solution $O_j = 24$ and resistances equal to $24/(24 - x)$ are obtained.

7. If $C_j = C_k = 24$, the solution is defined as $O_j = O_k = 12$ in line with the solutions if $C_j = C_k < 24$.

8. There are two main differences between the algorithm reported here and the algorithm reported in Cook and Yamagishi (1992). Firstly, in Cook and Yamagishi's algorithm suboptimal relations are updated differently then other exchange relations. Secondly, Cook and Yamagishi's algorithm stops if not only $O^m = O^{m-1}$ but also $C^m = C^{m-1}$. Notwithstanding these differences, both algorithms should result in the same predictions.

9. The author thanks Skvoretz for providing the computer program to generate the exchange networks, and for his permission to make use of all the networks up to size 9 generated with this algorithm.

10. A problem with binary integers as identifiers is that their length increases exponentially if the size of the network increases. One way to deal with this problem is to represent the exchange network by, for example, a hexadecimal integer. Skvoretz (1996) suggests another solution. He suggests to identify each network by three numbers, one for the number of nodes, one for the number of edges or exchange relations, and one for the ordering of the exchange network among the list of all exchange networks with the same number of nodes and edges. Using this identification system the *Line4* structure is identified by 4_3_2. However, a problem with the identification system suggested by Skvoretz (1996) is that a structure's identifier no longer determines the exact shape of the structure.

11. The author attempted to be complete in the overview. However, it is not improbable that one or a few studies have been overlooked.

12. Cook and Yamagishi (1992) predicted a 12-12 division in the *BE* relation in the *T* structure. This prediction is not in agreement with the equidependence principle described in the present paper. In the case of a 12-12 division, the relative gains of *B* and *E* are equal to 0 and 12 respectively.

13. Personal communication.

ACKNOWLEDGMENTS

The author is grateful to Shane Thye and John Skvoretz for their valuable suggestions to improve the manuscript.

REFERENCES

Bearman, P. (1997). Generalized exchange. *American Journal of Sociology, 102,* 1383–1415.

Berg, C., & Panther, S. (1998). Network exchange as a non-cooperative bargaining game (unpublished manuscript).

Bienenstock, E. J., & Bonachich, P. (1992). The core as a solution to exclusionary networks. *Social Networks, 14,* 231–243.

Bienenstock, E. J., & Bonacich, P. (1993). Game-theory models for exchange networks: Experimental results. *Sociological Perspectives, 36,* 117–135.

Bienenstock, E. J., & Bonachich, P. (1997). Network exchange as a cooperative game. *Rationality and Society, 9,* 37–65.

Blau, P. M. (1964). *Exchange and power in social life.* Wiley.

Bonacich, P. (1987). Power and centrality: A family of measures. *American Journal of Sociology, 92,* 1170–1182.

Bonacich, P. (1995). Four kinds of social dilemmas within exchange networks. *Current Research in Social Psychology, 1,* 1–7.

Bonacich, P. (1998a). A behavioral foundation for a structural theory of power in exchange networks. *Social Psychology Quarterly, 61,* 185–198.

Bonacich, P. (1998b). The evolutionary stability of strategies in exchange networks. *Current Research in Social Psychology, 3,* 12–34.

Bonacich, P. (1999a). The strength of weak power: A simulation study of network evolution (unpublished manuscript).

Bonacich, P. (1999b). An algebraic theory of strong power in negatively connected exchange networks. *Journal of Mathematical Sociology, 23,* 203–224.

Bonacich, P. (2000). Patterns of coalitions in exchange networks: An experimental study. *Rationality and Society, 12,* 353–373.

Bonacich, P., & Bienenstock, E. J. (1993). Assignment games, chromatic number, and exchange theory. *Journal of Mathematical Psychology, 17,* 243–259.

Bonacich, P., & Bienenstock, E. J. (1995). When rationality fails: Unstable exchange networks with empty cores. *Rationality and Society, 7,* 293–320.

Bonacich, P., & Bienenstock, E. J. (1997a). Strategy in exchange networks: Exploitation vs. accommodation. In: J. Szmatka, J. Skvoretz & J. Berger (Eds), *Status, Network, and Structure: Theory Construction and Theory Development.* Stanford: Stanford University Press.

Bonacich, P., & Bienenstock, E. J. (1997b). Latent classes in exchange networks: Sets of positions with common interests. *Journal of Mathematical Psychology, 22,* 1–28.

Bonacich, P., & Friedkin, N. E. (1998). Unequally valued exchange relations. *Social Psychology Quarterly, 61,* 160–171.

Borgatti, S. P., & Everett, M. G. (1992). Graph colorings and power in experimental exchange networks. *Social Networks, 14,* 287–308.

Braun, N., & Gautschi, T. (2000). Who gets how much in which relation? A non-cooperative bargaining approach to exchange networks (unpublished manuscript).

Burke, P. J. (1997). An identity model for network exchange. *American Sociological Review, 62,* 134–150.

Cook, K. S. (1982). Network structures from an exchange perspective. In: P. V. Marsden, & N. Lin (Eds), *Social Structure and Network Analysis* (pp. 177–199). Sage.

Cook, K. S. (1995). Social relationships and group processes. In: K. S. Cook, G. A. Fine & J. S. House (Eds), *Sociological Perspectives on Social Psychology* (pp. 203–235). Boston, MA: Allyn and Bacon.

Cook, K. S., & Emerson, R. M. (1978). Power, equity and commitment in exchange networks. *American Sociological Review, 43*, 721–739.

Cook, K. S., Emerson, R. M., Gillmore, M. R., & Yamagishi, T. (1983). The distribution of power in exchange networks: Theory and experimental results. *American Journal of Sociology, 89*, 275–305.

Cook, K. S., & Gillmore, M. R. (1984). Power, dependence, and coalitions. *Advances in Group Processes, 1*, 27–58.

Cook, K. S., Gillmore, M. R., & Yamagishi, T. (1986). Point and line vulnerability as bases for predicting the distribution of power in exchange networks: Reply to Willer. *American Journal of Sociology, 92*, 445–448.

Cook, K. S., Molm, L. D., & Yamagishi, T. (1993). Exchange relations and exchange networks: Recent developments in social exchange theory. In: J. Berger & M. Zelditch, Jr. (Eds), *Theoretical Research Programs: Studies in the Growth of Theory* (pp. 296–322). Stanford, CA: Stanford University Press.

Cook, K. S., & Yamagishi, T. (1992). Power in exchange networks: A power-dependence formulation. *Social Networks, 14*, 245–265.

Emerson, R. M. (1962). Power-dependence relations. *American Sociological Review, 27*, 31–40.

Emerson, R. M. (1972a). Exchange theory, Part I: A psychological basis for social exchange. In: J. Berger, M. Zelditch, Jr. & B. Anderson (Eds), *Sociological Theories in Progress* (Vol. 2, pp. 38–57). Boston: Houghton Mifflin.

Emerson, R. M. (1972b). Exchange theory, Part II: Exchange relations and networks. In: J. Berger, M. Zelditch, Jr. & B. Anderson (Eds), *Sociological Theories in Progress* (Vol. 2, pp. 58–87). Boston: Houghton Mifflin.

Emerson, R. M. (1976). Social exchange theory. *Annual Review of Sociology, 2*, 335–361.

Emerson, R. M. (1981). Social exchange theory. In: M. Rosenberg & R. H. Turner (Eds), *Social Psychology: Sociological Perspectives* (pp. 30–65). New York: Basic Books.

Friedkin, N. E. (1992). An expected value model of social power: Predictions for selected exchange networks. *Social Networks, 14*, 213–229.

Friedkin, N. E. (1993). An expected value model of social exchange outcomes. *Advances in Group Processes, 10*, 163–193.

Friedkin, N. E. (1995). The incidence of exchange networks. *Social Psychology Quarterly, 58*, 213–221.

Gillmore, M. R. (1987). Implications of generalized vs. restricted exchange. In: K. S. Cook (Ed.), *Social Exchange Theory* (pp. 179–189). Newbury Park, CA: Sage.

Heckathorn, D. D. (1978). A paradigm for bargaining and a test of two bargaining models. *Behavioral Science, 23*, 73–85.

Heckathorn, D. D. (1980). A unified model for bargaining and conflict. *Behavioral Science, 25*, 261–284.

Heckathorn, D. D. (1983). Extensions of power-dependence theory: The concept of resistance. *Social Forces, 61*, 1206–1231.

Homans, G. C. (1958). Social behavior as exchange. *American Journal of Sociology, 62*, 597–606.

Lawler, E. J., Thye, S. R., & Yoon, J. (2000). Emotion and group cohesion in productive exchange. *American Journal of Sociology, 106*, 616–657.

Lawler, E. J., & Yoon, J. (1998). Network structure and emotion in exchange relations. *American Sociological Review, 63*, 871–894.

Leik, R. K. (1992). New directions for network exchange theory: Strategic manipulation of network linkages. *Social Networks, 14,* 309–323.

Lovaglia, M. J., Skvoretz, J., Markovsky, B., & Willer, D. (1995a). Assessing fundamental power differences in exchange networks: Iterative GPI. *Current Research in Social Psychology, 1,* 8–15.

Lovaglia, M. J., Skvoretz, J., Willer, D., & Markovsky, B. (1995b). Negotiated exchanges in social networks. *Social Forces, 74,* 123–155.

Lucas, J. W., Younts, C. W., Lovaglia, M. J., & Markovsky, B. (2001). Lines of power in exchange networks. *Social Forces, 80,* 185–214.

Markovsky, B. (1987). Toward multilevel sociological theories: Simulations of actor and network effects. *Sociological Theory, 5,* 110–115.

Markovsky, B. (1992). Network exchange outcomes: Limits of predictability. *Social Networks, 14,* 267–286.

Markovsky, B. (1995). Developing an exchange network simulator. *Sociological Perspectives, 38,* 519–545.

Markovsky, B. (1997). Network games. *Rationality and Society, 9,* 67–90.

Markovsky, B., Skvoretz, J., Willer, D., Lovaglia, M. J., & Erger, J. (1993). The seeds of weak power: An extension of network exchange theory. *American Sociological Review, 58,* 197–209.

Markovsky, B., Willer, D., & Patton, T. (1988). Power relations in exchange networks. *American Sociological Review, 53,* 220–236.

Marsden, P. V. (1987). Elements of interactor dependence. In: K. S. Cook (Ed.), *Social Exchange Theory* (pp. 130–148). Newbury Park, CA: Sage.

Marsden, P. V., & Laumann, E. O. (1977). Collective action in a community elite: Exchange, influence resources, and issue resolution. In: R. J. Liebert & A. W. Imershein (Eds), *Power, Paradigms, and Community Research* (pp. 199–250). London: Sage.

Molm, L. D. (1997). *Coercive power in social exchange.* Cambridge: Cambridge University Press.

Molm, L. D., Peterson, G., & Takahashi, N. (1999). Power in negotiated and reciprocal exchange. *American Sociological Review, 64,* 876–890.

Molm, L. D., Peterson, G., & Takahashi, N. (2001). The value of exchange. *Social Forces, 79,* 159–185.

Molm, L. D., Takahashi, N., & Peterson, G. (2000). Risk and trust in social exchange: An experimental test of a classical proposition. *American Journal of Sociology, 105,* 1396–1427.

Nash, J. F. (1953). Two-person cooperative games. *Econometrica, 21,* 128–140.

Skvoretz, J. (1996). An algorithm to generate connected graphs. *Current Research in Social Psychology, 1,* 43–49.

Skvoretz, J., & Burkett, T. (1994). Information and the distribution of power in exchange networks. *Journal of Mathematical Sociology, 19,* 263–278.

Skvoretz, J., & Fararo, T. J. (1992). Power and network exchange: An essay toward theoretical unification. *Social Networks, 14,* 325–344.

Skvoretz, J., & Lovaglia, M. J. (1995). Who exchanges with whom: Structural determinants of exchange frequency in negotiated exchange networks. *Social Psychology Quarterly, 58,* 163–177.

Skvoretz, J., & Willer, D. (1991). Power in exchange networks: Setting and structural variations. *Social Psychology Quarterly, 54,* 224–238.

Skvoretz, J., & Willer, D. (1993). Exclusion and power: A test of four theories of power in exchange networks. *American Sociological Review, 58,* 801–818.

Skvoretz, J., Willer, D., & Fararo, T. J. (1993). Toward models of power development in exchange networks. *Sociological Perspectives, 36,* 95–115.

Skvoretz, J., & Zhang, P. (1997). Actors' responses to outcomes in exchange networks. *Sociological Perspectives, 40*, 183–197.

Stolte, J. F. (1988). From micro- to macro-exchange structure: Measuring power imbalance at the exchange network level. *Social Psychology Quarterly, 51*, 357–364.

Stolte, J. F. (1990). Power processes in structures of dependence and exchange. *Advances in Group Processes, 7*, 129–150.

Stolte, J. F., & Emerson, R. M. (1977). Structural inequality: Position and power in exchange structures. In: R. L. Hamblin & J. H. Kunkel (Eds), *Behavioral Theory in Sociology* (pp. 117–138). New Brunswick: Transaction Books.

Szmatka, J., Skvoretz, J., Sozanski, T., & Mazur, J. (1998). Conflict in networks. *Sociological Perspectives, 41*, 49–66.

Szmatka, J., & Willer, D. (1995). Exclusion, inclusion, and compound connection in exchange networks. *Social Psychology Quarterly, 58*, 123–132.

Takahashi, N. (2000). The emergence of generalized exchange. *American Journal of Sociology, 105*, 1105–1134.

Takahashi, N., & Yamagishi, T. (1993). Power in social exchange networks: Power-dependence theory vs. elementary theory. *Sociological Theory and Methods, 8*, 251–269 (in Japanese).

Thibaut, J., & Kelley, H. H. (1959). *The social psychology of groups*. New York: Wiley.

Thye, S. R. (2000). A status-value theory of power in exchange relations. *American Sociological Review, 65*, 407–432.

Thye, S. R., Lovaglia, M. J., & Markovsky, B. (1997). Responses to social exchange and social exclusion in networks. *Social Forces, 75*, 1031–1047.

Whitmeyer, J. M. (1997). Applying general equilibrium analysis & game theory to exchange networks. *Current Research in Social Psychology, 2*, 13–23.

Whitmeyer, J. M. (1999). Interest-network structures in exchange networks. *Sociological Perspectives, 42*, 23–47.

Whitmeyer, J. M. (1999). Convex preferences and power inequality in exchange networks: An experimental study. *Rationality and Society, 11*, 419–442.

Willer, D. (1984). Analysis and composition as theoretic procedures. *Journal of Mathematical Psychology, 10*, 241–269.

Willer, D. (1986). Vulnerability and the location of power positions: Comment on Cook, Emerson, Gillmore and Yamagishi. *American Journal of Sociology, 92*, 441–444.

Willer, D. (1987). *Theory and the empirical investigation of social structures*. New York: Gordon and Breach Science Publishers.

Willer, D. (1992). Predicting power in exchange networks: A brief history and introduction to the issues. *Social Networks, 14*, 187–211.

Willer, D. (Ed.) (1999). *Network exchange theory*. Westport, CT: Praeger Press.

Willer, D., & Anderson, B. (1981). *Networks, exchange and coercion: The elementary theory and its applications*. North Holland: Elsevier.

Willer, D., Lovaglia, M. J., & Markovsky, B. (1997). Power and influence: A theoretical bridge. *Social Forces, 76*, 571–603.

Willer, D., & Markovsky, B. (1993). Elementary theory: Its development and research program. In: J. Berger & M. Zelditch, Jr. (Eds), *Theoretical Research Programs: Studies in the Growth of Theory* (pp. 323–363). Stanford, CA: Stanford University Press.

Willer, D., Markovsky, B., & Patton, T. (1989). Power structures: Derivations and applications of elementary theory. In: J. Berger, M. Zelditch, Jr. & B. Anderson (Eds), *Sociological Theories in Progress* (Vol. 3, pp. 313–353). Boston: Houghton Mifflin.

Willer, D., & Patton, T. (1987). The development of network exchange theory. *Advances in Group Processes, 4*, 199–242.

Willer, D., & Simpson, B. (1999). A new method for finding power structures. In: D. Willer (Ed.), *Network Exchange Theory* (pp. 270–284). Westport, CT: Praeger Press.

Willer, D., & Skvoretz, J. (1997a). Network connection and exchange ratios: Theory, predictions, and experimental tests. *Advances in Group Processes, 14*, 199–234.

Willer, D., & Skvoretz, J. (1997b). Games and Structures. *Rationality and Society, 9*, 5–35.

Willer, D., & Szmatka, J. (1993). Cross-national experimental investigations of elementary theory: Implications for the generality of the theory and the autonomy of social structure. *Advances in Group Processes, 10*, 37–81.

Willer, R., & Willer, D. (2000). Exploring dynamic networks: Hypotheses and conjectures. *Social Networks, 22*, 251–272.

Yamagishi, T., & Cook, K. S. (1990). Power relations in exchange networks: A comment on network exchange theory. *American Sociological Review, 55*, 297–300.

Yamagishi, T., & Cook, K. S. (1993). Generalized exchange and social dilemmas. *Social Psychology Quarterly, 56*, 235–248.

Yamagishi, T., Gillmore, M. R., & Cook, K. S. (1988). Network connections and the distribution of power in exchange networks. *American Journal of Sociology, 93*, 833–851.

Yamaguchi, K. (1996). Power in networks of substitutable and complementary exchange relations: A rational-choice model and an analysis of power centralization. *American Sociological Review, 61*, 308–332.

Yamaguchi, K. (2000). Power in mixed exchange networks: A rational choice model. *Social Networks, 22*, 93–121.

POWER, STATUS, AND COLLECTIVE ACTION: DEVELOPING FUNDAMENTAL THEORIES TO ADDRESS A SUBSTANTIVE PROBLEM

Michael J. Lovaglia, Robb Willer and Lisa Troyer

ABSTRACT

We develop elements of Network Exchange and Expectation States Theories to explain the relationship between power and status. While power and status are highly correlated, demonstrating that power can be used to attain high status has proven difficult, perhaps because negative reactions to power use limit power users' influence. We propose three ways to reduce negative reactions to power use. One of them, philanthropy, suggests a solution to the "free-rider" problem in collective action. If philanthropic contributions increase status, then contributing to a public good may also. Thus, status attainment may be an incentive motivating public goods contributions.

INTRODUCTION

Fundamental theories of power in exchange networks and status in groups have developed in parallel research programs to the point where the relationship between power and status can be fruitfully investigated. We show how that relationship illuminates a substantive problem in sociological research, identifying

Power and Status
Advances in Group Processes, Volume 20, 105–131
© 2003 Published by Elsevier Ltd.
ISSN: 0882-6145/doi:10.1016/S0882-6145(03)20004-7

the incentive for individuals to contribute to public goods and thus their motivation to engage in collective action.

Our approach to theoretical development uses the insights of classical theory to formulate a testable theory that can be developed within a research program. Theoretical development in sociology has suffered from the inability of diverse practitioners to benefit from each other's work. A recent survey discovered that sociologists agree on the importance of the work of only three theorists, Marx, Weber and Durkheim (Markovsky, 2002). Appreciation of recent theory construction approaches may suffer from the inability of theorists to see how recent theories relate to the fundamental sociological processes of classical theory. Group processes researchers who study fundamental processes such as power and status can attempt to bridge the gap between classical theory and theory construction by incorporating classical ideas into the foundations of their developing theories. Not only will the likely result be more effective theory construction, but we also hope that more sociologists will see the value of theory construction and programmatic research.

We first develop the theoretical relationship between power and status, using ideas from classical theory to develop propositions that can be used to derive testable hypotheses. In addition, theoretical derivations suggest a new approach to the collective action problem of interest to a wide variety of sociologists and other social scientists.

POWER AND STATUS: A CONCEPTUAL APPROACH

C. Wright Mills observed that the powerful, wealthy and prestigious tend to be the same people (Mills, 1956). Those in power usually also have high social status. How power can be used to increase status remains unclear because those subjected to power react negatively?

To paraphrase Weber's famous definition, social power is the capacity to dominate social interaction, to impose one's will, overcoming the resistance of others (Weber, 1978 [1921]). Those exploited by power use, however, are unlikely to hold the power user in high regard. Power use, then, not only overcomes the resistance of others but also produces resistance in others to the power user's influence. The prestige, honor and respect that comprise high social status produce deference conferred at the discretion of others, which implies that high status cannot be obtained directly through force or sanctions. Power can be used to take resources but may not increase esteem and honor. Thus, a power user seeking to gain status from power use must first mitigate the resistance caused by power use.

We develop the theory that power can increase status if negative reactions to power use can be mitigated. Specifically, we propose that: (1) resources can be gained by using power on a few while its consequences are observed by many; (2) power users can present their power use as group-motivated, forestalling a negative reaction; and (3) with philanthropy, power users can donate to the common good a portion of the resources gained from power use, reducing perceptions of selfishness and greed. Moreover, voluntary contribution to the common good is the basis of collective action. We conclude by applying the theory to show how the desire to acquire status can motivate participation in collective action.

Theoretical Background

Power and status are two fundamental social processes whose importance can be traced to the origins of human society (Maryanski & Turner, 1992; Turner, 2000). Competitive power relations produce individuals who can survive in a hostile environment. Cooperative status hierarchies develop because groups of people working together can accomplish what no individual could accomplish alone: A cooperating group can dominate the strongest individual (Hobbes, 1996 [1651]). The fundamental push and pull of power and status, competition and cooperation, may have developed when relatively autonomous, individualistic primates evolved into human tribal groups as they adapted to the increasingly open conditions of the African savanna between eight and six million years ago (Maryanski & Turner, 1992; Turner, 2000).

Our basic understanding of power and status has been shaped by social theory. Kemper and Collins (1990) see power and status as distinct dimensions underlying the social-order, but the two dimensions are related. People in positions of power usually have high status, judges for example, or presidents. Moreover, the relationship between power and status seems to be causal, high-power gives rise to status. For example, Bierstedt (1950) concludes that Stalin was held in respect and even awe in the Soviet Union because he was first a man of power and despite having caused the deaths of millions of Soviets (Radzinsky, 1996).

Power takes precedence over status for several important social theorists. Marx (1967 [1867]) emphasized the fundamental importance of control of the means of production, the power to control resources and attain wealth, as the underlying dynamic of society. For Marx, high status is merely one side effect of power. Dahrendorf (1968) also sees power as fundamental to create and legitimate the social-order.

Social status, based on the esteem and honor in which a person is held by members of the status group, emerges as an important social dimension alongside power in Weber's analysis. For Weber, economic power as represented by property "is not always recognized as a status qualification, but in the long run it is, and with extraordinary regularity" (Gerth & Mills, 1958, p. 187). For Homans (1974) also, power consistently used over time produces higher status. Emerson (1962) proposed a causal link in that those low in power "give status" to those high in power to discourage additional power use.

   The relationship between power and status is thought to be reciprocal; status may also produce power. Blau (1964) saw power developing from a person's high status when those of lower status become increasingly dependent on the contributions of the high status person. That is, the contributions of high status people are expected to be more valuable than the contributions of others. Thye (2000) demonstrated that resources controlled by people assigned high status were worth more than comparable resources controlled by people assigned low status. Thus, high status produced a material advantage that is the basis of power.

How Power Compromises Status

Although Weber sees power regularly increasing status, he also hints that untrammeled power use can damage a power user's status: "The typical American Boss, as well as the big speculator, deliberately relinquishes social honor" (Gerth & Mills, 1958, p. 180). Using a position of power to gain wealth is seen as less than honorable. Lenski (1966, p. 52) notes, "honor is denied to those who rule by force alone." Similarly, Coleman (1990) viewed social status as an exchangeable good.[1] Social status could be adjusted to balance otherwise unequal transactions. A wealthy person might be able to buy prestige and honor. Brehm (1966) and Brehm and Brehm (1981) proposed the concept of reactance. Overt power use is perceived as an attempt to limit the freedom of those on whom power is used. Reactance occurs as those exploited resist the influence of the powerful, *decreasing* the status of a power user.

   Veblen (1898) developed the idea that people infer merit from displays of wealth. Conspicuous consumption is a way to show high ability. Wealth implies efficiency, hard work, in a word, merit. In modern times, it seems to matter little how the wealth was acquired, observers of property are most aware of the amount of wealth, not its roots. Although Veblen does caution, "the appearance of evil must be avoided to escape dispraise" (p. 190). The powerful must try to avoid appearing selfish, greedy, and arrogant. Escaping dispraise is more easily accomplished in modern times when the power user acquiring wealth is exposed "to a large and especially to a shifting, human environment whose approval is sought" (Veblen, 1898, p. 198).

A theory of power and status takes shape from these classical roots. Power produces wealth but also gives the appearance of selfishness, greed and arrogance. High status results from the perception that a person is capable and motivated to contribute to the common good. Wealth and success give the perception of high ability. Along with the perception of high ability, however, high status also requires the perception that high ability will be used to benefit others. Thus, having become wealthy from power use, the powerful can gain status by countering perceptions of selfishness.

A THEORY OF POWER AND STATUS

Using classical conceptions of power and status as a foundation, we use Network Exchange Theory and Status Characteristics and Expectation States Theories to develop a theory that relates power and status.

Defining Power, Influence, and Status

We follow Willer, Lovaglia and Markovsky (1997, p. 573) who define *power* as the "structurally determined potential for obtaining favored payoffs in relations where interests are opposed." Earlier theorists often defined power more broadly in ways that could include influence. For Heider (1958), power is a person's ability to accomplish something, to alter the environment. Wrong (1979) defines power as the capacity to produce intended and foreseen effects on others. Power, for Wrong, is identical with intended and effective influence.[2] Similarly, French and Raven (1968) define power in terms of influence. More narrow definitions of power such as the one we use have proven effective in developing formal theory and systematic empirical research.[3]

To distinguish influence from power, we define *influence* to occur when a person's opinion or behavior changes to conform to the suggestion of another without the threat of punishment or the promise of reward. For Zelditch (1992, p. 995), "what distinguishes power is that it involves external sanctions.... Influence, on the other hand, persuades B that X is right according to B's own interests." Influence uses persuasion, information and advice while power use employs force, coercion and sanctions (Mokken & Stokman, 1976).

We define *status* as a person's position in a group's prestige hierarchy.[4] An individual's status determines her influence. When a high-status person suggests a course of action, other group members are more likely to follow that suggestion because of their high expectations for the competence of the high-status person.

In matters affecting group goals, high-status members have influence to the extent that they are perceived as competent and oriented toward group goals rather than selfish goals (Ridgeway, 1982). Status, then, is a collective estimation of a person's worthiness in the context of the group (Berger, Fisek, Norman & Wagner, 1985; Podolny, 1993; Ridgeway, 1991; Thye, 2000).

Power and status arise in quite different ways. Power differences result when the interests of two people are opposed (Willer, Markovsky & Lovaglia, 1997). Status hierarchies emerge in task situations when the interests of group members coincide (Berger, Fisek, Norman & Zelditch, 1977). Complex, naturally occurring social situations often contain elements of both cooperation and competition. For example, employees may work together in groups to accomplish the goals of the organization while competing with each other for raises and promotions.

Power in Exchange Networks

In Network Exchange Theory, power occurs when a person's position in an exchange network allows her to exclude another person from profitable exchange.[5] The theory has been used to make precise predictions of subtle power differences in exchange networks (Lovaglia, Skvoretz, Willer & Markovsky, 1995).

Two qualitatively different kinds of power are produced in exchange networks. Markovsky, Willer and Patton (1988) studied what have become known as *strong-power* differences. Strong-power occurs when a person in one network position controls resources to the extent that people in other network positions must bid against each other for the privilege of participating in a profitable exchange. The bidding process produces gross differences in resources between those with a strong-power advantage and those with a strong-power disadvantage. A network position that is *high* strong-power will gain most of the available resources in exchange.

Proposition 1. The greater an actor's structural power, the greater the resources attained from exchange by that actor.

The prototypical strong-power network is a 3-actor line (3-line): A_1–B–A_2. In a 3-line network, the letters represent exchange positions with subscripts to distinguish isomorphic positions. The dashes connecting the letters represent exchange links. Thus, in the 3-line, A_1 may exchange with B, and A_2 may exchange with B, but A_1 may not exchange with A_2. If the network permits B to exchange with only one of the A positions at a time, then B is in a position to exclude one A from a profitable exchange. Over a series of exchange opportunities, the A positions must vie for exchange with **B**. To avoid being excluded from exchange, each **A** offers more and more to **B**. The result of **B**'s strong-power advantage is that eventually, the **A** actors offer **B** nearly all of the profit available to them.

Weak power produces subtler differences in exchange networks (Markovsky, Skvoretz, Willer, Lovaglia & Erger, 1993). Weak power occurs when a position is less likely to be excluded from exchange than is at least one of its trading partners. In contrast to strong-power, however, a weak-power trading advantage disappears as soon as the advantaged position realizes a profit greater than its partner does. In weak power networks *"no positions can consistently exclude others from exchanging without themselves suffering losses"* (Markovsky, Skovretz, Willer, Lovaglia & Erger, 1993, p. 201). The result is relatively small differences in profit between *high* weak-power and *low* weak-power positions.

The prototypical weak-power network is the 4-actor line (4-line): A_1–B_1–B_2–A_2. If the **B** actors may exchange with either an **A** or the other **B**, but not both, then the **B** positions have an advantage over the **A** positions. **B** positions can exclude **A** positions from exchange, the source of power in exchange networks. For example, suppose B_1 demands a little extra profit from A_1. If A_1 refuses, then B_1 can exchange with B_2, while A_1 is excluded from exchange. To avoid exclusion, a rational A_1 will offer B_1 a little more profit to avoid being left out. But as long as A_1 offers only a little more than an even split of the available profit, a rational B_1 will accept A_1's offer. That is because B_1 can expect no more than an equal split from B_2. A_1 and B_2 do not bid for B_1's attention in the weak power 4-line the way that **A** positions bid for **B**'s attention in the strong-power 3-line.

Strong-power and weak-power differences relate to our research in that observers of exchanges in strong-power networks may come to different conclusions about the extent of power being used than do observers of weak-power networks. Power use has been shown to produce negative reactions in those subjected to it. Willer, Lovaglia and Markovsky (1997) report that strong-power differences produced substantial negative reactions in participants subjected to power use in a strong-power network. Negative reactions to weak-power use have yet to be measured, but it seems reasonable to assume that negative reaction may vary with the extent of power use.

Proposition 2. The greater the resources attained through power use, the more negative the reaction to power use, including perceptions of selfishness and greed.

Observers might also feel differently about the fairness and selfishness of those using power to obtain resources in strong-power and weak-power networks. Perhaps the different perceptions of power in observers of weak-power and strong-power networks might give power users different degrees of influence over observers.

Status, Expectations and Influence

Status Characteristics and Expectation States Theories explain the processes that determine differences in influence among group members. Characterized by formal theoretical development and systematic empirical tests, the theory has been used to explain social inequality in a wide variety of settings but especially racial and gender inequality in work organizations and schools.[6] A group member's influence increases with the group's expectations for the member's contributions to group goals (Berger, Fisek, Norman & Zelditch, 1977).

Status characteristics such as gender, race, age, education and occupation have been shown to alter the influence of group members (Cohen & Roper, 1972; Pugh & Wahrman, 1983; Webster & Driskell, 1978). Members of advantaged categories such as white men are expected to contribute more to the group and attain more influence over group decisions than are other group members. Status characteristics imply status value. That is, a person with high states of status characteristics is valued because he is expected to contribute to group goals. These expectations in turn produce interaction patterns typical of status hierarchies: High status group members: (1) are given more opportunities to perform; (2) perform more; (3) are evaluated more highly for their performances; and (4) have more influence over other group members. Such outcomes then serve to reinforce expectations for contribution to the group (Berger, Connor & McKeown, 1974).

Expectation States as Cause and Consequence of Status

In Status Characteristics Theory, a valued state of some characteristic, being male for example, causes group members to form expectations for the high competence of a member possessing that state. Members who possess the valued state of the characteristic are then accorded respect and deference in the group. That is, possessing the valued state of a status characteristic produces expectations for contributions to the group.

Other expectation states theories make clear that expectations for contribution to group goals determine the prestige and honor of individuals, their status.[7] Group members are held in high regard *because* of their expected contributions. Status Value Theory explains that expectations for competence are used to justify unequal rewards for group members (Berger, Zelditch, Anderson & Cohen, 1972). Those expected to contribute more to the group are deemed worthier, that is, higher in status. Ridgeway (1991, p. 373) explains the causal role of expectation states in the creation of status hierarchies:

> This local status hierarchy results from and is maintained by the expectations the interactants develop about the likely usefulness of each interactant's contributions to the shared goal, compared to the contributions of the others. Once formed, this shared, often implicit order of performance expectations tends to become self-fulfilling by shaping an interactant's propensity to offer goal-related suggestions and the likelihood that others will attend to and positively evaluate those suggestions and accept influence from the interactant.

Proposition 3. The greater the expectations for an actor's contributions to the group, the greater that actor's status.

Influence as Cause and Consequence of Expectation States

Not only should high expectations for contribution increase a member's influence in the group, but influence should also increase expectations for contribution. Status characteristics theory explains how high-status group members gain influence even when no initial power differences exist. And while influence can be obtained in ways other than through high status – group identity for example (Kalkhoff & Barnum, 2000) – influence attempts and their acceptance are part of a process through which status differences are enacted (Fisek, Hamit & Norman, 1991). "Expectations both determine and are determined by these power and prestige behaviors" (Wagner & Berger, 1993, p. 27). Consistent behavioral interchanges typical of high and low status produce expectations that differentiate high-status and low-status actors. Through interaction, then, influence differences could produce differences in prestige and status over time (Berger & Zelditch, 1997).

Proposition 4. The greater the influence of an actor over others in a group, the greater the expectations for that actor's contribution to the group.

Resources as Cause and Consequence of Expectation States

Network Exchange Theory explains how access to resources confers power that increases rewards and resources. And while Status Value Theory explains how high expected contribution increases rewards and resources, two expectation states theories also explain the reverse causal direction.

Reward Expectations Theory (Berger, Fisek, Norman & Wagner, 1985), links rewards to expected contributions through "referential structures," taken-for-granted beliefs about the social world. In task situations, we commonly assume that rewards are related to contributions to group goals. Highly competent and productive people are supposed to be paid more. Conversely, highly paid people are expected to be more competent and productive (Ridgeway & Berger, 1988). Thus, people who are highly rewarded will also obtain influence over group decisions, expectations for contribution to the group, and high status.

Ridgeway's (1991, p. 375) Status Construction Theory ties resources to expected contributions more directly. She reasons that resources enable a member to contribute to many kinds of group goals:

> Superior exchangeable resources are likely to make a person appear to have a greater capacity to contribute usefully to a goal. This, in turn, makes that person appear more situationally competent independent of any individual ability. This appearance of situational competence should develop regardless of whether the resource rich individual is assumed to have earned or deserved his or her riches because of past contributions or innate ability. Furthermore, it should develop whether or not resource-rich people ever actually use their power, since it is the structural capacity to do so that gives the impression of competence in the situation.

Proposition 5. The greater an actor's resources, the greater will be the expectations for that actor's contributions to the group.

Several experimental tests support Status Construction Theory's assertion that differences in resources create status beliefs consistent with those differences and that such status beliefs can then be transferred to others (Ridgeway, Boyle, Kuipers & Robinson, 1998; Ridgeway & Erickson, 2000). Reward Expectations Theory supports a similar conclusion: A member's reward and resource levels alter group expectations for that member's contributions to the group. Those expectations then alter the group member's influence. Empirical studies have consistently found that an individual's rewards and resources alter that individual's influence (Bierhoff, Buck & Klein, 1986; Cook, 1975; Harrod, 1980; Stewart & Moore, 1992). Thus, it seemed logical for Lovaglia (1994) to propose that power use that results in increased rewards and resources would increase influence.

Issues of Scope

When Lovaglia (1995) measured influence following power use, he found no difference in influence between partners who had previously been high or low in power. One possible explanation is that power use may place a situation outside the scope of status characteristics and expectation states theories. The scope of a theory encompasses conditions under which the theory is proposed to apply (Walker & Cohen, 1985). In particular, status characteristics theory applies when group members are collectively oriented and task oriented.[8] That is, when group members feel that it is appropriate to consider the contributions of all group members in completing a group task. Moreover, all group members must be expected to work toward the same goal (Berger, Fisek, Norman & Zelditch, 1977). It is possible that power use interferes with perceptions that a group member is collectively oriented and will use her resources to accomplish group goals. Thus, expectations of competence would not necessarily generalize to greater expected contributions to the group.[9] The implication is that scope conditions can be partially violated with predictable effects on influence.

Following Walker and Cohen (1985), we see scope conditions as the minimum necessary conditions for Status Characteristics Theory to apply. Network exchange research designs contain elements of competition, where the interests and goals of competitors are opposed. A competitive exchange situation, however, can also contain elements of cooperation, where people work together on a cooperative task and are free to accept or reject advice without fear of sanctions. Viewing scope statements as describing necessary conditions, such mixed cooperative and competitive situations do not violate the scope of status characteristics theory. For example, Status Characteristics Theory has been shown to explain behavior in research and development teams in corporations where employees work together to accomplish team goals but also compete for raises and promotions (Cohen & Zhou, 1991). A research design that contains elements of both competition and cooperation but measures influence in a setting where team members work on a cooperative task will fall within the scope of Status Characteristics Theory.

Extending Expectation States Theories to Explain Effects of Power and Perceived Group Motivation

We build on Ridgeway's (1978, 1982) theory of perceived group motivation and status attainment to show how power relates to status. Ridgeway proposes that the group's perception of a member as group-oriented or self-oriented combines with the member's external status characteristics and perceived task competence to determine that member's status within the group.

Ridgeway (1978, 1982) proposed that expectations of high ability alone would not be sufficient to increase the status of a group member. Rather, people could attain high status only if they were expected to possess high ability and were also perceived to be motivated to help the group achieve its goals. Expectations of high ability will increase deference and status only to the extent that the group member is also perceived to be group-motivated rather than selfishly motivated (Ridgeway, 1982). That is, expectations of ability increases status only to the extent that the group member is trusted to use her ability to contribute to group goals rather than to selfish goals.

For Ridgeway (1982), people perceived to be selfish have less influence because their contributions are expected to be less valuable to the group. The selfish person cannot be trusted to cooperate, so her advice has less value, and she has less influence than she otherwise would. Ridgeway (1982) found that a group member who was perceived to be group-motivated had more influence over participants than did a group member who was perceived to be selfishly motivated. Her findings were replicated and extended by Shackelford, Wood and Worchel (1996).

Molm, Takahashi and Peterson (2000) define trust as, ". . . expectations that an exchange partner will behave benignly, based on an attribution of positive dispositions and intentions to the partner in a situation of uncertainty and risk" (p. 1402). Like Kollock (1994) and Yamagishi and Yamagishi (1996) they emphasize that attributions of trustworthiness arise in situations where one actor foregoes the opportunity to exploit another actor. Unequal structural power in exchange networks represents precisely such a situation. When an actor enjoys a structural advantage – either strong-power or weak-power – in an exchange network, the more she exploits that advantage, the lower the trust that others will place in her.

Recent research on the development of trust in exchange relations finds that ongoing exchange relations are accompanied by positive affect and commitment to engage in exchange with a particular partner (e.g. Kollock, 1994; Lawler & Yoon, 1993, 1996; Molm, Takahashi & Peterson, 2000; Yamagishi & Yamagishi, 1996). However, Lawler and Yoon (1998) found that increased positive affect and commitment resulted only from equal exchange relations. Exchange relations where power was unequal did not produce positive affect and commitment. That is, power use interferes with trust.

In addition, Lovaglia and Houser (1996) created negative emotional reactions by causing participants to lose out in an exchange setting. Participants who lost out in exchange were less influenced by a partner than were those who were satisfied with the exchange. Lovaglia and Houser also found that negative emotional reactions in general could reduce the influence of a partner. Thus, negative emotional reactions coinciding with perceptions that a high-power person is selfish could reduce a high-power person's influence. Willer, Lovaglia and Markovsky (1997) reported further evidence that negative emotional reactions could interfere with the influence of a high-power partner. They found that low-power participants in an exchange network reported the same negative emotional reactions reported by participants in Lovaglia and Houser's study who had lost out in exchange. Thus, power use by a partner created the same negative emotional reactions that had reduced the influence of a partner in Lovaglia and Houser's study. Willer, Lovaglia and Markovsky conclude that in the absence of a negative emotional reaction to power use, their evidence suggests that power use could increase influence.

Proposition 6. The greater the negative reactions to power use, including perceptions of selfishness and greed, the lower the influence of the powerful.

Mitigating Negative Reactions to Power Use

Power use may have two opposing effects on the influence of the power user. Increased expectations of the power user's competence my enhance influence, while increased perceptions of the power user's selfishness may decrease influence. Lovaglia (1994) proposed that people placed in high-power positions in an exchange setting would gain influence over people who had been placed in low-power positions. The difference in influence should continue after differences in power had been removed and people work together on a cooperative task. While Lovaglia (1995) found evidence that people thought their high-power partners were more competent than they thought their low-power partners were, high-power and low-power partners exerted the same amount of influence over participants in the study.

Lovaglia (1995) also noticed that power use produces negative emotional reactions in those on whom it is used. He proposed that emotional reactions might interfere with an expectation advantage that power would otherwise confer. His results suggest that negative reactions to power use can have an equal but opposite effect on a power user's influence. Lovaglia and Houser (1996) later demonstrated that negative emotional reactions could decrease influence. Moreover, they found that negative emotional reactions combine with effects of status characteristics in a way consistent with the combining principles of Status Characteristics Theory. Ridgeway (1982) demonstrated that expectations of competence and perceptions of group motivation combined to determine influence and expectations consistent with the combining principle of Status Characteristics Theory. An influence advantage could be dampened to the extent that a power user is expected to be selfish or greedy.

Proposition 7. Effects of resources and expected self-motivation combine to determine an actor's influence.

These seven propositions extend the predictions of Status Characteristics Theory to include the effects perceived group-motivation on influence. Propositions 8–10 suggest ways to mitigate negative reactions to power use.

Veblen's analysis, described in the Theoretical Background section, suggested that observers of wealth perceive the wealthy to be competent and successful while such observers ignore the manner in which wealth was acquired. He noted that in modern society, the group of observers who supply a person's reputation is large and shifting. Few are likely to be aware of the details of power used to acquire wealth. Thus, when power is used on a few to acquire wealth, but many observe the wealth that results, negative reactions will be avoided but expectations of competence maintained. Moreover, observers of power use may not feel the negative emotion or perceive the power user to be selfish in the same way as those who are directly exploited by the power user.

Proposition 8. The more directly a person is subjected to power use, the more self-motivated that person will perceive the power user to be.

Proposition 8 implies that a person directly subjected to power use will experience a strong negative reaction; whereas the negative reaction of an observer of power use who has not directly been subjected to it will be milder, while the power user will feel little or no negative reaction to power use.

In Ridgeway's (1982) study, participants worked with partners who presented themselves as group-motivated or selfishly motivated. When partners might be seeking higher status, those who presented themselves as group-motivated had more influence over participants than did partners who presented themselves as selfishly motivated. Ridgeway's (1982) results suggest that power users who present themselves as group-motivated might avoid creating the perception of selfishness and greed that produces a negative reaction in others.

Proposition 9. Self-presentation as group-motivated can reduce perceptions that a power user is selfishly motivated.

Coleman's proposal that status can be traded suggests that the powerful, having used their power to acquire wealth, could then use some of it to increase their status. Philanthropy would be one way to convert money to status. By contributing to the common good, power-users provide dramatic evidence of their group-motivation. Moreover, philanthropy can be seen as form of conspicuous consumption, evidence of wealth, success, and merit.

Proposition 10a. Philanthropy, voluntary contributions to a common good, reduces expectations of self-motivation and increases expectations for contribution to group goals.

DERIVATIONS FROM THE THEORY

The propositions of the theory can be combined to yield three derivations:

Power users can increase their status by influencing observers of power use. Power use produces resources (Proposition 1) that increase expectations for contribution (Proposition 4) and expected self-motivation (Proposition 2) that decreases influence (Proposition 6). Because the effects of resources and self-motivation combine (Proposition 7) and observers expect less self-motivation from power users than do those directly subjected to power (Proposition 8), the power user's influence increases over observers of power use. Finally, increased resources and influence increase the power user's status (Propositions 3–5) among observers.

Power users can increase their status through self-presentation as group-motivated. As the previous derivation shows, power use produces opposing gains and losses of influence that combine. Self-presentation as group-motivated, however, may reduce perceptions of self-motivation produced by power use (Proposition 9). Because the effects of resources and self-motivation combine (Proposition 7), reducing perceptions of self-motivation will increase influence (Proposition 6) and status (Propositions 3–5).

Power users can increase their status through voluntary contributions to a common good (philanthropy). Given that power use produces opposing gains and losses of influence that combine, using a portion of the resources produced by power use to contribute to a common good will reduce expectations of self-motivation (Proposition 10a) and increases the influence of the power user (Proposition 6), as well as the power user's status (Propositions 3–5) (Fig. 1).

Tests of these derivations are proceeding using an experimental setting that combines those currently in use by Network Exchange and Status Characteristics researchers. Power is first established in an exchange setting where participants observe or participate in exchanges in a strong-power or weak-power network, in either a high-power or low-power position. Then in a second phase, participants work together with one of the exchange partners from the first phase to accomplish a cooperative task with no power differences (Willer, Troyer & Lovaglia, 2001, 2002).

USING FUNDAMENTAL THEORIES TO EXPLAIN COLLECTIVE ACTION

Research on the collective action problem attempts to explain why individuals contribute to public goods when they can enjoy the benefits of collective action without contributing. The fundamental theory of power and status developed above

Proposition 1. The greater an actor's structural power, the greater the resources attained from exchange by that actor.

Proposition 2. The greater the resources attained through power use, the more negative the reaction to power use, including perceptions of selfishness and greed.

Proposition 3. The greater the expectations for an actor's contributions to the group, the greater that actor's status.

Proposition 4. The greater the influence of an actor over others in a group, the greater the expectations for that actor s contribution to the group.

Proposition 5. The greater an actor's resources, the greater will be the expectations for that actor's contributions to the group.

Proposition 6. The greater the negative reactions to power use, including perceptions of selfishness and greed, the lower the influence of the powerful.

Proposition 7. Effects of resources and expected self-motivation combine to determine an actor's influence.

Proposition 8. The more directly a person is subjected to power use, the more self-motivated that person will perceive the power user to be.

Proposition 9. Self-presentation as group motivated may reduce perceptions that a power user is selfishly motivated.

Proposition 10a. Philanthropy, voluntary contributions to a common good, reduces expectations of self-motivation and increases expectations for contribution to group goals.

Proposition 10b. Contribution to a public good increases expectations of the contributor's competence and perceptions of group motivation in a group that benefits from the public good.

Proposition 11. Status attainment has value to individuals.

Derivation 1. Power users can increase their status by influencing observers of power use.

Derivation 2. Power users can increase their status through self-presentation as group motivated.

Derivation 3. Power users can increase their status through voluntary contributions to a common good (philanthropy).

Derivation 4. Contribution to public goods increases the status of contributors.

Fig. 1.   Propositions and Derivations of a Theory Relating Power and Status.

suggests a solution to a substantive problem in sociology, the problem of collective action. Using Network Exchange Theory and Status Characteristics and Expectation States Theories to develop a theory of power and status led to the derivation that power users can increase their status through philanthropy, voluntary contributions to the common good. The theory proposes that voluntary contributions to the common good increase influence and status. Assuming that proposition is valid, then increasing status might be a good reason for individuals to contribute to public goods even though they can enjoy the material benefits of collective action without contributing. Further, because higher status increases the value of one's resources (Thye, 2000), the competition for higher status may pay material dividends as well.

Public Goods and the Collective Action Problem

Olson (1965) reasoned that self-interested, rational individuals will not contribute to the production of public goods. A rational individual may net higher marginal returns by not contributing and "free-riding" on the contributions of others. Because public goods are defined as non-excludable to members of a given group, an individual may enjoy the products of collective action without contributing. Collective action situations represent a social dilemma because of the conflict between group-level interests and individual interests. Although it is in any given individual's interest to free-ride on others' contributions, if all group members act in this way then no public good is produced and the group suffers.

Although public goods problems are frequently applied to social movements, collective action theory has wide application. To ask why it is that an individual would contribute to group goals instead of free-riding is to ask the fundamental social question of "why society?" Why and when do individuals come together in communities and collective endeavors? Olson's question presupposes the familiar Hobbesian view of the individual's plight in the state of nature as "solitary, poor, nasty, brutish, and short." Individuals do not instinctually come together, with individual suffering and collective welfare loss the natural result (Maryanski & Turner, 1992).

Collective action theory has also found broad applicability through the prisoner's dilemma game (Rapoport & Chammah, 1965).[10] The basic prisoner's dilemma game (PD) is essentially a 2-person, public goods situation.[11] The PD game models a social dilemma between two actors with choices to cooperate or defect. Regardless of what one's partner does, defection always provides a higher individual payoff. However, if both actors defect, the outcome is collectively suboptimal. The PD game represents a wide variety of cooperative situations and has been used to model such diverse settings as the nuclear arms race (Rapoport, 1960; Schelling, 1960) and defensive behavior of stickleback fish (Milinski, 1987).

Attempts to Explain Collective Action

Collective action has generated research in economics, political science, psychology, and sociology. Sociology's contribution has centered around formal models of collective action that indicate possible solutions to the dilemma (see Oliver, 1993, for a review). Several of these formal models use computer simulation to explore the consequences of different structural arrangements and actor attributes.

Research by Oliver and Marwell (1988) and Oliver et al. (1985) has employed simulation techniques to analyze variables that may make collective action more or less likely. Oliver and Marwell's research proposes the necessity of a small group of individuals, different in some respects from the rest of the group, to start a chain reaction of contribution that results in successful collective action.

Collective action research by Macy has primarily focused on the effects of different agent assumptions on collective action outcomes. Macy models agents, using a learning algorithm from Bush and Mosteller (1955), as backward-looking actors who generally tend to repeat rewarded behaviors and change behavior in the absence of reward. Across a series of papers Macy (1990, 1991a, b, 1993) demonstrated that successful collective action in repeated public goods settings can be modeled if researchers employ backward-looking, adaptive agents rather than highly complex, forward-looking, rational agents. As with many solutions to cooperation in the prisoner's dilemma, Macy's model only works for repeated collective action situations where success or failure of cooperation can be assessed. The assumption is that people cooperate because they have observed the success of prior cooperation.

Status as a Selective Incentive for Collective Action

If voluntary contribution to public goods is irrational, then why is contribution to public goods so common? Olson (1965) proposed the first solution to the collective action problem, arguing that collective action can obtain when selective incentives are available to individuals for contribution. That is, group members will absorb the marginal loss of contribution if they are compensated with an external reward (or avoidance of punishment), which makes contribution profitable.

If status attainment is a goal and contribution to public goods increases status, then status may be a selective incentive to contribute to public goods. Perhaps people cooperate in collective action because those who do attain higher status. The association between contribution to public goods and increased social status has been noted repeatedly (Chagnon, 1988; Tittle, 1977; Zahavi & Zahavi, 1997). Our theory of the fundamental relationship between power and status can help explain how contribution to public goods increases status.

Proposition 10b. Contribution to a public good increases expectations of the contributor's competence and perceptions of group motivation in a group that benefits from the public good.

As with philanthropy, contribution to a public good demonstrates competent contribution to group goals, and increases perceptions of group motivation. These, in turn, increase influence (Propositions 6 and 7) that results in increased status (Propositions 3–5).

For status to motivate contribution to public goods, status attainment must have value to individuals. Frank (1985) documented many social settings in which individuals choose increased status over higher rewards. Moreover, Thye (2000) has shown that high status increases the resources obtained from exchange. Not only is the prestige of high status a reward in itself, but it can also lead to increased resources and power.

Proposition 11. Status attainment has value to individuals.

If people value the prestige of high status and receive it for contributing to public goods, then individuals may contribute to collective action in order to gain status in the group.

Status and the Second-Order Free-Rider Problem

In some collective action settings the administration of selective incentives can itself present a collective action problem. Who would volunteer to do the work of monitoring individual contributions without individual incentives to do so? This is the second-order free-rider problem proposed by Oliver (1980). Identifying a selective incentive that motivates contribution to a public good may not be a theoretically complete solution to the collective action problem unless that selective incentive requires little or no administration. In some cases, the administration of selective incentives is a collective action that is costly to individual sanctioners. For example, civil defense monitors in the U.S. during World War II patrolled neighborhoods warning residents to black out their windows and turn off their lights at night. Volunteers worked hard to keep populated areas dark because just a few exposed lights could attract enemy bombers. In contrast, a Red Cross blood drive requires little reward for those who donate because only a small percentage of the population need comply to provide sufficient reserves.

Thus, a logical difficulty exists for theoretical solutions to social dilemmas that are predicated on selective incentives. In one solution, Heckathorn (1989) has shown that contribution at the second-order can offer a larger marginal return than first-order contribution, meaning that first-order free-riders may engage in hypocritical cooperation by enforcing contribution without actually contributing themselves. However, why it is that all group members do not free-ride at the second-order remains to be explained. Could a second-order social dilemma result if status operates as a selective incentive for first-order contribution to collective action?

Status as a collective action incentive avoids a second-order dilemma because no individual administration of status incentives is necessary. The incentive to vie for higher status is built into power and prestige structure of the group. High status is not only its own reward but increases access to resources (Thye, 2000). Moreover, the administration of status as a collective action incentive is costless because it is automatic. Status characteristics theory proposes that actors reorder status hierarchies based on all status-relevant information (Fisek et al., 1991), and further, that the expectations that combine to produce status hierarchies are largely unconscious (Berger et al., 1977). Thus, actors perceive no cost to administering status as a selective incentive. Status as an individual incentive to contribute to public goods, and thus as a motivator for collective action, represents a solution to the second-order collective action problem as well as the first.

CONCLUSION

We used classical conceptions of power and status as a foundation to bring together Network Exchange Theory and Status Characteristics and Expectation States Theories to explain how power can be used to attain high status. One proposed strategy through which power increases status, philanthropy, suggests a solution to the collective action problem that has engaged the interest of a wide variety of social scientists.

Status attainment and the access to resources it can provide could motivate individuals to contribute to public goods. The logic of this conclusion is compelling in that status obtains in those individuals expected to contribute most to the successful completion of group goals (Berger, Fisek, Norman & Wagner, 1985; Fisek, Hamit & Norman, 1991; Ridgeway, 1991), for which contribution to public goods provides direct evidence.

With a theory of power, status, and collective action in place, research can now investigate proposed relationships among them. Investigating whether contributing to collective action can increase the influence of contributors would be a good start. Participants could engage in collective action in a controlled setting in which some contribute more than others. Then in a second phase of the study, the influence of participants would be measured. Will those who contribute more to public goods in the first phase attain greater influence in the second phase?

With the caveat that theories are valid to the extent that they are embedded in an empirical research program that allows cumulative testing and development, our use of classical theoretical ideas in conjunction with the formal theoretical development of fundamental theories of power and status has produced a plausible solution to a substantive problem in sociological theory. Status attainment may be the motivation potentially rational individuals need to contribute to public goods in sufficient quantity to ensure successful collective action.

NOTES

1. But also see Coleman's (1963) critique of Parsons's (1963a, b) conceptions of power and influence as distinct circulating media analogous to money.

2. Willer, Lovaglia and Markovsky (1997) note that Wrong (1979) attributes the synonymous use of power and influence to the lack of a verb form for power in English. We cannot say that an organized crime boss "powered" a jury to vote for acquittal; instead we say that the crime boss "influenced" the jury. Exchange theories use the terms "power use" (Cook & Emerson, 1978) and "power exercise" (Willer & Anderson, 1981) to substitute for the verb form of power. Thus, power and influence need not be conflated.

3. See for example, Bacharach and Lawler (1980), Bienenstock and Bonacich (1993, 1997), Burke (1996), Cook and Emerson (1978), Cook, Emerson, Gillmore and Yamagishi (1983), Emerson (1962), Friedkin (1992, 1995), Lawler and Yoon (1993, 1996, 1998), Lovaglia, Skvoretz, Willer and Markovsky (1995), Markovsky, Skvoretz, Willer, Lovaglia and Erger (1993), Markovsky, Willer and Patton (1988), Molm (1990, 1997a, b), Molm, Peterson and Takahashi (1999), Skvoretz and Willer (1993), Walker, Thye, Simpson, Lovaglia, Willer and Markovsky (2000), Whitmeyer (1999).

4. Status characteristics theorists use the term *observable power and prestige order* of the group to encompass behavior produced by status differences including opportunities to perform, performances, evaluations and influence. Thus, the observable power and prestige order results from the interaction of group members, each with an individual status in the prestige hierarchy.

5. See Lovaglia (1999) for a thorough but non-technical description of the theory and related research.

6. See for example, Berger, Cohen and Zelditch (1972), Berger, Fisek, Norman and Zelditch (1977), Berger, Norman, Balkwell and Smith (1992), Cohen and Zhou (1991), Cohen, Lotan and Leechor (1989), Cohen and Roper (1972), Foschi, Lai and Sigerson (1994), Lovaglia and Houser (1996), Lovaglia, Lucas, Houser, Thye and Markovsky (1998),

Lucas (1999), Markovsky, Smith and Berger (1984), Pugh and Wahrman (1983), Ridgeway (1981, 1982, 1991), Ridgeway and Berger (1986), Ridgeway, Boyle, Kuipers and Robinson (1998), Stewart and Moore (1992), Troyer and Younts (1997), Webster and Driskell (1978), Webster and Hysom (1998), Webster and Sobieszek (1974), Webster and Whitmeyer (1999).

7. It is important to distinguish the concept of *status* from that of a *status characteristic*. Education, for example, is a status characteristic. University graduates are held in higher regard than high school graduates precisely because their contributions are expected to be more valuable. This does not preclude high school graduates who consistently make valuable contributions from increasing their status, gaining prestige and honor surpassing that of many university graduates.

8. The scope conditions of Network Exchange Theory are more inclusive than are those of Status Characteristics Theory. See Willer, Markovsky and Patton (1988) for a discussion of the scope of Network Exchange Theory.

9. This explanation was adopted by Willer, Markovsky and Lovaglia (1997) who proposed that emotional reactions to power use interfere with collective orientation, increasing resistance to influence. It fits Lovaglia's (1995) results but also rendered problematic future theoretical development. Exactly how to develop a theory when scope conditions can be partially violated is unclear.

10. The name "prisoners dilemma" comes from the police practice of separating partners in crime and offering each a deal to confess and implicate the other, who will then receive the maximum sentence. Unwilling to risk possible defection by their partner, one or the other soon confesses.

11. Accordingly, public goods problems are often viewed as n-person PD games. For a mathematical representation of the n-person PD game, see Komorita (1976).

ACKNOWLEDGMENTS

We thank the National Science Foundation (Grant SES-0096481) for supporting this research and acknowledge the helpful insights offered by Reef Youngreen and Ko Kuwambara.

REFERENCES

Bacharach, S. B., & Lawler, E. J. (1980). *Power and politics in organizations*. San Francisco: Jossey-Bass.

Berger, J., Cohen, B. P., & Zelditch, M., Jr. (1972). Status characteristics and social interaction. *American Sociological Review, 37*, 241–255.

Berger, J., Conner, T. L., & McKeown, W. L. (1974). Evaluations and the formation and maintenance of performance expectations. In: J. Berger, T. L. Conner & M. H. Fisek (Eds), *Expectation States Theory: A Theoretical Research Program* (pp. 27–51). Cambridge, MA: Winthrop.

Berger, J., Fisek, M. H., Norman, R. Z., & Wagner, D. G. (1985). Formation of reward expectations in status situations. In: J. Berger & M. Zelditch, Jr. (Eds), *Status Rewards and Influence* (pp. 215–261). San Francisco: Jossey-Bass.

Berger, J., Fisek, M. H., Norman, R. Z., & Zelditch, M., Jr. (1977). *Status characteristics and social interaction: An expectations states approach.* New York: Elsevier.

Berger, J., Norman, R. Z., Balkwell, J., & Smith, R. F. (1992). Status inconsistency in task situations: A test of four status processing principles. *American Sociological Review, 57*, 843–855.

Berger, J., Wagner, D. G., & Zelditch, M., Jr. (1985). Introduction: Expectation states theory: Review and assessment. In: J. Berger & M. Zeldtich, Jr. (Eds), *Status, Rewards and Influence: How Expectations Organize Behavior* (pp. 1–72). San Francisco: Jossey-Bass.

Berger, J., & Zelditch, M., Jr. (1997). Theoretical research programs: A reformulation. In: *Status, Network and Structure: Theory Development in Group Processes* (pp. 29–46). Stanford, CA: Stanford University Press.

Berger, J., Zelditch, M., Jr., Anderson, B., & Cohen, B. P. (1972). Structural aspects of distributive justice: A status-value formulation. In: J. Berger, M. Zelditch, Jr. & B. Anderson (Eds), *Sociological Theories in Progress* (Vol. 2). Boston: Houghton-Mifflin.

Bienenstock, E. J., & Bonacich, P. (1993). Game theory models for exchange networks: Experimental results. *Sociological Perspectives, 36*, 117–135.

Bienenstock, E. J., & Bonacich, P. (1997). Network exchange as a cooperative game. *Rationality and Society, 9*, 36–65.

Bierhoff, H. W., Buck, E., & Klein, R. (1986). Social context and perceived justice. In: H. W. Bierhoff, R. L. Cohen & J. Greenberg (Eds), *Justice in Social Relations* (pp. 165–185). New York: Plenum.

Bierstedt, R. (1950). An analysis of social power. *American Sociological Review, 15*, 161–184.

Blau, P. M. (1964). *Exchange and power in social life.* New York: Wiley.

Brehm, J. W. (1966). *A theory of psychological reactance.* New York: Academic Press.

Brehm, S. S., & Brehm, J. W. (1981). *Psychological reactance: A theory of freedom and control.* New York: Academic Press.

Burke, P. J. (1996). An identity model of network exchange. *American Sociological Review, 62*, 134–150.

Bush, R. R., & Mosteller, F. (1955). *Stochastic models of learning.* New York: Wiley.

Chagnon, N. A. (1988). Life histories, blood revenge, and warfare in tribal populations. *Science, 239*, 985–992.

Cohen, E. G., Lotan, R. A., & Leechor, C. (1989). Can classrooms learn? *Sociology of Education, 62*, 75–94.

Cohen, E. G., & Roper, S. S. (1972). Modification of interracial interaction disability: An application of status characteristics theory. *American Sociological Review, 37*, 648–655.

Cohen, B. P., & Zhou, X. (1991). Status processes in enduring work groups. *American Sociological Review, 56*, 179–188.

Coleman, J. S. (1963). Comment on the concept of influence. *Public Opinion Quarterly, 27*, 63–82.

Coleman, J. S. (1990). *Foundations of social theory.* London: Harvard University Press.

Cook, K. S. (1975). Expectations, evaluations and equity. *American Sociological Review, 40*, 372–388.

Cook, K. S., & Emerson, R. M. (1978). Power, equity and commitment in exchange networks. *American Sociological Review, 43*, 721–739.

Cook, K. S., Emerson, R. M., Gillmore, M. R., & Yamagishi, T. (1983). The distribution of power in exchange networks: Theory and experimental results. *American Journal of Sociology, 89*, 275–305.

Dahrendorf, R. (1968). In praise of Thrasymachus. In: R. Dahrendorf (Ed.), *Essays in the Theory of Society* (pp. 129–150). Stanford, CA: Stanford University Press.

Emerson, R. M. (1962). Power-dependence relations. *American Sociological Review, 27*, 282–298.

Fisek, M. H., Berger, J., & Norman, R. Z. (1991). Participation in heterogeneous and homogeneous groups: A theoretical integration. *American Journal of Sociology, 97*, 114–142.

Foschi, M., Lai, L., & Sigerson, K. (1994). Gender and double standards in the assessment of job applicants. *Social Psychology Quarterly, 57,* 326–339.

Frank, R. H. (1985). *Choosing the right pond.* New York: Oxford University Press.

French, J. R. P., Jr., & Raven, B. (1968). The bases of social power. In: D. Cartwright & A. Zander (Eds), *Group Dynamics* (pp. 259–269). New York: Harper & Row.

Friedkin, N. E. (1992). An expected value model of social power: Predictions for selected exchange networks. *Social Networks, 14,* 213–229.

Friedkin, N. E. (1995). The incidence of exchange networks. *Social Psychology Quarterly, 58,* 213–221.

Gerth, H. H., & Mills, C. W. (1958). *From Max Weber: Essays in sociology.* New York: Galaxy.

Harrod, W. J. (1980). Expectations from unequal rewards. *Social Psychology Quarterly, 43,* 126–130.

Heckathorn, D. D. (1989). Collective action and the second-order free-rider problem. *Rationality and Society, 1,* 78–100.

Heider, F. (1958). *The psychology of interpersonal relations.* New York: Wiley.

Hobbes, T. (1996 [1651]). Leviathan: Revised student edition. In: R. Tuck (Ed.). Cambridge: Cambridge University Press.

Homans, G. C. (1974). *Social behavior: Its elementary forms* (Rev. ed.). New York: Harcourt, Brace and Jovanovich.

Kalkhoff, W., & Barnum, C. (2000). The effects of status-organizing and social identity processes on patterns of social influence. *Social Psychology Quarterly, 63,* 95–115.

Kemper, T. D., & Collins, R. (1990). Dimensions of microinteraction. *American Journal of Sociology, 96,* 32–68.

Kollock, P. (1994). The emergence of exchange structures: An experimental study of uncertainty, commitment, and trust. *American Journal of Sociology, 100,* 315–345.

Komorita, S. S. (1976). A model of the n-person dilemma-type game. *Journal of Experimental Social Psychology, 12,* 357–373.

Lawler, E. J., & Yoon, J. (1993). Power and the emergence of commitment behavior in negotiated exchange. *American Sociological Review, 58,* 465–481.

Lawler, E. J., & Yoon, J. (1996). Commitment in exchange relations: Test of a theory of relational cohesion. *American Sociological Review, 61,* 89–108.

Lawler, E. J., & Yoon, J. (1998). Network structure and emotion in exchange relations. *American Sociological Review, 63,* 871–894.

Lenski, G. (1966). *Power and privilege: A theory of social stratification.* New York: McGraw-Hill.

Lovaglia, M. J. (1994). Relating power to status. *Advances in Group Process, 11,* 87–111.

Lovaglia, M. J. (1995). Power and status: Exchange, attribution and expectation states. *Small Group Research, 26,* 400–426.

Lovaglia, M. J. (1999). Understanding network exchange theory. In: E. J. Lawler, S. R. Thye, M. W. Macy & H. A. Walker (Eds), *Advances in Group Processes* (pp. 31–59). Stamford, CT: JAI Press.

Lovaglia, M. J., & Houser, J. A. (1996). Emotional reactions, status characteristics and social interaction. *American Sociological Review, 61,* 867–883.

Lovaglia, M. J., Lucas, J. W., Houser, J. A., Thye, S. R., & Markovsky, B. (1998). Status processes and mental ability test scores. *American Journal of Sociology, 104,* 198–228.

Lovaglia, M. J., Skvoretz, J., Willer, D., & Markovsky, B. (1995). Negotiated exchanges in social networks. *Social Forces, 74,* 123–155.

Lucas, J. W. (1999). Behavioral and emotional outcomes of leadership in task groups. *Social Forces, 78,* 747–776.

Macy, M. W. (1990). Learning theory and the logic of critical mass. *American Sociological Review, 55,* 809–826.

Macy, M. W. (1991a). Learning to cooperate: Stochastic and tacit collusion in social exchange. *American Journal of Sociology, 97*, 808–843.

Macy, M. W. (1991b). Chains of cooperation: Threshold effects in collective action. *American Sociological Review, 56*, 730–747.

Macy, M. W. (1993). Backward-looking social control. *American Sociological Review, 58*, 819–836.

Markovsky, B. (2002). Theory and methods in graduate education of sociologists. Presented to the Annual Meeting of the American Sociological Association. Chicago.

Markovsky, B., Smith, L. F., & Berger, J. (1984). Do status interventions persist? *American Sociological Review, 49*, 373–382.

Markovsky, B., Skvoretz, J., Willer, D., Lovaglia, M. J., & Erger, J. (1993). The seeds of weak power: An extension of network exchange theory. *American Sociological Review, 58*, 197–209.

Markovsky, B., Willer, D., & Patton, T. (1988). Power relations in exchange networks. *American Sociological Review, 53*, 220–236.

Marx, K. (1967 [1867]). *Capital*. International Publishers.

Maryanski, A., & Turner, J. H. (1992). *The social cage: Human nature and the evolution of society.* Stanford, CA: Stanford University Press.

Milinski, M. (1987). Tit For Tat in sticklebacks and the evolution of reciprocity. *Nature, 325*, 433–435.

Mills, C. W. (1956). *The power elite.* New York: Oxford.

Mokken, R. J., & Stokman, F. N. (1976). Power and influence and political phenomena. In: B. Barry (Ed.), *Power and Political Theory: Some European Perspectives* (pp. 33–54). New York: Wiley.

Molm, L. D. (1990). Structure, action and outcomes: The dynamics of power in exchange relations. *American Sociological Review, 55*, 427–447.

Molm, L. D. (1997a). Risk and power use: Constraints on the use of coercion in exchange. *American Sociological Review, 62*, 113–133.

Molm, L. D. (1997b). *Coercive power in social exchange.* Cambridge, England: Cambridge University Press.

Molm, L. D., Peterson, G., & Takahashi, N. (1999). Power in negotiated and reciprocal exchange. *American Sociological Review, 64*, 876–890.

Molm, L., Takahashi, D. N., & Peterson, G. (2000). Risk and trust in social exchange: An experimental test of a classical proposition. *American Journal of Sociology, 105*, 1396–1427.

Oliver, P. E. (1980). Rewards and punishments as selective incentives for collective action: Theoretical investigations. *American Journal of Sociology, 85*, 1356–1375.

Oliver, P. E. (1993). Formal models of collective action. *Annual Review of Sociology, 19*, 271–300.

Oliver, P. E., & Marwell, G. (1988). The paradox of group size in collective action: A theory of the critical mass II. *American Sociological Review, 53*, 1–8.

Oliver, P. E., Marwell, G., & Teixeira, R. (1985). A theory of the critical mass I. Interdependence, group heterogeneity, and the production of collective action. *American Journal of Sociology, 91*, 522–556.

Olson, M. (1965). *The logic of collective action: Public goods and the theory of groups.* Cambridge, MA: Harvard University Press.

Parsons, T. (1963a). On the concept of political power. *Proceedings of the American Philosophical Society, 107*, 232–262.

Parsons, T. (1963b). On the concept of influence. *Public Opinion Quarterly, 24*, 37–62.

Podolny, J. M. (1993). A status-based model of market competition. *American Journal of Sociology, 98*, 829–872.

Pugh, M. D., & Wahrman, R. (1983). Neutralizing sexism in mixed-sex groups: Do women have to be better than men? *American Journal of Sociology, 88*, 746–762.

Radzinsky, E. (1996). *Stalin*. New York: Doubleday.

Rapoport, A. (1960). *Fights, games, and debates*. Ann Arbor, MI: University of Michigan Press.

Rapoport, A., & Chammah, A. M. (1965). *Prisoner's dilemma*. Ann Arbor, MI: University of Michigan Press.

Ridgeway, C. L. (1978). Conformity, group-oriented motivation, and status attainment in small groups. *Social Psychology, 47*, 175–188.

Ridgeway, C. L. (1981). Noncomformity, Competence, and influence in groups: A test of two theories. *American Sociological Review, 46*, 333–347.

Ridgeway, C. L. (1982). Status in groups: The importance of motivation. *American Sociological Review, 47*, 76–88.

Ridgeway, C. L. (1991). The social construction of status value: Gender and other nominal characteristics. *Social Forces, 70*, 367–386.

Ridgeway, C. L., & Berger, J. (1986). Expectation, legitimation, and dominance behavior in task groups. *American Sociological Review, 51*, 603–617.

Ridgeway, C. L., & Berger, J. (1988). The legitimation of power and prestige orders in task groups. In: M. Webster, Jr. & M. Foschi (Eds), *Status Generalization: New Theory and Research* (pp. 207–231). Stanford, CA: Stanford University Press.

Ridgeway, C. L., Boyle, E. H., Kuipers, K. J., & Robinson, D. T. (1998). Resources and interaction in the development of status beliefs. *American Sociological Review, 63*, 331–350.

Ridgeway, C. L., & Erickson, K. G. (2000). Creating and spreading status beliefs. *American Journal of Sociology, 106*, 579–615.

Schelling, T. C. (1960). *The strategy of conflict*. Cambridge, MA: Harvard University Press.

Shackelford, S., Wood, W., & Worchel, S. (1996). Behavioral styles and the influence of women in mixed-sex groups. *Social Psychology Quarterly, 59*, 284–293.

Skvoretz, J., & Willer, D. (1993). Exclusion and power: A test of four theories of power in exchange networks. *American Sociological Review, 58*, 801–818.

Stewart, P. A., & Moore, J. C. (1992). Wage disparities and performance expectations. *Social Psychology Quarterly, 55*, 78–85.

Thye, S. R. (2000). A status value theory of power in exchange relations. *American Sociological Review, 65*, 407–432.

Tittle, C. R. (1977). Sanction fear and the maintenance of social order. *Social Forces, 55*, 579–596.

Troyer, L., & Younts, C. W. (1997). Whose expectations matter? The relative power of first- and second-order expectations in determining social influence. *American Journal of Sociology, 103*, 692–732.

Turner, J. H. (2000). *On the origins of human emotions*. Stanford, CA: Stanford University Press.

Veblen, T. (1898). The instinct of workmanship and the irksomeness of labor. *American Journal of Sociology, 4*, 187–201.

Wagner, D. G., & Berger, J. (1993). Status characteristics theory: The growth of a program. In: J. Berger & M. Zelditch, Jr. (Eds), *Theoretical Research Programs: Studies in the Growth of Theory* (pp. 23–63). Stanford, CA: Stanford University Press.

Walker, H. A., & Cohen, B. P. (1985). Scope statements: Imperatives for evaluating theory. *American Sociological Review, 50*, 288–301.

Walker, H. A., Thye, S. R., Simpson, B., Lovaglia, M. J., Willer, D., & Markovsky, B. (2000). Network exchange theory: Recent developments and new directions. *Social Psychology Quarterly*.

Weber, M. (1978 [1921]). *Economy and society*. In: G. Roth & C. Wittich (Eds). Berkeley: University of California Press.

Webster, M., Jr., & Driskell, J. E., Jr. (1978). Status generalization: A review and some new data. *American Sociological Review, 43*, 220–236.

Webster, M., Jr., & Hysom, S. J. (1998). Creating status characteristics. *American Sociological Review, 63*, 351–378.

Webster, M., Jr., & Sobieszek, B. I. (1974). *Sources of self-evaluation: A formal theory of significant others and social influence*. New York: Wiley.

Webster, M., Jr., & Whitmeyer, J. M. (1999). A theory of second-order expectations and behavior. *Social Psychology Quarterly, 62*, 17–31.

Whitmeyer, J. M. (1999). Convex preferences and power inequality in exchange networks: An experimental study. *Rationality and Society, 11*, 419–442.

Willer, D., & Anderson, B. (1981). *Networks, exchange and coercion*. Elsevier/Greenwood.

Willer, D., Lovaglia, M. J., & Markovsky, B. (1997). Power and influence: A theoretical bridge. *Social Forces, 76*, 571–603.

Willer, R., Troyer, L., & Lovaglia, M. J. (2001). Using power to elevate status: Observers of power use. Presented to the Annual Meeting of the American Sociological Association, Anaheim, CA (August).

Willer, R., Troyer, L., & Lovaglia, M. J. (2002). Power status and philanthropy. Paper presented at the XV World Congress of Sociology. Brisbane, Australia.

Wrong, D. H. (1979). *Power: Its forms, bases and uses*. Basil Blackwell.

Yamagishi, T., & Yamagishi, M. (1996). Trust and commitment in the United States and Japan. *Motivation and Emotion, 18*, 129–166.

Zahavi, A., & Zahavi, A. (1997). *The handicap principle: A missing piece of Darwin's puzzle*. New York: Oxford University Press.

Zelditch, M., Jr. (1992). Interpersonal power. In: E. F. Borgatta & M. L. Borgatta (Eds), *Encyclopedia of Sociology* (pp. 994–1001). New York: MacMillan.

REWARD EXPECTATIONS AND ALLOCATIVE BEHAVIORS: A MATHEMATICAL MODEL

M. Hamit Fişek and David G. Wagner

ABSTRACT

We present a specific mathematical model for predicting allocative behaviors in the context of reward expectations theory. We test the goodness of fit of the model to data from two empirical studies and demonstrate that it fits quite well. We also suggest alternative research uses for the model.

INTRODUCTION

Distributive justice – that is, social perceptions about the fairness of reward allocations to, or sharing of material or honorific resources between, individuals in social settings – has been of traditional concern for social psychologists (Adams, 1965; Homans, 1961; Jasso, 1980; Walster, Berscheid & Walster, 1976). One of the theoretical approaches to the study of distributive justice has been developed within the conceptual framework of expectation states theory (see Berger, 1988 for a review of expectation states theory). This approach has led to the development of a mathematical formulation of a theory of justice – the theory of reward expectations (Berger, Fisek, Norman & Wagner, 1985). This theory is an abstract and general theory. Although it is capable of making numerical predictions in general form, the application of the theory to any

Power and Status
Advances in Group Processes, Volume 20, 133–148
ISSN: 0882-6145/doi:10.1016/S0882-6145(03)20005-9

concrete social setting and to a specific type of allocative behavior requires that a specific model for the setting and type of behavior needs to be constructed. The purpose of this paper is to present one such model and to test it with the available relevant data.

THEORETICAL BACKGROUND

The theory of reward expectations is based on the theory of status characteristics and expectation states (Berger, Fisek, Norman & Zelditch, 1977) and shares the core assumptions of that theory as well as the mathematical representation. The scope of the theory, like that of status characteristics theory, is limited to situations where collectively oriented actors are working on valued tasks with well defined success and failure outcomes, and where the actors may be allocated goal objects. Such situations are called S situations, and graph theoretic structures are used to represent them. An initial S structure consists of three components, the actor, task, and reward components, all represented from the point of view of one actor, p, in the situation. That is, the S structure is represented as p perceives it, not in objective form. One such structure is represented in Fig. 1.

The actor component is a set of points, each representing an actor in the situation. In Fig. 1 the actor component includes the points representing actors p and o in the situation.

The task component consists of two other pairs of points: one pair represents the success and failure states of the task outcome, and the other the high and low states of the ability instrumental to task performance. The high and low states of the instrumental characteristic are respectively connected by lines representing their *relevance* to the success and failure outcomes. In Fig. 1 the task component includes the points representing success, $T(+)$, and failure, $T(-)$, at the task, those representing high ability, $C^*(+)$, and low ability, $C^*(-)$, at the task, together with the relevance lines establishing for p that $C^*(+)$ is instrumental to performing task T well and that $C^*(-)$ is instrumental to performing task T poorly.

The reward component similarly consists of two pairs of points: one pair representing high and low reward levels, and the other pair the high and low goal objects (i.e. actual concrete rewards, such as money, corner offices or country club memberships) allocated in the situation. The points representing the goal objects are connected to the corresponding points representing reward levels by relevance lines. In Fig. 1, the reward levels are represented by points $R(+)$ and $R(-)$ and the goal objects by points $GO(+)$ and $GO(-)$. The relevance lines indicate that p believes that high reward levels will be manifested with $GO(+)$ and low reward levels with $GO(-)$.

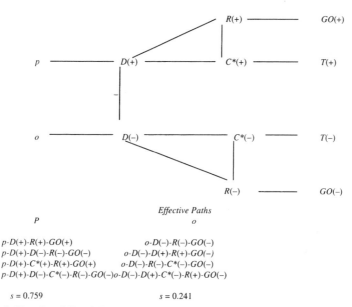

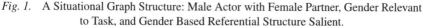

Fig. 1. A Situational Graph Structure: Male Actor with Female Partner, Gender Relevant to Task, and Gender Based Referential Structure Salient.

The task and reward components are connected by relevance lines from $C^*(+)$ to $R(+)$ and $C^*(-)$ to $R(-)$ representing the *ability referential structure* which will be described below.

The *salience assumption* specifies which status elements can become salient in the situation. The possible status elements are diffuse and specific status characteristics and goal objects, each of which is represented by a point. The status elements in Fig. 1 are the diffuse status states $D(+)$ and $D(-)$. The principle of salience states that if a status element is either directly relevant to the task or discriminates among the actors, it becomes salient in the situation. The actors are connected to the states of status elements they possess by possession lines, and status elements are connected by relevance lines between the elements of the task and reward components to which they are relevant. Thus, Fig. 1 represents p's belief that s/he possesses a higher diffuse status – $D(+)$ – than does actor o – $D(-)$, and that those status states are directly relevant to both levels of task ability – $C^*(+)$ and $C^*(-)$ respectively – and levels of *reward* – $R(+)$ and $R(-)$ respectively.

A *referential structure* is a socially validated belief which describes how rewards are allocated in the social system. In particular, *categorical* referential structures describe how states of status elements are associated with differences in reward levels. For example, p might have a socially validated belief that men are more highly paid then women. That is, p believes that, in general, being *male* – $D(+)$ – is associated with a high reward level – $R(+)$ – and being female – $D(-)$ – is associated with a low reward level – $D(-)$. The *activation of referential structures* assumption states that, if salient status characteristics are referentially associated with reward levels for p, then relevance lines will connect these status characteristics to the reward levels in situation S. Thus, the relevance lines between $D(+)$ and $R(+)$ and between $D(-)$ and $R(-)$ in Fig. 1 may represent activation of p's referential structure above. The *ability* referential structure describes how levels of ability are associated with reward levels: High ability actors are more highly rewarded than low ability actors. The ability referential structure is assumed to be salient in all situations where rewards are allocated. The relevance line representing the ability referential structure connects the task and reward componenets of the situational graph as decscibed above.

The *burden of proof* assumption describes how a possessed status element which is not initially task connected becomes so connected through the activation or induction of its associated expectation state. No connections based on burden of proof are represented in Fig. 1.

The *sequence of completion* assumption states that a given structure is further completed on the introduction of a new actor, new status information or a new task. As structures are completed older parts of the structures are retained as long as the actor remains in the task situation. Again, no new connections based on sequencing are included in Fig. 1.

Collectively, the salience, activation of referential structures, burden of proof and sequencing assumptions represent *structure completion processes*. That is, they explicate how the actor, status and task components may come to be related to each other in a single belief structure for p.

Given such a completed structure, paths linking each actor to the reward outcome states, that is the goal objects, are created. Figure 1 identifies the paths generated for p by the completed graph structure represented there. The list includes paths linking both actors p and o to both goal objects $GO(+)$ and $GO(-)$. These paths represent p's expectancies for actual rewards p and o should receive. They do *not* represent anything about actor o's expectancies.

The strength, or the contribution to expectations, of each path is given by a function, $f(i)$, of its length; the longer the path, the less its strength. Figure 1 includes paths of lengths 3, 4, and 5. Path strengths take on values in the interval $(0, 1)$. Actual numerical values are provided by Fisek, Norman and Nelson-Kilger (1992).

Paths may have different task significance. That is, some may suggest that the actor should receive a highly valued goal object, others that a less valued goal object is expected. Task significance is determined by the algebraic product of the signs of each line along the path (which are $+$ unless otherwise noted in the graph) and the sign of the outcome state at the end of the path. If the product is positive, the path has positive task significance; if the product is negative, the path has negative task significance. In figure all four paths connecting p to reward outcome states are positive.[1]

The *formation of aggregated expectation states assumption* states how paths are combined to compute expectations for actors. The paths for each actor are combined within like-signed subsets (that is, subsets of paths with the same task significance) according to the function,

$$f(i \cup j) = f(i) + f(j) - f(i)f(j),$$

and given the sign of the paths in the subset. The values of the two subsets are algebraically summed to yield the expectations for the actor.

Given expectation values for actors it is possible to generate different expectation measures such as the *expectation advantage*, which is the difference between an actor's expectations for self and another actor. For our purposes the *expectation standing* (Fisek, Berger & Norman, 1991), which is the share of an actor of the total expectations in a group is the more appropriate measure. The expectation standing s_i is defined as follows:

$$s_i = \frac{1 + e_i}{\sum(1 + e_j)}$$

The *basic expectation assumption* states that an actor's status related behaviors are functions of his appropriate expectation measure. In the context with which we are concerned here, the actor p's reward allocation behavior should be a function of p's reward expectation standing in the group.[2]

THE ALLOCATION FUNCTION

We will concentrate on one particular type of allocative behavior – the proportion of the total reward available to a task group allocated to self and others by the focal actor in the group. We will designate this quantity as, $P_i(R)$, the proportion of the rewards allocated to the ith actor in the power and prestige order of the group. We want to construct a function which, given the expectations for the members of a group, will predict $P_i(R)$.

The simplest such function would be the identity function, simply setting $P_i(R)$ equal to the expectation standing, s_i. However, we believe that this would not be satisfactory because it would imply that reward expectations are the only determinant of reward allocation. While we believe that reward expectations are the major determinant of allocation of rewards, we also believe that there are other factors which mediate the translation of reward expectations into allocative behaviors. As a simple example, the size of the group is probably such a mediating variable, we would expect that as group size gets larger, the allocation of rewards gets more in line with reward expectations. Other probably effective factors are, whether the group is working in a cooperative or competitive task environment (Sherif, 1966), and whether the group is embedded in an individualistic or collectivistic culture (Kagitçibasi, 1977). Therefore we would like our function to contain at least one parameter to account for the mediating effects.

The distributive justice literature contains a considerable amount of research on whether, and/or under what conditions, people prefer the equity norm or the equality norm (Aral & Sunar, 1977). This line of research, plus an insight provided by Wagner (1990, 1995) that reward expectations define the equitable distribution of rewards, provides the conceptual background for the function we propose. Our conception is that actors facing the task of allocating rewards incorporate concerns for both equity and equality. It is not a question of using one norm or the other, but rather a question of using both to different degrees.[3] The reward expectation standings give the equity distribution of rewards; the distribution of rewards under equality for a group of size n is simply $1/n$ of the reward for each actor; what we seek to generate is a distribution which is a weighted average of the two. In symbolic terms, using r_i, rather than $P_i(R)$ for simplicity, s_i for expectation standings, and ω for the weight parameter we have:

$$r_i = \omega s_i + (1 - \omega)\left(\frac{1}{n}\right)$$

Given a set of observed r_i values and s_i values for actors in task groups of the same size, working under similar task and cultural conditions, an OLS estimate can be obtained for ω in a straightforward way as follows. We want to minimize the sum of the differences between the observed r_i and the predicted reward proportions from the theoretical s_i values. This sum is a function of ω as below, where k is the number of different observations, and n is the group size.

$$F(\omega) = \sum_{i=1}^{k}\left[r_i - \left(\omega s_i + (1 - \omega)\left(\frac{1}{n}\right)\right)\right]^2$$

Taking the derivative of this function with respect to ω, simplifying, setting equal to zero, and solving for ω yields:

$$\omega = \frac{\sum r_i s_i - (1/n)\left(\sum r_i + \sum s_i\right) + k/n^2}{\sum s_i^2 - (2/n)\sum s_i + k/n^2}$$

All summations are indexed over i from 1 to k.

If the data contain values for all members of a group (or the averages for a number of groups for all positions) then this formula has a simpler form since the r_i and s_i will sum to one, and k is equal to n. This simplified formula is given below:

$$\omega = \frac{\sum r_i s_i - (1/n)}{\sum s_i^2 - (1/n)}$$

In this formula the summations are indexed over i from 1 to n.

EMPIRICAL EVIDENCE ON REWARD ALLOCATION

There are a considerable number of empirical studies, experimental, observational, and survey, on reward allocation in the literatures of the social sciences. These studies are mostly grouped in three distinct literatures: economics, cross-cultural psychology, and the group processes tradition in sociology.

Of the economic literature, the most relevant studies are the experimental studies of reward allocation (see Fehr & Schmidt, 1999, for a survey of these studies). However, we cannot use data from these studies to evaluate our model because as Fehr and Schmidt note, in these studies "The subjects enter the laboratory as equals, they do not know anything about each other, and they are allocated to different roles in the experiment at random" (Fehr & Schmidt, 1999, p. 822). Since there are no status differences between subjects, we cannot compute reward expectations for the subjects and the model cannot be applied. It may be possible to develop status interpretations for some of the roles the subjects in these experiments are assigned, however this body of literature is obviously not the place to start for assessing the empirical adequacy of our model.

Reward allocation studies in psychology primarily involve investigators working with the individualism/collectivism paradigm of cross-cultural psychology (see Kagitçibasi, 1977, for a review of this paradigm). These studies explore justice norm differences (i.e. equity vs. equality) in different cultures. Fischer (2001) provides a comprehensive survey, and meta-analysis, of these reward allocation studies. Unfortunately, for our purposes, the majority of these studies either have the subjects choose between equality and equity norms (e.g. Leung & Bond, 1984), or use a multiple item scale to measure norm preference (e.g. Kim, Park & Suzuki, 1990), rather than having the subjects actually allocate rewards. Thus we are unable to check out our model with the results of these studies.

We have located two studies in the cross-cultural psychology literature which actually have the subjects allocate rewards, Rusbult, Insko and Lin (1995), and Giacobbe-Miller, Miller and Victorov (1998). However, in both cases the authors report the results of the analyses they have done, rather than the actual allocation results, so that we are again unable to explore the fit of our model to their data.

Despite our inability to evaluate the goodness-of-fit of our data to the results of cross-cultural psychology studies, we think our model has the potential of being useful for such studies. As Fischer (2001) shows in his survey of these studies, there are inconsistencies in the results of these studies, and, as he concludes, there is need for further theoretical and empirical research. The idea underlying our model is that individuals do not prefer one norm over the other, but rather incorporate a balance between the two for a given situation. If this idea is correct, then forcing individuals to choose between the two could elicit erratic responses from subjects which in turn could be responsible for some of the inconsistent findings.

Further, even in the studies where subjects actually allocate rewards to a group of actors, the results are analyzed in terms of given target actors, either by regressing the target actor's inputs on the rewards he or she is assigned, or by doing the equivalent ANOVA. This type of analysis, while it obviously captures part of the effect, ignores an important aspect of the allocation situation, namely that it is a group phenomenon: An actor's rewards do not depend only on the actor's inputs, but also on the inputs of the other actors in the situation. Our model provides a measure, the parameter ω, of the relative weights assigned to the two allocation norms, taking into account all actors over whom the rewards are allocated. This measure can be computed for individual actors as well as for any given set of actors. As such it can provide a valuable research tool.

There are four empirical studies of reward allocation within the group processes tradition: Wagner (1990, 1995), Griffith, Sell and Parker (1993), Meeker and Elliot (1996). The Griffith and associates study manipulates among other variables "performance level," and removes any social status value that may be associated with performance. "The subjects were told that their performance on this task was not a measure of their abilities or talents; it reflected on only effort or concentration" (Griffith et al., 1993, p. 151). This is a manipulation which takes us beyond the scope conditions of status characteristics and expectation states theory (Berger et al., 1977) and we do not attempt to fit the model to the data of this study.

Meeker and Elliot (1996) also manipulated performance level, however as they work within the expectation states tradition, there is no dissociation of performance and status as in the case of Griffith et al. (1993). Therefore it should be possible to apply our model to their data. However, to do so requires a representation for "performance" in situational graphs. Developing such a representation is not a simple task and we do not attempt it in the process of an initial evaluation of our model.

The two Wagner (1990, 1995) studies are squarely within the expectation states tradition, and the experiments are performed in the standardized experimental situation associated with the expectation states theory (Berger et al., 1977). We will examine the results of these studies in detail.

THE WAGNER STUDIES

Wagner (1990, 1995) has conducted two experimental studies to test the basic predictions of reward expectations study, and to explore gender differences in reward preference. We will explore the fit of our function to this data set.

Both of these studies are carried out in the standardized experimental situation associated with expectation states theory. In this situation the usual design involves a first phase where status conditions are manipulated, and a second phase where there is team interaction with two subjects interacting on a decision making task, and the subjects acceptance or rejection of influence is measured. The Wagner experiments follow this general design, but have different measurements added at the end of the experiment. The following question is put to the subjects:

> given the opportunity at the end of today's study to allocate the group reward for your team in this study, what percentages do you think you will assign to yourself and to your partner? Please make sure that the percentages add up to 100%)
> _____% Allocation to self.
> _____% Allocation to partner.
>   100% TOTAL.

It is this final measurement, together with the status manipulations in the first phase, which are of interest to us.

In the first study, the subjects are given a test of a fictional ability and the results of the test are reported to the subjects. They then interact on a task supposedly involving the ability on which were tested. Finally, the subjects answer the allocation question. There are four experimental conditions:

  (i) HS – The subject is lead to believe that he or she did very well on the test and her partner did very poorly.
 (ii) LS – The subject is lead to believe that he or she did very poorly on the test and her partner did very well.

(iii) ES – The subject is lead to believe that both he or she and the partner did average on the test.
(iv) IS – The subjects are given two tests, and the subject is told that he/she did very well on one test and very poorly on the other while his/her partner had exactly the opposite results.

Both male and female subjects were used, but the experimental "teams" are always same sex. To allow for the possibility that the weight parameter of our function may be gender dependent we will treat males and females as different experimental conditions, thus for our purposes this experiment has eight conditions.

Since gender never becomes salient in these experimental conditions, and there are no other differentiating diffuse status characteristics, no categorical referential structure can become salient. Thus only the basic ability referential structure is salient and the graphs for the different conditions are straightforward.

The procedure for the second experiment is the same as in the first experiment with minor manipulation differences. All teams are mixed sex, that is all males have female partners, and all females have male partners. There are three different manipulations:

(i) DSC Only – The results of the initial test are not reported to the subjects; all they know is that their partner is of the opposite sex.
(ii) Relevant DSC – Again test results are not reported but subjects are told that gender is relevant to the ability involved, with men being usually better than women on this task.
(iii) Inconsistent DSC – The same gender relevance manipulation is applied but test results are also reported with the female doing very well and the male quite poorly.

Again we have six conditions to work with. In these conditions since gender is salient we assume that a categorical referential structure based on gender such that males receive higher rewards than females becomes salient. The graph shown in Fig. 1 is in fact the S-graph for the relevant DSC condition. As can be seen, the referential structure links the male state of gender, $D(+)$, with the high reward level state, $R(+)$, and the female state of gender, $D(-)$, with the low reward level state, $R(-)$. The figure gives a complete enumeration of the paths and the resulting reward expectation standing values. p is connected to the task outcomes by four positive paths of lengths 3, 4, 4, 5, and o is connected to the task outcomes, by the same number of paths of the same lengths, but which are negative. Thus p's reward expectation standing is computed to be 0.759, and o's to be 0.241.

THE FIT OF THE MODEL

We pool together the data from the two Wagner studies and organize them in two subsets as the male and female data. Each set consists of three conditions from the second study and four from the first. We estimate for each set separately. The values we obtain are 0.626 for the males, and 0.517 for the females. These values are in line with the idea that women are more inclined toward equality then men.

The estimation of the parameter ω actually constitutes the first test of the model: The model does not mathematically constrain the parameter to (0, 1), the fact that our estimates are actually in the conceptually acceptable range is an indication that the model fits to the extent that the observed allocated proportions are indeed in between the reward expectation standings and equal allocation proportions.

Using these values we predict the reward allocations for each experimental condition. These predictions are given in Table 1. We use the square of the

Table 1. The Fit of the Function to the Wagner Data.

Condition[a]	s_i	Predicted r_i	Observed r_i	Difference
Males				
Gender only	0.705	0.628	0.608	0.020
Gender relevant	0.759	0.662	0.671	−0.009
Inconsistent ability	0.500	0.500	0.518	−0.018
High vs. low ability	0.705	0.628	0.647	−0.019
Low vs. high ability	0.295	0.372	0.381	−0.009
Equal abilities	0.500	0.500	0.502	−0.002
Inconsistent abilities	0.500	0.500	0.513	−0.013

$\omega = 0.626$; $r^2 = 0.983$[b]; $F = 295.149$; df = 1, 4[c]; $p < 0.0000$

Females				
Gender only	0.295	0.394	0.458	−0.064
Gender relevant	0.241	0.366	0.363	0.003
Inconsistent ability	0.500	0.500	0.551	−0.051
High vs. low ability	0.705	0.606	0.617	−0.011
Low vs. high ability	0.295	0.394	0.345	0.049
Equal abilities	0.500	0.500	0.5	0.000
Inconsistent abilities	0.500	0.500	0.484	0.016

$\omega = 0.517$; $r^2 = 0.842$; $F = 26.610$; df = 1, 4[c]; $p = 0.007$

Males and females combined: $r^2 = 0.926$; $F = 150.368$; df = 1, 10[d]; $p < 0.0000$

[a] The number of subjects in each condition is 20.
[b] All reported correlations are between the observed and predicted values.
[c] The second degree of freedom is reduced by one because of the estimated parameter.
[d] The second degree of freedom is reduced by 2 because of the two estimated parameters.

correlation of observed and predicted values as our measure of goodness of fit. The squared correlation for the male subjects is 0.983, which is as high a value as could possibly be expected. This result is highly significant even with a sample as small as this one – we have just seven observations.

The squared correlation of the observed and predicted reward allocations for the females is 0.842, this value is not as high as in the case of males, but it is adequately high by any social science standard, and highly statistically significant. An examination of the deviations by conditions reveals the reason why the correlation is not as high as for males. The two highest deviations occur for the two conditions of the second study, the "gender only" and "inconsistent ability" conditions. The prediction for the third condition, the "gender relevant" condition is quite good. In this study we assumed that a gender based categorical referential structure was salient. Apparently it is only salient in the gender relevant case, when there is no explicit relevance or when other information contradicts its relevance, the referential structure does not become salient.

The squared correlation of observed and predicted reward allocations for both sets of conditions combined is 0.926. We conclude that our function fits this set of data quite well at the aggregate level. However, further analyses at the individual subject level can provide additional information on the adequacy of our model.

We cannot perform goodness-of-fit tests at the individual subject level because our data consists of a single data point for each subject, and estimating omega at the individual level removes the single degree of freedom, assuring a perfect fit. However, other analyses are possible. We have already noted that estimation of the omega parameter constitutes a preliminary test of the model; for the model to make substantive sense omega must be in the interval $(0, 1)$, yielding a weighted average of the equity and equality values. In equivalent terms, for the model to be acceptable its predictions must be between the point of equality (i.e. 0.5 for two-person groups), and the reward expectation standing of the actor. Looking at Table 1, we see, first of all, that for six of the 14 conditions the expectation standing is actually 0.5; consequently, omega estimation cannot be done for subjects in these conditions. For the remaining eight conditions the width of the interval between 0.5 and the expectation standing is either 0.205 (six conditions) or 0.259 (two conditions). Thus, the model is expected to make predictions in a fairly narrow interval, about one fourth the range for predictions. We can

Table 2.   Sign Test for Acceptable ω Estimation.

Number of cases	160
Number of failures	24
z	−8.933
p	0.000000

Table 3. Correlations of Individual Responses with Group Predictions.

Gender	Males		Females
r	0.743		0.701
r^2	0.552		0.491
F	96.156		75.101
df		1.78	
p	0.000000		0.000000

estimate omega for each subject in these eight conditions and see the frequency of mis-estimates. The results are given in Table 2.

In 24 cases out of 180, omega estimates are out of bounds. We have noted that the acceptable interval is about one fourth of the range of predictions; however, since we would not expect predictions close to the limiting values of 0 and 1, the sign test for the null hypothesis that the prediction is as likely to be outside as inside the acceptable interval is probably a fair test of the model. As the table shows, the z value obtained is quite extreme and the null hypothesis is strongly rejected in favor of the model.

Although we cannot estimate omega at the individual subject level and meaningfully make individual predictions, we can use estimates at the group level to make predictions for the individual subjects (that is making the same prediction for all subjects in the same condition). The correlations of such predictions and the observed values are given in Table 3.

The correlations are quite high. The model explains fully half the variance in the individual data, and the probabilities associated with the correlations are infinitesimally small. Our conclusion is that the model is also adequate at the individual subject level.

There is one further analysis we can carry out at the individual subject level. We have remarked on the difference in omegas between males and females. The individual omega estimates allow us to test if the considerable apparent difference is actually statistically significant. The results are given in Table 4.

Table 4. t-Test for Gender Difference on ω.

Gender	Males		Females
Mean ω^*	0.621		0.516
Standard deviation	0.465		0.483
t		1.411	
df		158	
p		0.160	

Interestingly, the difference actually falls quite short of significance. This is obviously because the variance of omega in both groups is very high; the magnitude of the standard deviation is almost equal to the magnitude of the mean in both groups. The issue of whether there are gender differences in the omega value remains open.

CONCLUDING REMARKS

We have presented a specific function for predicting allocative behaviors in the context of reward expectations theory. We have explored how well this function works with data from two empirical studies, and found it to work quite well at both the aggregate and individual levels. We believe this function increases the number different concrete settings and different types of allocative behaviors the theory can be applied to, and therefore increases the testability of the theory.

We are intrigued by the apparent difference in function parameter values for male and female subjects, even though high variances in those values prevent the difference from reaching statistical significance. One of the implications made explicit in the Wagner (1990, 1995) studies was that a general assumption in the literature on gender differences that men prefer equity norms and women prefer equality norms was inaccurate. The studies showed quite clearly that both men and women engage in reward allocation behavior that is a function of expectation standing. What looks like an equality norm may be seen as a reflection of equal expectation standing; what looks like an equity norm may be seen as a reflection of differentiated expectation standing. Wagner interpreted these results as suggesting that equity and equality are not in fact distinct norms, but merely implications of the absence or presence respectively of differentiation in expectation standing.

The analysis presented here suggests a slightly different interpretation of Wagner's results. While there is no gender-based preference for equity or equality norms per se, there may still be gender-based differences in the degree to which either norm is emphasized. Equity and equality may still be seen as functions of the nature of the actors' expectation standing, but the degree of differentiation may be affected by the a priori importance attached to equal reward distribution in the situation. Difference in the importance so attached may flow from group size, task environment, or any of a variety of other factors, including gender.[4] A combination of these factors may, in fact, be responsible for the high variances in parameter value we have reported.

Of course, it is important to be cautious in evaluating the support for our function on the basis of only two experimental studies. Nevertheless, the results so far suggest that the function may be used to predict reward allocation behaviors in a variety of different situations. It should provide a measure of differences in allocation behavior among members of the same population based on their expectation standing and between members of different populations, based on the weight attached to equal distributions in each population. Thus we believe we have developed a multiple-use research tool which should help generate justice research.

NOTES

1. Note the negative line connecting $D(+)$ and $D(-)$ in the second and fourth paths listed. Together with the negative outcome states at the end of both lines, the signs cancel and the path is positive. Such paths may be thought of as reflecting p's expectancies that p should *not* $(-)$ receive the low $(-)$ reward outcome.

2. The reward expectation theory also includes a series of theorems derived from the basic assumptions outlined above. These derivations deal with such issues as the implications of combining multiple referential structures, the interdependence of task and reward expectations, the significance for the power of status characteristics of associating them with referential structures, and the use of actual reward allocations to generate expectations for task and reward expectations. Although there is a significant amount of research that supports these theorems, research directly testing most of them remains to be done. Since they yield no current data for us to consider in developing our function, we will not consider these theorems here. However, as new data of this sort is generated, we expect it to provide further opportunities for evaluating the function we develop here.

3. A second interpretation of the conception is that the equality norm serves as a baseline for all allocation behaviors and that the equity norm takes on greater or lesser importance relative to the baseline depending on the kinds of mediating conditions we have mentioned. In substantive terms this would mean that actors may enter most situations assuming that rewards will be distributed equally, but that expectation standing and mediating factors may alter that assumption. This is an interpretation particularly congenial to the second author.

4. To test this interpretation Wagner would have had to include a condition involving *no* status or ability manipulation in one of his studies. A significant difference between the allocation behaviors of men and women in this condition would support it; the lack of a difference would be more consistent with Wagner's original interpretation. A test of this difference, as well as of other implications of the function, are in preparation.

ACKNOWLEDGMENTS

An earlier version of this paper was presented at the Annual Meeting of the American Sociological Association in Chicago, August 16–19, 2002. We would like to thank Erkut Özbay for help with the development of the model and to acknowledge support for M. Hamit Fisek's work from the Turkish Academy of Sciences and the Bogaziçi University Research Fund (Project No. 00B702).

REFERENCES

Adams, J. S. (1965). Inequity in social exchange. In: L. Berkowitz (Ed.), *Advances in Experimental Social Psychology*. New York: Academic Press.

Aral, S. O., & Sunar, D. G. (1977). Interaction and justice norms, a cross cultural comparison. *The Journal of Social Psychology, 101*, 175–186.

Berger, J. (1988). Directions in expectation states research. In: M. Webster, Jr. & M. Foschi (Eds), *Status Generalization* (pp. 450–476). Stanford, CA: Stanford University Press.

Berger, J., Fisek, M. H., Norman, R. Z., & Wagner, D. G. (1985). Formation of reward expectations in status situations. In: J. Berger & M. Zelditch, Jr. (Eds), *Status, Rewards, and Influence* (pp. 215–261). San Francisco: Jossey-Bass.

Berger, J., Fisek, M. H., Norman, R. Z., & Zelditch, M., Jr. (1977). *Status characteristics and social interaction*. New York: Elsevier.

Fehr, E., & Schmidt, K. M. (1999). A theory of fairness, competition, and cooperation. *The Quarterly Journal of Economics, 114*, 817–868.

Fischer, R. (2001). Reward allocation and culture: A meta-analytical review (unpublished manuscript). University of Sussex.

Fisek, M. H., Berger, J., & Norman, R. Z. (1991). Participation in heterogeneous and homogeneous groups: A theoretical integration. *American Journal of Sociology, 97*(1), 114–142.

Fisek, M. H., Norman, R. Z., & Nelson-Kilger, M. (1992). Status characteristics and expectation states theory: A priori model parameters and test. *Journal of Mathematical Sociology, 16*, 285–303.

Giacobbe-Miller, J. K., Miller, D. J., & Victorov, V. I. (1998). A comparison of Russian and U.S. pay allocation decisions, distributive justice judgements, and productivity under different payment conditions. *Personnel Psychology, 51*, 137–143.

Griffith, W. I., Sell, J., & Parker, M. J. (1993). Self-interested vs. third party allocation of rewards. *Social Psychology Quarterly, 59*, 294–301.

Homans, G. C. (1961). *Social behavior: Its elementary forms*. New York: Harcourt Brace & World.

Jasso, G. (1980). A new theory of distributive justice. *American Sociological Review, 45*, 3–32.

Kagitçibasi, Ç. (1977). Individualism and collectivism. In: J. W. Berry, M. H. Segall & Ç. Kagitçibasi (Eds), *Handbook of Cross-Cultural Psychology* (Vol. 3, pp. 1–50). Boston: Allyn and Bacon.

Kim, K. I., Park, H., & Suzuki, N. (1990). Reward allocations in the United States, Japan, and Korea: A comparison of individualistic and collectivistic cultures. *Academy of Management Journal, 33*, 188–198.

Leung, K., & Bond, M. H. (1984). The impact of cultural collectivism on reward allocation. *Journal of Personality and Social Psychology, 47*.

Meeker, B. F., & Elliot, C. G. (1966). Reward allocations, gender, and task performance. *Social Psychology Quarterly, 56*, 148–155.

Rusbult, C. E., Insko, C. A., & Lin, Y. W. (1995). Seniority-based reward allocation in the United States and Taiwan. *Social Psychology Quarterly, 58*, 13–30.

Sherif, M. (1966). *Group conflict and cooperation*. London: Routledge & Kegan Paul.

Walster, E., Berscheid, E., & Walster, G. W. (1976). New directions in equity research. In: L. Berkowitz & E. Walster (Eds), *Equity Theory: Towards a General Theory of Social Interaction* (pp. 226–235). New York: Academic Press.

Wagner, D. G. (1990). Gender differences in reward preference: A status-based account. *Small Group Research, 26*, 353–371.

Wagner, D. G. (1995). Reward preferences in mixed-sex interaction (unpublished manuscript). Department of Sociology, State University of New York at Albany.

THE ROLE OF SOCIAL IDENTITY PROCESSES IN STATUS CONSTRUCTION

Lisa Troyer

ABSTRACT

According to status construction theory, a social attribute becomes imbued with status value through its association with valued resources. Yet, explanations for such associations have received scant attention. I propose that social identity processes may lead agents controlling resources to over-allocate to in-group members. This generates a doubly dissimilar situation in which actors are differentiated both with respect to a nominal characteristic and resources, leading the characteristic to become imbued with status value. I find support for this elaboration in a sample of newly founded organizations. I discuss the implications of this elaboration for further developments in status construction theory.

INTRODUCTION

Where does status come from? Status, the perceived value of an actor in a social system (as manifested in the prestige, respect, and esteem the person garners), is a ubiquitous feature of society. Although the question of how status arises has been theoretically addressed across the history of theorizing in the expectation states theoretical research program (e.g. Berger, Cohen & Zelditch, 1972;

Power and Status
Advances in Group Processes, Volume 20, 149–172
ISSN: 0882-6145/doi:10.1016/S0882-6145(03)20006-0

Berger, Fisek, Norman & Zelditch, 1977), only recently have more refined statements and empirical studies of the question begun to surface (e.g. Ridgeway, 1991, 1997; Ridgeway & Balkwell, 1997; Ridgeway, Boyle, Kuipers & Robinison, 1998; Ridgeway & Erickson, 2000; Webster & Hysom, 1998). In this chapter, I briefly review the theoretical arguments regarding the genesis of status and focus on a particular component of status construction: local culture. Existing theories of status construction link the emergence of status value to the coincidence of resources with a state of a nominal characteristic. I add to this line of theorizing by describing how status value may arise through social identity processes. I examine the role that social identity may play in constructing status in an empirical investigation of status variation across organizational cultures.

STATUS CHARACTERISTICS THEORY AND STATUS CONSTRUCTION

Because status characteristics theory is thoroughly summarized elsewhere in this volume (e.g. Webster's chapter), I provide only a cursory overview here. A branch of the expectation states theoretical research program (Berger et al., 1977), status characteristics theory, describes the process through which differently evaluated states of an attribute generate a hierarchy of prestige and influence in a task-oriented and collectively oriented group. This hierarchy is referred to as the group's "power and prestige order." Occupying a more positively evaluated state of an attribute engenders higher status for an individual. That is, the actor is more socially valued. This social value corresponds to beliefs regarding the general competence of the actor: more valued actors are believed to be more competent than less valued actors. Beliefs about general competence are translated to corresponding expectations regarding specific task-relevant ability. Actors who are believed to be more generally competent are also expected to have more ability relevant to the particular task on which a group is working, relative to actors who are believed to be less generally competent. These competency expectations are acted upon such that, compared to lower status group members, higher status members are given more opportunities to participate, are more likely to seize participation opportunities, and are more likely to receive positive evaluations of their contributions to the group's work. Furthermore, higher status group members come to generate more influence in the group's work than lower status members.

The attributes that initially differentiate actors and lead to a power and prestige order are status characteristics. There are two types of status characteristics, diffuse and specific. Specific status characteristics refer to particular abilities. For instance, math aptitude reflects whether a person has more or less math ability. When members of a social group value having more ability over having less ability, then the ability is a specific status characteristic. If some members of the group have more of the particular ability than others (i.e. the members of the group are differentiated with respect to the ability), then the characteristic will become salient in the group and a catalyst for the processes described above leading to the construction of a power and prestige order in the group. In contrast, diffuse status characteristics are not initially linked to differentials in ability. Rather, diffuse characteristics arise from nominal attributes of group members, such as gender, race, age, and other demographic categories. Like specific status characteristics, however, the theory indicates that different states of a diffuse characteristic may be differentially valued in a social system. For instance, in U.S. society, the nominal attribute, sex, is widely conceptualized as involving two states: male and female. Additionally, in U.S. society, males tend to be more highly valued than females. This valuing is manifested in a variety of ways, including pay differentials between men and women working at the same job. It is important to emphasize that status characteristics theory does not directly address whether such differential valuing on the basis of nominal characteristics is appropriate, right, or ethical. Rather, the theory recognizes the de facto situation: such differential valuing does occur.

When states of a nominal attribute are initially accorded differential value, then the characteristic is a diffuse status characteristic, and if members of the group occupy different states of the characteristic (i.e. they are differentiated with respect to the characteristic), then it becomes a salient basis for the status processes the theory describes. That is, compared to lower status others, actors occupying the more valued, higher status state of the characteristic will be believed to be more generally competent, will be expected to have more task-relevant skill, will be accorded more opportunities to contribute to the group task, will be more positively evaluated, and will be more influential in the group. Thus, they will come to occupy higher positions in the group's power and prestige order. Through this chain of arguments, the theory describes how actors who are more socially valued come to exercise greater influence in the group, *even when the attribute that initially generates the value has no explicitly known relevance to the task on which the group is working.* It is this latter point that has captured the attention of researchers, it begs the question, "How does a nominal characteristic come to be imbued with status value?"

Ridgeway (1991) provided the first theoretical statement on status construction processes that addresses how a nominal characteristic develops status value. According to Ridgeway's status construction theory, states of a nominal attribute that initially lack evaluative connotations become associated with valued resources.

This association occurs through interactions with, or observations of interactions of actors. The value accorded the existing resources transfers to the state of the nominal characteristic the actors occupy. Thus, for example, an individual occupying the state "A" of a nominal characterstic, N, designated N_A, may be interacting with the individual occupying state "B" of the same characteristic, N_B. If N_A also possesses more of some exchangeable resource (which is already valued in the social system), than N_B possesses, then through a process of (mis)attribution, the actors associate the value of the resources possessed by each actor with the general competency expectations for each. These expectations are acted upon, leading to more dominance on the part of the actor with more of the valued resource and more positive evaluations of this actor's contributions to the group, compared to the actor with less of the valued resource. That is, the power and prestige order in the local interaction will develop around initial differences in the possession of resources. Through repeated interactions in which a particular state of the nominal characteristic is associated with advantage in the power and prestige order, the advantaged state of the characteristic will become imbued with status value in the local interaction. That is, the state will come to be more socially valued in the interactions. Furthermore, drawing on work on status transfer (e.g. Markovsky, Smith & Berger, 1984; Pugh & Wahrman, 1983) Ridgeway argues that actors will carry these newly constructed values and beliefs into future interactions with others in which the nominal characteristic is salient. Through these processes of association, (mis)attribution, and status transfer, the nominal characteristic will become a status characteristic. Over time, the status value associated with the nominal characteristic diffuses through the social system (Ridgeway & Balkwell, 1997). Consequently, it becomes a status characteristic in the broader social system.

Ridgeway (1991) refers to the interactions involving the association of a state of a nominal characteristic with the possession of valued resources as a "doubly dissimilar" situation, which is sufficient for status construction processes to begin. By this, she means that the potential for status construction is present if actors (1) are dissimilar with respect to the amounts of a socially valued resources they initial possess in an interaction setting; and (2) are dissimilar with respect to some nominal characteristic. Ridgeway et al. (1998) conducted an experimental test of the processes described by status construction theory and found strong support for the hypothesis that a status characteristic is constructed when actors are doubly dissimilar with respect to resources and an initially unevaluated nominal characteristic and interact in task-oriented and collectively oriented groups (see also, Ridgeway & Erickson, 2000).

Webster and Hysom (1998) offer an extension of Ridgeway's (1991) theory.[1] Of particular importance for the further elaboration that I will offer, Webster and

Hysom draw on status-reward theory (e.g. Berger et al., 1985; Webster, 1984) to articulate how valued resources become associated with performance expectations. According to status-reward theory, actors who are expected to be more competent at a task should also expected to be differentially rewarded, such that more competent actors should receive more rewards than less competent actors. This expectation should be realized in the possession of "goal objects," socially preferred outcomes for actors in a situation. The concept of a "goal object" is an important and general one. A goal object can be tangible (e.g. money, a prize) or intangible (e.g. recognition, a title). The key point is that the possession of the goal object is an expected outcome of competence. Webster and Hysom propose that the valued resources central to Ridgeway's theory are goal objects, and through a kind of "reverse-reasoning" process, actors in a doubly dissimiliar interaction setting will reach the conclusion that the actor with more of the valued goal object (i.e. more of the valued resource) must be competent. In part, this may correspond to "just world" beliefs; that is, in a just world, rewards are distributed to individuals who deserve them, and individuals who are more competent are more deserving. As Webster and Hysom note, integrating status construction theory with status-reward theory generates a more general theory of status construction. This is because it allows for the possibility that status may be constructed through the association of nominal characteristics with not only tangible resources that are valued, but also with intangible resources.

Both Ridgeway's (1991) original statement and the extension by Webster and Hysom (1998) suggest that variation in how goal objects (whether tangible or intangible) are distributed across social systems may affect which nominal characteristics become status characteristics, and which states of nominal characteristics come to denote higher status and which denote lower status. This directs attention to the mechanisms through which goal objects are distributed. In fact, the first of four structural conditions that Ridgeway asserts are sufficient for the initiation of a status construction process is the unequal distribution of an exchangeable resource in a population. While there may be stochastic processes involved in generating an unequal distribution of resources or interaction processes related to structural conditions, as Ridgeway proposes (drawing on Blau, 1977), there may also be other social processes involved that are linked to other sociocultural features of the social system. In particular, I propose that key actors may oversee allocations of either or both intangible goal objects (e.g. titles) and tangible goal objects (e.g. money) that are central to the construction of status. Moreover, through social identity processes (e.g. Tajfel & Turner, 1979), the allocators may come to favor one state of a nominal characteristic over others, leading them to over-allocate the goal objects to occupants of the favored state. The status construction processes articulated by Webster and Hysom and Ridgeway will lead others within the social system to associate the category receiving the over-allocation with greater value, and thus accord occupants of the category higher status.

SOCIAL IDENTITY THEORY

Social identity theory describes how social group membership affects actors' perceptions and behaviors. Early studies by Tajfel and colleagues (e.g. Tajfel, 1959, 1969, 1970; Tajfel, Sheikh & Gardner, 1964; Tajfel & Wilkes, 1963) demonstrated that actors perceive more similarities among objects categorized in the same group and more differences in objects categorized into different groups. These researchers further argued that this categorization phenomenon could explain stereotypes and in-group/out-group dynamics. In particular, Tajfel (1974, 1981) and Tajfel and Turner (1979) showed that (1) individuals seek social categorization to provide themselves with meaningful self-definitions; and (2) individuals tend to seek to assign the social categories to which they belong more positive definitions than other social categories of which they are not members. Social identity researchers argue that these outcomes are based on a self-enhancement motive: individuals seek meaningful, positive self-identities, which are developed by developing favorable definitions of others who share the same attributes. Furthermore, Tajfel and his colleagues showed that members tended to engage in actions that favor members of their own social categories and disadvantage members of other social categories. For instance, they found that actors would assign more resources to in-group members and fewer resources to out-group members (irrespective of the actions or behaviors of the in-group and out-group members).

From this foundation, Turner (1985, 1991) developed self-categorization theory, in which he argued that the self is comprised of cognitive representations that correspond to social group memberships. The salience of a category, however, depends on its mental accessibility; the more an actor is prompted to think in terms of the category, the more salient it will be. Salience, in turn, determines the likelihood that actions will be taken in reference to the category. Drawing on the self-enhancement motive of social identity theory, Turner and colleagues (e.g. Hogg & Turner, 1987; Turner, 1991; Turner & Oakes, 1989) proposed that social categorization processes can lead actors to be more or less accepting of social influence. More specifically, actors will be more inclined to accept that opinions and ideas of in-group members than out-group members. Acceptance of in-group member positions signals a positive evaluation of those group members, and hence one's self. Furthermore, agreement among in-group members reduces uncertainty, since it is taken as an indicator of the "true" state of an issue.

Empirical research has confirmed the operation of social identity processes (e.g. Hogg & Turner, 1987; Kalkhoff & Barnum, 2000). In addition, Kalkhoff and Barnum (2000) explored the relative power of status-organizing processes and social identity processes in determining social influence and found that both processes appear to have equally strong effects on social influence: actors are more accepting of social influence from higher than lower status actors and more accepting of influence from in-group than out-group members. Furthermore, the processes appear to operate concurrently. For example, Kalkhoff and Barnum found that being higher status increased the influence of an actor over both in- and out-group members, and being an in-group member increased influence over both higher and lower status actors.

At the heart of both status construction and social identity processes is the notion of social value. In the case of status construction theory, the distribution of goal objects determines the social value of attributes. Although Ridgeway and Balkwell (1997) have suggested that population distributions of resources are key to understanding social construction, less systematic attention has been paid to factors that may affect these distributions. Social identity theory, however, provides important clues. Social identity theory posits that rewards are more likely to be distributed to in-group members. Consequently, according to social identity theory, agents who control goal objects are more likely to distribute the goal objects to individuals who share a salient social category membership with them. Thus, to the extent that actors controlling goal objects occupy different social categories across social systems, we would expect to find very different distributions, and hence different status systems.

For instance, imagine an actor occupying a particular state of a nominal characteristic, N_A, in a social system, S_I. Additionally, imagine an agent who controls the allocation of a goal object in that system who also occupies the N_A state of the characteristic, and other actors occupying other states of the nominal characteristic (e.g. N_B, N_C, N_D). In this system, social identity theory posits that the allocator will distribute more of the goal object to the actor sharing the same state of the nominal characteristic, N_A, than to the other actors in the social system occupying other states of the nominal characteristic, N_B, N_C, N_D. Thus, through the status construction processes described earlier, the N_A state of the nominal characteristic will be imbued with more status than the other states of the nominal characteristic. Now, imagine an alternative social system, S_{II} in which the allocator occupies the N_B, state of the nominal characteristic. In this system, the allocator is more likely to distribute more of the goal object to another occupying the N_B state in the social system, than those occupying the N_A state. Consequently, in this second social system, N_B will become imbued with status value. Therefore, agents charged with overseeing the allocation of goal objects in a social system may become important determinants of the construction of status.

These arguments correspond to work by Willer, Lovaglia and Markovsky (1997) and Thye (2000) linking power and status. These researchers propose that powerful actors (i.e. those able to extract more resources from a social system) are viewed as more competent, are more influential, and are granted higher status, compared to less powerful actors. Also, resources controlled by higher status actors are more valued than those controlled by lower status actors, engendering more power to the higher status actors. My arguments and those of Willer et al. and Thye both highlight the central role that resource allocations play in status construction. While Willer et al. and Thye propose that position in an exchange network is a critical determinant of resource allocations, I add that social identity processes may play an important role.[2]

These insights on the role of agents who oversee goal object allocations are not terribly compelling in isolation and may initially seem overly contrived. Yet, they beg the question of whether different social systems in which different characteristics that assume different degrees of status value can concurrently exist. Recently, Foschi and Lapointe (2002) conducted an experiment that clearly demonstrated that gender was not operating as a status characteristic in their sample of Canadian university students. In another experiment, conducted around the same time, Hopcroft (2002) reports clear evidence that gender was operating as a status characteristic in a sample of U.S. university students. Foschi and Lapointe, as well as Hopcroft note that the status value of gender may be changing in societies. The point is that there is evidence that social systems may differ in whether particular characteristics are imbued with status value, and the status value accorded a characteristic may change over time as also noted by Webster & Hysom (1998, footnote 14). Whether agents charged with overseeing goal object allocations can affect status construction processes, however, requires (1) identifying social systems in which agents have such control; and (2) assessing whether their own associations with particular categories affect the manner in which goal objects are distributed in the system. One type of a social system that might fit these criteria is an organization. I turn now to a discussion of organization research, which generates insights on how different cultures (i.e. systems of meanings, values, and beliefs) may emerge in different organizations.

ORGANIZATIONAL CULTURE

Organization theorists have long recognized that different organizations develop distinct cultures. Although organization theorists do not seem to have reached a consensus regarding exactly what organizational culture is or how it evolves (e.g. Ebers, 1995; Martin, 2002), in general, the study of organizational culture focuses on the different norms, values, and meanings that guide behavior in the workplace (e.g. Kunda, 1992; Pettigrew, 1979). In part, the lack of consensus that characterizes research on organizational culture may reflect the fact that culture itself is a multidimensional concept, and as such, different dimensions of the concept may reflect different theoretical processes. Further difficulty may arise from the fact that research indicates that, even within an industry, the values and norms that define organizational culture may vary widely (e.g. Chatman & Jen, 1994; Deal & Kennedy, 1982; Ebers, 1995; O'Reilly, Chatman & Caldwell, 1991).

Despite the differences, there is some consensus regarding the role that culture plays in organizations. In particular, a key focus of research on organizational culture is on how it functions as a system of social control; a means through which rewards and punishments are distributed, not only to encourage certain behaviors and outcomes, but also to define the boundaries of the organization by determining what is valued. Thus, the notion of the allocation of rewards and punishments – how they are allocated and to whom – represents an important avenue for understanding organizational culture.

Several researchers have noted the key role that managers, executives, and founders play in determining the values that permeate an organization's culture (e.g. Barnard, 1938; Deal & Kennedy, 1982; O'Reilly & Chatman, 1995; Tannenbaum, Weschler & Massarik, 1961). Furthermore, reward systems have long been recognized as critical determinants of organizational culture because of the role they play in determining employees' behaviors (e.g. Biggart, 1989; O'Reilly & Chatman, 1995). It may be that the ability of organizational leaders to control reward systems is a key mechanism through which they affect culture, including which social attributes are recognized as higher status. Researchers have also suggested that the effect of reward allocations on forming the values that constitute an organization's culture and leaders' control of them are likely to be most pronounced at the early stages of an organization's existence (e.g. Deal & Kennedy, 1982; Peters, 1978). Thus, newly founded organizations may represent social systems that are particularly amenable to the observation of status construction processes.

THEORETICAL INTEGRATION: STATUS CONSTRUCTION, SOCIAL IDENTITY, AND ORGANIZATIONAL CULTURE

As this discussion has suggested, values are an important component of organizational culture that are, in part, determined by how rewards are allocated. As such, actors who control those allocations may play critical roles in determining the cultural values that emerge in organizations. More specifically, leaders at early stages in an organization's existence are likely to both control reward allocations and, as such, be key figures in determining what and who is valued in an organization (e.g. Baron & Newman, 1990). Insofar as status represents one dimension of the value system characterizing organizations, these insights may be applied to the construction of status in organizations. That is, status construction processes may occur in organizations as a part of the social construction of the organizational culture. Furthermore, these processes may be linked to social identity processes. First, according to social identity theory, actors value in-group members more than out-group members. In an organizational setting, this suggests the following proposition:

Proposition 1. Employees who are members of the same social categories as organizational leaders will be valued more by the leaders than employees who are not members of the same social categories as the leaders.

Second, social identity theory suggests that the differential valuing of in-group members over out-group members will result in over-allocation of rewards to in-group members and under-allocation of rewards to out-group members. In an organizational setting, this suggests the following proposition:

Proposition 2. Employees who are members of the same social categories as organizational leaders will receive more rewards (i.e. goal objects) from the leaders, than employees who are not members of the same social categories as the leaders.

Third, according to status construction theory, the social categories that reflect an advantageous allocation are more likely to become imbued with status value than those that do not reflect this advantage throughout the social system. Within an organization, this suggests the following proposition:

Proposition 3. Employees who receive more rewards will be granted higher status than those who receive fewer rewards.

From P2 and P3, the following can be derived:

Proposition 4. Employees who are members of the same social categories as organizational leaders will be granted higher status than those who are not members of the same social categories as leaders.

In summary, these arguments suggest that the social categories occupied by organizational leaders are a key determinant of the allocation of rewards in organizations, with employees who occupy the same category as the leader receiving more rewards than those not occupying the same category as the leader. If rewards are allocated in a manner that favors those in the leader's social category, then this establishes the "doubly-dissimilar" situation, which serves as a catalyst for status construction processes in social systems. The social categorization of the employees receiving more rewards will become imbued with status value, such that affiliation with the category will correspond to possessing the more-valued state of a status characteristic (i.e. engendering higher status for those possessing the more-valued state), and lack of affiliation with the category will correspond to possessing the less-valued state of the status characteristic (i.e. engendering lower status for those possessing the less-valued state). In other words, a new status characteristic may be constructed in the organization, which has an effect that is independent of other existing status characteristics that may be common to organizations such as educational attainment or occupational prestige. I now turn to an empirical study that I conducted to test these arguments.

AN EMPIRICAL INVESTIGATION OF STATUS CONSTRUCTION IN NEW ORGANIZATIONS

I conducted a survey of employees and founders of organizations that had been in existence (as determined by date of legal incorporation) for less than three years. Newly founded organizations may be particularly amenable to the observation of status construction processes arising through social identity dynamics that I have described above. This is because newly founded organizations tend to be heavily influenced by their founders (Baron & Newman, 1990; Deal & Kennedy, 1982; Peters, 1978). Additionally, the relative effects of founders, who tend to be highly active key leaders in the organization, may be more pronounced than other effects, like isomorphic tendencies arising from institutional pressures (DiMaggio & Powell, 1983), market demands, and stratification within the broader culture in which an organization is embedded (e.g. Konrad & Pfeffer, 1990), each of which may affect the value of particular social categories in the workplace.

An important process that occurs in the early stages of founding is determining who will fill what roles in the organization. While many factors go into the hiring and placement process, educational background represents both a common and highly salient factor in recruitment decisions. Educational background refers to the area in which an individual obtains certification or a degree (e.g. engineering, humanities, computer science, social sciences, physical sciences, biological sciences). Hiring decisions often reflect the perceptions of key stakeholders in the organization regarding the need for the skills corresponding to a potential hire's educational background. Thus, educational background reflects a social dimension that is likely to be accorded more or less value in an organization. Furthermore, an individual's educational background reflects membership in a social category that may or may not be shared by others in the organization. Thus, I examined how educational background is perceived by founders, how it is rewarded, and how other members of the newly founded organization come to perceive occupants of different educational backgrounds as a means of investigating the elaboration of status construction theory through social identity processes that I described earlier. On the basis of the arguments I set forth in this elaboration, I offer the following empirical hypotheses, which parallel the four propositions that I presented earlier:

Hypothesis 1. Individuals whose educational backgrounds coincide with a founder's educational background will be valued more by the founder than individuals whose educational backgrounds differ from the founder's.

Hypothesis 2. Individuals who have educational backgrounds that are more valued by a founder will receive higher salaries than individuals who have educational backgrounds that are less valued by a founder.

Hypothesis 3. Individuals who receive higher salaries will be accorded more respect in the organization by non-founding members of the organization than individuals who receive lower salaries.

Hypothesis 4. Individuals whose educational backgrounds coincide with a founder's educational background will be accorded more respect in the organization by non-founding members of the organization than individuals whose educational backgrounds do not coincide with a founder's educational background.

Thus, similarity to the founder in terms of educational background will lead to a higher resource allocation in the form of salary. This establishes the doubly-dissimilar situation whereby educational background becomes a status characteristic within the organization, and those sharing the founder's background are assigned the higher state of the characteristic (and more respect from others, a manifestation of higher status), while those not sharing the founder's background are assigned the lower state of the characteristic (and less respect from others, a manifestation of lower status).

Method

I surveyed members and founders of 35 "dot-com" organizations. The sample of organizations began as a convenience sample (reflecting organizations whose members were personal contacts of mine), which was supplemented through snowball methodologies (i.e. I asked contacts in the existing sample of organizations to suggest others that may be interested in participating in the study). The organizations were all in high-tech industries related to the Web and Intemet (e.g. Intemet Service Providers, Web design companies, software companies, network companies). I emphasized that participation in the survey was voluntary (there was no incentive for participating). Employees completed questionnaires anonymously. Founders, however, were not anonymous, since each company in the survey had only one founder. The survey was conducted over a 12-month period. At the time the survey was administered in each organization, the organization had not been in existence for more than three years.

In two of the organizations, the response rate was less than 30%, and in one of these two, the founder elected not to answer several questions. Thus, I did not include data from these two organizations in my analyses. Across the remaining 33 organizations, the response rate among founders was 100% and among employees it was about 85%. This amounted to a total of 507 employee respondents and 33 founder respondents. The organizations ranged in size from four to 34 employees, with a mean of 18.06 employees.

The questionnaires were completed first by employees.[3] The employees were asked to indicate their educational background by describing the training, certification, and/or degree that they had received in an educational context. If a respondent did not feel that she/he had received any training or degree in an educational context, then she/he was instructed to indicate "no training." I then re-coded the responses into one of the following categories: engineering, computer science/programming, physical/mathematical sciences, social sciences, biological sciences, management sciences, finance/accounting, law, humanities, and "none" (for respondents who indicated that they had not received any training). Additionally, employees were asked to indicate the highest level of education they had completed (1 = high school degree of equivalent (e.g. GED), 2 = two years of college or an associate degree, 3 = four years of college or a bachelor degree, 4 = some graduate school, 5 = master degree or professional graduate degree (e.g. J.D.), 6 = doctoral degree). Respondents were also asked to indicate their net salary and official job title in the organization. On the basis of their job titles, I assigned each respondent an occupational prestige score based on the Nakao–Hodge–Treas occupational prestige scores (Nakao & Treas, 1992). Also, respondents were given a list of all of the employees (except the founder) in the organization and were asked to indicate the degree of respect that they had for the input that each employee provided in group discussions within the organization. The response system for this item was a seven-point scale ranging from 1 = "Absolutely No Respect" to 7 = "Highest Degree of Respect I Give Any Employee."

Founders completed their questionnaires after I had recoded the educational background of the employees. Founders were asked to indicate their own educational background by categorizing it into one of the categories described above that resulted from the recoding (each founder was asked to rate only those categories that were represented by employees in his[4] organization). Additionally, founders were asked to rate the value of each category of educational background in terms of its importance to the kind of work that the organization conducted. The response system for these ratings was 1 = "Not at All Important" to 7 = "Extremely Important."

Results

Descriptive statistics for the variables of interest are provided in Tables 1a and 1b. These tables reveal some interesting results, which are important for this study.

Table 1a. Frequencies, Means, and Standard Deviations for Educational Attainment and Occupational Prestige Score of Employees ($n = 507$).

Variable and Category	Frequency
Educational attainment	
1 = No college	5
2 = Two years of college or associate degree	13
3 = Four years of college or bachelor degree	339
4 = Some graduate school	85
5 = Master degree	63
6 = Doctoral degree	2
Mean (S.D.)	3.38 (0.79)
Occupational prestige score	
31	8
34	4
39	47
52	28
59	31
61	161
64	69
70	45
73	20
74	83
75	11
Mean (S.D.)	61.77 (10.73)

Table 1b. Frequency of Employees ($n = 507$) and Founders ($n = 33$) in Educational Background Categories, Mean of Founder's Value of Educational Background (Standard Deviation in Parentheses).

Educational Background	Frequency of Employees	Frequency of Founders	Mean (S.D.) of Founder's Value of Educational Background
Engineering	107	5	5.72 (0.92)
Computer programming	162	7	5.69 (1.04)
Physical sciences & mathematics	45	5	5.27 (1.44)
Finance & accounting	58	7	5.93 (1.30)
Biological sciences	14	0	3.79 (1.42)
Management sciences	35	3	6.2 (1.11)
Social sciences	30	3	4.07 (1.82)
Humanities	28	0	2.75 (1.27)
None	15	0	1.13 (0.35)
Law	13	3	6.15 (1.57)

First, as Table 1a indicates, the sample for these analyses is relatively highly educated; approximately 96% of the employees sampled had completed four or more years of college. Moreover, they represent a relatively professionalized sample, with approximately 77% of the employees falling into occupational prestige groups corresponding to professional or managerial occupations.

Table 1b also reveals interesting distributions in the data. Given that organizations in "dot-com" industries were sampled, it is not surprising that a very large percentage of the respondents have backgrounds in information, technical, and physical sciences (about 62%). Similarly, it is not surprising that these backgrounds are relatively highly valued (all above 5.5 on a 7-point scale). This also corresponds to the large percentage of founders with these backgrounds (approximately 52%). Furthermore, given that occupational prestige is generally associated with attorneys, the high valuing of employees with a law background may not be surprising. Also, as expected, employees lacking educational training are not highly valued. It is interesting to note that those with humanities backgrounds are also not highly valued. Finally, business backgrounds appear to be relatively highly valued, while those with a social science background fall at nearly exactly the median. The high valuing of those with business backgrounds may reflect the relatively large percentage of founders (approximately 30%) that also fall into these categories.

The social category membership of interest that I am investigating in this study is educational background. In particular, I am interested in whether founders perceive their own educational background as more valuable than other

Table 2.   Effects of Educational Attainment, Occupational Prestige, and
Founder's Valuing of Educational Background on Relative Salary ($n = 507$).

Variable	Coefficient	Standard Error	t
Intercept	−0.342	0.257	−1.330
Educational attainment	0.056	0.044	1.012
Occupational prestige	0.014	0.004	3.287*
Founder's valuing of educational background	0.347	0.028	12.362*

$F(3, 503) = 87.367, p < 0.05$. Adj $R^2 = 0.339$.
*$p < 0.001$.

educational backgrounds. For each organization, I took the mean of the values
founders assigned to the backgrounds that were not the same as their own. Thus,
for each organization, I operationalized in-group valuing (i.e. value of founder's
educational background) as the founder's rating of his own educational background, and I operationalized out-group valuing (i.e. value of other educational
backgrounds) as the mean of the founder's rating of other educational backgrounds. A t-test showed that founders valued their own educational background
significantly more than others ($t(52) = 10.80, p < 0.001$, in-group mean $= 6.80$,
out-group mean $= 4.90$).[5] Although this supports Hypothesis 1, it may be misleading insofar as founders may consider some educational backgrounds closer to
their own than others. For instance, founders with an educational background in
engineering may consider computer programmers and physical scientists as a part
of their in-group, but others (like social scientists and humanists) as members of
an out-group. Unfortunately, in these data, I can not distinguish which educational
groups founders consider as part of their in-group. Consequently, while there
is support for Hypothesis 1, the results should be accepted cautiously and finer
analyses should be pursued in order to assess this hypothesis more systematically.

To examine the second hypothesis, that employees who have educational
backgrounds that are more valued by founders will receive higher salaries than
employees who have educational backgrounds that are less valued by founders, I
conducted a regression analysis. Prior to the analysis, I assigned each respondent
the rating the founder had assigned the educational background of the respondent.
I calculated the salary quartile into which each respondent fell within her/his
organization (since I am treating the organization as a social system). I then
regressed salary quartile (reverse-coded for purposes of interpretation) on value of
educational background, controlling for occupational prestige and level of education, since these factors are well-recognized determinants of salary. The results of
this analysis are provided in Table 2 (means, standard deviations, and correlations
for all variables in the regression analyses are provided in the Appendix).

The results in Table 2 provide striking support for the hypothesis that founder valuing of the educational background of an employee has a positive effect on the employee's relative salary within the organization. This effect holds even when well-recognized determinants of salary like educational attainment and occupational prestige are included in the analysis. The fact that educational attainment does not have a significant effect on an employee's relative salary within an organization is curious. Yet, this may be due to the relative homogeneity in the sample with respect to educational attainment. As indicated in Table 1a, the majority of respondents have a four-year college degree or higher (with most at the four-year degree level). Very few have less than a four-year college education. Nonetheless, this analysis provides strong support for the claim that individuals who control resource allocations allocate more of the resources to in-group members than out-group members.

The third hypothesis, that individuals who receive higher salaries will be accorded more respect than individuals who receive lower salaries, was also examined through a regression. For this analysis, I operationalized the respect a focal employee was accorded by taking the mean of other employees' respect ratings for the focal employee. This value was then regressed on the employee's standardized salary, controlling for occupational prestige and level of education. The results of this analysis appear in Table 3.

As Table 3 indicates, this analysis supports Hypothesis 3. The higher an employee's salary, the more respect that other employees reported according him/her. This relationship holds even when controlling for occupational prestige and educational attainment, recognized variables affecting status. Occupational prestige did not, however, have the anticipated effect on salary.

This may reflect the relatively narrow range of occupations represented in the organizations. Across the 33 organizations included in the analysis, only 11 occupational prestige categories were represented. Furthermore, it may be

Table 3. Effects of Employee's Educational Attainment, Occupational Prestige, and Salary on Degree of Respect Accorded to an Employee ($n = 507$).

Variable	Coefficient	Standard Error	t
Intercept	2.310	0.305	7.567
Educational attainment	0.140	0.654	2.137[*]
Occupational prestige	−0.003	0.005	−0.505
Relative salary	0.905	0.047	19.446[***]

$F(3, 503) = 152.978, p < 0.001$. Adj $R^2 = 0.474$.
[*]$p < 0.05$.
[***]$p < 0.001$.

that the job titles of employees (and hence differences in occupational prestige) are less salient to employees than educational attainment and the function (i.e. programmer, Web designer, financial controller, customer service agent) that an employee fulfills in the organization. Again, this highlights the need for further finer-grained research that takes into account the meaning of occupations, education, and salary to employees. Yet, it also provides strong support for the link between the acquisition of valued goal objects and status.

The fourth hypothesis explicitly links social categorization with status in the context of educational background. To test this hypothesis, I added a dummy variable operationalizing shared social categorization with the founder to the regression equation that tested Hypothesis 3. Thus, this analysis assesses the relationship between an employee's membership in the founder's social category (as represented by educational background) and the respect the employee receives in the organization, controlling for relative salary, occupational prestige, and educational attainment. The results of this analysis are presented in Table 4.

This result provides very strong support for the arguments on status construction that I have presented. Membership in the founder's social category is strongly related to the degree of respect other employees accord an individual in the organization. This relationship holds even when salary is controlled and other known status markers like occupational prestige and educational attainment are controlled. It is interesting to note that once again, occupational prestige fails to have an effect on status value (as operationalized by respect). Together, however, the tests of Hypotheses 1–4 are highly supportive of the status construction arguments that I have posited.

Table 4. Effects of Membership in Founder's Social Category[a], Relative Salary, Occupational Prestige, and Educational Attainment on Degree of Respect Accorded to an Employee ($n = 507$).

Variable	Coefficient	Standard Error	t
Intercept	6.603	0.391	16.898[**]
Membership in founder's social category[a]	0.403	0.137	2.938[*]
Relative salary	0.859	0.047	17.634[***]
Occupational prestige	−0.003	0.005	−0.590
Educational attainment	0.162	0.065	2.484[*]

$F(4, 502) = 118.600, p < 0.001$. Adj $R^2 = 0.482$.

[a] "Membership in Founder's Social Category" is a dummy variable coded "1" if the employee's educational background was the same as the founder's, and coded "0" if the employee's educational background was not the same as the founder's.

[*] $p < 0.05$.
[**] $p < 0.01$.
[***] $p < 0.001$.

DISCUSSION

Despite the support that this investigation offers for the hypotheses I proposed, and hence the elaboration of status construction theory that I am presenting, there are several limitations. Most notably, this is a small sample of a particular type of organization: newly founded "dot-coms." While I selected the sample frame for strategic reasons (i.e. because I wanted to examine status construction in a new social system with minimal historical influences), this is a serious limitation that begs the issue of how status construction processes may be influenced by factors both within and outside of the social system. For instance, it is possible that employees are selecting into particular organizations on the basis of shared values. It may be that employees whose values (including status values) are inconsistent with those of established organizations gravitate toward newer organizations with less firmly established cultures. In these data, I have no measures that allow me to examine whether employees' initial perceptions of status value at the point of hiring did or did not favor the social categories of the founder (and it is quite plausible to suspect that they would). This limitation, however, does not mean that status construction is not occurring. It means that employees may have a propensity to support a particular pattern of status construction. Moreover, the results are a compelling example of how different status value systems may emerge across different social systems. As Table 1b indicates, founders did have quite varying backgrounds. Thus, for instance, a finance background may engender higher status in one organization but not others. An interesting question this raises is whether employees who exit the organization carry status beliefs that are developed within the organization to subsequent work environments (and the conditions under which such beliefs may be strengthened or may decay over time).

I also note that dynamic changes in the organization's environment may play an important role in status construction (and change) processes. In particular, we might expect that as more indicators of performance become available over time (e.g. the quality and volume of an employee's work), then new factors may affect the status-value assigned to a state of a nominal characteristic like educational background. Furthermore, the longer an organization exists, the more likely it is to be subjected to external pressures from the environment. In particular, market forces may have a stronger effect on the salaries that are paid to employees of different backgrounds, and institutional processes may lead to isomorphic tendencies in the relation between educational background and salary across organizations. I could not, however, explore these dynamics in the data I examined.

This latter limitation, however, suggests interesting avenues for further elaboration of status construction theory that may link it to macro social dynamics. Whether a status construction "survives" over time may depend on (1) whether the construction holds in other social systems; and (2) the extent of dependence between the focal social system and others. These contingencies reflect insights from organization theories, including institutional theory, resource dependence theory, and population ecology theory. Institutional theory (DiMaggio & Powell, 1983; Meyer & Rowan, 1977) describes the effect of social and cultural environments on organizations. Institutional theorists recognize that organizations are embedded in a broader social environment that imposes existing taken-for-granted structures and processes on the organization. Indeed, the values and taken-for-granted structures and routines that come to characterize organizations are often those that already characterize other organizations in the environment. Failing to conform to these conventions threatens an organization's legitimacy. Without legitimacy, organizations will have difficulty acquiring the resources and support they need from other agents and organizations in their environment. Moreover, as noted by resource dependence theorists, without resources and support, organizations can not survive (Pfeffer & Salancik, 1978).

Extending these insights from institutional theory to status construction within a social system suggests that the nominal characteristics that become candidates for status construction and the values assigned to different states may depend on how common similar constructions are in other social systems and the degree of dependence between social systems. Highly interdependent social systems are likely to develop similar status value systems.

Furthermore, status value systems may reflect structures that are more or less conducive to the ability of a social system to compete for scarce resources. According to population ecology theorists (Hannan & Carroll, 1992), organizational forms that are more successful at facilitating the acquisition of scarce resources from the environment endure and are replicated over time and across organizations, while those that are less successful in facilitating resource acquisition "die." Death occurs when organizations embodying the forms cease to exist and the forms are no longer replicated among new organizations.

These ideas can be extended to status construction processes. Some nominal characteristics that become transformed to status characteristics may facilitate the acquisition of critical resources in a social system (e.g. political alliances, economic support, acquisition of raw materials), while others may hinder the acquisition of such resources. Those that facilitate resource acquisition may persist, while those that do not may die. Thus, over time, there may be increasing homogeneity in the kinds of nominal characteristics that become and survive as status characteristics. Also, however, this suggests another interesting point: social systems themselves may become imbued with status value, in part, because of the status constructions that have occurred within the system. This status value may become the basis on which the system accrues further resources (like political and economic support). My point is that the status construction processes that I and others have described may correspond to a more general multi-level theory that elucidates not only how individuals gain power and prestige, but also how groups and societies rise to positions of power and prestige in a broader system. That is, status construction theory may be on the verge of identifying general mechanisms that span levels of social analysis, making it an ideal candidate for a multi-level theory (e.g. Markovsky, 1997).

In conclusion, Ridgeway's (1991) groundbreaking work on status construction theory along with important elaborations by Webster and Hysom (1998) represent one of the most important advances in the expectation states program of theoretical research in the last decade. In this paper, I have tried to further this work by theoretically articulating how social identity processes may affect status construction processes. Preliminary research supports the arguments I have offered. This lends insight on how different status value systems may emerge in different social systems. Perhaps more importantly, however, the research and arguments presented here suggest further avenues of theorizing and research that might be pursued to continue to advance this important line of work.

NOTES

1. Webster and Hysom (1998) offered two additional extensions of status construction theory: (1) how status is constructed through interaction among initially undifferentiated group members; and (2) how status is constructed through the association of behavior with personality attributes. Since these are less germane to my elaboration of status construction processes, I do not review these extensions here.

2. These are not necessarily competing arguments. In fact, network position may be a function of social identity (e.g. exchange partners may be those with whom one shares an identity). An interesting avenue for future research may involve assessing the role of social identity in the configuration of exchange networks.

3. The questionnaires had 28 questions. For the purposes of this paper, however, I only describe the items relevant to analyses involving the hypotheses I have offered. The questionnaire took respondents about 15 minutes to complete, which may explain the high response rate.

4. All of the founders were male.

5. For this analysis, there were three organizations in which the founder's educational background was not shared by any of the employees. These organizations were excluded from this analysis, leaving ratings from founders of 30 organizations for analysis.

ACKNOWLEDGMENTS

The analyses I conducted was partially supported by a University of Iowa Old Gold Summer Fellowship. I am grateful to the participants in the Social Psychology Brown Bag at the University of Wisconsin, Department of Sociology, who provided extremely useful comments on an earlier presentation of this work.

Additionally, I greatly appreciate the constructive evaluation of this paper by the volume editors, Shane Thye and John Skvoretz. Their suggestions substantially improved this work. Finally, I thank the many organizations and their employees who generously participated in the research that I described, but must remain anonymous. Without them, this work would not have been possible.

REFERENCES

Barnard, C. I. (1938). *The functions of the executive*. Cambridge, MA: Harvard University Press.

Baron, J. N., & Newman, A. E. (1990). For what it's worth: Organizations, occupations, and the value of work done by women and nonwhites. *American Sociological Review, 55*, 155–175.

Berger, J., Cohen, B. P., & Zelditch, M., Jr. (1972). Status characteristics and social interaction. *American Sociological Review, 37*, 241–255.

Berger, J., Fisek, M. H., Norman, R. Z., & Zelditch, M., Jr. (1977). *Status characteristics and social interaction: An expectation-states approach*. New York, NY: Elsevier.

Berger, J., Fisek, M. H., Norman, R. Z., & Wagner, D. G. (1985). Formation of reward expectations in status situations. In: J. Berger & M. Zelditch, Jr. (Eds), *Status, Rewards, and Influence: How Expectations Organize Behavior* (pp. 215–261). San Francisco, CA: Jossey-Bass.

Biggart, N. W. (1989). *Charismatic capitalism: Direct selling organizations in America*. Chicago, IL: University of Chicago Press.

Blau, P. (1977). *Inequality and heterogeneity: A primitive theory of social structure*. New York, NY: Free Press.

Chatman, J., & Jen, K. A. (1994). Assessing the relationship between industry characteristics and organizational culture: How different can you be? *Academy of Management Journal, 37*, 522–553.

Deal, T. E., & Kennedy, A. A. (1982). *Corporate cultures: Rites and rituals of corporate life*. Reading, MA: Addison-Wesley.

DiMaggio, P. J., & Powell, W. W. (1983). The iron cage revisited: Institutional isomorphism and collective rationality in organizational fields. *American Sociological Review, 48*, 147–160.

Ebers, M. (1995). The framing of organizational cultures. In: S. B. Bacharach, P. Gagliardi & B. Mundell (Eds), *Research in the Sociology of Organizations: Studies of Organizations in the European Tradition* (Vol. 13, pp. 129–170). Greenwich, CT: JAI Press.

Foschi, M., & Lapointe, V. (2002). On conditional hypotheses and gender as a status characteristic. *Social Psychology Quarterly, 65*, 146–162.

Hannan, M. T., & Carroll, G. R. (1992). *Dynamics of organizational populations: Density, competition, and legitimation*. New York, NY: Oxford University Press.

Hogg, M. A., & Turner, J. C. (1987). Intergroup behaviour, self-stereotypinig, and the salience of social categories. *British Journal of Sociology, 26*, 325–340.

Hopcroft, R. (2002). Is gender still a status characteristic? *Current Research in Social Psychology, 7*, 339–346. http://www.uiowa.edu/~grpproc/

Kalkhoff, W., & Barnum, C. (2000). The effects of status-organizing and social identity processes on patterns of social influence. *Social Psychology Quarterly, 63*, 95–115.

Konrad, A. M., & Pfeffer, J. (1990). Do you get what you deserve? Factors affecting the relationship between productivity and pay. *Administrative Science Quarterly, 35*, 258–285.

Kunda, G. (1992). *Engineering culture: Control and commitment in a high-tech corporation*. Philadelphia, PA: Temple University Press.

Markovsky, B. (1997). Building and testing multilevel theories. In: J. Szmatka, J. Skvoretz & J. Berger (Eds), *Status, Network, and Structure: Theory Development in Group Processes* (pp. 13–28). Stanford, CA: Stanford University Press.

Markovsky, B., Smith, L. F., & Berger, J. (1984). Do status interventions persist? *American Sociological Review, 49*, 373–382.

Martin, J. (2002). *Organizational culture: Mapping the terrain.* Thousand Oaks, CA: Sage.

Meyer, J. W., & Rowan, B. (1977). Institutionalized organizations: Formal structures as myth and ceremony. *American Journal of Sociology, 83*, 340–363.

Nakao, K., & Treas, J. (1992). The 1989 socioeconomic index of occupations: Construction from the 1989 Occupational Prestige Scores. General Social Survey Methodological Report No. 74. Chicago, IL: National Opinion Research Consortium (NORC).

O'Reilly, C. A., & Chatman, J. A. (1995). Culture as social control: Corporations, cults, and commitment. In: B. M. Staw & L. L. Cummings (Eds), *Research in Organizational Behavior* (Vol. 18, pp. 157–200). Greenwich, CT: JAI Press.

O'Reilly, C. A., Chatman, J., & Caldwell, D. F. (1991). People and organizational culture: A profile comparison approach to assessing person-organization fit. *Academy of Management Journal, 34*, 487–516.

Peters, T. J. (1978). Symbols, patterns, and settings: An optimistic case for getting things done. *Organizational Dynamics, 7*, 3–23.

Pettigrew, A. M. (1979). On studying organizational cultures. *Administrative Science Quarterly, 24*, 570–581.

Pfeffer, J., & Salancik, G. (1978). *The external control of organizations: A resource dependence perspective.* New York, NY: Harper and Row.

Pugh, M. D., & Wahrman, R. (1983). Neutralizing sexism in mixed-sex groups: Do women have to be better than men? *American Journal of Sociology, 88*, 746–762.

Ridgeway, C. L. (1991). The social construction of status value: Gender and other nominal characteristics. *Social Forces, 70*, 367–386.

Ridgeway, C. L. (1997). Where do status beliefs come from? New developments. In: J. Szmatka, J. Skvoretz & J. Berger (Eds), *Status, Network, and Structure: Theory Development in Group Processes* (pp. 137–158). Stanford, CA: Stanford University Press.

Ridgeway, C. L., & Balkwell, J. W. (1997). Group processes and the diffusion of status beliefs. *Social Psychology Quarterly, 60*, 14–31.

Ridgeway, C. L., Boyle, E. H., Kuipers, K., & Robinson, D. (1998). How do status beliefs develop? The role of resources and interactional experience. *American Sociological Review, 63*, 331–350.

Ridgeway, C. L., & Erickson, K. G. (2000). Creating and spreading status beliefs. *American Journal of Sociology, 106*, 579–615.

Tajfel, H. (1959). Quantitative judgment in social perception. *British Journal of Psychology, 50*, 16–29.

Tajfel, H. (1969). Cognitive aspects of prejudice. *Journal of Social Issues, 25*, 79–97.

Tajfel, H. (1970). Experiments in intergroup discrimination. *Scientific American, 223*, 96–102.

Tajfel, H. (1974). Social identity and intergroup behaviour. *Social Science Information, 13*, 6593.

Tajfel, H. (1981). *Human groups and social categories: Studies in social psychology.* Cambridge, UK: Cambridge University Press.

Tajfel, H., Sheikh, A. A., & Gardner, R. C. (1964). Content of stereotypes and the inference of similarity between members of stereotyped groups. *Acta Psychologica, 22*, 191–201.

Tajfel, H., & Turner, J. C. (1979). An integrative theory of intergroup conflict. In: W. G. Austin & S. Worchel (Eds), *The Social Psychology of Intergroup Relations* (pp. 33–47). Monterey, CA: Brooks-Cole.

Tajfel, H., & Wilkes, A. L. (1963). Classification and quantitative judgement. *British Journal of Psychology, S4*, 101–114.

Tannenbaum, R., Weschler, I. R., & Maasarik, F. (1961). *Leadership and organization: A behavioral science approach.* New York, NY: McGraw-Hill.

Thye, S. R. (2000). A status value theory of power in exchange relations. *American Sociological Review, 65*, 407–432.

Turner, J. C. (1985). Social categorization and the self-concept: A social cognitive theory of group behaviour. In: E. J. Lawler (Ed.), *Advances in Group Processes: Theory and Research* (Vol. 2, pp. 77–122). Greenwich, CT: JAI Press.

Turner, J. C. (1991). *Social influence.* Milton Keynes: Open University Press.

Turner, J. C., & Oakes, P. J. (1989). Self categorization theory and social influence. In: P. B. Paulus (Ed.), *The Psychology of Group Influence* (pp. 233–275). Hillsdale, NJ: Erlbaum.

Webster, M., Jr. (1984). Social structures and the sense of justice. In: S. B. Bacharach & E. J. Lawler (Eds), *Research in the Sociology of Organizations* (Vol. 3, pp. 59–94). Greenwich, CT: JAI Press.

Webster, M., & Hysom, S. J. (1998). Creating status characteristics. *American Sociological Review, 63*, 351–378.

Willer, D., Lovaglia, M. J., & Markovsky, B. (1997). Power and influence: A theoretical bridge. *Social Forces, 76*, 571–603.

APPENDIX

Means, standard deviations (S.D.) and correlations for variables in regression analyses ($n = 508$).

Variable	Mean (S.D.)	(1)	(2)	(3)	(4)	(5)
(1) Educational attainment	3.38 (0.79)	–	–	–		–
(2) Occupational prestige	61.77 (10.73)	0.34	–	–		–
(3) Salary quartile[a]	2.55 (1.12)	0.23	0.36	–		–
(4) Membership in founder's social category[b]	0.16 (0.37)	−0.03	0.11	0.32	–	–
(5) Founder's valuing of educational background	5.29 (1.61)	0.28	0.43	0.57	0.43	–
(6) Degree of respect accorded employee	4.94 (1.49)	0.22	0.25	0.69	0.30	0.41

[a] Reverse-coded (i.e. 4 = highest salary quartile; 1 = lowest salary quartile).

[b] "Membership in Founder's Social Category" is a dummy variable coded "1" if the employee's educational background was the same as the founder's, and coded "0" if the employee's educational background was not the same as the founder's (mean corresponds to percentage of employees sharing founder's social category).

WORKING ON STATUS PUZZLES

Murray Webster Jr.

INTRODUCTION: PUZZLES AS GUIDES TO UNDERSTANDING

Basic science, sometimes called "curiosity-driven research" at the National Science Foundation and other places, starts with a question that somehow stays in the mind, nagging for an answer. Such questions really are "puzzles"; they arise in an intellectual field or context, asking someone to fit pieces to an improving but incomplete picture of the social world. What makes a worthwhile puzzle is a missing part in understanding the picture, or a new piece of knowledge that does not seem to fit among other parts. Sometimes creative theorists can imagine a solution to one of the holes in the puzzle. If they are also empirical scientists, they devise ways to get evidence bearing on their ideas, and some of those ideas survive to give more complete and detailed pictures of the world. This chapter is the story of puzzles and provisional solutions to them, developed by dozens of men and women investigating status processes and status structures, using a coherent perspective, for over half a century.[1]

The story begins at Harvard University's Department of Social Relations in the 1940s, in an extraordinarily rich environment of sociologists, social and clinical psychologists, a statistician, psychologists, and cultural anthropologists who, for several reasons, were supremely influential in the development of social science in the U.S.[2] Two members of that department, Robert Freed Bales and Talcott Parsons, sought to understand how social systems of all sizes develop. Parsons focused on the structure and development of entire societies, and Bales focused on structure and development of small face to face groups. They believed that

Power and Status
Advances in Group Processes, Volume 20, 173–215
Copyright © 2003 by Elsevier Ltd.
ISSN: 0882-6145/doi:10.1016/S0882-6145(03)20007-2

the social processes would be analytically similar at both ends of the scale; small groups seemed to be microcosms of societies.

At the beginning, most of the theoretical terms we now take for granted in the study of status processes – status characteristics, power and prestige structures, action opportunities, salience, and many more – had not yet been formulated. The study of groups and group processes was still largely phenomenological and holistic. That is, investigators were trying to describe and understand what the groups were like and what happened in them. Few attempted to conceptualize abstractly, to focus on certain aspects while leaving others for possible later study. The terms and concepts were close to everyday language, and there was little difference between observation of a phenomenon and naming of it. For instance, the everyday term "asks for information," which now we think of as an instance of the abstract concept of giving an action opportunity was still just asking for information. Without abstract conceptualization, there was no recognition that "asks for information" and pausing and nodding while looking at someone had important similarities. Yet in concrete and historical terms, early investigators made remarkable strides figuring out methods of reliable observation and recording of behavior, and they developed research settings and operations that remain valuable.

The groups Bales observed closely from 1945 to 1954 have become so well known that such groups still are called Bales groups.[3] A Bales group has from two to (about) twenty members; it encompasses the range of sizes in which people can interact face to face and keep track of each other as distinct individuals (instead of, for instance, "members of the crowd" or "a fan club"). Bales and his research assistants would assemble groups, usually Harvard undergraduate volunteers, and would try to preserve complete records of their interaction by observing and recording (either in the same room or through a one-way mirror) *initiator*, *content*, and *recipient* of interaction. Initiation means a person speaks or makes a meaningful gesture such as looking expectantly at someone; recipient refers to the person to whom an initiation is directed. Content was scored according to a 12-category system,[4] including "asks for information," "gives suggestion," and "shows agreement."

Two obvious abstract features of Bales groups are that they are (1) task focused – they are given a problem to solve; and (2) collectively oriented – everyone must take everyone else's ideas into account.[5] In those two features, Bales groups resemble many common natural groups, such as committees, work teams, sport teams, and juries. Natural groups with a socio-emotional focus – cocktail parties, gossip sessions, and romantic liaisons – are different.

Observations by Bales and his assistants provide voluminous records of what happened during group meetings. Indeed, they probably come close to attaining Bales' goal of being able to reconstruct every significant occurrence during the meetings. The next piece of the puzzle is to develop understanding of the general form of the interaction. Many such attempts, seemingly promising at the time, did not in themselves succeed, though some gave rise to more successful efforts later.[6] One, Bales' "harmonic distribution model," describes a puzzle that many scholars returned to repeatedly over succeeding decades.

To describe patterns of interaction, nothing could seem more natural than an idea Bales and his associates worked with for several years in which they liken conversational patterns to ripples generated by a stone dropped into a still lake. A large ripple moves outward from where the stone dropped, followed by ripples of diminishing size until the water is still again. Metaphorically, if Person No. 1 directs an act (e.g. a question) to Person No. 2, there is a high probability, though not a certainty, that No. 2 then will direct an act to No. 1 (e.g. an answer); that generates another likelihood of an act from No. 1 to No. 2 (e.g. an evaluation or an agreement); and so on until the sequence plays out. Then a new sequence begins, and so it continues for the duration of the group meeting. Empirically, the number of initiations (acts) of the second-ranked individual would be half that of the first-ranked, the third-ranked would be half that of the second-ranked, and so on. Unfortunately, when this very plausible model was applied to data from 1,343 groups of sizes 3 through 8, its predicted patterns differed significantly from observations (Bales, Strodtbeck, Mills & Roseborough, 1951).

Though empirically unsuccessful, the harmonic distribution model had valuable consequences. It focused attention on how often each person participates as a significant fact, and the empirical test demonstrates that even plausible ideas need comparison with actuality before we conclude that we understand how the world really is. The broad question of how to create a theoretical description of the process by which interaction proceeds was certainly at the forefront of issues then – as it is today. As with an incomplete jigsaw puzzle, the vacant area was apparent and the general shape of the needed pieces was known; the challenge was to find pieces that fit in the existing field.

The remainder of this chapter is organized around some of the puzzles that prompted theoretical and empirical investigation in the six decades since 1950. To the investigators involved, the puzzles were deeply fascinating; I hope I am able to convey some of their passion in this outline of their intellectual history.

THE 1950s: INEQUALITY, ABSTRACTION, AND PERFORMANCE EXPECTATIONS

Joseph Berger, a graduate student of Bales, approached the study of small groups quite differently from his mentor. While Bales hoped to get a full understanding of groups "in the round," Berger wished to focus on features abstracted from observation, and to develop general propositions that would explain those features and predict novel features of similar situations.

Significant questions – at least to Berger – at the time included the following.

(1) What are the significant features of inequality in Bales-type discussion groups?
(2) What scope conditions are important for the inequality to appear?
(3) What theoretical propositions allow the inequality to be explained or predicted?
(4) [And later] What sort of empirical setting can be used to test novel predictions from theoretical ideas developed in answer to question No. 3?

Berger's approach begins with a widely known feature of Bales groups, though it had not then been conceptualized abstractly. Although group members start without noticeable differentiation – as Harvard undergraduates, they were alike on age, gender, skin color, educational level, SES, and virtually any other characteristic – they regularly developed a structure of inequality. That structure was evident in different measures, some behavioral (time talking, influence exerted, being chosen as leader) and some subjective (thought to have good ideas, seen as persuasive). So regular is the inequality in these groups that, after Berger described and analyzed it, has become known as one of the most reliable findings in social science. Inequality in Bales-type groups is:

• General; few groups do not show some differentiation after a short period (i.e. within the first 50 acts out of a typical 750 acts in a group).
• Transitive and reciprocal; ranking on any measure of inequality is regular, and where reciprocity is possible, such as speaking and being addressed, a person's rank on being addressed corresponds closely to her or his rank on speaking.
• Stable and persistent; once it emerges, the ranking tends to persist throughout the meeting, and at subsequent meetings if the group meets more than once.
• Consistent; the different kinds of inequality correlate highly with each other.

Berger's doctoral thesis (1958) proposed that those phenomena were produced by an underlying structure of *performance expectation states* (then called "expectation sets") that emerged during the interaction process. The thesis also lays out an abstract conception of interaction cycles: *action opportunities, performance outputs, unit evaluations*, and *agreement or disagreement*. Later (Berger & Snell, 1961) the concept *acceptance or rejection of influence* was added to the list of what is now called the "power and prestige structure" of the group. This perspective continues to guide theoretical research today (Fisek, Berger & Norman, 1995; Webster, Whitmeyer & Rashotte, 2003).

Expectation states are a theoretical construct, not completely defined explicitly nor directly observable, but having consequences that may be predicted and measured. For instance, the higher the relative expectations associated with one individual as compared to another, the more likely the first person is to attempt to solve a group's problem, the more likely his problem solving attempt is to receive positive evaluations and agreement, the less likely he is to accept influence in case of disagreement, and the more likely he is to enjoy all the subjective assessments such as perceived ability and leadership potential. Expectation states arise through interaction, primarily through differential participation rates and evaluation processes. Whatever results in positive evaluations increases the chances that high expectations will get associated with an individual, and whatever results in negative evaluations increases the chances that low expectations will become attached to him or her. Expectations are not necessarily conscious, though they may sometimes be accessed through questionnaires and interviews.[7]

Berger's work thus abstracts features of the interaction process, focusing on problem solving attempts, unit evaluations, agreements and disagreements, acceptance and rejection of influence, and choices for leadership positions. Other acts such as social and emotional responses are irrelevant, noise to the expectation formation process and behavioral features of interest.[8] This simplifying and abstracting approach directs attention to such questions as how to show expectation creation and governance of behavior, and how to understand the way the processes unfold. The first set of issues involves operations and measurement, and the second set involves modeling the process.

For observations, Berger developed an experimental design that came to be called the standard experiment for studying expectation (and later, status) processes.[9] The experiment creates the simplest possible situation in which these processes may occur: a group of two participants, one or more tasks with binary choices, and clear evaluative information. It require developing some new tasks unrelated to known tasks in order to remove effects of pre-existing expectations, and controlling interaction by using machines to slow down and limit the possible range of actions.

The standard experiment was developed with two phases corresponding roughly to introducing independent and measuring dependent variables. In phase 1, for instance, individuals may receive controlled evaluations to induce formation of expectation patterns; in phase 2, their expectations may be measured by introducing controlled disagreements and recording the proportion of disagreements resolved in favor of self, or $P(s)$, which directly reflects relative expectations.

By the end of the 1950s, the outlines of the standard experiment had been developed; it was used in experiments first reported by Camilleri and Berger (1967; see also Balkwell, 2001) and several tasks meeting various requirements had been developed for other experiments. Successive modeling attempts showed alternative ways to describe the formation and effects of performance expectations

(Berger & Conner, 1969, 1974; Berger, Conner & McKeown, 1969; Berger & Snell, 1961; Conner, 1966).

Theoretically, Berger's work provided the foundation for an abstract understanding of processes and structures evident in Bales groups. It treats the emergent inequality structure as the most significant feature of those groups, and seeks to understand facts and processes that lead to its creation, maintenance, and possible disintegration. In terms of the questions at the top of this section, by the end of the 1950s the picture included these parts.

(1) Discussion group inequality centered on task-focused interaction. It is manifested in interaction and perceptions that are highly intercorrelated and may be termed a group's *power and prestige structure*. Interaction components include *action opportunities, performance outputs*, positive and negative *unit evaluations*, and acceptance or rejection of *influence*. Perceptual elements include *estimations of social worth and importance, ability*, and *fitness for leadership*.

(2) Conditions for emergence of a power and prestige inequality structure include: *task focus, collective orientation*, and a *unitary group task*.

(3) Propositions were not fully developed at this stage, but it was clear that they centered about the basic sequence of interaction: an action opportunity appears, it might be followed by a performance output, which might be followed by a unit evaluation and influence.

(4) A standard experimental design first used by Camilleri and Berger (1967), with modification and development, continues to be useful. It simplifies a discussion group to give the clearest visibility to the assumed theoretical processes. For instance, the design used only two group members, the smallest size in which interaction and influence can occur, and individuals worked together on a series of problems. The design instantiates scope and initial conditions of the theory and permitted all the abstract features of interaction to occur.

THE 1960s: STATUS CHARACTERISTICS AND EXPECTATION STATES

Questions addressed in the 1960s appeared fairly simple and easier to answer than those formulated in the preceding decade. Yet some of them needed more than this one decade for satisfactory answers. They include:

(1) Can mathematical models represent the formation of performance expectation states? What benefits accrue from formulating such models?

(2) How can models represent observable behavior resulting from performance expectation states? What additional factors (besides expectations) would behavioral models need to incorporate?

(3) How do we understand the inequality process in heterogeneous groups, including

    (a) Does the inequality develop in the same way?

    (b) Are the inequality processes simpler or more complicated than they are for initially homogeneous groups?

This decade introduced the study of status characteristics and interaction, and a proliferation of theories using those concepts that continues today. Recall that individuals in the original Bales groups were unusually homogeneous in terms of virtually all noticeable characteristics. That is what makes the inevitable differentiation of those groups so notable. However in natural groups, wide diversity of membership is much more common. For instance, jurors or committee members differ in age, occupation, gender, educational level, skin color, and many other characteristics.

Heterogeneous groups also displayed power and prestige differentiation, and the differentiation quite predictably followed the differentiation on external characteristics. That is, if a characteristic (e.g. education) typically carries social advantages and disadvantages in society, those inequalities seemed to be "imported" to the face to face group. That effect had been widely reported (though with historical explanations unique to each group studied), and it appeared whether the characteristic was plausibly related to the task at hand (e.g. Air Force rank and visual perception; Torrance, 1954) or not (e.g. occupation and jury position; Strodtbeck, James & Hawkins, 1957; or skin color and arithmetic skill; Katz, Roberts & Robinson, 1965).

Two differences between homogeneous and heterogeneous groups are significant in the ways they develop power and prestige structures. First, in homogeneous groups, the structure may differentiate gradually, becoming apparent after five or ten minutes of discussion. Heterogeneous groups showed differentiation from the very outset of interaction. Whatever the process that creates power and prestige inequality in heterogeneous groups, it does not involve extended interaction sequences to develop. The second difference is that heterogeneous groups seldom develop the two types of leaders that Bales and others had thought were universal. In that view, the highest interactor, who was also the most influential (called "the task leader"), was generally not the best liked. That makes intuitive sense, for initiating problem solutions, evaluating others, and rejecting influence all can hurt others' feelings. In (homogeneous) Bales groups, the second-highest on interaction and influence usually was the best liked; Bales called this person the "social-emotional leader." Gordon Lewis (1972; see also Kadane & Lewis, 1969) showed that differentiation of task and social-emotional leaders, far from being universal, occurred only in initially homogeneous groups. In heterogeneous groups, the task leader is also the best liked, thus combining both types of leadership. In other words, when there is some external differentiating principle consistent with the internal power and prestige structure, group members do not seem to resent the power and influence exerted by the group leader as they do when the power and prestige inequality emerges from an initial state of equality. Homogeneous groups often display a "status struggle" in early stages, and several individuals attempt to attain positions of high interaction and influence. Status struggles usually are absent in initially differentiated, heterogeneous groups. The difference seems to be what later came to be called "legitimation": there was a "reason" why a person became leader, and hence, she or he is not resented in heterogeneous groups.

Findings from a wide range to heterogeneous groups working on many different tasks could be understood if we knew that actors formed expectations for each other consistent with their society's evaluation of their status characteristics. In 1966; Berger, Cohen and Zelditch presented a theory claiming that unless the relevance of a particular status characteristic is dissociated or successfully challenged as irrelevant to their task, they will treat it as relevant and associate expectations with themselves and each other consistent with their ranking on the status characteristic. This way of stating the claim is often called "burden of proof": the burden of proof is upon showing that a characteristic is *not* relevant to a task, rather than the other way around. The extended theory, called "status characteristics and expectation states theory," provided a single, coherent explanation for a large range of empirical findings. Status heterogeneous groups are much more common than homogeneous groups such as Bales studied.

In 1965, James C. Moore (published 1968) conducted the first experimental tests of the new ideas. He also developed some new tasks, and a way to create status differences in the laboratory that has been adapted for virtually all subsequent status experiments.[10] In Moore's studies, pairs of participants, both women from a junior (community) college entered the laboratory. Moore took care to prevent them from seeing each other, and when they were seated facing him but with a partition between them, he looked at both and said "I see we have two young women in our group today, one from California Junior College, and one from Stanford University." That sentence, from the point of view of each participant, created a status advantage for her partner. Contrasting high status conditions described one participant as a student at California High School. The salient status dimension might be called educational level or academic prestige. Moore's results showed that status, whether or not linked to the experimental task, created performance expectations as predicted.

That same year, Berger and colleagues began an ambitious set of experiments in a different setting, using a different status characteristic (Berger, Cohen & Zelditch, 1972). Those experiments were conducted in a laboratory constructed for the purpose in an unused building at Travis Air Force Base. While the cooperation and support of the Air Force were notable, still, conditions were hardly ideal. The Vietnam War was expanding and troop carrier planes took off every few minutes from a nearby runway. Even using microphones and headsets to read instructions for the experiment, experimenters often had to wait until the ambient noise level dropped enough for participants to hear. All participants were Air Force staff sergeants; the purported partner was Airman Third Class William Mason, Staff Sergeant William Mason, or Captain William Mason. Moore's manipulation created the status structures for the various conditions of the experiment, and again, results supported predictions. Thus we had information supporting the explanation for group structuring in heterogeneous groups. The extended theory was general; it was indifferent to the specific status characteristic or group task involved, so long as those met the definitions of the terms in the theory. Furthermore, the theory is indifferent to *which* characteristics a given society may treat as meeting the definition of a status characteristic. All societies seem to treat gender as status (and all favor men), but skin color may not universally be a status characteristic. In Israel, Ashkenazi or Sephardic ethnicity is a status characteristic (Yuchtmann-Yaar & Semyonov, 1979), though that distinction would attract little notice in the U.S. The point is that the theory does *not* claim that any particular characteristic is a status characteristic as defined; rather, it says that *if* a particular characteristic meets the definition of a status characteristic, certain behavioral consequences follow.

At the end of the 1960s, great strides in theoretical understanding and empirical techniques were evident. In terms of the questions at the start of this decade, knowledge had developed in these ways.

(1) Modeling expectation formation. The first model (Berger-Snell, 1961) was a Markov state model, and it still is consistent with our understanding of how interaction leads to formation of performance expectations in homogeneous groups. Among its features:
  (a) It uses the mathematical idea of "states," conditions having different observable manifestations. States are the five possible relative expectation relations: $(0\,0)$, $(+\,-)$, $(-\,+)$, $(+\,+)$, and $(-\,-)$.
  (b) Like all Markov models, prediction requires only knowledge of the immediately prior state and the transition probabilities. This keeps calculation (e.g. for a 25-trial experiment) to manageable size.

(c) The model was extensible, permitting variants (e.g. Berger, Conner & McKeown, 1969) for two- and three-person interaction situations.

(2) Modeling behavior. The Camilleri-Berger decision making model proved quite good at predicting influence behavior in the evolving experimental situation. Besides expectation states, it incorporates additional factors affecting behavior: desire for self-presentation (or self-consistency), desire to please the other group member, and desire to please the experimenter. These motives still are recognized, especially when the experimental design is used to study additional processes beyond expectations (as in Thye, 1999; Troyer, Younts & Kalkhoff, 2001, below), and in a behavioral translation model presented in 1977.

(3) For heterogeneous groups, the 1966 theory represents the general notion of status generalization, and the models describe expectation formation from external status differentiation without interaction sequences.

THE 1970s: THE GENERAL THEORY OF STATUS ORGANIZING PROCESSES AND SOME MODELS; NEW STATUS-RELATED PROCESSES; AND APPLIED RESEARCH PROGRAMS

By 1970, the generalization from expectation states theory to the theory of status characteristics and expectation states was well under way, and the basic process of status generalization was empirically documented. That success led to interest in using the processes for practical purposes. At the same time, theoretical puzzles remained.

Questions in this decade included:

(1) [Beyond the "big two"] Can the theory adequately predict features of mixed-race and mixed-gender interaction, such as interaction subordination and superiority?

(2) [Applied] How can the theory guide intervention for practical purposes?
  (a) What problems faced by ethnic minority children in classrooms can be addressed as status problems?
  (b) What interventions might be useful in correcting them?
  (c) How can the theory be used to analyze the Pygmalion Effect in classrooms (a widely discussed phenomenon in this decade)?

(3) [Theoretical] How can the theory be generalized to handle cases of two or more status characteristics simultaneously?

    (a) Do they combine?
        (i) If so, how? That is, what is the mathematical form of the combining process?
    (b) Or, do individuals eliminate one or more characteristic when possible?
        (i) If so, what conditions determine whether a characteristic is eliminated?
(4) [Theoretical] Is it useful to distinguish degrees of relevance among status characteristics; that is, are some more "relevant" to performance at the task and thus they have greater effect than others upon specific performance expectations?
    (a) If it proves useful to distinguish degrees of relevance, how can we modify the theory to do that?

Logically, though not always historically, theoretical development precedes instantiation and application, so we begin with that. Theoretically, the extraordinary achievement was the theory and model published by Berger, Fisek, Norman and Zelditch (1977) that constituted a great extension of the theory of status, and provided theoretical and behavioral models for analyzing status situations and predicting behavior. Because this work is well known, I will briefly describe its consequences for knowledge rather than explicating the theory. Wagner and Berger (2002) trace the ideas as they developed in a number of related theory groups.

The Problem of Combining Two or More Status Characteristics

As soon as the 1966 theory of status and expectations appeared, it was apparent to most investigators that the next task was to confront the more difficult question of multiple characteristics. How could we understand jury interaction between, say, a black woman physician and a white male laborer? As it happened, the theory was extended twice. In 1974, a provisional extension (Berger & Hamit Fisek, 1974) allowed for analyzing and predicting in conditions of two characteristics, and both of the characteristics could either equate actors (that is, they might both be high or both low on one), or differentiate them. It was not until 1977 that a satisfactory general theory appeared.

Complex status situations of two or more characteristics entail three major issues, and several smaller ones. Two significant problems are: (1) What is the general form of the combining process? and (2) is it possible (or necessary) to specify conditions under which combining takes a different form?

Multi-characteristic situations received considerable time and effort in the decade after the 1966 theory appeared. At that time, an idea common in the large literature on "status consistency" was that actors try to maximize their status by focusing on whatever status characteristics favor them and making other statuses irrelevant. Thus the hypothetical man above would try to emphasize skin color and gender, and the woman would try to emphasize occupation. In 1970, Berger and Fisek published results of an experiment in which pairs of actors were differentiated by two characteristics, C_1 and C_2. Either the focal actor was high on both while the partner was low on both (HH-LL), or the reverse (LL-HH), or one actor was high on C_1 and the other was high on C_2 (HL-LH). Results showed that resultant expectations, and thus behavior, were created by *both* characteristics; there was no evidence that actors selectively processed information to give themselves a status advantage. Thus theory extension efforts pursued the idea that all salient status information was combined; none ignored or eliminated.

A second experiment (Berger, Fisek & Crosbie, 1970) added two conditions to permit further examination of the maximization hypothesis, and they also create asymmetric status relations to explore whether there is something "special" about the symmetries of the first three conditions. Data for these new conditions were ordered in among the first three conditions, showing again that a simple combining mechanism accounts for the aggregate expectations formed.

A third and final experiment in this series (Berger & Hamit Fisek, 1974; Berger, Fisek & Freese, 1976) addressed the issue of how status generalization proceeds. In this one, actors were differentiated by a single characteristic (H-L) or (L-H), and the characteristic either was made directly relevant to the task, or its relevance was unspecified. In the first two conditions, the task used to create the status difference was said to be known as strongly related to the criterion task; in the latter two conditions, the relevance of the tasks was said to be unknown. Status generalization proceeded in all four conditions, but more strongly when direct relevance was induced.

Results from those three experiments enabled creation of the first generalization of the 1966 theory (Berger & Hamit Fisek, 1974). By comparison with the first theory, the 1974 theory:

- Handles either one or two consistent or inconsistent status characteristics simultaneously;
- Provides a consistent, general explanation for how any status characteristic – skill, gender, etc. – affects behavior through structures of performance expectations;
- Distinguishes directly relevant status information from information of unknown relevance, and predicts greater effects from the former.

In hindsight, the remaining shortcomings of the 1974 theory are easy to see; for instance, it handles only two characteristics at a time. However given the enormous influence of such ideas as status consistency, self-maximization and cognitive simplification in other areas of group process research, the view promoted in this extension – that all information is used, and combined, was hardly obvious, and it was surprising at the time.

The General Theory and Model

The third formulation appeared in 1977, and it represents an enormous advance over the 1966 and 1974 theories. It builds on the idea first presented in 1974, distinguishes diffuse and specific status characteristics, and it also permits analyzing and predicting behavior in status situations containing any number of both kinds. Further, it analyzes situations containing any number of actors, and some of the actors may be noninteracting, called "referent actors." Status situations may be symmetric or asymmetric, and actors may be linked to the criterion task in many ways having different, specific degrees of relevance.

Of special interest is a new idea on how multiple items of status information get processed to develop aggregate expectations, roughly comparable to the economic idea of diminishing marginal utility. Generally: (1) a single piece of inconsistent status information against a field of consistently evaluated states has greater effect than it would by itself; and (2) each additional consistently valued status element has less effect than the preceding element. Thus (1) a black woman college graduate gains more status from the educational level than a white male would; and (2) the effect of adding "college graduate" after already noting that someone is white, male, highly paid, and tall is less than that educational characteristic would have by itself. While the theory's aggregation mechanism is easy to understand, it is somewhat counter-intuitive, and is far from the only possible way status information might be combined.[11]

Along with the new theory, the 1977 book presents two models. The first is a graph model of the theory, usable to predict aggregate expectations associated with an individual in simple or complex status situations.[12] The second is a specific behavioral model applying only to antecedent conditions of the standard experiment. It translates expectations associated with individuals into influence rejection. Both models are widely used. They have been fruitful, in the sense of stimulating variants for different situations (e.g. Balkwell, 1991a, 2001; Fisek et al., 1995; Simpson & Walker, 2002).

In the first independent empirical test of the new theory, Webster and Driskell (1978) found good confirmation of the theory's precise predictions (quantitative rather than ordinal predictions), in an experiment in which actors were differentiated by race and ability in different combinations. Meeker and Weitzel-O'Neill (1977) showed that many advantages and disadvantages associated with gender were likely to be status effects rather than effects of different gender-linked socialization patterns.

The definitive assessment of the theory's combining mechanism (Berger, Norman, Balkwell & Smith, 1992) used a complicated 7-condition experiment, and data from 322 subjects. It compares four alternate models of status processing: the theory's aggregation mechanism; the elimination and maximization mechanism described above[13]; a consistency model in which each actor responds to the majority of characteristics she/he possesses; and a simple canceling model, in which the high state of one characteristic would cancel the low state of another, making both irrelevant to overall expectations. Results strongly supported the theory's aggregation mechanism, though it is neither the simplest nor the most intuitive mechanism.

Simplifying Assumptions Regarding Status Characteristics

The theory tells when status information will be salient, and it predicts that all salient status information will be used; none is ignored or eliminated. It treats all status information as equal in creating aggregate expectations, assuming there is no difference in relevance of the characteristics. Gender for instance, has the same effect on expectations as skin color, and beauty has the same effect as skill at a contrived laboratory task, assuming all have the same degree of task relevance. Further, status characteristics take only three values: relatively high, equal, and relatively low. That is, considering a pair of actors, one may be higher or lower than the other, or they may be equal; finer graded differences do not appear in the calculations.

Treating all status elements alike, and allowing them to take on only ordinal values, of course, mean that the theory's view of status structures is simpler than the way the world actually is. Those are simplifying assumptions, not claims about the world or any particular social system. To date, no strong reason exists to encourage making the theory more "realistic." The simplifications have not prevented the theory's making highly accurate predictions in complex situations. Without some predictive failure, efforts to "complicate" the theory have little payoff.

Balkwell (2001) thoroughly reviewed the question of using graded characteristics to modify the theory, and the effect such modification would have on its predictive success. His strong conclusion is that such modification, far from improving predictions, actually would reduce predictive success by any of the reasonable models he considered. Nothing in the theory denies that people *could* make finely graded status distinctions. The issue is whether they actually *do* make them in typical group circumstances, and Balkwell shows that they do not.[14]

A related issue, whether diffuse and specific status characteristics have equal effects on expectations, also merits attention. Freese and Cohen (1973), as well as Foddy and Smithson (1996, 1999) that Balkwell (2001) analyzed in detail, suggested that specific characteristics might be more "diagnostic." That is, specific characteristics generally refer to abilities, such as "Nobel Economist," or "CPA"; therefore we might expect them to more readily generalize to expectations for task abilities. On the other hand, Simpson and Walker (2002) argue that diffuse characteristics, being more enduring and generally carrying greater social definitions of worthiness, might be stronger. At present, there exists no persuasive evidence that the theory needs any such modification to improve prediction, though related efforts to find a useful modification may continue.

Are status characteristics equal? Of course they are not. It is possible to find situations where, say, gender matters much more than skin color, or vice versa. The theory does not treat all characteristics as equal in cases such as differing relevance (e.g. gender typing of tasks), or when goal objects are associated with the characteristics. Yet for simple cases where those effects do not occur, the theory has not been modified to reflect differential emphasis because it has done so well at predicting behavior – in other words, there has been no need to do so, if the criterion is accurate prediction. If one wanted to modify the theory to satisfy an esthetic preference for realism, a host of new problems would appear, high among them, stating conditions under which the significance of a particular status characteristic changes. *When* does color matter more than, say, gender or accounting expertise; that is, under what abstract conditions or in what abstractly-defined types of social systems? If the significance of a characteristic differs according to as yet unknown conditions, what about the combining mechanism? Is it particularly disadvantageous to be a black woman in some kinds of systems, and are there other systems in which there is no disadvantage to being a woman so long as one is a white woman? Absent predictive failures, theoretical complication would entail large costs in complexity.

New Research Programs

During the 1970s, status researchers developed independent research programs at several institutions. The investigations proceeded independently, often with coordination and almost always with consultation among the various researchers. That semi-independent pattern proved to be a good one for stimulating and pursuing new directions while taking advantage of technological developments, theoretical advances, and cumulative findings from different subject populations at different locations.

Sources of Self-Evaluation

In 1967, Webster and Sobieszek began a series of sequential experimental studies of conditions under which actors incorporate outside evaluations into their own expectation states; that is, when do they use external evaluations and when they ignore them? This work has relevance to questions of self esteem, a more global concept that attracted considerable attention at that time.[15] This research program adapted ideas on Significant Others, a terms originally used by the psychiatrist Harry Stack Sullivan (1947) to mean someone whose opinions were particularly important to a growing child. While Sullivan did not specify abstract characteristics for qualifying as a significant other, so far as performance expectations were concerned, it seemed likely that having high ability to do the task would be one important qualification.

The source program showed that evaluations coming from an actor thought to have high ability to do the task are influential, whether the evaluator's ability is based on test scores or on status characteristics. If an actor has low ability or low status, he or she is likely to be ignored. The acceptance process is simple; there is no tendency to maximize the self-concept by selectively using evaluations, and the evaluative information from multiple sources is combined according to the theory's aggregation proposition. Results of the source program are collected in a book (Webster & Sobieszek, 1974), and some more recent research is reported by Ilardi and McMahon (1988).

The Webster-Sobieszek program led to a program of applied research by Doris Entwisle and Webster (see Entwisle, 1978; Entwisle & Webster, 1974). The researchers set out to show that the source of evaluations process operates in elementary school classrooms, and that it can produce self-fulfilling prophecies when a teacher's high or low expectations for a student later translate into consistent performance by the student.[16] Entwisle and Webster showed that it was possible to intervene using the evaluation – expectation process to raise selected children's expectations.

Multiple Standards for Evaluation

Martha Foschi and her many students have studied the development and operation of standards for judging success and failure; a detailed summary and overview is Foschi (2000). The overall concern is with situations where individuals are treated with differing standards depending on who they are, especially when all individuals provide the same evidence regarding the attribute being assessed.

Elizabeth Cohen's Applied Program

Beginning in the 1960s, Elizabeth G. Cohen and her many students and colleagues developed and elaborated a program applying ideas of status generalization to elementary school classrooms.[17] This program differs from the more modest and analytic program of Entwisle and Webster in that it is more heavily focused on outcomes. Cohen began with an interest in finding ways to reduce the "interracial interaction disability" seen in many classrooms, and marked by a lack of participation and influence by children with a status disadvantage. Her research led her to develop a number of effective treatments, including

- Role determination. Designating disadvantaged children as "teachers" and advantaged as "learners," and having the teachers explain something to learners.
- Multiple abilities. Emphasizing that task completion requires a variety of different skills, and it would be unrealistic to expect that anyone will have them all, or that anyone will lack them all.
- Norms. Requiring all members of task groups to participate, and to evaluate their own and each others' contributions, both positively and negatively, as appropriate.

Cohen has also suggested modifications in the structure of classroom instruction, and participatory learning, and she has implemented them in schools in the U.S. and several other countries. One finding not directly predicted by the theory is that increasing participation of all children leads to higher scores on standardized tests – an outcome perhaps of greater interest to school administrators than any precise theoretical analysis of classroom interaction. The research program continues (a recent summary is Cohen & Lotan, 1997).

When Cohen began her work in the 1960s, little was known theoretically about status processes. From the insight that classroom disadvantages were linked to performance expectations, Cohen began investigating ways to overcome them, and that led her to the idea of adding on additional characteristics to compensate for ethnic disadvantage. All of this predated appearance of the first theory treating multiple characteristics (Berger & Hamit Fisek, 1974), and Cohen's work was crucial in guiding the way that theory developed.

A second major intellectual contribution of Cohen's work was evident by the end of the 1970s. Theory development had not been directly concerned with developing applications and interventions as Cohen was, and it was not clear whether classroom analogues could be developed that would have some of the same effects as laboratory manipulations. But beyond that, neither the theory nor laboratory experience gave clear reason to expect that intervening in the status generalization process would affect factors that educators recognized as important. Thus when Cohen was able to show improvements in test scores as the result of her work, she tapped into something educators understood and cared deeply about, and that demonstration was crucial in obtaining the support and access needed for much of her applied research program (Cohen, 1988).

Returning to the questions at the top of this section, understanding had developed by the end of the 1970s in these ways:

(1) Webster and Driskell (1978) and Meeker and Weitzel-O'Neill (1977) showed that significant features of mixed-race and mixed-gender interaction varied in ways predictable from the theory of status characteristics and expectation states.
(2) Elizabeth G. Cohen showed that the general theory was useful in understanding many features of what she came to call "interracial interaction disability." She also developed many successful interventions, some of which were rigorously based on the theory (e.g. using multiple characteristics to overcome problems) and some of which went beyond strict derivations from the theory (activating countervailing norms of participation). The Entwisle-Webster research program explicated the mechanism behind the Pygmalion Effect: action opportunities and unit evaluations differentially directed towards some students; and resulting changes in their self-expectations that led to increased likelihoods of accepting action opportunities and making performances attempts.
(3) A fully general theory for multiple characteristics was achieved with the 1977 version.
(4) Degrees of relevance, taken up in the 1974 theory, also was resolved at the 1977 version. Up through the conduct of the Travis experiments (Berger et al., 1972), most thinking was that status characteristics would have identical effects if (1) they simply became salient; (2) they were culturally defined as relevant in "most cases"; and (3) they were known relevant in the immediate specific case. However in the 1977 version of the theory, those cases were seen to have increasing degrees of effect on performance expectations: (1) < (2) < (3).[18]

THE 1980s: INSTANTIATION, REWARD
EXPECTATIONS AND LEGITIMACY

Theoretical and empirical efforts continued into the next decade, but what most characterizes the 1980s, I think, is proliferation of topics addressed using the general perspective. Prominent questions in this decade included:

(1) What other socially important characteristics besides "the big two" of race and gender might usefully be treated as diffuse or specific status characteristics?

(2) What other elements of social life besides performance do individuals form expectations for? Rewards? Legitimacy?

(3) When do individuals treat a power and prestige structure as legitimate; that is, treat the particular form of inequality as right and proper?

    (a) How does a structure acquire legitimacy? How does a legitimate structure lose legitimacy?

    (b) What behavioral and other consequences follow when a structure acquires legitimacy? When it loses legitimacy?

Thus much work on status processes in the 1980s explored and developed ideas implied by the 1977 theory. However some work went off in new directions and some of these new paths proved to be fruitful. This work addresses topics beyond the original domain addressed by status generalization processes, enlarging the range of application of ideas and principles to deal with new issues. Proliferant theories, formulated within the same family of concepts and principles, do not conflict; they address different issues, so they ask and answer different questions. Their foci differ. In this section I describe two bodies of proliferating work, reward expectations and legitimate group structures.

Reward Expectations

Structured groups often involve not only performance but rewards of one type or another: wage and salary differences are common instances. In such groups, individuals typically come to anticipate certain levels of reward allocations for themselves and others, much as they typically anticipate certain levels of performance. In other words, they develop reward expectations from processes analogous to the processes developing performance expectations. Berger, Fisek, Norman and Wagner (1985) presented a theory of reward expectations that argued, essentially, that group members will come to expect that their relative rankings on reward allocations will correspond to their rankings on performance capacity: the most capable person is expected to receive the greatest reward, the next most capable receives the second-ranked allocation, and so on.

Without going deeply into the structure or implications of this theory, we should note that it relies on an idea that reward expectations and performance expectations are interrelated. Change in one should, thus, entail change in the other. If someone's performance improves, she/he will come to expect improved rewards. A bit less obvious is the reverse process, which will figure in theoretical developments up through the present decade: if someone's rewards improve, that person and others have a tendency to infer higher performance expectations for him or her. Indeed, when this theory was formulated, an experimental study by Cook (1975) had already shown that giving differential rewards (payments) to participants created differentiated performance expectations – high expectations for those highly paid, low for those receiving low pay.

The theory of reward expectations grew out of an earlier conceptualization of what were called "distributive justice processes," usually analyzed in exchange theory terms in the 1960s and 1970s. Berger, Zelditch, Anderson and Cohen (1972) analyzed the exchange view and identified four problems with it:

(1) It does not conceptualize status value – distinct from consummatory value – such as honors, reserved parking places, flat-screen computer monitors, and corner offices.
(2) There is no unique and precise conception of justice. Thus small differences, e.g. in weekly wages, often have great importance to those involved.
(3) There also is no unique and plausible conception of injustice. Actors need a social comparison that came to be called a *referential structure* describing relations between characteristics and outcomes in the external world before justice comparisons become possible.
(4) There is no way to explain either the sources of justice feelings, or the strong moral feelings regarding injustice. How can it happen, for instance, that *both women and men* can sometimes feel it is fair for men to be paid more (Jasso & Rossi, 1977)? With a referential structure, normative feelings become understandable; what *is* in the larger world *ought to be* in the local system.

Next, they developed the alternative status-value theory of justice processes that incorporated a referential structure. The 1972 theory included "goal objects" rather than "rewards" to emphasize the significance of status aspects of justice. An experimental study by Webster and Smith (1978) showed good evidence for the new theory. Continuing work on justice processes has led to a theory of how status processes can lead to the construction of referential structures (Berger, Ridgeway & Zelditch, 2002).

Both the idea of status value and the need for a stable comparison structure are incorporated in the 1985 theory of reward expectations. Stable comparisons appear importantly in theories of legitimate and illegitimate group structures, to which we turn next. The reward expectation process and status value of goal objects also are key in theories of how status characteristics get constructed (Ridgeway, 1991, 2000).

Legitimate Social Structures

Several scholars in group processes, as well as scholars from other areas of social science, have investigated what makes social structures legitimate, conditions under which legitimacy is conferred and lost, and effects of legitimacy in social relations.

Zelditch and Walker (1984) showed that it is useful to consider three elements of structures, actors, positions, and behaviors, each of which can be a separate object of legitimacy concerns. Legitimate exercise of power, which means in accord with group norms, gives a powerful actor greater likelihood of inducing compliance, and entails less need for coercive power. Compliance is voluntary given consent of the governed, even when a particular individual might prefer not to comply. By increasing the likelihood of compliance, legitimacy increases a group's stability.

Zelditch and Walker added the important idea that *validity*, collective support of others for the norms promoting compliance, is essential to generate legitimacy. By contrast, individual level belief in the structure was neither necessary nor sufficient to produce legitimacy. Thus, the collective nature of legitimacy was established, as opposed to a basis in individuals' value systems. People comply, and believe they should comply, when they also believe others hold values supporting compliance – and not usually otherwise. With legitimation, status positions based on performance expectations acquire a moral quality such that behavior inconsistent with those positions becomes "outrageous," something "that should not happen." Thus in a legitimate structure, a low status person who does not comply, or a high status person who does not direct, is behaving inappropriately, and is likely to incur social sanctions aimed at restoring a consistent relationship between position and behavior.

Building on Zelditch and Walker's (1984) work, Ridgeway and Berger (1986) and Ridgeway (1989) showed that the extent to which group members treat a status order as legitimate affects the type of power used, as well as the overall need to use power to effect compliance.

Next, they considered how a status order acquires a sense of legitimacy, or fails to do so. The key to understanding legitimation processes in Ridgeway and Berger's theory is to see status position as a reward for whose distribution individuals develop expectations. They come to believe, for instance, that someone for whom high expectations are held in the larger social setting *ought to* also receive the goal object of high status. When such beliefs are consensual in a group, its power and prestige structure has acquired legitimacy. The legitimation process thus is a reward expectation process, requiring a stable referential structure linking status characteristics with social position. If individuals believe that, in general, the world grants high social position to those making more task contributions and withholds social position from those making few contributions, then once a structure of performance expectations arises in their group, individuals will come to see a congruent status structure as legitimate, and any deviation from congruence in the status structure as illegitimate.

An interesting consequence of this theory is the following. In all kinds of groups, the expectation-based power and prestige structure is created by the same status generalization mechanism. Thus we might expect that individuals in all kinds of groups would use performance-based arguments to justify the status structure or the reward structure. However they are more likely to do that when their status order has acquired legitimacy. Thus legitimacy has additional consequences, most significantly, the generation of norms justifying and objectifying the status order. In simple terms, people refer to understandings that certain positions "ought to" go to certain people and certain rewards "ought to" go to certain positions. Emergent norms make the status order explicit, clearly pointing out to everyone the basis for it in performance competence. Norm emergence appears to be fostered by repeated, patterned, interaction inequality, and by occasional norm violations requiring correction.

Berger, Ridgeway, Fisek and Norman (1998) returned to issues of legitimate structures, seeking to specify conditions that foster and other conditions that weaken legitimacy of status structures. They developed a more comprehensive theoretical understanding of how structures may either acquire or lose legitimacy. Their approach is a multi-level theory that uses cultural information (referential structures) to provide social validation (legitimacy) of group hierarchies. It emphasizes the status value of legitimacy, including the honorific significance of status structures and of deference. This constitutes a considerable expansion of scope, and the general theory accounts for a wide range of phenomena; among them, the stability of legitimate structures, the impact of evaluations on de-legitimation, and effects of status consistency and inconsistency on legitimacy processes. The theory includes derivation of six theorems, each having several parts, and those theorems could generate a host of testable hypotheses for different kinds of social structures. The derivations await empirical assessment.

Returning to the questions at the beginning of this section and this decade:

(1) Documented status characteristics included:
   (a) Beauty is a diffuse status characteristic (Webster & Driskell, 1983).
   (b) Reading ability, local popularity, and participating in a school lunch program are instances of specific status characteristics (Cohen & Lotan, 1997).

(c) Johnson (1995) theorized that sexual orientation (heterosexual or homosexual) often was a diffuse status characteristic, an idea confirmed empirically by Webster, Hysom and Fullmer (1998).

(2) Extending the theory of status processes to include reward expectations was contemplated as early as the 1960, but the 1985 theory of reward expectations was the first satisfactory link of performance expectations and reward expectations. The "reverse process" (Berger et al., 1985, pp. 251–252; Cook, 1975) by which differentially distributed goal objects can affect performance expectations, became more important than was anticipated at the time, especially as a fundamental mechanism in the construction of status characteristics (Ridgeway, 1991, 2000).

(3) The theory of legitimacy that several scholars contributed to in the 1980s predicts that structures in which the power and prestige position is consistent with performance expectation states will be treated as legitimate by participants and will be stable, and deviations from that condition will be treated as not legitimate and will be unstable.

THE 1990s: MODELING STATUS PROCESSES, RELATED PROCESSES, AND THE CONSTRUCTION OF STATUS CHARACTERISTICS

The final decade of the 20th century was marked by posing some puzzles that proved more difficult than almost anyone anticipated at the time. These include developing mathematical models, using the approach to investigate auxiliary processes, and understanding the fundamental processes by which status is created and diffused throughout a population. Some questions investigated included:

(1) How can a dynamic model be constructed to represent the creation and maintenance of power and prestige structures in either homogeneous or heterogeneous groups?
   (a) What benefits – new derivations, new processes, improved predictions, reduced indeterminacy – make new models desirable?
(2) What makes *status* characteristics in particular societies? That is, how do characteristics acquire invidious qualities and performance significance?
   (b) Once a characteristic acquires status significance, how does its new meaning spread through a social system?
(3) What other processes may be triggered by status generalization? For instance, how do status processes affect the inference and assignment of personality traits to self and others?

Skvoretz and Fararo's E-State Structural Model

This work matured in the 1990s; precursors can be found as early as Skvoretz (1981), continuing through refinements and extensions (Fararo & Skvoretz, 1986, 1988; Fararo, Skvoretz & Kosaka, 1994; Skvoretz, 1985; Skvoretz & Fararo, 1996; Skvoretz, Webster & Whitmeyer, 1999).

John Skvoretz and Thomas Fararo set themselves the tasks of developing alternate models of status organizing processes in groups, including returning to Fisek's concerns with emergence of structure in large groups. Their work relies on two main means by which such groups develop power and prestige structures: externally, from status differentiation, and internally, through behavior patterns. Thus their models apply to both homogeneous and heterogeneous groups. They focus on group structure, measured by participation rates using unobserved "e-states" having the same properties as expectation states in status organizing theories. Interestingly, the models were elaborated and modified from earlier models constructed for animal groups: chickens (Chase, 1980, 1982), macaques (Barchas & Mendoza, 1984) and other primates (Mazur, 1973, 1985).[19]

Three virtues of Skvoretz-Fararo model are (1) it is fully dynamic, modeling the process of status evolution as well as its outcome; (2) it applies readily to groups of any size; and (3) it incorporates Chase's "bystander effect" that becomes particularly significant in larger groups. Being able to apply the model to groups of any size often makes it simpler to use than the 1977 theory and model of status generalization, which requires pairwise comparisons of individuals in order to predict behavior. The Skvoretz-Fararo model predicts interaction rates for all ordered actors in a group. The bystander effect has some similarities to referent actors in the 1977 general theory, but bystanders form expectation states, while referent actors do not (or at least the theory is indeterminate as to the question of whether referent actors form expectation states).

The model's bystander effect predicts expectation formation (or e-state formation) by an actor who does not himself interact, but who witnesses interaction among others. The bystander effect predicts an initial value of "average" for one's own expectations, and allows that to be modified either by interaction or by witnessing others' interaction patterns. In twelve-person jury, one or more individuals are unlikely ever to participate much in the deliberation. However according to this model, they would form expectations based on their observations of others.

Two empirical consequences of the bystander effect are derivable, one now empirically confirmed and the second at present untested. The confirmed effect is that the bystander effect promotes group structuring faster than would occur without it (Skvoretz et al., 1999). (Without the bystander effect, structure emerges fully only when every group member has interacted and thereby formed expectation states.)

The other implication of the bystander effect is intriguing. Imagine a large group in which one or two people participate never or hardly at all. Those who never participate have no influence on the group discussion and they rank at the bottom of the power and prestige structure. We might infer therefore that they hold the lowest self-expectations in the group, because expectations are the main factor affecting participation rates. However the bystander parameter in the Skvoretz-Fararo model takes "average" as the initial e-state for an individual. Because non-participating individuals have witnessed actors influencing each other, the bystanders will, according to the model, form e-states for themselves intermediate to the e-states they associate with influential and non-influential interactants. In other words, from participation rates alone we would predict very low expectations for bystanders; from the Skvoretz-Fararo model, we would predict intermediate expectations for them. That differentiating prediction awaits empirical assessment.

Balkwell's Model Transforming Expectations to Behavior

Many investigators have extended status and expectation state explanations to a wide range of phenomena. James Balkwell (1991a) developed an alternate model for translating expectations to behavior.

Balkwell's model uses behavior increments, a theoretical continuous variable, from a baseline of behavior output at the theoretical point where an actor's expectations are perfectly unknown. The model itself is abstract, and it may be instantiated with any sort of behavior. Balkwell showed how the model might be instantiated for three kinds of situations: the influence behavior measured among dyads in the standard experimental design, participation rates in homogeneous (Bales) groups, and participation in heterogeneous groups. With appropriate interpretations for each setting, Balkwell shows that his model predicts outcome behavior very well in all three kinds of settings. More generally, Balkwell's model provides a single, consistent, theoretically derived way to apply theories of status processes across diverse kinds of behavior and social settings. It requires no discontinuity between dyads and larger groups, and it conforms to intuitive ideas about how individuals perceive each other and process status information.

Behavior Interchange Patterns and Social Positions

The same year Balkwell presented his translation model, Fisek, Berger and Norman (1991) also undertook to integrate status and behavior processes within a single theoretical formulation and model. This work has some similarities with Balkwell's, and each approach has some unique features. Balkwell's translation model could be interpreted for almost any kind of power and prestige behavior, while Fisek et al.'s model is best suited to participation in discussion groups. On the other hand, Fisek et al. incorporate ideas about reward expectations and legitimation that are absent in Balkwell's model. For cases within the scope of both models, both provide excellent fits to data.

A later undertaking by Fisek, Berger and Norman (1995) integrates ideas from the source theory program of Webster and Sobieszek (1974) described above with ideas on status generalization. This effort also introduces a new element, "valued role," to the basic status generalization graph model. Another new theoretical idea in this model became significant for theories of second-order expectations described below. It is the idea of variable line lengths in status diagrams, which, of course, will affect the lengths of paths containing such lines. Fisek et al. used variable line lengths to represent possession of a characteristic that is less than certain; for instance, based upon an evaluator's claims. Since the evaluator is likely but not certain to be right, the possession line is longer – "weaker" – than it would be if the interactant knew for certain that she/he possessed the ability level the source announces.

Gerber's Study of Personality Attributions among Police

Gwendolyn Gerber (1996, 2001) studied two-person police car teams in New York City over several years. Among other accomplishments, she documented how police form impressions of each other at work, and how status relations affect the personalities they attribute to themselves and others.

Police officers regard gender and longevity on the force as especially significant characteristics. In a two-person mixed gender team, the woman would take the lower status position. In a same-gender team, the person newer to the force was lower status. From discussion group and other research involving open interaction situations, we know that status differences affect not only the amount of participation, but also the kinds of participation individuals display. Among other differences, high status people tend to pro-act in task-focused categories of interaction; low status people tend to react in social-emotional categories. Furthermore, the levels and kinds of interaction tend to change as a person moves from a situation of, say, low status into another situation where she/he has a status advantage. Thus these behaviors are functions of status position rather than of some more enduring traits or innate differences among people.

Gerber's insight was that those different behaviors, predictable from an officer's status position in a team, will be noticed and interpreted by them. Police tend not, however, to see the behaviors as outcomes of status processes, but rather as cues to the "personalities" of the individuals involved. That is, the officers themselves see these behaviors as revealing "what type of person I am" or "what type my partner is." So when the officers are asked to characterize themselves and their partners, they may say things like: [higher status officer] "I tend to rush in and take charge, giving orders, controlling the situation. My partner is more sympathetic and understanding, and he helps people deal with their feelings in these situations."

What Gerber saw and documented is no less than watching the social creation of people, as they develop ideas about who they are and who their partners are. Status differences produce patterns of behavior, those patterns are noticed by the officers but are coded as cues to personality types, and they thus form conclusions about what sort of person each of them is.

Constructing Status Characteristics

Probably everyone who works with status characteristics has wondered at some time what gives them their special social significance. Why do people attach such importance to gender, occupational prestige, skin color, or age of others? The question arises most pointedly when an investigator is documenting undeserved interaction benefits or disabilities based on status. Often status generalization processes are undesirable, socially and morally, and a concern with them often is part of an interest in finding ways to reduce or eliminate their status significance.

In most cases the question is not about conscious prejudice, for generally we do not think people reason, for instance, "I am a woman and he is a man, and therefore he probably understands this jury case better than I do." Thus it would give little useful information simply to ask people why they think gender or skin color has status significance. But the question remains.

Cecilia Ridgeway, in a series of theoretical and empirical papers, develops a theory of the construction of status characteristics (Ridgeway, 1991, 1997a, b, 2000; Ridgeway & Balkwell, 1997; Ridgeway, Boyle, Kuipers & Robinson, 1998; Ridgeway & Erickson, 2001).

In outline, Ridgeway's approach uses ideas from reward expectations theories to show that process is sufficient to create status value. If a social system contains two or more distinct groups of individuals, and two or more distinct levels of social rewards, and if, further, individuals observe a more or less regular association of certain types of people with certain levels of rewards, that process will suffice to add status value to the characteristics of the people. To say the same thing less abstractly, if people notice that men regularly receive higher pay than women, they will treat the association as somehow causal: "There must be some reason for it," and that reason must be that men are more deserving. Thus Ridgeway's theory posits a way in which differential rewards can attach evaluative and moral significance to characteristics of people.

The process is effective and will diffuse without a strong relationship; it is not necessary for all or even most members of one group to receive greater rewards. A surprisingly small discrepancy, however, acts as an "engine" that continually creates and reinforces the status construction. Ordinary interaction causes status beliefs to diffuse rapidly throughout a system (Ridgeway & Balkwell, 1997).

Inspired by Ridgeway's path-breaking work, Webster and Hysom (1998) sought to generalize the theory by tracing other means by which status characteristics can be created. They showed, for instance, that the reward expectations theory posits a more general process than Ridgeway had identified up to that point. The favored group need not receive more exchangeable rewards such as money; status valued rewards such as esteem will also work. Thus some status characteristics that we do not usually think of as linked to money, such as beauty and sexual orientation, can be created through regular association with differential levels of esteem. A second generalization shows that behavior patterns of influence and deference can create status characteristics even in absence of any material or status-valued rewards.

A very illuminating analysis by Ridgeway (1997b) shows how gender produces and then reproduces patterns of inequality in business organizations. This analysis is particularly valuable because it shows how gender inequality can persist and spread even in the face of laws prohibiting it and in the absence of intentional sexism. Mueller, Mulinge and Glass (2002) applied Ridgeway's analysis of the conservation of gender inequality to agricultural workers in Kenya, and found evidence for the processes Ridgeway analyzed. They found, for instance, that women field workers (who seldom work side by side with men) did not encounter the sorts of status disadvantages experienced by women who worked as nominal equals with men in a research institute (office or laboratory setting). The latter group of women might be expected to show disadvantages of status generalization processes, as they contrast with male co-workers. By contrast, field workers usually do not appear in mixed-gender groups, and so their gender would not become *salient* in theoretical terms. Thus, they experience fewer or no such status disadvantages.

To the questions posed above:

(1) Three dynamic models of status processes developed during the 1990s: the Balkwell (1991b) model, the Skvoretz-Fararo (1996) model, and the

Fisek-Berger-Norman (1995) model. All account well for the process of status ordering, and all yield determinate empirical derivations for test.

(2) Status construction theory accounts for the creation of status characteristics through the regular association of a nominal (unevaluated) characteristic with differential levels of goal objects (Ridgeway, 2000).

(3) Gerber (2001) showed how interaction patterns that are created by status inequality get interpreted as revealing dispositions. Thus status-based interaction patterns turn into personality attributions.

THE NEW CENTURY: EXTENDING THE THEORY AND INTEGRATING ADDITIONAL GROUP PROCESSES – CUES, SECOND-ORDER EXPECTATIONS, SENTIMENTS, AND POWER

In the first decade of the 21st century, research involving status processes appears to be entering a mature period of normal science. By that I mean the work is salient in research of diverse groups of sociologists, including those who never do it, those who occasionally do it, and those of us who mainly who do it. For the second group of sociologists, status process research occupies some of their efforts, and other research topics occupy the rest of their efforts. For the largest group, the majority of sociologists whose primary interests lie elsewhere, status research has become recognized; its outlines are known and accepted as a significant part of the study of group processes. It is part of the intellectual landscape of 21st century sociology. By this decade's end, there will surely be more puzzles, more provisional answers, and more clarity on the big picture of what we know.

Elaboration: Status Cues

Berger, Webster, Ridgeway and Rosenholtz (1986) introduced the term "status cues" to name the markers or identifiers people use to recognize the statuses we possess. Status cues are divided into "categorical," identifying social categories such as female, white, college graduate, and "task," identifying behaviors signifying skill or lack thereof at the group work, such as verbal latency, eye gaze, and posture. Cues are divided into "indicative," overt claims to possess a characteristic, such as "I am a physician," and "expressive," requiring inference on the part of an observer, such as inferring ethnicity from dialect of a telephone voice.

The questions leading to the statement on cues include such issues as how individuals recognize the status characteristics they possess – in other words, how do differentiating characteristics become salient in a group – and why do the same people often behave quite differently (in terms of status-relevant actions) in different settings – for instance, why many women speak more softly with more verbal qualifiers and hedges in mixed gender groups than they do in groups of all women?

Quite a few empirical studies (including Balkwell & Berger, 1996; Ridgeway, Berger & Smith, 1986; Sev'er, 1989; Tuzlak, 1988; Tuzlak & Moore, 1984), show interactions of status, cues, and group structures. The intervening factor appears to be expectation states, which are affected by levels of all sorts of cues and in turn, affect the production of task cues. Remaining questions include

(1) Whether all types of cues are equally effective at affecting expectations, or whether, for instance, task cues have greater effects than categorical cues. If cues are added to status graphs as additional elements, it seems reasonable that task cues would be relevant either to specific ability (C^*) or to task success or failure (T). Categorical cues would be relevant to activating states of D's or C's, which would then connect to T through status generalization – through induced intervening elements Γ or τ. If that is the they way cues work, then paths for categorical cues would be longer than those for task cues, and hence, categorical cues would have weaker effects on individuals' aggregate expectations.

(2) How individuals process inconsistent cues; for example, when a person pounds on the table and shouts (expressive cues), "I am *not* angry!" (indicative cue). Many writers in the symbolic interaction tradition would conclude that expressive cues are more informative, perhaps because they seem to be less under conscious control. That conjecture, along with specification of necessary conditions, awaits empirical confirmation.

Elaboration: Second-Order Expectations

James C. Moore (1985) proposed the term "second-order expectations" for known opinions of others; illustrated in phrases such as "I know you think you can do this task better than I can, but I have no opinion about that as yet." That formulation leads to the question of how and under what conditions expressed second-order expectations become accepted and incorporated into one's own ("first-order") expectations. Moore showed that one mechanism for acceptance was being required to act in accord with the second-order beliefs; for instance, being required to accept leadership because the other person was unwilling to do so.

Lisa Troyer and her students (Troyer & Younts, 1997; Troyer, Younts & Kalkhoff, 2001) pursued this general topic, adding theoretical ideas and empirical confirmation. In their view, second-order information is most useful when it contradicts other information such as the distribution of status characteristics in a situation. For instance, if a focal person possesses the high state of some status characteristic, mechanisms of status generalization will cause that person to form high self-expectations. Second-order information contradicting that becomes salient new information, and it therefore gets aggregated with the expectations formed from the status advantage.

Webster and Whitmeyer (1999) developed a theory making explicit some of the links in the presumed chain of how second-order information is used, and along the way, they modified some of the ideas in Moore's work. We borrowed the idea of variable line lengths developed by Fisek et al. (1995) to represent the effect of second-order information in status graphs. Results of experimental tests of the Webster-Whitmeyer model (Webster, Whitmeyer & Rashotte, 2003) confirm the predicted ordering of conditions.

Meanwhile, Fisek, Berger and Moore (2002) have analyzed several more studies conducted by Moore and his colleagues. Their data show good support for their model, although they are about equally well represented by the Webster-Whitmeyer model. While there are some differences in detail among the three lines of research, overall they show comparable effects of expressed opinions from a co-interactant. Differentiating predictions are matters of precision.

In the work on second-order expectations, the meaning of the term has changed from its meaning in Moore (1985). Recent work actually studies the effect of communicated opinions, or imputations, from an interacting partner. What that partner actually thinks (more precisely, the expectations that partner actually holds) is irrelevant; this theory and research studies effects of communication from others having various characteristics. However in just a few years, our understanding of the process has improved considerably.

Integration: Power and Position

Shane Thye (1999, 2000; also see Willer, Lovaglia & Markovsky, 1997) has pioneered in bringing together ideas from theoretical studies of power and status processes. *Power*, generally understood to mean the ability to exact behavioral compliance, is often distinguished from *influence*, meaning the ability to induce another person *willingly* to behave in a certain way; Willer et al. (1997) make that distinction, and Thye uses it in his work. One behavioral consequence of status and expectation processes is influence; that is, getting compliance with one's suggestions because others accept them as correct. And one of the behavioral consequences of occupying a "strong" position in network bargaining experiments is power; that is, getting others to accept less favorable divisions of points or winnings than they otherwise would accept. How do status processes and structural power position interact? At present, only some of the questions in this line of investigation have confirmed answers.

Thye's experimental results showed that high status subjects won greater resources than low status; that goods (poker chips) held by high status subjects were valued more highly than if held by low status subjects; and that high status subjects were more frequently chosen as preferred exchange partners than low status subjects. What those studies show is that status gets translated into power; that is, that actors who have a status advantage seem also to get a power advantage. The key may be to understand that "power" in network studies is measured as winnings. Because most goods, including the poker chips in these experiments, have both consummatory (e.g. monetary) value and status (non-transferable) value, what seems to happen in that the high or low status value (position) of the holder of a poker chip spreads to the chip. Thus the overall value – exchange value plus status value – of a chip held by a high status person is greater than the value of the chip held by a low status person. Beyond showing that status confers power, these studies provide a mechanism to explain how that works.

The links between power and position, on the one hand, and status on the other, are only beginning to be mapped out. Thye's research program opens many new theoretical issues, and one outcome of this work is likely to be specification of conditions under which status and power operate independently, and other conditions under which they interact.

Integrations: Sentiments

While P(s) has proven to be a good laboratory measure of expectations, we have known at least since Camilleri and Berger's (1967) experiments that expectations are not the only factor that produces influence. Independent of expectations for task skill, one might, for instance, be more willing to accept influence from a liked partner, or less willing to accept influence from a disliked partner. Thus both expectations and sentiment might lead to the same behavioral outcome. Further, we might expect them to be additive: P(s) or influence rejection should be highest when one holds high relative expectations for self and dislikes the partner, and lowest when one holds low relative expectations and likes the partner.

How best to conceptualize sentiment effects in status situations revolves about two possible mechanisms. Either sentiment is part of the status generalization process – it constitutes an element in the aggregate expectations – or sentiment intervenes between expectations and their measurement. Both processes are intuitively plausible. The first might be represented when someone thinks a loved child or a pet is smarter than an outside observer would say. The second might be represented when a politician refuses to accept influence from another, even though conceding that the other probably is right, because of dislike.

Two kinds of studies have addressed the interaction of sentiment and status, behavioral and subjective. In behavioral studies (e.g. Bianchi, 2003; Driskell & Webster, 1997), the dependent variable is the P(s) measure of expectations described earlier. In subjective studies the dependent variable is responses on questionnaires about relative expectations (e.g. Lovaglia & Houser, 1996; Lucas & Lovaglia, 1998; Shelly, 1993, 2001). In general, behavior studies support the idea that sentiment and status organizing are separate processes; that is, sentiments may intervene in the expression of status processes, but they do not affect aggregate expectations. Subjective studies show the opposite: sentiments do affect aggregate expectations, a process Shelly (2001) has modeled. At this time we simply have not fully answered the constitutive vs. mediating views. This is an area where more empirical study, perhaps following additional theoretical work, is essential for answering the question.

OUTREACH WITH KNOWLEDGE RELATED TO STATUS PROCESSES

The puzzles that drive investigations into status and related processes have sustained a growing research program for more than half a century now. While specialists develop knowledge that is not immediately part of the culture of every educated person, outreach, too, is important. Status researchers believe their work has value for understanding and improving aspects of the social world. Several scholars have applied theories of status and related processes for useful ends. New opportunities for outreach appear almost daily.

An Anecdote on Gender

Meeker and Weitzel-O'Neil (1977) convincingly demonstrated that many interaction disadvantages associated with being female are better explained as status effects than as, for instance, results of socialization. Balkwell and Berger (1996) showed in detail what sorts of gender-linked interpersonal behaviors are properly seen as status effects. Ridgeway (1997b) detailed numerous ways in which gender-related inequalities are reproduced and diffused in organizations, even without deliberate attempts to keep women and men unequal, and often despite concerted efforts to produce equality. Most readers know all these things. Most lay people and many social scientists do not.

In the 1980s, I gave a talk to a group of clinical psychologists about structural and interpersonal inequality associated with gender. At the end, a psychologist came up and said "You seem like a nice man, but at the beginning when you said that it is higher status to be male than female, I got so angry I'm afraid I don't remember anything else you said." I was stunned, and probably didn't say much that was helpful in reply. Here is what I wish I had said.

> Gender is a status characteristic in American society, and in all other societies anthropologists have reported. To say that men receive social advantages denied to women hardly seems like new information to me. But I am far from an apologist for the way things are. To document and analyze how things are is a first step in figuring out how to change them. Elizabeth G. Cohen's work with elementary school children is exemplary here. She used theoretical analysis to figure out what was happening, and used theoretical principles to change things. Many of us study status processes with an eye to finding ways to reduce or eliminate undesirable inequalities. A few investigators do both basic and applied work, but most of us specialize in one or the other. However the goals of promoting egalitarianism and blocking status generalization where it is undesirable – and using and directing status generalization where it is helpful – are probably universal. If we are to improve our world, we must get beyond merely viewing it with outrage (or with satisfaction), and begin to deal with the "why" questions. When we understand causal mechanisms, we gain the ability to intervene in ways that actually can make a difference. The alternative, impotent outrage, is easier, but it does no good.

The Nature and Value of Social Engineering

Jonathan Turner (1998) issued a vivid call for more social engineering and less empty speculation. Most sociological researchers, certainly including group process researchers, should applaud his call, for it would focus us on important theoretical issues and away from debating what this or that great man "really said." Intervention requires theories stated logically and clearly enough that determinate predictions are possible.

Following Turner's call would have benefits far beyond improving our theories, though that would surely be a wonderful outcome. It would also improve the quality of our analysis of existing situations, and get us beyond the empty moralizing that so turns off our students. Too much sociology is conducted by getting surface data that show some kind of inequality, and then concluding that "This should not be!" A good starting point, but useless if not followed up with analysis, theory, and test.

Men often are promoted faster than women and they are paid more for similar work. Teachers often judge Hispanic children's performance lower than comparable performances by Anglo children. The U.S. Army considers homosexuality incompatible with military service. Employers will choose a man over a woman with equal qualification scores. Essays supposedly written by attractive children receive higher marks than the same essays supposedly written by ugly children. Black car buyers end up paying higher prices than white buyers at the same dealers. This is the world we live in. Unfortunately, most of the time the analysis stops there. Lenin's famous question is pertinent: "But what is to be done?" Outrage is a normal human response to many situations, but by now it has grown old in sociology. We need to move on, and we have many theoretical tools that can help in that. Theories of status organizing processes have been – and can be in the future – used to analyze situations and improve the social world. Many researchers have fitted pieces into this puzzle; many exciting new puzzles are all around us.

SUMMARY AND CONCLUSIONS

In this selective review, I have traced part of the development of understanding about performance expectation states and status processes. In the 1940s, Bales and his collaborator Parsons sought to understand how social structures emerged and evolved in small task focused groups. While Bales' ideas and observations have been very useful and influential for many purposes, it is Berger's initial conception of abstract components of interaction and the theoretical construct "expectation state" that launched the remainder of the work surveyed here.

In the 1950s, abstraction was unusual in social science, and working out some implications of the method was important for later work. By the 1960s, research techniques and additional abstract work made it possible to generalize the theory to include status processes in heterogeneous groups. As a consequence, the issues of multiple characteristics and combining logically appeared, and by 1977 the general theoretical explanation was available.

Elaboration and variation constituted most efforts in the 1980s. Sometimes these involved issues suggested by other areas of research (as reward expectations overlapped with some issues in distributive justice), and sometimes the issues arose without such context. In the 1990s investigators developed new models incorporating theoretical ideas and improvements. In the present decade, they added topics interacting with status, such as personality attribution and power, and developed ideas on second-order expectations, personality attributions, and sentiment processes. Maybe by tomorrow, certainly by the end of this decade, we will know a great deal more about some of these topics, and imaginative scientists will have opened some new puzzles in this extremely productive research tradition.

NOTES

1. I will not include all research into status processes, nor all of the families of related theories that make up this diverse theoretical research program. Rather I focus on a few puzzles, sustained investigations, and some provisional gains to understanding. Excellent encyclopedic histories of the program are available in Wagner and Berger (1993, 2002).

2. The Department and Laboratory of Social Relations at Harvard was founded with a Ford Foundation grant by Talcott Parsons, Gordon W. Allport, Henry A. Murray, Clyde M. Kluckhohn, and Samuel A. Stouffer; Bales' (1999) book is dedicated to their memory.

3. For complete description of Bales groups, please see Bales (1970).

4. The categories classified behavioral acts dealing with what were then seen as universal problems of social systems: Adaptation, Goal Attainment, Integration, and Latency. Bales (1999, p. 166) later recalled kidding from a colleague that the 12 categories he eventually settled upon matched the number of rows in the IBM computer punch cards used to hold data.

5. A third important feature, that the members were remarkably *homogeneous*, becomes significant in the 1960s when attention turns to status generalization processes and in the 1980s with interest in legitimacy.

6. Many ideas and terms that Bales and his associates developed in the 1940s and 1950s persist today in business school curricula: for instance the idea that problem-solving groups pass through "phases" including information gathering ("brainstorming"), evaluation, narrowing of focus, agreeing on a solution, and implementing the solution; or the terms "pro-active" and "reactive," which were used to describe initiated problem solving or responding to others' questions, respectively. See, for instance, Bales (1953) and Heinecke and Bales (1953).

7. Fisek and Ofshe (1970) showed that expectation formation and behavioral inequality *precede* rather than *follow* cognitive awareness of differential abilities; they also occur when individuals never show awareness of any differential ability levels among group members.

8. Lindenberg (1997) argues that decline in interest in the field that used to be called "small groups" was caused by lack of theories adequate to the task of treating the groups holistically. Since the 1960s, at least, study has focused on one or more group processes, or on one or more kinds of group structures. These more abstract and limited theoretical exercises have proved very fruitful.

9. It is described in Berger, Fisek, Norman and Zelditch (1977, pp. 43–48) and in Webster and Sobieszek (1974, Appendix 1).

10. An unpublished technical report in 1965, "Three Tasks for Small Groups Experiments" by Thomas L. Conner, describes properties of tasks that were in use at that time and that have been adapted for many subsequent experiments.

11. Status situations are first decomposed into univalent subsets. Attenuation occurs as information aggregates within subsets. Finally, the positive and negative subsets are combined to determine overall performance expectations.

12. The graph model has been enormously useful for calculating expectation values that the theory predicts for virtually any structure of status characteristics. Balkwell (1991a) discusses variant ways of estimating status effects using the graph model. Whitmeyer (2000) developed an algorithm that, with the graph model, permits quick and easy calculation of expectation values for actors in any symmetric status situation. Walker (2000) generalized Whitmeyer's program to permit calculations for asymmetric situations.

13. Further consideration of elimination without any presumption of purposive maximization, along with analysis of several relevant experiments, is available in Balkwell (1991b).

14. Balkwell (2001, p. 112) notes: "It may be comforting to believe that people process finely graded social information so as to use its full richness, but this assumption consistently has been shown wanting." Also, "Overlooked in this reasoning is its implicit claim that human beings have the information-processing capacity of powerful computers, which much research in cognitive social psychology refutes . . . ." (p. 101).

15. High self esteem was widely thought to have all sorts of positive consequences, from reducing school dropout rates to preventing teen pregnancy.

16. *Pygmalion in the Classroom* (Rosenthal & Jacobson, 1968), an enormously influential study, had documented such effects, though without putting them into theoretical context, and analyzing such phenomena was a prime concern behind the Entwisle-Webster research program.

17. Cohen (1968) was an early report of this research; and Cohen (1971) was the first published report. However Cohen's work began several years earlier, before the 1966 theory was published, though of course she was informed about theoretical work as it developed before publication. Cohen's work contributed significantly to theory development, as described below.

18. This may be easier to see using the graph model of the theory. In case (1), an actor gets connected to outcome states of T through given and inferred paths to D, Γ, and C^*. Case (2) has that path and an additional path through a referent actor. In case (3), the actor is linked directly to C^* and the generalization path through D becomes irrelevant. Multiple paths (case 2) and shorter paths (case 3) have greater effects on expectations, thus predicting the stated ordering of effects.

19. Developing models describing processes that generate, maintain, or change social structures in all these kinds of groups makes quite clear that, whatever the cognitive status of expectation states in humans, equivalent structures surely are not conscious in, say, chickens!

REFERENCES

Bales, R. F. (1953). The equilibrium problem in small groups. In: T. Parsons, R. F. Bales & E. H. Shils (Eds), *Working Papers in the Theory of Action* (pp. 111–161). Glencoe, IL: Free Press.

Bales, R. F. (1970). *Personality and interpersonal behavior*. New York: Holt, Rinehart and Winston.

Bales, R. F. (1999). *Social interaction systems: Theory and measurement*. New Brunswick, NJ: Transaction.

Bales, R. F., Strodtbeck, F. L., Mills, T. M., & Roseborough, M. E. (1951). Channels of communication in small groups. *American Sociological Review, 16*, 461–468.

Balkwell, J. W. (1991a). From expectations to behavior: A general translation function. *American Sociological Review, 56*, 355–369.

Balkwell, J. W. (1991b). Status characteristics and social interaction: An assessment of theoretical variants. In: E. J. Lawler, B. Markovsky, C. L. Ridgeway & H. A. Walkers (Eds), *Advances in Group Processes* (Vol. 8, pp. 135–176). Greenwich, CT: JAI.

Balkwell, J. W. (2001). How do actors in task-oriented situations process finely graded differences in ability? *Sociological Focus, 34*, 97–115.

Balkwell, J. W., & Berger, J. (1996). Gender, status, and behavior in task situations. *Social Psychology Quarterly, 59*, 278–283.

Barchas, P. R., & Mendoza, S. P. (1984). Emergent hierarchical relationships in rhesus macaques: An application of Chase's model. In: P. R. Barchas (Ed.), *Social Hierarchies: Essays Toward a Sociophysiological Perspective* (pp. 81–95). Westport, CT: Greenwood Press.

Berger, J. (1958). Relations between performance, rewards, and action-opportunities in small problem-solving groups. Doctoral dissertation, Harvard University, Cambridge, MA.

Berger, J., Cohen, B. P., & Zelditch, M., Jr. (1966). Status characteristics and expectation states. In: J. Berger, M. Zelditch, Jr. & B. Anderson (Eds), *Sociological Theories in Progress* (Vol. 1, pp. 29–46). Boston: Houghton-Mifflin.

Berger, J., & Conner, T. L. (1969). Performance expectations and behavior in small groups. *Acta Sociologica, 12*, 186–198.

Berger, J., & Conner, T. L. (1974). Performance expectations and behavior in small groups: A revised formulation. In: J. Berger, T. L. Conner & M. H. Fisek (Eds), *Expectation States Theory: A Theoretical Research Program* (pp. 85–109). Cambridge, MA: Winthrop.

Berger, J., Conner, T. L., & McKeown, W. L. (1969). Evaluations and the formation and maintenance of performance expectations. *Human Relations, 22*, 481–502.

Berger, J., & Hamit Fisek, M. (1974). A generalization of the theory of status characteristics and expectation states. In: J. Berger, T. L. Conner & M. H. Fisek (Eds), *Expectation States Theory: A Theoretical Research Program* (Chap. 6, pp. 163–205). Cambridge, MA: Winthrop.

Berger, J., Hamit Fisek, M., & Crosbie, P. V. (1970). Multi-characteristic status situations and the determination of power and prestige orders. Technical Report No. 35, Laboratory for Social Research, Stanford University.

Berger, J., Hamit Fisek, M., & Freese, L. (1976). Paths of relevance and the determination of power and prestige orders. *Pacific Sociological Review, 19*, 45–62.

Berger, J., Hamit Fisek, M., Norman, R. Z., & Wagner, D. G. (1985). Formation of reward expectations in status situations. In: J. Berger & M. Zelditch, Jr. (Eds), *Status Rewards and Influence* (pp. 2156–2261). San Francisco: Jossey-Bass.

Berger, J., Hamit Fisek, M., Norman, R. Z., & Zelditch, M., Jr. (1977). *Status characteristics and social interaction: An expectation states approach*. New York: Elsevier.

Berger, J., Norman, R. Z., Balkwell, J., & Smith, R. F. (1992). Status inconsistency in task situations: A test of four status processing principles. *American Sociological Review, 57*, 243–255.

Berger, J., Ridgeway, C. L., Hamit Fisek, M., & Norman, R. Z. (1998). The legitimation and delegitimation of power and prestige orders. *American Sociological Review, 63*, 379–405.

Berger, J., Ridgeway, C. L., & Zelditch, M., Jr. (2002). Construction of status and referential structures. *Sociological Theory, 20*, 157–179.

Berger, J., & Snell, J. L. (1961). A stochastic theory for self-other expectations. Technical Report No. 1, Laboratory for Social Research, Stanford University.

Berger, J., Webster, M., Jr., Ridgeway, C. L., & Rosenholtz, S. J. (1986). Status cues, expectations and behavior. In: E. J. Lawler (Ed.), *Advances in Group Processes* (Vol. 3, pp. 1–22). Greenwich, CT: JAI Press.

Berger, J., Zelditch, M., Jr., Anderson, B., & Cohen, B. P. (1972). Structural aspects of distributive justice: A status-value formulation. In: J. Berger, M. Delditch, Jr. & B. Anderson (Eds), *Sociological Theories in Progress* (Vol. 2, pp. 119–146). Boston: Houghton-Mifflin.

Bianchi, A. J. (2003). Examining sentiments effect on status: Constitutive and moderator models. Unpublished manuscript available from the author at Department of Sociology, Kent State University, Kent, OH, 39 pp.

Camilleri, S. F., & Berger, J. (1967). Decision making and social influence: A model and an experimental test. *Sociometry*, *30*, 365–378.

Chase, I. D. (1980). Social process and hierarchy formation in small groups: A comparative perspective. *American Sociological Review*, *45*, 905–924.

Chase, I. D. (1982). Dynamics of hierarchy formation: The sequential development of dominance relationships. *Behaviour*, *80*, 218–239.

Cohen, E. G. (1968). Interracial interaction disability. Technical Report No. 1, School of Education, Stanford University, Stanford, CA.

Cohen, E. G. (1971). Interracial interaction disability: A problem for integrated education. *Urban Education* (January), 336–356.

Cohen, E. G. (1988). Can expectations for competence be altered in the classroom? In: M. Webster, Jr. & M. Foschi (Eds), *Status Generalization: New Theory and Research* (pp. 27–54). Stanford, CA: Stanford University Press.

Cohen, E. G., & Lotan, R. A. (Eds) (1997). *Working for equity in heterogeneous classrooms*. New York: Columbia University Teachers Press.

Conner, T. L. (1966). Continual disagreement and the assignment of self-other performance expectations. Unpublished Ph.D. dissertation, Department of Sociology, Stanford University, Stanford, CA.

Cook, K. S. (1975). Expectations, evaluations and equity. *American Sociological Review*, *40*, 372–388.

Driskell, J. E., & Webster, M., Jr. (1997). Status and sentiment in task groups. In: J. Szmatka, J. Skvoretz & J. Berger (Eds), *Status, Network and Structure: Theory Development in Group Processes* (pp. 179–200). Stanford, CA: Stanford University Press.

Entwisle, D. R., & Webster, M., Jr. (1974). Raising children's expectations for their own performance. In: J. Berger, T. L. Conner & M. Hamit Fisek (Eds), *Expectation States Theory: A Theoretical Research Program* (pp. 211–243). Cambridge, MA: Winthrop.

Entwisle, D. R. (1978). Raising expectations indirectly. *Social Forces*, *57*(1), 257–264.

Fararo, T. J., & Skvoretz, J. (1986). E-state structuralism: A theoretical method. *American Sociological Review*, *51*, 591–602.

Fararo, T. J., & Skvoretz, J. (1988). Dynamics of the formation of stable dominance structures. In: M. Webster, Jr. & M. Foschi (Eds), *Status Generalization: New Theory and Research* (pp. 327–350). Stanford, CA: Stanford University Press.

Fararo, T. J., Skvoretz, J., & Kosaka, K. (1994). Advances in E-state structuralism: Further studies in dominance structure formation. *Social Networks*, *16*, 233–265.

Fisek, M. H., Berger, J., & Moore, J. C. (2002). Evaluations, enactment, and expectations. *Social Psychology Quarterly*, *65*, 329–345.

Fisek, M. H., Berger, J., & Norman, R. Z. (1991). Participation in heterogeneous and homogeneous groups: A theoretical integration. *American Journal of Sociology*, *97*, 114–142.

Fisek, M. H., Berger, J., & Norman, R. Z. (1995). Evaluations and the formation of expectations. *American Journal of Sociology, 101*, 721–746.

Fisek, M. H., & Ofshe, R. (1970). The process of status evolution. *Sociometry, 33*, 327–346.

Foddy, M., & Smithson, M. (1996). Relative ability, paths of relevance, and influence in task-oriented groups. *Social Psychology Quarterly, 59*, 140–153.

Foddy, M., & Smithson, M. (1999). Can gender inequalities be eliminated? *Social Psychology Quarterly, 65*, 329–345.

Foschi, M. (2000). Double standards for competence: Theory and research. In: *Annual Review of Sociology* (Vol. 26, pp. 21–42). Palo Alto, CA: Annual Reviews.

Freese, L., & Cohen, B. P. (1973). Eliminating status generalization. *Sociometry, 36*, 177–198.

Gerber, G. L. (1996). Status in same-gender and mixed-gender police dyads: Effects on personality attribution. *Social Psychology Quarterly, 59*, 350–363.

Gerber, G. L. (2001). *Women and men police officers: Status, gender, and personality.* Westport, CT: Praeger.

Heinecke, C., & Bales, R. F. (1953). Developmental trends in the structure of small groups. *Sociometry, 16*, 7–38.

Ilardi, B., & McMahon, A. M. (1988). Organizational legitimacy and performance evaluation. In: E. J. Lawler & B. Markovsky (Eds), *Advances in Group Processes* (Vol. 5, pp. 217–244). Greenwich, CT: JAI Press.

Jasso, G., & Rossi, P. H. (1977). Distributive justice and earned income. *American Sociological Review, 42*, 639–651.

Johnson, C. (1995). Sexual orientation as a diffuse status characteristic: Implications for small group interaction. In: B. Markovsky, M. J. Lovaglia & K. Heimer (Eds), *Advances in Group Processes* (Vol. 12, pp. 115–137). Greenwich, CT: JAI Press.

Kadane, J., & Lewis, G. H. (1969). The distribution of participation in group discussions. *American Sociological Review, 34*, 71–73.

Katz, I., Roberts, O., & Robinson, J. (1965). Effects of task difficulty, race of administrator, and instructions of digit-symbol performance of Negroes. *Journal of Personality and Social Psychology, 2*, 53–69.

Lewis, G. H. (1972). Role differentiation. *American Sociological Review, 37*, 424–434.

Lindenberg, S. (1997). Grounding groups in theory: Functional, cognitive, and structural interdependencies. In: B. Markovsky, M. J. Lovaglia & L. Troyer (Eds), *Advances in Group Processes* (Vol. 14, pp. 281–331). Greenwich, CT: JAI Press.

Lovaglia, M., & Houser, J. (1996). Emotional reactions and status in groups. *American Sociological Review, 61*, 867–883.

Lucas, J. W., & Lovaglia, M. J. (1998). Leadership status, gender, group size, and emotion in face-to-face groups. *Sociological Perspectives, 41*, 617–637.

Mazur, A. (1973). A cross-species comparison of status in small established groups. *American Sociological Review, 38*, 513–530.

Mazur, A. (1985). A biosocial model of status in face-to-face primate groups. *Social Forces, 64*, 377–402.

Meeker, B., & Weitzel-O'Neill, P. A. (1977). Sex roles and interpersonal behavior in task-oriented groups. *American Sociological Review, 42*, 91–105.

Moore, J. C. (1968). Status and influence in small group interactions. *Sociometry, 31*, 47–63.

Moore, J. C. (1985). Role enactment and self-identity. In: J. Berger & M. Zelditch, Jr. (Eds), *Status, Rewards, and Influence* (pp. 262–316). San Francisco: Jossey-Bass.

Mueller, C. W., Mulinge, M., & Glass, J. (2002). Interactional processes and gender workplace inequalities. *Social Psychology Quarterly, 65*, 163–188.

Ridgeway, C. L. (1989). Understanding legitimation in informal status orders. In: J. Berger, M. Zelditch, Jr. & B. Anderson (Eds), *Sociological Theories in Progress: New Formulations* (pp. 131–159). Newbury Park, CA: Sage.

Ridgeway, C. L. (1991). The social construction of status value: Gender and other nominal character-istics. *Social Forces, 70*, 367–386.

Ridgeway, C. L. (1997a). Where do status-value beliefs come from? New developments. In: J. Szmatka, J. Skvoretz & J. Berger (Eds), *Status, Networks and Structure: Theory Development in Group Processes* (pp. 137–158). Stanford, CA: Stanford University Press.

Ridgeway, C. L. (1997b). Interaction and the conservation of gender inequality: Considering employ-ment. *American Sociological Review, 62*, 218–235.

Ridgeway, C. L. (2000). The formation of status beliefs: Improving status construction theory. In: S. R Thye, E. J. Lawler, M. W. Macy & H. A Walker (Eds), *Advances in Group Processes* (Vol. 17, pp. 77–102). Stamford, CT: JAI Press.

Ridgeway, C. L., & & Balkwell, J. W. (1997). Group processes and the diffusion of status-beliefs. *Social Psychology Quarterly, 60*, 14–31.

Ridgeway, C. L., & Berger, J. (1986). Expectations, legitimation, and dominance behavior in task groups. *American Sociological Review, 51*, 603–617.

Ridgeway, C. L., Berger, J., & Smith, R. (1986). Nonverbal cues and status: An expectation states approach. *American Journal of Sociology, 90*, 955–978.

Ridgeway, C. L., Boyle, E. H., Kuipers, K. J., & Robinson, D. T. (1998). How do status beliefs develop? The role of resources and interactional experience. *American Sociological Review, 63*, 331–350.

Ridgeway, C. L., & Erickson, K. (2001). Creating and spreading status beliefs. *American Journal of Sociology*.

Rosenthal, R., & Jacobson, L. F. (1968). *Pygmalion in the classroom.* New York: Holt, Rinehart and Winston.

Sev'er, A. (1989). Simultaneous effects of status and task cues: Combining, eliminating, or buffering? *Social Psychology Quarterly, 52*, 327–335.

Shelly, R. K. (1993). How sentiments organize interaction. In: E. J. Lawler, B. Markovsky & J. O'Brien (Eds), *Advances in Group Processes* (Vol. 10, pp. 113–132). Greenwich, CT: JAI Press.

Shelly, R. K. (2001). How performance expectations arise from sentiments. *Social Psychology Quar-terly, 64*, 72–87.

Simpson, B., & Walker, H. A. (2002). Status characteristics and performance expectations: A refor-mulation. *Sociological Theory, 20*, 24–40.

Skvoretz, J. (1981). Extending expectation states theory: Comparative status models of participation in N person groups. *Social Forces, 59*, 752–770.

Skvoretz, J. (1985). Status characteristics, expectation states, and participation in N person task groups. In: J. Berger & M. Zelditch, Jr. (Eds), *Status, Rewards and Influence* (pp. 163–188). San Francisco: Jossey-Bass.

Skvoretz, J., & Fararo, T. J. (1996). Status and participation in task groups: A dynamic network model. *American Journal of Sociology, 101*, 1366–1414.

Skvoretz, J., Webster, M., Jr., & Whitmeyer, J. (1999). Status orders in task discussion groups. In: S. R. Thye, E. J. Lawler, M. W. Macy & H. A. Walker (Eds), *Advances in Group Processes* (Vol. 16, pp. 199–218). Greenwich, CT: JAI Press.

Strodtbeck, F. L., James, R. M., & Hawkins, C. (1957). Social status in jury deliberations. *American Sociological Review, 22*, 714–719.

Sullivan, H. S. (1947). *Conceptions of modern psychiatry.* Washington, DC: William H. White Psychiatric Foundation.

Thye, S. R. (1999). Status influence and status value. In: D. Willer (Ed.), *Network Exchange Theory* (pp. 248–255). Westport, CT: Praeger.

Thye, S. R. (2000). A status value theory of power in exchange relations. *American Sociological Review*, *65*, 407–432.

Torrance, E. P. (1954). Some consequences of power differences on decision making in permanent and temporary three-man groups. *Research Studies* (State College of Washington, Pullman), *22*, 130–140.

Troyer, L., & Younts, C. W. (1997). Whose expectations matter? The relative power of first-order and second-order expectations in determining social influence. *American Journal of Sociology*, *103*, 692–732.

Troyer, L., Younts, C. W., & Kalkhoff, W. (2001). Clarifying the theory of second-order expectations: The correspondence between motives for interaction and actors' orientation toward group interaction. *Social Psychology Quarterly*, *64*, 128–145.

Turner, J. (1998). Must sociological theory and sociological practice be so far apart? A polemical answer. *Sociological Perspectives*, *41*, 243–258.

Tuzlak, A. (1988). Boomerang effects: Status and demeanor over time. In: M. Webster, Jr. & M. Foschi (Eds), *Status Generalization: New Theory and Research* (pp. 261–274). Stanford, CA: Stanford University Press.

Tuzlak, A., & & Moore, J. C. (1984). Status, demeanor, and influence: An empirical assessment. *Social Psychology Quarterly*, *47*, 178–183.

Wagner, D. G., & Berger, J. (1993). Status characteristics theory: The growth of a program. In: J. Berger & M. Zelditch, Jr. (Eds), *Theoretical Research Programs: Studies in the Growth of Theory* (pp. 23–63). Stanford, CA: Stanford University Press.

Wagner, D. G., & Berger, J. (2002). Expectation states theory: An evolving research program. In: J. Berger & M. Zelditch, Jr. (Eds), *New Directions in Contemporary Sociological Theory* (Chap. 3, pp. 41–76). New York: Rowman and Littlefield.

Walker, H. A. (2000). A program for calculating P(S) in complex, asymmetric status structures. *Contemporary Research in Social Psychology*, *4*, 113–124. http://www.uiowa.edu/~grpproc/crisp/crisp.html

Webster, M., Jr., & Driskell, J., Jr. (1978). Status generalization: A review and some new data. *American Sociological Review*, *43*, 220–236.

Webster, M., Jr., & Driskell, J., Jr. (1983). Beauty as status. *American Journal of Sociology*, *89*, 140–165.

Webster, M., Jr., & Hysom, S. J. (1998). Creating status characteristics. *American Sociological Review*, *63*, 351–378.

Webster, M., Jr., Hysom, S., & Fullmer, E. M. (1998). Sexual orientation as status. In: E. J. Lawler, J. Skvoretz & J. Szmatka (Eds), *Advances in Group Processes* (Vol. 15, pp. 1–21). Stamford, CT: JAI.

Webster, M., Jr., & Smith, L. F. (1978). Justice and revolutionary coalitions: A test of two theories. *American Journal of Sociology*, *84*, 267–292.

Webster, M., Jr., & Sobieszek, B. (1974). *Sources of self-evaluation: A theory of significant others and social influence*. New York: Wiley-Interscience.

Webster, M., Jr., & Whitmeyer, J. M. (1999). A theory of second-order expectations and behavior. *Social Psychology Quarterly*, *62*, 17–31.

Webster, M., Jr., Whitmeyer, J., Rashotte, L. (2003). Status claims, second-order expectations, and inequality in groups. Paper presented at the annual meetings of the American Sociological Association, Atlanta, GA.

Whitmeyer, J. (2000). A program for calculating P(S) in complex, symmetric status structures. *Current Research in Social Psychology*, *3*, 64–68. http://www.uiowa.edu/~grpproc/crisp/crisp.html

Willer, D., Lovaglia, M. J., & Markovsky, B. (1997). Power and influence: A theoretical bridge. *Social Forces*, *76*, 571–603.

Yuchtmann-Yaar, E., & Semyonov, M. (1979). Ethnic inequality in Israeli schools and sports: An expectation-states approach. *American Journal of Sociology*, *85*, 576–590.

Zelditch, M., Jr., & Walker, H. A. (1984). Legitimacy and the stability of authority. In: E. J. Lawler (Ed.), *Advances in Group Processes* (Vol. 1, pp. 1–27). Greenwich, CT: JAI.

THE LEGITIMACY OF REGIMES

Morris Zelditch and Henry A. Walker

ABSTRACT

A centuries-long history of theory and research shows that every authority system tries to cultivate a belief in its legitimacy. This paper focuses on the legitimation of regimes – social relationships and the rules that govern them. We use existing theory and research to identify a basic legitimation assumption that includes four conditions necessary to establish legitimacy. We also identify four corollaries of the assumption and use our own published and unpublished laboratory research to show (1) how successful experimental procedures satisfy the assumption's conditions, and (2) how the failure of experimental procedures to establish legitimacy violate the assumption and its corollaries.

INTRODUCTION

Every authority system tries to cultivate a belief in its legitimacy (Weber, 1918 [1968], p. 213). In Weber's classic analysis, legitimacy enhances the efficiency and effectiveness of authority systems by eliminating or reducing an authority figure's need to exercise power to secure compliance. Systems claim legitimacy by appealing to tradition, charismatic figures, or rational-legal principles. But Weber's explication makes clear that the ideal typical bases on which authority systems build and substantiate their claims to legitimacy must themselves possess legitimacy. Weber's discussion leaves two questions unanswered: First, how, and under what conditions, is first-order legitimacy established (Berger & Luckmann,

Power and Status
Advances in Group Processes, Volume 20, 217–249
Copyright © by 2003 Elsevier Ltd.
All rights of reproduction in any form reserved
ISSN: 0882-6145/doi:10.1016/S0882-6145(03)20008-4

1966)?[1] Second, how and under what conditions do first-order legitimations establish the legitimacy of systems whose legitimacy has not been established or, if established, is contested? This paper addresses the second of these questions.

The present paper builds on a centuries-long history of theory and research and on our own research program which spans the greater part of three decades (Walker & Zelditch, 1993). We describe our understandings of legitimacy processes and develop a basic legitimation assumption. We discuss findings from our research (much of it previously unpublished), that illustrate the power of the assumption. We show how successful research protocols satisfy the assumption's conditions and corollaries and show how those that violate the basic legitimation assumption either fail to create legitimacy or substantially weaken previously established legitimacy.

THE LEGITIMACY OF REGIMES

Weber (1918 [1968]) distinguished domination[2] from power but contemporary usage (e.g. in organizational behavior), has conflated the terms. Authority *means* legitimate power for many social scientists (Scott, 1981, p. 280). To avoid confusion and loss of clarity, we substitute the term *regime* to refer to social relationships (including authority relations), and the principles that govern them. (See Keohane & Nye, 1977, p. 19, for a similar usage.)

> **Definition 1** *(Regime)*. A regime, R, is a system consisting of positions, relations between positions and a set of rules governing R. System rules include criteria for role occupancy, role enactment, and interaction among roles.

Legitimacy is vital to the smooth functioning of all social relationships. The assertion is certainly true of hierarchical authority relations and those that display other forms of inequality (e.g. unequal economic relations). Recent history provides many examples of new regimes whose legitimacy must be established and established regimes in which legitimacy is contested.

American military forces entered Afghanistan in November 2001 as part of President George W. Bush's "war on terror." U.S. forces secured major urban areas in short order with the assistance of a hodge-podge of regional and local militias and, eventually, Afghanistan created a civilian government. But the new government and its leader faced an ageless question: How would the new regime establish its legitimacy (Lipset, 1959, 1963)? Ironically, the invasion of Afghanistan strengthened the legitimacy of George W. Bush's fledgling administration.

George W. Bush assumed the office of President on January 20, 2001. His inauguration followed a catastrophic election and a series of events, unprecedented in American history, that ended with the Electoral College's certification of a Bush "victory" in December 2000. A sitting Vice-President won a majority of votes cast in a country whose citizens subscribe to the principle of majority rule. Bush won a majority of votes in the Electoral College – under a constitutionally established procedure – but only after he had won a 5–4 decision in the U.S. Supreme Court. Justices who supported Bush's position had been appointed by presidents who shared his Republican affiliation. At his inauguration, many Americans openly questioned the legitimacy of the election, Electoral College procedures, the Supreme Court, and the new President's occupancy of the highest executive office in the land.

These examples show why legitimacy is important to political institutions but they also raise crucial theoretical questions: Under what conditions can a post-Taliban Afghani government establish its legitimacy? What are the conditions that permitted George W. Bush's administration to gain a greater sense of legitimacy after its invasion of Afghanistan? More generally, is it possible to identify universal conditions that separately or jointly establish the legitimacy of new regimes or substantiate the claims of regimes whose legitimacy is contested? For answers, we turn to an overview of the multiple-source, multiple-object theory of legitimacy that informs our research.

CONSENSUS, CONFLICT, AND CONTEMPORARY LEGITIMACY THEORY

Historically, theories of legitimacy were built on either consensus or conflict frameworks but Max Weber (1918 [1968]) skillfully melded the two approaches (Zelditch, 2001a). Weber argued that social order rests on twin pillars of collectively-established and individually-accepted legitimacy. Collectively-established legitimacy, or *validity*, exists when norms, values, beliefs, and procedures are treated as matters of objective fact.[3] At the individual level, actors may accept and support norms, values, beliefs, and procedures as desirable or proper – as the way things ought to be (Homans, 1974).

Dornbusch and Scott (1975) effected the conceptual separation of validity and *propriety* (their term for individual-level legitimacy). In their elaboration of Weber's ideas, Dornbusch and Scott pointed out that those who failed to attribute propriety to elements of social orders, would still comply if they oriented their actions to the validity of authority systems. Furthermore, Dornbusch and Scott asserted that validity was buttressed by the support of higher order authorities (*authorization*), or the support of the masses (consensus or *endorsement*).

Systematic research supports the basic claims of Weber's analysis and extensions and explications offered by Dornbusch and Scott (1975) and Zelditch and Walker (1984). (See summaries in Walker & Zelditch, 1993; Zelditch & Walker, 2000.) At the individual level, actors comply with authority systems to which they attribute propriety. Otherwise, they resist compliance. On the other hand, valid authority systems secure compliance in two ways. First, they affect compliance directly; valid authority systems establish the boundaries of legitimate or *moral* behavior. The "fact" of their legitimacy is buttressed by the presumption of authorization and endorsement (Thomas et al., 1986; Walker et al., 1986). Second, valid authority influences compliance indirectly. Valid systems influence individuals to attribute propriety to the norms, beliefs, practices, and procedures that define it. More important, our research shows that in instances of conflict between the two types of legitimation, validity has the more powerful effects (Walker et al., 1988, 1991).

From Demand Characteristics to a Basic Legitimation Assumption

Our initial thinking about legitimation processes and our earliest efforts to vary legitimacy experimentally were guided by a *demand characteristic assumption*. The assumption was the germ from which our program of research on legitimacy and the stability of authority grew. The striking results obtained by Orne (1962; Orne & Evans, 1965), and similar results by Frank (1944), seemed to imply that the authority of an experimenter (E), backed by a subject's (S) belief in science, could produce virtually any behavior, however meaningless, and make it "legitimate."

Many researchers considered demand characteristics a source of experimenter "bias" (Adair, 1973). In turn, experimenter bias could generate results that lend credibility to invalid theoretical arguments. One of our earliest insights was that demand characteristics were not necessarily a matter of experimenter "bias" because they were constant across all conditions in an experiment. Nevertheless, the idea of demand characteristics seemed to imply that the meaning, purpose, and understanding of what is appropriate (or legitimate) in a laboratory is created by the verbal and non-verbal acts of E and *only* by them. Hence, it seemed that an experimenter could use the legitimacy of science and his or her role in it to make any element of a laboratory study either legitimate or illegitimate and study its consequences. We state the assumption in a general form but stress two points: (1) our work was guided by a version of the assumption that was limited to situations governed by the legitimacy of scientific research. (2) our research experiences are inconsistent with the restricted version of the assumption and, consequently, with the more general statement.

Assumption 1 *(Demand Characteristic Assumption)*. If an actor believes another is an authority on the rules of a practice and is engaged in but does not know the rules of the practice, then the values, norms, beliefs, practices and procedures created or established by an authority figure and only those are legitimate.

Several of our early attempts to establish legitimacy or illegitimacy in the laboratory failed and some of the "new" findings we present in this paper bring evidence to bear on the demand characteristics assumption. Our early failures led eventually to the ideas we describe as a basic legitimation assumption.

We argue that traditional and contemporary theories of legitimacy, and research that supports them, imply a basic legitimation assumption. Elements of the basic legitimation assumption (BLA) are culled from a survey of theories of legitimacy beginning with Thucydides (423B.C.[1954]) and Aristotle (c. 335–323B.C.[1946]), through Machiavelli (1517 [1940a], 1532 [1940b]), Locke (1690 [1960]), Rousseau (1762 [1948]), and Marx (Marx & Engels, 1845–1847 [1976]), to Gramsci (1947 [1971]), Parsons (1958 [1960]), Lipset (1959) and Habermas (1975). (See Zelditch, 2001a.) The literature implies that an authority system's claims to legitimacy will be unsuccessful unless (1) there is general consensus on the norms, values, beliefs, practices, and procedures to which the regime appeals; (2) any benefits to which the regime appeals are either in the common interest or can be made universal; (3) any beliefs to which the regime appeals are generally treated as matters of objective fact; and (4) the values, norms, beliefs, practices and/or procedures to which the regime appeals are consonant with the nature, conditions, and consequences of the system.

Consensus on norms, values, practices, etc., is important for establishing legitimacy because it represents endorsement (i.e. consent of the governed). However, it is the perception of consensus rather than objective consensus that is important to the satisfaction of claims to legitimacy. Regimes that generate high levels of dissensus are often quite stable if dissensus is not expressed publicly. Public silence permits individual members to maintain their disquietude while presuming that others fail to speak out because they approve (i.e. they endorse norms, values, etc.).

Authority systems have difficulty legitimizing norms, values, and practices that serve the interests of a few. Human groups establish regimes to provide benefits to those within their domains of authority. Legitimacy is more easily established if policies benefit the commonweal or, if they can claim universality when benefits flow disproportionately to special interests. As an example, a political economy like that in the U.S. establishes a wide gap between haves and have nots and ought to provoke widespread discontent among have nots. However, class divisions in the U.S. are substantially weaker than those in other countries with similar political economies. We suggest that the differences are due, in part, to a belief system that glorifies the possibility of long-distance (i.e. rags-to-riches), mobility within the American occupational structure (Blau & Duncan, 1967, p. 434). Put simply, the regime is legitimized by an ideology that holds out the possibility that *anyone* can join the ranks of the economically well off.

Authority systems are also more likely to sustain claims to legitimacy if they can establish supporting beliefs that are treated as matters of objective fact. We point again to the importance of *beliefs about mobility* to the legitimacy of economic stratification in the U.S. Lipset and Bendix's (1959) classic study of comparative mobility found that U.S. rates of intergenerational mobility were similar to those in five other industrialized nations. However, subsequent research showed that, historically, long-distance mobility was substantially more likely in the U.S. than in most European countries. Not surprisingly, Americans believe more strongly than Europeans that they "can make it" without governmental assistance (Lipset, 1996). The "fact" of long-distance mobility and public exposure to archetypal examples like Oprah Winfrey, Sam Walton, or Bill Clinton sustain system legitimacy despite the fact that rates of upward *and* downward mobility are remarkably similar.

Finally, a regime is more able to sustain its claims to legitimacy if the beliefs, values, and procedures on which such claims rest articulate well with the nature, conditions, and consequences of the system. Lipset (1963) documents the crises that faced the new American nation as it made its debut near the end of the 18th century. The nation survived and established its legitimacy because, in part, the actions it took and the outcomes it realized in those early crises were consistent with the beliefs, values, and laws on which its sovereignty was founded.

We argue that the four conditions are necessary for establishing legitimacy, not causes of it. However, given a legitimating "formula" that links undefined or contested elements of a regime to accepted values (from Mosca, 1896 [1939]), they are jointly sufficient and can be thought of as a single assumption. The claims may apply to other elements of social life but in this paper we only apply them to the legitimacy of regimes. We define two additional terms before we combine the four claims in a single assumption.

Definition 2 *(Accepted Legitimating Elements).* Elements of a social situation including norms, values, beliefs, practices and procedures are accepted legitimating elements (ALE), if members of the collectivity believe they are consensually accepted by others in R's domain.

Definition 3 *(Regime-Legitimating Formula).* A formula is a regime-legitimating formula (RLF), if for some regime, R, or for some component of R, ALEs imply it either logically or empirically and in turn the formula logically or empirically implies R's legitimacy.

The relationship between ALEs and Regime Legitimating Formulae provide the support that permits RLFs to establish the legitimacy of systems that lack it and to strengthen the legitimacy of authority systems whose legitimacy is contested. The conditions under which RLFs and their associated ALEs establish the legitimacy of authority systems are stated formally in the Basic Legitimation Assumption:

Assumption 2 *(Basic Legitimation Assumption)*. Given a regime-legitimating formula (RLF) of a regime, R, the undefined or contested elements of R acquire the legitimacy of ALEs if and only if:

Condition 1 *(Consensus)*. The elements to which a RLF appeals are consensually accepted (i.e. they are ALEs), within R's domain;

Condition 2 *(Impartiality)*. Any benefit of R to which a RLF appeals is either in the group interest or, if the appeal is to self-interest, it can be made universal;[4]

Condition 3 *(Objectification)*. Any belief to which a RLF appeals is an ALE and is treated as a matter of objective fact; and

Condition 4 *(Consonance)*. Any ALE to which a RLF appeals is consonant with the nature, conditions, and consequences of R.

COROLLARIES OF THE BASIC LEGITIMATION ASSUMPTION

We identify other principles from the general literature but most are corollaries of the BLA, including:

Corollary 1 *(Spread of Legitimacy)*. If the conditions of the BLA are satisfied, the legitimacy of ALEs spreads to any elements of R to which they are linked;

Corollary 2 *(Conservation of Legitimacy)*. Undefined or contested elements of a social situation (i.e. those that are not ALEs), cannot establish (or strengthen) legitimacy;

Corollary 3 *(Effectiveness)*. If G is an accepted goal of a group, any element of R that is instrumental to G is legitimate in the group;

Corollary 4 *(Mystification)*. If the consequences of R are not in the interests of the group or are not universalizable, a RLF legitimates R only if R's consequences are masked.

In late 2001, the second Bush administration took actions on behalf of the American people (impartiality), actions that were defined consensually as prerogatives of the Office of the President (consensus). Moreover, substantial numbers of Americans treated the "threat of terrorism" as a matter of objective fact (objectification). Finally, the apparent decisiveness of American military action in Afghanistan suggested that the new administration's actions were instrumental to meeting the country's goals with respect to the demands of nation states in the new millennium (effectiveness). The contested President's public approval ratings reached stratospheric numbers and his legitimacy as President appeared secure.

OBJECTIVES

The balance of the present paper is an examination of the BLA and its corollaries in the light of the successes and, in particular, the failures of our many attempts to systematically vary legitimacy in two dozen experiments. Most of those experiments were concerned with studying the consequences of legitimacy not with creating it. (For summaries of various stages of this research and additional references, see Walker & Zelditch, 1993; Zelditch, 2001b; Zelditch & Walker, 1984, 2000; Zelditch et al., 1983.) The analyses we offer are by-products of that research, some previously published, but much of it unpublished. We examine results of (1) unsuccessful pretests of eventually successful experimental manip- ulations; (2) experiments that failed because our procedures did not establish the required initial conditions; and (3) preliminary, criterion phases of experiments that guided selection and interpretation of experimental manipulations that succeeded.

Scope

The analyses that follow examine only the legitimacy of regimes; we neglect the legitimacy of acts and persons. Even with respect to regimes, we have nothing at all to say about procedures, simply because we never attempted to manipulate them. Furthermore, we have nothing to say about the motives actors have for making claims to legitimacy. Finally, the present paper says little about the conse- quences of legitimacy, except where necessary to interpret the success or failure of manipulations of its causes. Throughout, we are concerned with the method- ological rigor (i.e. validity in the measurement sense), of attempts to manipulate legitimacy, not with the effects of manipulations on behavior or on the stability of authority.

EVIDENCE FOR A BASIC LEGITIMATION ASSUMPTION

We use the structure of the BLA to organize our analyses. With the exception of the demand characteristics assumption, there is a section for each condition and each corollary in the order given above. Because the failure of most of our efforts to vary legitimacy by means of demand characteristics was closely related to the evidence in support of the effectiveness hypothesis (Corollary 3), we treat findings relevant to the demand characteristics assumption only in that section.

Consensus

The hypothesis that legitimacy depends on consensus dates at least from Aristotle's *Politics* (335–323B.C. [1946]) and is found in all theories of legitimacy since, whether consensus theories (e.g. Linz, 1978; Lipset, 1959; Parsons, 1958 [1960]; Rousseau, 1762 [1948]), conflict theories (e.g. Machiavelli, 1517 [1940a], 1532 [1940b]; Marx (Marx & Engels, 1845–1847 [1976]), or hybrid combinations of the two (Habermas, 1975; Weber, 1918 [1968]).[5]

Nothing in our research casts doubt on the assumption that legitimacy depends on collective consensus. We varied consensual validity in two experiments, one designed to study the acceptance of justifications for unexpected, untoward acts (Massey, Freeman & Zelditch, 1997), the other to study justifications offered for the legitimacy of regimes (Zelditch & Floyd, 1998a, b).[6] In both, the experimenter (E), offered justification for violating expectations. The experiments used a commons dilemma setting in which pairs of Ss harvested water resources, monitored by a "water monitor" (WM) who, owing to a rigged election, was expected to use a fixed rule to replenish their local reserves of water from a general water reserve. (See Table 1 for brief descriptions of the two basic protocols used by the studies we review.) The WM violated the rule twice in five trials of the experiment by not replenishing S's local reserve at all. WM justified its rule violations at the fifth trial of the experiment.

In Massey et al. (1997), the justifications offered had been previously determined to be either consensually valid, ambiguous, or consensually invalid by an independent sample of Ss drawn from the same population. Respondents volunteered the best and worst accounts they could think of for violating expectations in the experiment. A second sample drawn from the same population rated these justifications on a seven-point scale from most to least acceptable. Analysis of

Table 1. Summary of Protocols for Information Exchange and Tragedy of the
Commons Settings.

Information Exchange Setting

The standardized experimental setting employs a communication network comprised of five
positions or nodes. The most common version is a centralized network with four connections, each
of which connects one of four peripheral nodes with a central node. (See the Bavelas (1950)
"wheel" structure.)

Ss enter the setting to work a problem solving task that requires communication among all
positions. S can occupy a peripheral position, the central position, or rarely, S can be an objective
observer of the network. Experimental instructions create inequality by awarding a bonus to the first
position transmitting a correct answer to E. The network structure ensures that the central position
will complete problems first. E establishes procedures (rules of the game), that permit a majority of
network members to change the structure. Experimental treatments are designed to vary the
legitimacy of either structural-based inequality or of attempts to change the structure. In a typical
study, the principal dependent measure is the timing of an S's initiation of a procedure to change the
structure. (See Walker, 1979, or Walker et al., 1986, for complete descriptions of the basic setting.)

Tragedy of the Commons Setting

The standardized setting is a computerized version of the tragedy of the commons. Two Ss are
assigned to separate rooms and are seated at computer terminals. Each S is responsible for releasing
water to its community from a finite reserve. S is told to balance its community's needs against the
needs of both communities. S could release as much water as it wished within the limit of existing
supplies. (That is, water reserves could be depleted if either S released "too much.) Ss were not
aware of how much water the other S released on a given trial. Local reserves were replenished after
every trial by a water monitor (WM), a pre-programmed computer stimulate.

Ss presume that they will work at the task for three rounds of ten trials each. A rigged election
before criterion trials ensures that Ss and WM approve a fixed rate of replenishment. That is, WM is
bound by a consensually valid rule. WM violates the rule on four of ten trials in the first (and only)
round. Ss and WM were permitted to communicate. The setting was designed to study ideas raised
by Scott and Lyman's theory of accounts. Experiments focus on, for example, (1) the nature of
questions Ss ask WM concerning its violations of rules, or (2) Ss' reactions to WM's justifications
for violations of rules. (See Massey et al., 1997 for a complete description of the basic setting.)

---

these scores rank-ordered the sample of justifications from best to worst and
measured the consensus with which the ratings were made.

There was consensus that the best justification for the WM's violation of S's
expectations was that, "The general reserve is in danger of running out. We have
to cut back now." Respondent consensus judged "I changed my mind about the
vote" as the worst. The validity of, "We should wait for bad times to dig into our
reserves," was ambiguous. It ranked about in the middle of the order, with a low
level of consensus.

Ss judged the WM's offerings of consensually valid justifications as significantly more legitimate than WM's offerings of consensually invalid justifications.

Furthermore, the legitimacy of WM's who offered ambiguous justifications, which were not consensual, was more vulnerable to the countervailing effects of status and power than it was for those offering either consensually valid or invalid justifications (Massey et al., 1997).

The effects of consensual validity are not direct as they were in some of our earlier studies that used peer endorsement to create consensus (see Walker et al., 1986). Rather, the effects are indirect through propriety and can be understood as the product of processes similar to those described by situated identity theorists (Alexander & Rudd, 1984). Ss are not aware that a majority of others like them believe the justifications to be valid or invalid. Instead, as persons who share the same background and are exposed to the same situation, they seem to attribute similar meanings to justifications as do the independent judges. Put simply, they share a collectively-established vocabulary of motives.

Zelditch and Floyd (1998a, b) also used the commons dilemma setting to study the legitimation of regimes under conditions of dissensus. Their criterion phase used a vignette simulation of conditions created by Massey et al. (1997) but the study cast doubt on the necessity of consensus. Half the Ss were asked to offer defenses of a WM's valid justifications. The other half were asked to defend a WM whose invalid justifications had been challenged. WMs were challenged with respect to either: (1) their claim of discretionary authority; (2) their right to disregard the vote; or (3) their claims about the importance of conservation.

A WM's invalid justification cast doubt on consensus but led Ss to assume that there was no consensus *with respect to a particular issue* rather than a complete lack of consensus. Ss presumed consensus on other issues and offered justifications based on different premises. Thus, if challenged, they simply looked elsewhere for consensus. When they had doubts about consensus on particular issues, Ss's default position assumed general consensus. They behaved as if the legitimacy of regimes is sustainable if consensus can be found anywhere in a situation, even if not everywhere (Zelditch & Floyd, 1998a, b).

The fact that, without absolute consensus, S still found a way to justify WM's behavior does not mean that consensus is not a necessary condition of legitimacy. It merely suggests that the concept needs to be more precisely defined. The idea is notoriously ambiguous (Rossi & Berk, 1985). It has never been clear whether unanimity, a majority, or simply a plurality is necessary to claim consensus. Additionally, it is not clear how much actors have to agree and on how many features of a situation they must agree to claim consensus.

We found that near consensus was sufficient. Ss treated situations as consensual even when there was less than 100% agreement. For example, we varied agreement among two Ss in the commons dilemma situation and studied the effect on legitimation of the WM. Given disagreement between S and a WM, *who* the other S agreed with was decisive in determining where consensus lay in the experiment (Zelditch & Floyd, 1998a). Even when there were only three actors, one dissenter was not necessarily evidence of lack of consensus about the legitimacy of WM's actions; it simply signaled disagreement. Ss also defined consensus in terms of what they believed to be collective agreement, rather than what they personally believed was right. Ss recognized that the WM had ignored a rule that had been adopted by majority vote. They claimed that they would have consulted others before failing to replenish a local community's water reserve even as they offered what they believed were valid justifications for disregarding the agreement (Zelditch & Floyd, 1998b).

Finally, we found that, at least in this particular situation, consensus was issue specific. Ss who doubted consensus with respect to one premise of a regime justification merely went on to search for consensus elsewhere in the situation (Zelditch & Floyd, 1998a, b).

This last finding requires not only refining the concept of consensus but also its scope of application. Issue-specific consensus would have been impossible if Ss had been presented with a situation structured by a tightly integrated set of ALEs on which one could draw to justify violations. But results from the criterion phase of Massey et al. (1997) had already given evidence that the situation was a mix of consensus and dissensus (i.e. uncontested and contested norms, values, and procedures). Hence dissensus about some elements in the system did not necessarily imply dissensus about every other element in it. Had definitions of the situation been complete and coherent, dissensus anywhere would have meant dissensus everywhere. Near, collective consensus would still have been all that legitimacy required, but only if Ss everywhere agreed.

Thus, consensus is a necessary condition of legitimation but the concept of consensus required by the condition is a minimalist one: It is sufficient if nearly all agree, if a particular individual believes others agree even if she/he does not, and consensus is specific to each issue. Consensus is an impossible condition to satisfy if the entire structure of pre-given values is a tightly integrated whole and there is dissensus anywhere in it. But if it is not a complete, coherent whole, all legitimacy requires is consensus somewhere in it.

The Common Interest: Impartiality

Like consensus, the hypothesis that a self-serving justification fails to legitimate a regime, even delegitimates it, is the foundation of theories as disparate as Rousseau's social contract theory (Rousseau, 1762 [1948]), Marx's theory of ideology (Marx & Engels, 1845–1847 [1976]; also Abercrombie, Hill & Turner, 1980; Gouldner, 1976), and Machiavelli's mystification theory (Machiavelli, 1517 [1940a], 1532 [1940b]; also Mosca, 1896 [1963]; Pareto, 1916 [1963], Vol. 3). If a regime legitimating formula (RLF), does appeal to self-interest, it legitimates a regime only if it is in the general interest (as in Smith, 1776) or is universalizable (i.e. only if interchanging self and other in no way alters who is advantaged), (from Kant, 1785 [1969]). Put another way, self-interest can legitimize a regime only if the playing field is level, as in the rules of competitive games such as chess or bridge. A claim to legitimacy cannot be based on an appeal to the interest of some but not others in a group.

We found support for this hypothesis in a failed experiment the purpose of which was to test Corollary 4, the mystification hypothesis (Zelditch et al., 1984). In this experiment, S assisted E in monitoring the performance of five confederates in a centralized information exchange network. A bonus was distributed inequitably (because access to it depended on position in the network) but it was possible to change the structure of the network by majority vote. Ss were assigned to a 2 × 2 (interest × regime purpose) design. Half the Ss had a vested interest in the outcome because they were paid an amount equal to that of the highest paid position they were monitoring for E. The other half had no interest in the network structure. Ss were told that previous research had shown that the network structure was the most efficient for the task. Regime purpose was varied by telling half the Ss that the procedure for changing the network structure had been retained to maintain comparability with previous research. E was now concerned to study detailed patterns of information flow that did not become stable until the eighth problem had been solved. E left the lab but told Ss he would return after the eighth problem was completed to measure the pattern of information flow. S was responsible, among other things, for deciding whether to hold an election to change the structure of the network if a motion to change it was made and seconded.

The purpose of the experiment was to test a theory of nondecisions (see Bachrach & Baratz, 1962, 1963, 1970; Zelditch et al., 1983). Its main hypothesis was that, for any S who had a vested interest in a centralized communication network, the legitimating myth of the experiment would justify suppressing attempts to change the network structure. As a result, S's self-interest was masked and the rate at which S suppressed elections should increase. But the legitimacy manipulation failed to mask self-interest, making it unacceptable for Ss to suppress elections. In the best-fitting "nested by value" model,[7] the legitimating myth, rather than raising the odds of preventing elections, significantly reduced them when interest was present compared with when it was absent (Zelditch et al., 1984).

Examination of post-session questionnaires and interviews showed that our manipulation of legitimacy failed to suppress elections because it failed to mask self-interest. We studied S's post-session approval of the network, the bonus, and the amount of the bonus, and S's opinion of other team members' approval of the network and bonus. Taking all five measures together, the investigators found that interest had a main effect on each of them (aggregate $\chi^2 = 18.65$, df $= 5$, $p < 0.01$); legitimacy had a significant effect in the absence of interest (aggregate $\chi^2 = 11.36$, df $= 5$, $p < 0.05$); but legitimacy had no effect in the presence of interest ($\chi^2 = 3.76$, df $= 5$, $p =$ n.s.). For all five items, the parameter for legitimacy's effect in the presence of interest was less than the parameter for interest alone and in four of the five it was less than the parameter for the effect of legitimacy in the absence of interest (Zelditch et al., 1984).

That it would have been transparently self-serving to deploy the legitimacy manipulation of the experiment to justify suppressing an election is reflected in the two measures concerned with what "others" thought. Absent interest, the odds of thinking that others would feel a bonus was appropriate were 10.2 times greater when legitimacy was present than when it was absent ($\chi^2 = 4.31$, df $= 1$, $p < 0.05$). The odds of thinking that others would approve a centralized communication network were 5.8 times greater when legitimacy was present than when it was absent ($\chi^2 = 4.17$, df $= 1$, $p < 0.05$). But the effect of legitimacy vanished in the presence of interest. (In the case of other's approval of the bonus, $\chi^2 = 0.00$, df $= 1$, $p =$ n.s. In the case of others' approval of the network, $\chi^2 = 0.32$, df $= 1$, $p =$ n.s. Zelditch et al., 1984.)

This supports the impartiality condition as far as it goes. Absent impartiality, a RLF does not legitimate R. But the BLA holds that, Conditions 1, 3, and 4 being equal, if impartiality *is* satisfied a RLF does legitimate R. Up to this point, we have no evidence that a legitimacy manipulation that masked self-interest would have legitimated the centralized communication network.

Studies of offers of justifications (Massey et al., 1997; Zelditch & Floyd, 1998a, b) provide another kind of evidence in support of the impartiality condition. In those studies, Ss appealed to group interests rather than special interests even when E explicitly legitimated self-interest. In contrast to our other studies, we found an anomaly: The commons dilemma setting satisfied the condition of universalizability but universalizability was not sufficient to legitimate self-interest.

Each S was responsible for the water reserves of a community, was instructed to maximize their community's water resources, and was awarded points for doing so. But each was also asked to balance the community's interests against the collective interest in conservation of a general reserve shared with another community.

The criterion phase of Massey et al. (1997) gave a sample of valid and invalid justifications for violating the expectation that a monitor of the general reserve would replenish each community's local reserve on each trial of the experiment. An ex post facto analysis of these justifications, for purposes of the present paper, found that appeals to the group interest were favored over appeals to self-interest and this was as true of invalid as valid justifications.

Using a single phrase as a unit of measure, we found that Ss appealed to the common interest in 13 of 59 unit-clauses in valid justifications (22%) and nine of 35 in invalid justifications (26%), an insignificant difference. But there were two kinds of appeals to self interest: Some were positive (e.g. appeals to the community's advantage), some were negative (e.g. accusing communities of selfishness, which therefore justified the WM's behavior). Positive appeals to self-interest occurred only twice, once in valid and once in invalid justifications. Accusations of selfishness were more common, nine in valid justifications (15%), six in invalid justifications (17%), again an insignificant difference. Pooling the two conditions, there were 11 appeals to the common interest and 7.5 appeals to the selfishness of partial interests for every positive appeal to self-interest (Massey et al., 1997*; Zelditch & Floyd, 1998b*).[8]

The criterion phase of Zelditch and Floyd (1998a, b) gave us a sample of defenses against challenges to the justifications actually employed in the first experiment. One of the study's purposes was to compare the content of justifications of justifications (meta-justifications) to that of justifications of acts, on the hypothesis that meta-justifications defend rules that are taken-for-granted and, therefore, are unmentioned by justifications of acts. And in fact the result was a sample of justifications of rules (i.e. of regime justifications).

Regime-justifications revealed the same pattern as justifications of acts. Appeals to group interest were favored over appeals to self-interest and appeared about as often in defense of invalid as valid justifications. They appealed to the group interest 115 times in 223 unit clauses in defense of valid justifications (52%) and 60 times in 142 clauses in defense of invalid justifications (42%) ($\chi^2 = 13.02$, df $= 1, p = $ n.s.). There was a small but significant difference in appeals to positive self-interest, which was appealed to less often when justifications were invalid. When the justification defended was invalid, and consensus was in doubt, 2% of clauses made a positive appeal to self-interest. When the justification defended was valid, and consensus was not in doubt, 7% of clauses made a positive appeal to self-interest ($\chi^2 = 3.94$, df $= 1, p < 0.05$). On the other hand, accusations of self-ishness occurred about equally in the two conditions, 5% in defense of valid justifications, 6% in defense of invalid justifications. Pooling the two conditions, the ratio of common appeals to positive appeals to self-interest is about 11.67 to 1, with one accusatory use of self-interest for each appeal to positive self-interest (Zelditch & Floyd, 1998b*).

Although they reveal the same pattern, regime-justifications appealed to the group interest even more than justifications of acts. Forty-eight percent of unit clauses in the former appealed to the common interest, compared to 23% in the latter ($\chi^2 = 18.38$, df = 1, $p < 0.001$). On the other hand, while the ratio of appeals to the common interest to positive appeals to self-interest is about the same in the two, the ratio of negative to positive appeals to self-interest is greater for justifications of acts (7.5 to 1) than regimes (1 to 1.11), ($\chi^2 = 5.36$, df = 1, $p < 0.05$) (Zelditch & Floyd, 1998b*).

Clearly, impartiality is a necessary condition of legitimation. The anomaly here is not impartiality, but universalizability. In the commons dilemma experiments, the situation satisfies universalizability, but it is not sufficient to legitimate self-interest. This does not mean that it is not possible to legitimate self-interest. But it does mean that it is not sufficient for E to just say it is so. Furthermore, at least in mixed-motive situations, appeals to universalizability are not by themselves sufficient to legitimate self-interest. What undermines the legitimacy of self-interest in the commons dilemma experiments is that if either or both of the communities is self-interested at the expense of the common interest, self-interest is illegitimate, no matter what E says and no matter how level the playing field. In competitive games, like bridge or chess, universalizability is sufficient to create legitimacy. In order to legitimate self-interest in mixed-motive situations both universalizability and the group interest must be satisfied, or at least self-interest must be consistent with the general welfare.[9]

Objectification

Many justifications of regimes include beliefs about matters of fact. For example, some justifications depend on "effectiveness" claims (see Corollary 3). In the information exchange setting, the idea that "A centralized communication network is the most efficient way of performing the group task," legitimates the network by citing its effectiveness. A similar claim is offered in the commons dilemma setting (i.e. "the amount of water is finite"). But the capacity of beliefs about matters of fact to legitimate a regime depends on the extent to which they are objectified (Berger & Luckmann, 1966). They (1) must reflect externalized, matters of "what is" as opposed to personal opinion (e.g. "what I think"), and (2) must be publicly validated by agreement with others. To the extent that beliefs are objectified, they are given in the nature of things. They can be used either to legitimate or delegitimate a regime. Natural laws – either God's or science's – have historically been used in both ways, as in the U.S. Declaration of Independence.

Offers of justifications for acts and regimes in the criterion phases of the two commons dilemma experiments provide useful data bearing on objectification. They show, first, that it is a factor in creating legitimacy in general and, second, that it is an important factor specifically for the legitimation of regimes.

We divided the sample of Massey et al.'s (1997) justifications of unwarranted acts at the median into valid and invalid justifications (without regard to consensus) and each clause in each justification was coded as either an "I" clause, indicating an opinion, or an "is" clause, indicating a matter of objective fact. The proportion of "I" clauses should be inversely proportional to the objectification of the sample of justifications. Among Massey et al.'s (1997) valid justifications, 15.25% of clauses used "I" compared to 42.86% among their invalid justifications ($\chi^2 = 8.80$, df $= 1, p < 0.01$) (Massey et al., 1997*; Zelditch & Floyd, 1998b*).

After coding Zelditch and Floyd's (1998a) regime-justifications in the same way, we found that Ss actually used "I" in three very different ways. First, 29% of Ss (in the valid and invalid conditions combined) used "I" as identity-work (i.e. to refer to their position in the regime and its duties, which became "my duties"). There were more of these in defense of an invalid (39%) than valid (22%) regime justification ($\chi^2 = 12.19$, df $= 1, p < 0.01$). Second, 4% of all Ss used "I" in "power trips" (e.g. "I do what I want."). All of these were in defense of an invalid regime justification (26% of such defenses). They essentially concede dissensus and resist the "need" for legitimacy. Only the third way of using "I" expressed personal opinions, as in "I think that . . . ." There were very few of these in defense of either valid or invalid regime justifications – 12% of clauses in defense of an invalid regime justification, 8% in defense of a valid regime justification ($\chi^2 = 0.83$, df $= 1, p =$ n.s.), 10% in the two conditions combined. This is proportionately fewer than we found in valid justifications of acts (15.25%) but the difference was not statistically significant ($\chi^2 = 1.38$, df $= 1, p =$ n.s. Zelditch & Floyd, 1998b*).

Consonance

In a sense, a claim to legitimacy applies general principles to a particular case. Crisis theories of legitimacy (e.g. Habermas, 1975), have called attention to the fact that, if the particular case is not an instance of the general principle that legitimates it, the claim to legitimacy fails to legitimate the particular case. Habermas's example is that an appeal to principles grounded in 19th century liberalism does not legitimate monopoly capitalism.

Two attempts to legitimate the bonus awarded for the fastest solution to the group task in the information exchange setting supported this hypothesis. In one,

S was in a peripheral position of a centralized communication network with a simulated confederate at the center (Lineweber et al., 1982). In this setting, the bonus was almost always perceived to be inequitable because it was very large and, because the network structure ensured that the center position would always win it. We attempted to legitimate the bonus by telling half the Ss that "we have specially selected the person who occupies the orange position," where "orange" was the color code for the person at the center of the network. "We have chosen a person for the orange position who is both experienced at the problems on which your group will be working and is very adept at the solution of these problems. In fact, the person who is orange in your group has demonstrated a performance level in the top 1% of all the people who have worked on these problems over the past year and a half."

This had the predicted effect of suppressing attempts to change the network structure but it was not our successful manipulation of the equity of the bonus that produced this effect. Five post-session questionnaire items were used to check the manipulation of equity. Four of the five did not differ significantly by condition. Orange was thought about equally able in both the equity and inequity conditions. Ss in both conditions thought team earnings should be divided equally, that the bonus was much too high, and that E should change the communication network in future experiments. The only item differentiating the two conditions was the appropriateness of the bonus. But even responses to this item differed only marginally between conditions. In the equity condition, only four Ss (20%) thought the bonus appropriate. This raised the mean propriety of the bonus, on a scale that ranged from 1 = very appropriate to 5 = very inappropriate, from 4.84 to 4.25. In neither case was the bonus very appropriate.

In post-session interviews Ss in the equity condition explained their responses by offering (often spontaneously) that, although orange was very able, the task was so simple that ability was irrelevant. Forty percent of Ss offered this explanation before they were asked for one and 75% offered it when asked. It is clear from these results that we did not successfully establish the propriety or individually-accepted legitimacy of the bonus (Lineweber et al., 1982).[10]

We also attempted to legitimate the bonus in an experiment in which S was at the center of the network, with (simulated) confederates in the peripheral positions (Zelditch & Walker, 2000). In this experiment we instructed half the Ss that "of course, in a centralized network like the one you are in today, the bonus will most often be won by the person in the center of the communication system. But that's OK, because in a centralized network, the person in the center does more work than any other person."

The effect was not much different: The bonus was marginally, though significantly, more appropriate in the equity than the inequity condition, but the equity manipulation increased the propriety of the bonus by less than a point. Of six measures of the legitimacy of the bonus, there were no significant differences in the responses of Ss in the equity and inequity conditions for four of them. Ss thought the bonus more appropriate in the equity conditions. But they thought the amount of the bonus much too high, and, in post-session interviews, they said that the task was too simple to require much effort (Zelditch & Walker, 2000*).

Thus, the premises of the manipulation were not consonant with the particular case they were intended to legitimate and the manipulation failed of its purpose. This is consistent with the consonance condition of the BLA as far as it goes, but leaves open the question of whether a consonant manipulation would have legitimated the bonus.

FOUR COROLLARIES OF THE BASIC LEGITIMATION ASSUMPTION

The Spread of Legitimacy

The BLA implies that the effect of a RLF is to spread the legitimacy of accepted legitimating elements (ALEs) to undefined or contested elements of R. This, in turn, implies that the effect of a RLF on compliance, support, riot, and revolution, is indirect rather than direct, through its effect on the attitudes and orientations of actors towards R.

This hypothesis was supported by an experiment designed to determine how validity (in the Weberian sense), affected change-attempts in the information exchange setting (Walker et al., 1988). In this experiment S was in a peripheral position of a centralized communication network. A bonus was awarded for the first correct solution reported to E. The bonus was inequitable because the communication network was centralized but it was possible to change the structure of the network by majority vote. Half the Ss heard a legitimacy manipulation that emphasized the efficiency of centralized networks and told Ss that E's objective was to study the pattern of the flow of information which did not become stable until eight of ten problems had been completed. E told Ss he would leave the lab and return to measure the flow after the eighth problem. Half the Ss had their attitudes toward the network measured before the manipulation of the bonus and those of the other half were measured after it. In the best-fitting model of this experiment, the manipulation of legitimacy had a direct effect on Ss beliefs about the propriety of the network, which in turn had a direct (inhibiting) effect on S's behavior in the experiment. The effect of the manipulation on the propriety of the network, in turn, was due to its emphasis on the efficiency of the network for the task of the experiment (Walker et al., 1988, 1991).

The legitimacy manipulation had two distinguishable features, its emphasis on efficiency and its implied directive, "don't change this network." The second was created by instructions that E's objective was to study patterns of information flow which could only be studied if S did not change the network structure before the eighth of ten trials. Nor can there be any doubt that the manipulation directly inhibited S from attempting to change the network. But independent of this effect, there was a significant difference in S's belief in the efficiency of the network between the legitimacy and baseline conditions ($U = 48.5$, $z = 4.10$, $p < 0.000$)[11] and this difference was correlated with the propriety of the network ($r_s = 73$, $t = 6.58$, df $= 38$, $p < 0.000$ Walker et al., 1988*). An alternative model, assuming that behavior explained propriety rather than propriety behavior, was rejected as inconsistent with the data (Walker et al., 1988). Thus, the evidence supported the hypothesis that legitimacy spread from E's manipulation, through its effect on beliefs in the network's efficiency, to the propriety of the network, independent of any direct effect on the inhibition of protest by S.

The inequity created in this setting by the bonus manipulation also spread to the propriety of the network – a reminder that the BLA can be used to delegitimate as well as legitimate regimes. The structure of the network was causally related to the inequity of the bonus. The illegitimacy of the bonus spread along this causal path, dampening the legitimacy of the network. Before the bonus manipulation, Ss in the peripheral positions of the network consistently believed its structure proper. Aggregated over Ss in the baseline condition of five experiments for which a measure of network propriety was available before the bonus manipulation, mean approval of the centralized communication network was 2.06 on a scale from 1 = very high approval to 5 = very low approval. The bonus, on the other hand, was improper even before any critical trials. We aggregated data for the baseline conditions of two experiments which measured propriety of the bonus immediately after the bonus manipulation. The mean approval rating was 4.25 (5 = very inappropriate). But all Ss understood that the network structure was one of the reasons that the bonus was inequitable. The bonus manipulation therefore had the effect of significantly reducing the propriety of the network when it was measured immediately after the bonus manipulation, even before any critical trials of the experiment. After the bonus, mean approval of the network was 2.65, a difference that was statistically significant ($U = 127$, $z = 1.98$, $p = 0.024$ Walker et al., 1988*) This was confirmed by the results of two subsequent experiments in which it was possible to compare the propriety of the network with and without the bonus. (For the first of these $U = 19$, $z = 5.24$, $p < 0.001$; for the second, $U = 127.5$, $z = 1.96$, $p = 0.025$ Walker et al., 1989*.)

The manipulation of the bonus also had two distinguishable features. It was inequitable because it was so large and because "the bonus will be paid to the member of the team who reports the correct answer first," which in a centralized network would always be the person at the center of it. It was also justified by saying that "we think you can work a little faster," which in itself could have undermined S's faith in the efficiency of the network. Thus, it might have been the effect of the bonus manipulation on belief in the network's efficiency rather than the spread of its illegitimacy that explained the effect of the bonus on the propriety of the network. However, if this is so, the effect was through S's belief in the efficiency of the network. To control for this effect, we did a two-way analysis of variance by ranks on baseline data reported by Walker et al. (1988). Holding efficiency constant, the propriety of the bonus had an independent effect on the propriety of the network ($\chi^2 = 12.38$, df $= 2, p < 0.01$ Walker et al., 1988*). No doubt the inequity of the bonus had a direct effect on the pressure to change the structure of the network, but it also had an indirect effect, through its negative effect on the propriety of the network.

Thus, Corollary 1 is supported by evidence that the mechanism by which a claim to legitimacy has its effect is through the spread of legitimacy from ALEs to unaccepted elements of a regime to which they are linked. But the BLA is too spare to account for one feature of our findings: in five of our experiments, we used the bonus and legitimacy manipulations and the effects of both spread, in the same experiment. The BLA does not take multiple sources of legitimacy into account although most regimes have multiple sources of legitimacy (Easton, 1965). An adequate formulation of the BLA needs to answer the question of how they combine.

The formulation most consistent with the evidence of these experiments is that multiple sources of legitimation have independent, and therefore additive, effects on the spread of legitimacy.[12] A two-way analysis of variance by ranks of the effects of the efficiency of the network and the propriety of the bonus on the propriety of the network – mentioned above – found that efficiency had a positive effect. It increased the propriety of the network independent of the propriety of the bonus. Propriety of the bonus had a negative, decreasing effect on the propriety of the network, independent of the efficiency of the network and the two effects were additive (data are from the baseline condition of Walker et al., 1988*). These data were from Ss in the peripheral positions of centralized networks in the information exchange setting. The finding was further supported by a two-way analysis of variance by ranks on data, also from baseline conditions, of the effects of network efficiency and the propriety of the bonus on the propriety of the network for Ss assisting E in E's office ($\chi^2 = 11.61$, df $= 2, p < 0.01$ Zelditch et al., 1984*) and for Ss at the center of the network. (In the latter case, the data are aggregated over the baseline conditions of two experiments ($\chi^2 = 148.11$, df $= 4, p < 0.001$).) (See Zelditch & Walker, 2000*.)

The Conservation of Legitimacy

A pre-given structure of socially accepted values, norms, beliefs, practices and procedures (ALEs) is a necessary condition of legitimation. Legitimacy cannot be created de novo, out of nothing. There are many instances in which what is required is agreement in a particular situation about the goals of the group. But even in these cases the beliefs that connect a particular regime to attainment of agreed-on goals must themselves have some pre-given acceptance. New bases of legitimacy do emerge, as science, for example, displaced religion as the grounds for "natural" law in the enlightenment, or, as Stryker shows, came to compete with legal rationalities in legitimating contemporary legal institutions (Stryker, 1994). But before science can ground a belief as a matter of unquestioned fact it must itself come to be accepted as an element of the pre-given structure of ALEs in a given society. To legitimate undefined or contested elements of a regime something must already be accepted somewhere.

It is again on offers of regime-justifications in the commons dilemma setting that we draw for evidence for this hypothesis. Responding to challenged justifications, Ss deployed largely stereotyped defenses of them. Few Ss gave complete accounts because most took one or more of their premises so much for granted that they went without saying. But an analysis that grouped together those defenses that formed a single, coherent logical progression, found that there were typically two, in one case three, pre-given, standardized defenses against each challenge (Zelditch & Floyd, 1998b).

One challenge was to justify a discretionary regime. One defense was that, "The water supply is non-renewable and in danger of running out, hence must be conserved. Self-monitoring is inadequate to assure conservation because one cannot be sure everyone will voluntarily participate. Therefore, someone has to be in control and the water monitor is the only one who sees what both communities are doing and knows how much is left in the general reserve." Alternatively, "The water monitor's goal is to make sure that the water supply lasts as long as possible and has a duty to be fair, to act in the interests of both communities."

Challenged to justify a WM's disregard of the majority's vote, one defense was that, "The vote did not take into account that water would run out so fast and did not take the general welfare into account." The other was that, "This is an emergency and in an emergency one may override a vote if it is in the interests of the general welfare, which in this case it is."

Challenged to justify conservation, there were three variants of what was essentially one defense, that conservation was vital to the survival of the species. One variant was specific to the experiment, a second to water, the third to all natural resources.

The validity of the justification defended made a difference to the number of defenses offered, but not to their content. Ss used the same arguments whether or not the justification defended was valid, hence whether or not they had reason to doubt consensus. Excluding "power trips," in which no defense was offered, 89% of all defenses used one or more premises from one of the pre-given, standardized regime-justifications (Zelditch & Floyd, 1998b). Thus, one can say that pre-given, stereotyped accounts provide the resources that enable, but also constrain, the vocabulary of the legitimation of regimes.

Effectiveness

One source of a regime's legitimacy is its effectiveness as a means to the agreed-on ends of the group: To the extent that a group accepts a goal, if the regime is instrumental to achieving the goal it is accepted as legitimate by the group (Linz, 1978; Lipset, 1959). We used it often and found repeated support for this hypothesis throughout the two dozen experiments with which we are concerned in the present paper. However, it was not the hypothesis with which we started. We began, as we stated earlier, with a demand characteristics hypothesis. It was the failures of this hypothesis, and the ways in which we had to reformulate it, that provide much of the support for the effectiveness hypothesis.

Subjects who volunteer for experiments tend to have faith in science and in experiments as means to the ends of science. An experiment can be conceived as a social practice in Wittgenstein's sense of the term (Wittgenstein, 1958). By definition, a practice is a rule-governed activity. Because Ss are unfamiliar with the practice, they enter the experiment ready to accept whatever E says in his/her instructions about the rules of the practice. E's directives are much like the rules inside the cover of the box in which any chess set is sold. The demand characteristics of an experiment (Orne, 1962; Orne & Evans, 1965) are simply the rules of the practice. The instructions given by E to S define the meaning of acts in the experiment and which acts do and do not have meaning in it.

To begin with, we understood this to mean that, literally, anything goes, that we could make anything legitimate or illegitimate by the way we wrote E's instructions. Our objective was to discover how legitimacy shaped the logic of collective action. Our first attempts to accomplish the purpose consisted simply in telling S, in an information exchange setting, that a centralized communication network was selected for study by E because it was the best way of accomplishing the group's task. We supposed that S believed in science; that S would accept whatever E said as science; hence, if E said a centralized network was the best means to the group's ends, then even if it caused inequity, S would be less likely to attempt change when compared with a control group in which S was told that the centralized network was randomly chosen.

On the other hand, the bonus manipulation was introduced by saying that, "We think you can work a little faster," which Ss took to mean that a centralized network was not in fact the best structure for the task, and, because E was searching for the best structure, it was consistent with E's goals to change that structure to one that might be better (Walker, 1979).

We pre-tested a succession of manipulations that strengthened the emphasis on the efficiency of a centralized network, with an elaborate history of scientific research on such networks, a chart of this history posted in each S's experimental cubicle, and repetition of the claim in the summary of E's instructions to S. None of this accomplished the purpose of legitimating a centralized network in the face of the bonus manipulation, which continued to say to S that E's purpose was to find the best structure. The instructions suggested that, despite previous research to the contrary, a centralized network was not the best structure. Hence, it was consistent with E's purposes in the experiment for S to find a better structure. Ss continued to think this way through seven versions of the manipulation until finally we simply changed their understanding of E's objectives in the experiment. The manipulation that legitimated a centralized network continued to emphasize its scientifically verified efficiency but it also informed S that E's *new* objective was to measure detailed patterns of information flow that did not stabilize until S had completed eight (out of 10) problems and that E would return after eight problems to measure them. Thus, stability of the network's structure became in-strumental to E's purposes and Ss, who always began the experiment by believing a centralized network efficient, hence a legitimate means to the task goals of the group, continued to believe it proper in the legitimacy conditions of these exper-iments and in consequence resisted pressure to change it (Thomas et al., 1986; Walker et al., 1988).

It might be argued that all that we did was directly command Ss to resist change and they followed E's instructions because they believed in the authority of E. But that argument is not consistent with our earlier experience, nor in fact any subsequent experience, with manipulating legitimacy in these experiments. It is true as far as it goes, but its limit is that such a directive is itself legitimate if and only if it is consistent with what S understands to be E's larger purposes in the experiment. Of the demand characteristics hypothesis, what remains true is that E's purposes determine what is legitimate in an experiment and anything that either has no meaning in light of E's purposes or disrupts that meaning is illegitimate. Anything consistent with that meaning in the light of E's legitimate purposes is also legitimate. The demand characteristics hypothesis holds only if at the same time all four conditions of the BLA are satisfied. Anything that satisfies the BLA goes, but nothing goes that fails to satisfy its conditions.

The ways that the demand characteristics hypothesis failed consistently supported the effectiveness hypothesis. If a centralized network is efficient, and therefore instrumental to the group's task goals, then it is proper. If it is not efficient it is improper and S's attempt to find a more efficient structure is legitimate because the search is instrumental to E's objectives for the experiment – objectives that are legitimized in the name of science. If network stability rather than efficiency is instrumental to E's purposes, a centralized network is proper and Ss resist pressures to change it.

Support for the effectiveness hypothesis was also found in an experiment in a multi-level hierarchy in which middle-level supervisors, whose function was to maximize the productivity of two teams playing a word game, assessed a penalty for under-achievement. In this experiment, the legitimacy of the position, person, and/or act was varied, and payment of the penalty was made anonymous, without any surveillance by either S's superior or E. The dependent variable was the amount of the penalty actually paid (Walker et al., 2002).

This experiment found that legitimacy of position, person, and act each had independent effects on the amount of the penalty paid. Illegitimacy of position and person substantially decreased the amount paid but compliance was much greater when the act – the amount S was actually penalized – was illegitimate than when position or person was illegitimate (Walker et al., 2002).

A replication of the experiment tested the hypothesis that compliance with the illegitimate act was due to an artifact of the timing of the penalties, but found that only a small part of the result was an artifact (Erlin & McLean, 1989). Erlin and McLean also asked Ss to account for the behavior of the middle manager. In all conditions, a majority of Ss legitimated penalties as an institution although in all conditions they felt the actual penalties were unfair because they had been randomly timed. Regardless of condition, the account offered for the middle manager's behavior was that the goal of the team was productivity, that incentives for performance were instrumental to productivity and, therefore, the incentives used by the middle manager were legitimate. Where the amount of the penalty was illegitimate but S had paid it, Ss were asked why they had complied. The Ss often offered demand characteristics accounts of their behavior. But if demand characteristics actually explained S's behavior, there would have been more compliance than there was in the illegitimate position and illegitimate person conditions of the experiment. Although ex post facto, the effectiveness hypothesis proved to be a better explanation: Where the amount of the penalty was illegitimate, the rate of compliance differed significantly if S offered an effectiveness account for the middle manager's behavior ($\chi^2 = 5.11, p < 0.05$ (Erlin & McLean, 1989*)).

Mystification

A claim to legitimacy cannot be based on an appeal to the interest of some but not others in a group (from the impartiality condition). If the motive for making the claim is self-interest, the claim will fail to legitimate R if its motive is transparent; it legitimates R only if the motive is masked. (From Machiavelli, 1517 [1940a], 1532 [1940b]; see also Mosca, 1896 [1939]; Pareto, 1916 [1963], Vol. 3.) Demystification of a claim, unmasking the interest that lies behind it, de-legitimates a regime.

In the section that describes work relevant to common interest above, we have already described our attempt to test this hypothesis, motivated by its role in Bachrach and Baratz's theory of non-decisions (Bachrach & Baratz, 1962, 1963, 1970). We constructed a logit model of their theory for an information exchange setting in which S assisted E in monitoring five confederates in a centralized communication network (Zelditch et al., 1984). Recall that half the Ss were paid a flat fee for their participation, half an amount keyed to the pay of the highest paid position in the network they monitored. Half also overheard E's manipulation of the legitimacy of the centralized network, half did not. S had the duty to decide whether to hold an election if there was a motion to change the structure of the network. The logit model constructed for this situation predicted (1) that self-interest would have a main effect on the odds of vetoing an election. Because Bachrach and Baratz assumed that, absent self-interest, legitimacy was epiphenomenal, the model assumed (2) that legitimacy would have no main effect on vetoing an election. But (3) if interest were present, legitimacy would magnify the effect of interest on the odds of vetoing an election, because, by hypothesis, the legitimating myth of the experiment would mask the self-interested character of S's motives, enabling S to legitimately justify suppressing a motion to change the structure of the network.

This nested-by-value[13] model was rejected because an additive model fit as well and was simpler (Zelditch et al., 1983). But we also found that, for the nested-by-value model that best fit the data, the effect of legitimacy on the odds of vetoing an election was significantly less, not more, when interest was present than when it was absent (Zelditch et al., 1984). This, in turn, was attributed to the transparency of S's motives, exhibited in the fact that, absent interest, legitimacy increased S's perception that others approved the bonus and network in post-session questionnaires, but had no effect when interest was present.

Thus, the data supported the need to mask self-interest, but stopped short of showing that were interest masked, mystification would legitimate a regime.

CONCLUSIONS

We offer several conclusions from this line of research. First, we considerably over-estimated the power of demand characteristics. Authority figures have the power to define meaning, purpose, and appropriateness but in our experiments they do not have the power to establish the legitimacy of anything that E designates. We found that the demand characteristics hypothesis holds only if it satisfies the conditions of the BLA. As with any regime, the authority of an experimenter must itself be established and maintained. Anything E says in an experiment goes if it satisfies the conditions of the BLA, but nothing goes that fails to satisfy them.

Second, we found it necessary to make three minor elaborations of the BLA. We found general support for the objectification and consonance conditions, but made minor refinements in the consensus and impartiality conditions. With respect to consensus, we found it necessary to refine both the definition of the concept and the scope of its application. Unless the pre-given structure of values, norms, beliefs, practices, and procedures from which a claim to legitimacy draws its premises is so well integrated that dissensus anywhere in it is dissensus everywhere, near, collective, specific consensus is all that is necessary. For impartiality, if self-interests are involved, at least in mixed-motive situations, universalizability is not sufficient for impartiality. Impartiality also requires that self-interest is in the group interest.

We found strong support for the effectiveness hypothesis among the BLA's corollaries. Regimes that are effective for the goals, first of all of S, but also of E, are legitimate. A regime that is ineffective for the goals of either of the two is not. The data also supported the conservation and mystification corollaries as far as they went, but did not go quite far enough. When offering regime-legitimating formulae, Ss deployed mostly old bottles. But we have no evidence that their attempts at legitimation would have failed had they deployed new bottles. Absent mystification, a self-serving legitimation failed, but we have no evidence that a less transparent mask would have succeeded.

The spread of legitimacy corollary proved to be more complicated than expected. It was supported by everything we have found about legitimacy, but the BLA does not adequately account for the complexity of regimes. Extending the

BLA to multiple sources of legitimacy required some idea of how they combine. We found that each source of legitimacy spread independently along a path of causal implication, paths combining additively in their effect on the legitimacy of regimes.

To sum up, we begin with consensus as we define it with respect to accepted legitimating elements (ALEs) and regime-legitimating formulae (RLFs) (Definitions 2 and 3). Then, given a RLF for a regime R, the undefined or contested elements of R acquire the legitimacy of the ALEs on which a RLF depends if and only if: (1) (Consensus) There is consensual acceptance of any potential legitimating elements (i.e. they are ALEs), to which RLF appeals within the domain of R. In the absence of consensus, there exists an ALE, independent of other ALEs, that implies or is implied by R. (2) (Impartiality) Any benefit of R to which a RLF appeals is (a) in the group interest, under cooperative conditions; (b) universalizable, under competitive conditions; or (c) both in the group interest and universalizable under mixed-motive conditions. (3) (Objectification) Any belief to which a RLF appeals is consensually accepted as a matter of objective fact. Finally, (4) (Consonance) Any ALE to which a RLF appeals is consonant with the nature, conditions, and consequences of R. Given two or more RLFs, the effect of each RLF is independent of any other.

NOTES

1. We borrow the term, "first-order legitimation," from Berger and Luckmann (1966, p. 92) and use it to describe nascent legitimation.

2. Weber's term is *Herrschaft* and his exposition makes clear that domination may or may not be legitimate.

3. "Collectively-establsihed" in the sense that a focal actor believes that others accept and support the legitimacy of norms, beliefs, etc. The focal actor does not have to accept or attribute legitimacy to them.

4. The assumption surveys the world from the point of view of members of a focal system (i.e. the conception is system specific). Any interests to which it refers are perceived rather than "real" interests.

5. An exception is Easton (1965, pp. 195–198), where very little consensus is required about very little.

6. See the Appendix for a catalog of studies from which the data we describe are drawn.

7. A "nested by value" model is a logit model in which one or more independent variables has no main effect but does interact with other independent variables in determining the dependent variable (Stokes et al., 2000, pp. 391–395).

8. We use an asterisk to show that a result is based on subsequent analysis of data originally reported in the citation given. Massey et al. (1997) did not report the data analysis that led to its manipulations but some of those data were analyzed in Zelditch and Floyd (1998b). The analyses carried out specifically for this paper were undertaken after both studies were completed.

9. We find parallels in current geopolitics. American citizens enthusiastically supported U.S. intervention in Afghanistan. Historically, successful military campaigns have strengthened the legitimacy and popularity of leaders (i.e. a result that satisfies a president's self interest). The Afghanistan campaign was viewed broadly as crucial to the security of every American. On the other hand, as we write, the specter of a war on Iraq is more contentious. Claims that such a campaign is in the public interest are met with skepticism and must compete with beliefs that the campaign is fueled by the combined interests of economic actors (blood for oil), and a president's self interest (a loyal son and former oilman completing his former oilman and presidential father's unfinished business).

10. Why, then, did the two conditions differ in rates of change attempts? Post-hoc analysis of the data showed that the equity manipulation did legitimate both orange's behavior and the structure of the network. In both conditions of the experiment, orange "took charge." In the equity condition, this was legitimated by E's instruction that orange had superior experience and skill. Because the manipulation also legitimated the structure of the network, changing it was seen by S as disrupting the smooth performance of the task. Together, these two effects diminished the magnitude of the pressure to change induced by the otherwise improper bonus in the equity condition (Lineweber et al., 1982).

11. Measured by the Mann-Whitney U-test rather than t because the distribution of propriety was so skewed.

12. We have repeatedly found that the legitimacy of authority cancels the destabilizing effects of inequity (e.g. Zelditch et al., 1983; Zelditch & Walker, 1984) and a study of the legitimacy of acts, persons, and positions has also found that each of them had an independent effect on compliance (Walker et al., 2002). But the present findings focus on the spread of legitimacy to different elements of the regime rather than the effects of the legitimacy of different elements of the regime on behavior.

13. The term that describes a logit model of this kind. See Note 4.

ACKNOWLEDGMENTS

We gratefully acknowledge the support of NSF grants SOC 7817434, SES 8420238, and SES 8712097. In addition, we are grateful for the assistance of Terry Amburgey, Dorine Barr-Bryan, Christopher Erlin, Anthony Floyd, Joan Ford, Sabrina Freeman, Edward Gilliland, William A. Harris, Jon Hooper, David Lineweber, Tormod Lunde, Kathy Lyman, Kelly Massey, Bonnie McLean, Valerie C. Montoya, Larry Rogers, Louise Smith-Donals, Paula S. Taylor, George M. Thomas, Valerie Valdez and Kelly Wong.

REFERENCES

Abercrombie, N., Hill, S., & Turner, B. S. (1980). *The dominant ideology thesis*. London: George Allen and Unwin.

Adair, J. G. (1973). *The human subject: The social psychology of the psychological experiment*. Boston: Little, Brown.

Alexander, C. N., & Rudd, J. (1984). Predicting behaviors from situated identities. *Social Psychology Quarterly, 47*, 172–177.

Aristotle. c. 335–323B. C. (1946) *Politics*. Oxford: Oxford University Press.

Bachrach, P., & Baratz, M. S. (1962). Two faces of power. *American Political Science Review, 56*, 947–952.

Bachrach, P., & Baratz, M. S. (1963). Decisions and nondecisions: An analytical framework. *American Political Science Review, 57*, 632–642.

Bachrach, P., & Baratz, M. S. (1970). *Power and poverty*. Oxford: Oxford University Press.

Bavelas, A. (1950). Communications patterns in task-oriented groups. *Journal of the Acoustical Society of America, 22*, 725–730.

Berger, P., & Luckmann, T. (1966). *The social construction of reality*. New York: Doubleday.

Blau, P. M., & Duncan, O. D. (1967). *The American occupational structure*. New York: Wiley.

Easton, D. (1965). *A systems analysis of political life*. New York: Wiley.

Erlin, H. C. W., & McLean, B. J. (1989). Normalizing illegitimate acts. Unpublished honors thesis, Department of Sociology, Stanford University, Stanford, CA.

Frank, J. D. (1944). Experimental studies of personal pressure and resistance. *Journal of Gen. Psychology, 30*, 23–64.

Gouldner, A. W. (1976). *The dialectic of ideology and technology: The origins, grammar, and future of ideology*. New York: Oxford University Press.

Gramsci, A. (1947 [1971]). *Selections from the prison notebooks*. New York: International Publishers.

Habermas, J. (1975). *Legitimation crisis*. Boston: Beacon Press.

Homans, G. C. (1974). *Social behavior*. New York: Harcourt, Brace and Jovanovich.

Kant, I. (1785 [1969]). *Foundations of the metaphysics of morals*. New York: Macmillan.

Keohane, R. O., & Nye, J. S. (1977). *Power and interdependence*. Boston: Little, Brown and Company.

Lineweber, D. C., Barr-Bryan, D., & Zelditch, M. (1982). Effects of a legitimate authority's justification of inequality on the mobilization of revolutionary coalitions. Technical Report No. 84, Laboratory for Social Research, Stanford University, Stanford, CA.

Linz, J. J. (1978). Crisis, breakdown, and re-equilibration. In: J. J. Linz & A. Stepan (Eds), *The Breakdown of Democratic Regimes* (Vol. 1). Baltimore: Johns Hopkins University Press.

Lipset, S. M. (1959). Some social requisites of democracy: Economic development and political legitimacy. *American Political Science Review, 53*, 69–105.

Lipset, S. M. (1963). *The first new nation*. New York: Basic Books.

Lipset, S. M. (1996). *American exceptionalism*. New York: Norton.

Lipset, S. M., & Bendix, R. (1959). *Social mobility in industrial society*. Berkeley: University of California Press.

Locke, J. (1690 [1960]). *Two treatises on government*. Cambridge: Cambridge University Press.

Machiavelli, N. (1517 [1940a]). *Discourses on the first ten books of Titus Livius*. New York: Modern Library.

Machiavelli, N. (1532 [1940b]). *The prince*. New York: Modern Library.

Marx, K., & Engels, F. (1845–1847 [1976]). *The German ideology*. In: Karl Marx & Frederick Engels (Eds), *Collected Works* (Vol. 5, pp. 19–539). New York: International Publishers.

Massey, K., Freeman, S., & Zelditch, M. (1997). Status, power, and accounts. *Social Psychology Quarterly, 60*, 238–251.

Mosca, G. (1896 [1939]). *The ruling class*. New York: McGraw Hill.

Orne, M. T. (1962). On the social psychology of the psychological experiment. *American Psychologist, 17*, 776–783.

Orne, M. T., & Evans, F. J. (1965). Social control in the psychological experiment. *Journal of Personality and Social Psychology, 1,* 189–200.

Pareto, V. (1916 [1963]). *The mind and society: A treatise on general sociology.* New York: Dover.

Parsons, T. (1958 [1960]). Authority, legitimation, and political action. In: T. Parsons (Ed.), *Structure and Process in Modern Societies* (pp. 170–198). Glencoe, IL: Free Press.

Rossi, P., & Berk, R. A. (1985). Varieties of normative consensus. *American Sociological Review, 33,* 46–62.

Rousseau, J. J. (1762 [1948]). *The social contract.* New York: Oxford University Press.

Scott, W. R. (1981). *Organizations: Rational, natural, and open systems.* Englewood Cliffs, NJ: Prentice-Hall.

Smith, A. (1776). *An inquiry into the nature and causes of the wealth of nations.* London: Strahan and Cadell.

Stokes, M. E., Davis, C. S., & Koch, G. G. (2000). *Categorical data analysis using the SAS system* (2nd ed.). Cary, NC: SAS Institute.

Stryker, R. (1994). Rules, resources, and legitimacy processes: Some implications for social conflict, order, and change. *American Journal of Sociology, 99,* 847–910.

Thomas, G. M., Walker, H. A., & Zelditch, M. (1986). Legitimacy and collective action. *Social Forces, 65,* 378–404.

Thucydides [423BC] (1954). *History of the Peloponnesian war.* R. Warner (Trans.). London: Penguin Books.

Walker, H. A. (1979). The effects of legitimacy on the inhibition of structural change (Unpublished Ph.D. Dissertation). Stanford University.

Walker, H. A., Rogers, L., Lyman, K., & Zelditch, M. (1989). Legitimacy and the support of revolutionary coalitions. Working Paper No. 89-3, Center for Sociological Research, Stanford University, Stanford, CA.

Walker, H. A., Rogers, L., Thomas, G. M., & Zelditch, M. (1991). Legitimating collective action: Theory and experimental results. *Research in Political Sociology, 5,* 1–25.

Walker, H. A., Rogers, L., & Zelditch, M. (1988). Legitimacy and collective action: A research note. *Social Forces, 67,* 216–228.

Walker, H. A., Rogers, L., & Zelditch, M. (2002). Acts, persons, positions, and institutions: Legitimating multiple objects and compliance with authority. In: S. Chew & J. D. Knottnerus (Eds), *Structure, Culture, and History* (pp. 323–339). Lanham, MD: Rowman & Littlefield.

Walker, H. A., Thomas, G. M., & Zelditch, M. (1986). Legitimation, endorsement, and stability. *Social Forces, 64,* 620–643.

Walker, H. A., & Zelditch, M. (1993). Power, legitimacy, and the stability of authority: A theoretical research program. In: J. Berger & M. Zelditch (Eds), *Theoretical Research Programs: Studies in the Growth of Theory* (pp. 364–381). Stanford, CA: Stanford University Press.

Weber, M. (1918 [1968]). Economy and society. In: G. Roth & C. Wittich (Eds). Berkeley, CA: California University Press.

Wittgenstein, L. (1958). *Philosophical investigations* (2nd ed.). Oxford: Blackwell.

Zelditch, M. (2001a). Theories of legitimacy. In: J. Jost & B. Major (Eds), *The Psychology of Legitimacy.* New York: Cambridge University Press.

Zelditch, M. (2001b). Processes of legitimation: Recent developments and new directions. *Social Psychology Quarterly, 64,* 4–17.

Zelditch, M., & Floyd, A. S. (1998a). Negotiating consensus. Presented at the Meeting of the International Sociological Association, Montreal, Canada.

Zelditch, M., & Floyd, A. S. (1998b). Consensus, dissensus, and justification. In: J. Berger & M. Zelditch (Eds), *Status, Power, and Legitimacy* (pp. 339–368). New Brunswick, NJ: Transaction.

Zelditch, M., Gilliland, E., & Thomas, G. M. (1984). Legitimacy of redistributive agendas. Paper formerly titled "An Experimental Study of the Mobilization of Bias." Working Paper No. 84-8, Center for Sociological Research, Stanford University, Stanford, CA.

Zelditch, M., Harris, W. A., Thomas, G. M., & Walker, H. A. (1983). Decisions, nondecisions, and metadecisions. In: L. Kriesberg (Ed.), *Research in Social Movements, Conflict, and Change* (Vol. 5, pp. 1–32). Greenwich, CT: JAI Press.

Zelditch, M., & Walker, H. A. (1984). Legitimacy and the stability of authority. *Advances in Group Processes: Theory and Research, 1*, 1–25.

Zelditch, M., & Walker, H. A. (2000). Normative regulation of power. *Advances in Group Processes, 17*, 155–178.

APPENDIX

Catalog of Studies Used in an Assessment of the Basic
Legitimation Assumption (BLA)

Condition or Corollary of BLA	Studies (Listed Chronologically)
Consensus	Massey et al. (1997) (TOC)[a] Walker et al. (1986) (IE) Zelditch and Floyd (1998a, b) (TOC)
Common interest, impartiality	Zelditch et al. (1984) (IE) Massey et al. (1997) (TOC) Zelditch and Floyd (1998a, b) (TOC)
Objectification	Massey et al. (1997) (TOC) Zelditch and Floyd (1998a, b) (TOC)
Consonance	Lineweber et al. (1982) (IE) Zelditch and Walker (2000) (IE)
Spread of legitimacy	Zelditch et al. (1984) (IE) Walker et al. (1988) (IE) Walker et al. (1989) (IE) Zelditch and Walker (2000) (IE)
Conservation of legitimacy Effectiveness	Zelditch and Floyd (1998b) (TOC) Walker (1979) (IE) Thomas et al. (1986) (IE) Walker et al. (1988) (IE) Erlin and McLean (1989) (IE) Walker et al. (2002) (IE)

APPENDIX *(Continued)*

Mystification	Zelditch et al. (1983) (IE)
	Zelditch et al. (1984) (IE)

[a] Abbreviations refer to basic protocol, either information exchange (IE) or tragedy of the commons (TOC).

CONSIDERATION OF LEGITIMACY PROCESSES IN TEASING OUT TWO PUZZLES IN THE STATUS LITERATURE

Cathryn Johnson

ABSTRACT

In this paper, I show how a consideration of legitimacy processes is of theoretical use in addressing two current issues in status research. First, I investigate under what conditions the contrast between the sex composition of a work group and the sex composition of an organization's authority structure may trigger the salience of gender status in task groups. I argue that this contrast will make gender status salient when an evaluation from an authority figure outside the group creates inconsistency and uncertainty in the current status structure within the group. Delegitimation of a superior is one such process that produces this inconsistency and uncertainty. Second, I examine under what conditions status position compared to identity will more likely stimulate behavior among work group members. I argue that the legitimation of the superior and the group's status order reduce the likelihood that group members will pursue status inconsistent, identity behaviors. Delegitimation, however, increases opportunities for acting in identity consistent ways and reduces the costs for doing so, thus enhancing the likelihood of identity-based behaviors.

Power and Status
Advances in Group Processes, Volume 20, 251–284
ISSN: 0882-6145/doi:10.1016/S0882-6145(03)20009-6

INTRODUCTION

Over the last two decades in the group processes area, scholars have developed legitimacy theories and tests of these theories that strive to show how legitimacy processes operate in informal task groups and work groups within organizations (e.g. Berger et al., 1998; Ridgeway & Berger, 1986; Ridgeway et al., 1994; Walker & Zelditch, 1993; Zelditch & Walker, 1984). In addition, researchers have made strides in showing how legitimacy processes interface with other processes to explain behavior in groups. For example, Ridgeway and Berger (1986) and Berger et al. (1998) examined how status and legitimacy processes operate simultaneously in informal task groups and how these processes affect interaction (see also Berger & Zelditch, 1998). Zeditch and Walker (2000), in an impressive set of studies, examine the conditions under which norms regulate the use of power by authorities. As well, using Zelditch and Walker's work on legitimacy and Bacharach and Lawler's theory of tactical choice in bargaining, Rebecca Ford and I examined how legitimacy processes and dimensions of dependence power (Emerson, 1962, 1972) affect perceptions of power, tactical choices, and emotional responses to a conflict between superiors and their subordinates (Ford & Johnson, 1998; Johnson & Ford, 1996; Johnson et al., 2000). And Karen Hegtvedt and I (2000) examined how legitimacy processes inform the main body of work in distributive and procedural justice.

In this paper, I attempt to show how a consideration of legitimacy processes is of theoretical use in addressing two current issues in status research. In the first section, I examine how legitimacy processes help us tease out when gender status may become salient in work groups within organizations. As we know, gender status typically becomes salient either when group members differentiate on gender or when the group task is gender-typed (Berger et al., 1980; also see Foschi & Lapointe (2002) for a discussion of gender status salience). As Ridgeway (1988; Ridgeway & Diekema, 1992) suggested, however, maybe information on gender status also becomes usable in groups depending on the sex composition of an organization's authority structure. I investigate under what conditions gender status may get triggered in organizational contexts, and show how one such condition, legitimation/delegitimation of an authority, is a key factor in solving this puzzle.

In the second section, I show how a consideration of legitimacy processes helps us tease out when members are more likely to express status-based or identity-based behaviors in work groups. In these groups, the status positions that actors hold often determine their behavior (such as superior and subordinate), but just as likely, members' identities that are personally embraced self identities may also influence how they behave (such as gender or control identities). I investigate under what conditions status position compared to identity will be more likely to stimulate behavior, and show how one such condition, legitimation/delegitimation of an authority, represents an initial key factor in solving this puzzle.

In each section below, I first provide an overview of the relevant theories. I then discuss the puzzle in the status literature and provide necessary background information. Finally, I provide a theoretical analysis of how bringing legitimacy processes into the theoretical mix provides an initial key step to address the issue. In both sections, the theoretical analysis applies to work groups consisting of superior/subordinate relationships within organizational settings.

GENDER STATUS, LEGITIMACY, AND ORGANIZATIONAL SEX COMPOSITION

Background on Status Characteristics Theory

Status characteristics theory (SCT) focuses on how status hierarchies develop and stabilize in decision-making groups (Berger et al., 1977; Berger et al., 1980; Wagner & Berger, 1993). It examines how status characteristics organize interaction in task groups where members are collectively oriented. A status characteristic is a feature of an actor that influences members' beliefs about one another. It has at least two states that are differentially evaluated, where one state is generally considered to be more highly esteemed and honored than another. Expectation states are considered specific if they apply to performance in a specific situation or general if not restricted to a defined situation. These expectations are estimates about how well a member will perform on a task compared to other members. There are two types of status characteristics. Diffuse status characteristics have at least two states that are differentially valued in the larger society, and are associated with general and specific performance expectations, such as gender, race, age, and physical attractiveness. For example, members who possess a high state of a status characteristic, such as whites in a mixed-racial group, are expected to do better than members who possess the low state within the group, e.g. blacks. Specific status characteristics, such as math ability and legal expertise, have two or more differentially valued states with expectations for performance related directly to the task, if the task involves these abilities (Berger et al., 1980).

The theory applies to the following conditions: (1) members value the task, that is, they perceive it as having at least two possible outcomes, success or failure, neither due to chance exclusively; (2) members are task-oriented, that is, they are motivated to do well on the task; and (3) members are collectively oriented in that they are willing to take into account each other's ideas in finding a solution to the task. In addition, the theory specifies five assumptions that help us connect members' status characteristics to their rank in the group's status hierarchy (Berger, Fisek & Norman, 1989). The first assumption states that information on status characteristics becomes salient when group members differentiate on that characteristic or when the task is directly relevant to the characteristic (e.g. a sex-typed task). The second assumption assumes that actors will consider status characteristics salient and use this information to order interaction unless they are convinced that these characteristics are not relevant to the task (called burden of proof). The third assumption specifies how the sequence in interaction is restructured in groups when a new member joins a group. This structure develops as the new member initiates a task or engages in interaction with a member as stated by the salience and burden of proof assumptions.

The fourth assumption explains how actors combine all relevant status information, although often they are unlikely to be aware of this process. Actors act as if they combine all positive status information (specified as a value of $e+$), and all negative information (specified as a value of $e-$). This combining is subject to attenuation. That is, each additional piece of positive information adds less to $e+$ than did information preceding it; each additional piece of negative information subtracts less from $e-$ than does information that precedes it. To calculate aggregated expectations for an actor, $e+$ and $e-$ are summed. Then, the subtraction of the aggregated expectations of an actor from those of another actor provides that actor's expectation advantage or disadvantage relative to that other (i.e., $e_p - e_0$). The fifth assumption specifies the relationship between expectation advantages and disadvantages and status rank. An actor's position in the status hierarchy relative to an other is a direct function of his or her expectation advantage or disadvantage relative to that other.

The theory examines how these status characteristics are related to: (1) the frequency of members' task behavior such as giving opinions or suggestions; (2) the expression of socioemotional behavior (e.g. positive and negative responses to opinions such as complementing, showing consideration, or withdrawing); and (3) who has more influence in the group (Wagner & Berger, 1993, 1997; Webster & Foschi, 1988). High status members are more likely than low status members to offer their opinions, receive positive evaluations, and achieve influence. There is substantial evidence to support this theory (see, for example, Wagner & Berger, 1997; Webster & Foschi, 1988).

A large portion of work in SCT is devoted to the effects of gender status on task group interaction. Gender is often a diffuse status characteristic that becomes salient either when members differentiate on gender as in a mixed-sex group or when the task at hand is relevant to cultural stereotypes of gender (e.g. sewing or auto mechanics) (Dovidio et al., 1988; Karakowsky & Siegel, 1999; Wood & Karten, 1986). As a result of salience of gender status in task situations, men in general are thought to be more competent than women on any given task and, therefore, they tend to offer more opinions and be more influential than women. Many studies confirm the effects of gender status in mixed-sex groups (see Wagner & Berger (1997) for a review). The evidence is mixed, however, for same-sex groups.

In contrast to the case of mixed-sex groups, SCT suggests that gender status will not be salient in all-female or all-male groups, given a gender neutral task, because members do not differentiate on gender. Without a contrast, members should not be particularly aware of their gender and, as a result, gender status should not affect their performance expectations. Therefore, status hierarchies in same-sex groups should be based on individual differences and should develop and stabilize in a similar fashion. The evidence for the original statement of SCT, however, is mixed. Some studies show that stereotypic gender differences exist between men and women in same-sex groups (Anderson & Blanchard, 1982; Carli, 1989, 1991; Piliavin & Martin, 1978). Men in all-male groups are slightly more task-oriented and directive than women in all-female groups; women are more likely to agree, smile, and use positive socioemotional behaviors more often than men. Other studies find no gender differences between men and women in same-sex groups in amount of task and directive behavior (Johnson et al., 1996; Shelly & Munroe, 1999; Wagner & Berger, 1997).[1] Johnson et al. (1996) found no gender differences in task and directive behavior, but did find some differences in the expression of agreements (i.e. higher for women) and use of counterarguments (i.e. higher for men). Carli (1990) also found gender differences in the use of verbal reinforcers and intensifiers (socioemotional behavior) between same-sex groups, with higher rates in women's than men's task groups. Typical explanations for this inconsistent evidence are the operation of gender stereotypic expectations for greater communality and efforts to overcome the legitimacy problems created by women's lower status (Ridgeway & Smith-Lovin, 1999).

To address these inconsistencies Ridgeway (1988; Ridgeway & Diekema, 1992) extended status characteristics theory by proposing another intriguing way that gender status may become salient in task groups, in addition to when members differentiate on gender or when the task is gender-typed. It may be that gender status becomes usable even in all-female groups embedded in an otherwise male-dominated organization (see also Fennell et al., 1978). Based on Kanter's work, Ridgeway considers an organization male-dominated when men fill at least 75% of the top authority positions (Kanter, 1977; Ridgeway, 1988; Ridgeway & Diekema, 1992). In male-dominated settings, all-female groups, such as all-female groups located in lower echelons of the organization with male supervisors, are charged with a task within a predominately male authority structure. As a result, the contrast between the all-female group and the male authority structure makes the lower status of being female rather than male salient, causing members to form lower performance expectations for themselves at the task relative to a male implied other. In contrast, Ridgeway suggests that gender status should not be salient in all-female groups in female-dominated organizations or in all-male groups in male-dominated organizations, given a gender neutral task, because there is no contrast between the sex composition of the group and that of the authority structure. In addition, gender status should be salient in all-male groups in female-dominated organizations (a rarity), but here, the contrast will provide an expectation advantage for the men.

Ridgeway (1988) assumes that members of task groups in general will be task oriented. Therefore, despite their low performance expectations, members in all-female groups within male-dominated organizations will grapple with the task by engaging in task and directive behaviors by making task suggestions, giving opinions, and procedural suggestions. Owing to the presence of low expectations, however, they should be hesitant in these behaviors and in the course of the group's interaction, engage in fewer of these behaviors than members in all-female groups in female-dominated organizations. These groups do not struggle with shared low expectations and so engage more freely and actively in these behaviors.

Therefore, as a result of salience of gender status, women in all-female groups within female-dominated organizations should have higher rates of directive and task behavior than women in all-female groups within male-dominated organizations. They should also have rates of these behaviors similar to those of men in all-male groups within male-dominated organizations.

The Puzzle: Does Gender Status Get Triggered by Organizational Sex Composition?

The evidence for Ridgeway's extension is mixed. Johnson et al. (1996) failed to find evidence for this extension, finding instead support for the original statement of SCT; there were no gender differences in directive and task behaviors (as well as positive socioemotional behaviors) between all-male and all-female groups, regardless of the sex composition of the organization's authority structure. Johnson et al. (1998), however, found limited evidence for Ridgeway's extension: women in all-female groups within a female-dominated organization were less tentative in presenting their ideas than women in all-female groups within a male-dominated organization. These studies represent only the initial tests of the extension and these results stem from a field experiment where other factors were not easily controlled (i.e. comparing interaction in same-sex groups within male- and female-dominated colleges).

There are at least two possible ways to interpret these results. First, the contrast between organizational sex composition and sex composition of a group simply may not be a mechanism whereby gender status becomes salient. I believe, however, that this conclusion is premature. We know from organizational studies that an organization's sex composition affects individuals' career mobility (Cohen et al., 1999; Ibarra, 1997), access to social networks (Burt, 1992; Ibarra, 1995, 1997; Spreitzer, 1996), and mental well-being (Jackson et al., 1995 who also focus on racial composition). As Reskin (1993) notes, "The organizational distribution of men and women strongly affects their psychological and economic rewards" (p. 711). Second, therefore, it may be that a better way to address this puzzle is to examine *under what conditions* the contrast between the sex composition of the task group and the sex composition of the organization will *trigger* gender status. I believe that a promising place to begin this investigation is to examine how legitimacy processes (i.e. legitimation an delegitimation processes) may trigger gender salience in some situations. In the following section, I first summarize the basic tenets of legitimacy theory, and then I offer a theoretical analysis of how legitimacy processes may trigger gender status in task groups within particular organizational contexts (Johnson & Lupo, 2000).

The Analysis: The Triggering Effect of Legitimacy Processes

Overview of Legitimacy Theory

Ridgeway and Berger (1986) and Berger et al. (1998), building on status theories, describe the process by which legitimation and delegitimation is created in task groups. In their theory legitimacy refers to the process by which members come to believe that a task group's power and prestige order (i.e., the status hierarchy) is collectively supported by the members.

Key to the Ridgeway and Berger (1986) and Berger et al. (1985) argument is the activation of various types of referential structures – socially shared systems of beliefs relating states of status characteristics and task outcomes or rewards to expectations for valued status positions. They discuss three elements that characterize actors in a situation and related referential beliefs. The diffuse status characteristics of group members prompt realization of categorical structures that suggest that individuals of one level of a status characteristic have higher positions than others (e.g. men occupy higher status positions). Specific status characteristics of group members trigger ability structures indicating that individuals who do better at the task are in higher status positions. And, reward or outcome characteristics, which often take the form of evaluations, correspond to outcome structures prescribing that actors who have higher evaluations will occupy higher positions in the status order.

Ridgeway and Berger (1986) and Berger et al. (1998) suggest that when referential beliefs are activated in a group, they give rise to expectations for valued status positions in that group. That is, group members form expectations regarding who should occupy higher status positions in the group. Just as group members draw on referential beliefs to form assumptions about the distribution of status in the group, they also create assumptions regarding the type of status order they expect other group members will support. Because group members presumably draw on the same referential beliefs, each actor believes that the other actors share their same expectations. Therefore, they are likely to treat each other in accordance with their shared status expectations. In doing so, they act as if the positions held in the group actually carry the differences in status value implied by their expectations for valued status positions. Group members thus tend to behave in ways that validate the status order. As these behaviors confirm the status order, they create a presumption of collective normative support for the order. These expectations, then, determine the distribution of deferential behaviors by the group members (Berger et al., 1998).

Ridgeway and Berger (1986) suggest that the structural condition that drives the process of legitimation mentioned above is the differentiation of expectations for valued status positions. The greater the differentiation in status expectations, the greater the likelihood that the power and prestige order will be perceived as legitimate by group members. Several studies provide support for this claim (Ridgeway et al., 1994; Ridgeway et al., 1995).[2]

Extending this idea, Berger et al. (1998) suggest that power and prestige orders may differ in the degree to which they are consistent and comprehensive. These elements of a status structure affect the degree of differentiation of expectations for valued status positions, and this differentiation shapes the legitimation process. A *consistent status structure* is one in which each actor has a consistent set of status characteristics (i.e. all high or all low) in the situation. For example, in formal work groups, if a manager has been assigned this position based on his experience, has status symbols consistent with his position, and has received a high level of rewards for his work by an external source, and a subordinate is believed to have less experience and is given less positively evaluated status symbols and a low level of rewards, the structure is said to be consistent. In this case, evaluations and expectations of task capacity and possession of valued positions are consistent. In an inconsistent structure the actors possess some oppositely evaluated states of status characteristics, such as when a manager has been assigned this position based on his experience, but is believed to be less skilled at the immediate task relative to his subordinates. The greater the degree of consistency, the greater the differentiation among actors for expectations for valued status positions and therefore, the greater the likelihood that the status hierarchy will become legitimated (i.e. believed to be collectively supported by the members).

Status structures also vary in their comprehensiveness. In a fully consistent structure, adding a new salient characteristic that is consistent with others creates a status structure that is more comprehensive than the original structure. In this case, each additional consistent status element reinforces the evaluations and expectations that are already associated with the status characteristics of the existing structure. A structure where actors differentiate consistently on five characteristics is more comprehensive than one in which actors differ only on two characteristics. The more comprehensive the structure, the more differentiation among actors for expectations for value status positions and, hence, the greater the likelihood that the power and prestige structure will be legitimated.

Just as status hierarchies may become legitimated, they also may become delegitimated. Delegitimation occurs when the order of performance expectations becomes incongruent or inversely related to the initially legitimated status hierarchy (Berger et al., 1998). For example, delegitimation occurs when group members work on new tasks that require new skills, making new status distinctions salient, or when there are explicit inconsistent evaluations of the actors' performances on the task. Typically, these evaluations come from an external source or authority figure who has a right to do this evaluation.

The Situation
Our analysis applies to situations that meet the following scope conditions. First, groups members in work settings are both task-focused and collectively-oriented (conditions fundamental to SCT). That is, group members come together to work on a task, take into account each other's opinions, and aim for overall task success. Second, the task group is embedded in an organizational structure that has at least three levels of authority. This allows us to examine how legitimation from an authority outside the group (in our case, authorization of a superior) affects interaction between the superior and the subordinates within the group. Hence, we need a structure that contains a three level, A-B-C, authority structure. There are other ways to study legitimation, but we begin by examining how authorization (i.e. support from an authority figure A above B) affects interaction between B (i.e. superior within the group) and C (i.e. his or her subordinates).

In addition, our analysis applies to situations that have the following elements. First, members of the task group are differentiated by at least two differentially valued formal positions, such as superior and subordinate. This characteristic epitomizes one of the most common ways in which organizations differentiate their members. Superiors compared to subordinates have access to more information and have more responsibilities, including making final decisions and instructing and monitoring the subordinates in their tasks. Subordinates, on the other hand, perform a variety of tasks directed by the superior. Second, an external legitimate authority within the organization, but outside the superior-subordinate task group, appoints the individual in the superior role. Third, group members believe that the external authority figure bases the appointment of the superior on the individual's work experience and previous responsibilities. Fourth, rewards (i.e. rewards in terms of both monetary value and/or status value) are consistent with a member's formal position. Thus, the superior receives higher pay, a better office, and more privileges than the subordinates. Fifth, only the superior's work is being explicitly evaluated, and all members are aware of this evaluation. Finally, the beliefs and expectations associated with the three referential structures (categorical, ability, and outcome) are held in common and accepted by all actors in the situation (Ridgeway & Berger, 1986).

Our analysis assumes that legitimation and delegitimation of the leader and the power and prestige order are created within the group as members apply these stable cultural beliefs to their immediate situation of action (Berger et al., 1998; Ridgeway & Berger, 1986). Thus the group itself interactionally constructs legitimation and delegitimation from facts in the immediate situation. These processes are situationally constructed, yet constrained by the pre-given structure (Zelditch & Floyd, 1998; Walker & Zelditch, 1993).

Given the above elements, imagine an all-female work group charged with a task from an external authority figure. For example, a manager and her subordinates are asked by the manager to develop a sales/marketing strategy for a marketing company or design a new community service project for a grocery store. In this situation, we presume that formal position acts as a diffuse status characteristic (Johnson & Lupo, 2000; Willer et al., 1997). Superiors possess the highly valued state and subordinates possess the less valued state. In addition, the superior receives rewards (rewards of both monetary and status value) that are more highly valued than the rewards of subordinates, and is assigned to her position by an external authority figure, based on previous experience. Formal position, rewards, and experience are indirectly linked to task outcome. Formal position is linked through general expectation states and instrumental ability; goal objects are linked through reward levels and instrumental ability; and previous managerial experience, only indirectly related to the current task, is linked through specific performance expectations and abstract task ability. (see Fig. 1 for a graph representation of these relationships.) According to SCT, performance expectations determine the directive behaviors, participation levels, and relative influence of group members. In this situation, superiors have a clear expectation advantage over subordinates

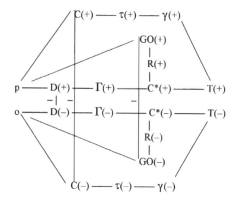

p–Superior; o–Subordinate

D Diffuse Status Characteristic: D+ (superior position), D- (subordinate position)

Γ General Performance Expectations: Γ+ (high perceived competence at most tasks), Γ-,(low perceived competence at most tasks)

C* Instrumental Ability: C*+ (high instrumental ability), C*- (low instrumental ability)

T Task Outcome States: T+ (successful task outcome), T- (failure at task outcome)

C Specific Status Characteristic: C+ (positively evaluated state of experience), C- (negatively evaluated state of experience)

τ Specific Performance Expectations: τ+ (high relative ability), τ- (low relative ability)

γ Abstract Task Ability: γ+ (high abstract task ability), γ- (low abstract task ability)

GO Goal Objects: GO+ (specific instances of preferred rewards), GO- (specific instances of non-referred rewards)

R Reward States: R+ (high levels of rewards), R- (low level of rewards)

*Note: Dimensionality exists between opposite states of a salient status characteristic or goal object. This is a negative relationship. Dimensionality reflects the idea that if an actor possesses one state of a status characteristic or goal object, then possessing the other state is thereby precluded.

Fig. 1. Graph Representation of Superior-Subordinate Relationship.*

(based on the combining principle – three positive pieces of status information for the superior and three negative pieces (relatively) for the subordinates). Therefore, superiors should participate more and be more directive and influential than subordinates.

Also, we assume that valued status positions emerge at the same time as the formation of performance expectations (Ridgeway & Berger, 1986). In our situation, formal position is the object of legitimation (Ridgeway, 1989). The referential structure for the diffuse status characteristic, formal position, implies that superiors are typically expected to occupy more valued positions. Similarly, people typically believe that superiors are more skilled at tasks, especially managerial ones, than subordinates. Thus expectations for both the diffuse status characteristic and the specific characteristic (managerial skill) favor the superior for the valued position. As a consequence, the superior is likely to be more directive and influential than the subordinates (Berger et al., 1998; Ridgeway & Berger, 1986). Berger et al. (1998) also argue that expectations for formal positions determine the distribution of deferential behaviors such as esteem, respect, and honor, which may be communicated verbally or non-verbally. As a result of the distribution of expectations for valued positions, subordinates are likely to engage in more deferential behaviors than individuals in the superior position.

After completion of a series of tasks, imagine that the manager's work on a major group project is evaluated in terms of success/support or failure/lack of support by the external authority, and the subordinates are aware of this evaluation. Here, drawing upon the work of Zelditch and Walker (1984) and Walker and Zelditch (1993) on legitimacy processes in organizations, the manager is either authorized or deauthorized.[3] Authorization involves the transfer of resources of support to the authority from organizational members at higher levels. When authorized, for example, the manager's work is positively evaluated and supported by an external authority, and she and her subordinates are given resources based on the manager's work on the prior task. When deauthorized, her work is negatively evaluated and not supported; thus the group does not receive resources. Authorization and deauthorization represent instances of legitimation and delegitimation respectively. Deauthorization is one common way that an individual in a superior position may lose status and face a loss in legitimacy (Berger et al., 1998). After this evaluation, imagine that the group is again charged with a task by the authority figure where the manager is responsible for the success or failure of the group task.

The Triggering Effect of Legitimacy

Ridgeway's original argument suggests that, in the above situation, gender status will become salient in all-female groups within a male authority structure, but not within a female authority structure. Therefore, female superiors in groups in male-dominated settings will have an expectation disadvantage relative to female superiors in female-dominated settings. This disadvantage, in turn, will have an effect on behavior and perceptions. We argue, however, that the simple contrast between the sex composition of the authority structure and the sex composition of the group is not strong enough to make gender salient for everyday interaction in typical work groups (Johnson & Lupo, 2000). In this case, gender is only a background identity primed by the contrast with the authority structure, but not relevant for interaction. Work setting identities, such as manager and subordinate, reside in the foreground for actors (Ridgeway, 1997). We argue that, as long as there is consistency and stability (i.e. no information that contradicts the power and prestige order), the sex composition of the authority structure should have little effect on directive and deferential behavior or perceptions of legitimacy of the superior.

The contrast between the authority structure and the group composition, however, may make gender status salient when there is some event that triggers the relevance of this contrast. As Ridgeway (1997) suggests, although gender status may not be initially salient in workplace settings, it can easily be triggered by events in interaction. Similar to Bacharach and Lawler's (1980, 1981) idea that the ambiguous, uncertain nature of conflict in organizations makes actors aware of their relative power in the situation, we argue that one way this contrast may become relevant is by an event that causes inconsistency and uncertainty in the order of performance expectations. Only some kind of threat to the existing power and prestige order, in addition to this contrast, may trigger gender status beliefs.

One type of event that may make the contrast between the group sex composition and the authority structure trigger the salience of gender status is delegitimation (Johnson & Lupo, 2000). Using our task situation, in all-female groups within male- and female-dominated organizations, deauthorization (an instance of delegitimation) creates an inconsistency between the ordering of performance expectations and expectations for valued formal positions in the prior task and their ordering in the current task, thus destabilizing the power and prestige order. In all-female groups in male-dominated organizations, however, deauthorization, in combination with the contrast between the sex composition of the group and the sex composition of the organization's authority structure, serve to trigger gender status beliefs in the group. In all-female groups in female-dominated organizations, there is no contrast based on sex, and therefore, deuathorization will not trigger gender status beliefs. Why would the combination of deauthorization and the contrast between the sex composition of the group and that of the authority structure trigger gender salience?

In male-dominated work contexts, gender stereotypes, diffuse in nature, have an opportunity to become construed as relevant for interaction for women superiors. A key element of gender stereotypes relevant to workplace settings is gender status beliefs. These beliefs cause both men and women to implicitly expect or expect that others will expect greater competence from men than from women, given that all else is equal in the situation (Ridgeway, 1997). When women superiors are deauthorized, they will search for explanations for this negative evaluation. One initial cause that will be assessed by both the superior and her subordinates will be something about her gender status, that is, something about being a woman. Individuals who hold lower states of a status characteristic such as gender and race, are more likely to implicitly expect or expect that others will expect that the reason for this negative evaluation is something, at least partially, about their status. Men and whites, on the other hand for example, do not necessarily search for explanations simply based on their status of gender or race. Cultural assumptions about women' general competence relative to men's competence makes the likelihood of women questioning their competence based on their status much more likely than men questioning their abilities based on being men. We argue that female members in both male-dominated and female-dominated organizations will search for reasons for deauthorization, such as poor decision-making choices or ineffective leadership style of the superior. In male-dominated contexts, however, female members are charged with tasks within a male authority structure. This contrast between the group and the larger authority structure (where a contrast is a fundamental condition for the salience of gender status) provides the context/opportunity in which gender status beliefs may become construed as relevant/salient if some event triggers their salience. Deauthorization is one such event that triggers a search for explanations for poor performance. In all-female groups within female-dominated organizations, no such contrast exists and, therefore, gender status should not be triggered by deauthorization. Other reasons will be assessed, but not the questioning of competence based simply on being a woman.

Unlike deauthorization, under conditions of authorization (an instance of legitimation), an explicitly positive evaluation of a superior's performance by an external authority figure should not trigger gender status beliefs, even in male-dominated authority structures. Authorization does not create any inconsistency or uncertainty in the original power and prestige order and the expectations for performances or rewards on the current task. In fact, authorization serves to further strengthen the already consistent status structure, making it more comprehensive. Competence is not called into question and, therefore, there is no reason to search for reasons for incompetence. Gender status beliefs, therefore, should not become salient for legitimated women superiors with female subordinates, either in female-dominated or male-dominated organizations. Modifying Ridgeway's contrast argument, therefore, we offer the following auxiliary assumption:

Uncertainty-Contrast argument. The contrast between the sex composition of an organization's authority structure and the sex composition of the group will make gender status salient only when evaluations from an authority figure create some inconsistency and uncertainty in the current status structure of the task group.

Drawing on status processes and the uncertainty-contrast argument, we suggest that the process of deauthorization and the salience of gender status will be operating in all-female groups within male-dominated organizations. Each will have independent negative effects on members' performance expectations. Dauthorization, however, will have a stronger effect than gender on expectations.

Deauthorization will have a direct effect on expectations for task success because an evaluation of the performance on the first task is directly relevant to perceived instrumental ability on the current similar task. Also, deauthorization often includes denial of resources as a result of prior task performance. Therefore, deauthorization will also have an indirect effect on instrumental ability through rewards. Gender will be indirectly related to task skill through general performance expectations. In addition, in all-female groups in a female-dominated organization, explicit lack of support of a woman superior by an external authority figure will not serve to trigger gender status beliefs because there is no contrast to trigger gender salience, a fundamental condition for the salience of gender status. The effects of deauthorization mentioned above, however, should occur. (see Fig. 2 for a graph representation.) Based on our analysis, then, we suggest the following statement:

Statement 1. The expectation advantage for performance of deauthorized female superiors over their subordinates in male-dominated organizations will be less than that of deauthorized female superiors over their subordinates in female-dominated organizations. Organizational sex composition should have no effect on the expectation advantage of authorized female superiors over their subordinates.

Applying legitimacy theory, in all-female groups in male-dominated organizations, deauthorization and gender status should have equal negative direct effects on expectations for valued formal positions for the superior in the current task. Deauthorization will have direct effects on these expectations through the activation of outcome referential structures and gender status will have direct effects through activation of categorical referential structures. In all-female groups in female-dominated organizations, deauthorization will not serve to trigger gender salience, but the effects of deauthorization on expectations for valued formal positions should occur. Therefore:

Statement 2. The expectation advantage for valued formal status positions of deauthorized female superiors over their subordinates in male-dominated organizations will be less than that of deauthorized female superiors over their subordinates in female-dominated organizations. Organizational sex composition will have no effect on these expectations of authorized female superiors over their subordinates.

Statements 1 and 2 explicitly argue that there will be an interaction between authorization/deauthorization and the sex composition of the workplace context. Under conditions of authorization, organizational sex composition will have no effect on members' expectations for performance and for formal status positions. There is no event that questions the competence of female superiors in

2.A: Authorized Conditions in Male-Dominated and Female-Dominated Organizations

2.B: Deauthorized Condition with Female Superior in Male-Dominated Organization

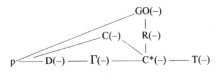

2.C: Deauthorized Condition with Female Superior in Female-Dominated Organization

p--superior
D Diffuse status characteristic: D+ (superior position), D- (subordinate position)
Γ General Performance Expectations: Γ+ (high perceived competence at most tasks), Γ-,(low perceived competence at most tasks)
C* Instrumental Ability: C*+ (high instrumental ability), C*- (low instrumental ability)
T Task Outcome States: T+ (successful task outcome), T- (failure at task outcome)
C Specific Status Characteristic: C+ (positively evaluated state), C- (negatively evaluated state)
GO Goal Objects: GO+ (specific instances of preferred rewards), GO- (specific instances of non-preferred rewards)
R Reward states: R+ (high levels of rewards), R- (low level of rewards)

Fig. 2.   Graph Representation of Effects Authorization/Deauthorization and Gender.

these groups. Under conditions of deauthorization, however, organizational sex composition will have an effect. Gender status beliefs will be salient in all-female groups in male-dominated organizations as a result of the triggering effect of gender by deauthorization; these beliefs will not be salient in female-dominated organizations as explained above because there is no contrast based on sex between the group and the authority structure.

Drawing upon status and legitimacy theories' arguments about the relationship between an expectation advantage for performance/valued status positions and actual behavior, the following sample hypotheses could be tested. First, authorized female superiors in male-dominated organizations will initiate action and exhibit amounts of directive behavior similar to authorized female superiors in female-dominated organizations. Deauthorized female superiors in male-dominated organizations are likely to talk less and use fewer directive behaviors than deauthorized female superiors in female-dominated organizations. Second, subordinates with authorized female superiors in male-dominated organizations will exhibit deference behaviors toward their superior similar to subordinates with authorized female superiors in female-dominated organizations. Subordinates with deauthorized female superiors in male-dominated organizations are likely to express fewer deference behaviors toward the superior than subordinates with deauthorized female superiors in female-dominated organizations. Third, subordinates with authorized female superiors in male-dominated organizations are as likely as those with authorized female superiors in female-dominated organizations to perceive their superior as the right and proper person for the superior position. Subordinates with deauthorized female superiors in male-dominated organizations are less likely to perceive their superior as the proper person for the superior position than subordinates with deauthorized female superior in female-dominated organizations.

Our analysis also suggests that women superiors in male-dominated settings who face delegitimation will more quickly internalize feelings of low competence and confidence compared to women superiors in female-dominated settings. The effects of delegitimation will be heightened for women superiors when the sex composition of the authority structure is predominately male. We suggest, therefore, that authorized female superiors in male-dominated organizations will perceive themselves as similarly proper to authorized female superiors in female-dominated organizations. Deauthorized female superiors in male-dominated organizations are less likely to perceive themselves as the right and proper person for the superior position than deauthorized female superiors in female-dominated organizations.

STATUS, IDENTITY, AND LEGITIMACY

Distinct theories in social psychology stress either the importance of status positions or self-meanings in predicting behavior in groups. Such theories argue that status or identity, respectively, are produced and maintained in interaction. As shown in the first section, status characteristics theory shows how actors internalize implicit expectations for behavior associated with their social positions (Berger et al., 1966). In comparison to SCT, identity theory (IT) (Burke, 1991; Stryker, 1968; Stryker & Serpe, 1982) suggests that individuals engage in behaviors similar in meaning to their identities to maintain consistency in their self-concept (Burke & Reitzes, 1991). When individuals face a discrepancy between their self view and how they perceive others to view them, they act to control their own perceptions in order to regain consistency. Attempts to regain consistency occur when people have the *opportunity* in a situation to challenge identity discrepant views.

In this section, I examine how status position and identity may affect the behavior of superiors and their subordinates in organizational work groups. In this theoretical analysis, I specify *the conditions under which* status position compared to identity will more likely be expressed in task group situations. Similar to the section above, I show how legitimacy of a superior and ultimately the status order is one such condition. In this theoretical analysis, I focus specifically on situations in which each member's status position and identity are inconsistent. In these situations, status position and identity may prescribe conflicting behaviors in the task setting. For example, superiors with feminine identities and subordinates with masculine identities have identities inconsistent with their status position. Inconsistency results in status position prescribing behaviors that conflict with those customary for gender identity. Examining inconsistent situations allows us to tease out the effects of status position and identity on behaviors.

Focusing on situations involving discrepancies between an individual's status position and identity, with legitimation, the costs of failing to fulfill status-based expectations may be too high to allow expression of identity-based behavior. In contrast, in the absence of such collective support for an authority figure and status order, group members are more likely to act in ways consistent with their identity as a result of greater opportunities to challenge the status order. This analysis of the effects of legitimacy on the likelihood of status- and/or identity-based behavior shows how ideas drawn from SCT and IT could be used to provide a more comprehensive explanation for behavior in groups than either theory alone.

To accomplish this task, I first provide an overview of identity theory and its predecessors. Then, I consider recent research that examines both status and identity processes simultaneously. Finally, drawing on SCT, IT, and legitimacy theories, I summarize my work with Lupo and Hegtvedt (Johnson et al., 2001) that integrates ideas from SCT and IT by providing predictions on how status, identity, and legitimacy are related in work settings.

Background on Identity Theories

Status Positions and Identities

In groups, members' status positions stem from salient status characteristics (e.g., superior/subordinate; male/female) in the task situation (Berger et al., 1980).

Generally, status positions are situationally determined, consensually agreed upon, and carry status value. They shape behavior whether or not the individuals embrace them as the "real me."[4] Status positions, then, are socially and consensually based. In contrast, a member's identity refers to a self-view or self-definition that may derive from social roles, group memberships, social categories, or various character traits (e.g. masculine vs. feminine; controlling vs. submissive) (Stryker, 1980). Typically, many identities, particularly those that are personally embraced self identities, are stable across situations, although they may be inactive in a particular situation. The expression and importance of an identity, then, may vary situationally.

Although conceptually distinct, the relationship between status and identity is complex and may be characterized in at least three ways. First, some identities (e.g. control identity) are clearly not statuses per se. Second, some identities may reflect an actor's status position. For example, a woman's occupation may become central to her self-identification. Likewise, race or ethnicity may be an important part self-identification. Not all statuses, however, become identities for all people. For some people, occupation may be irrelevant to their self view even though they hold an occupation, and not all members of minority groups transform their pride in group membership into a part of their personally embraced identity.[5] And third, some characteristics such as gender can be considered a status position, an identity, or both simultaneously (Balkwell & Berger, 1996; Johnson et al., 2001; Stets & Burke, 1996).

Identity Theory
As self-definitions or self-characterizations, identities represent "the various meanings attached to oneself by self and others" (Gecas & Burke, 1995, p. 42). Identities help individuals to frame interaction by providing meaning for their actions and situations that are shared by others (Mead, 1934; Stryker & Serpe, 1982). Individuals hold particular identities at any given point in time and they often desire consistency between how they view themselves and how they think others view them (Swann et al., 1989).

Burke (1991) and Stets and Burke (1996) conceptualizes identities as cybernetic control systems that maintain congruency between one's self-perceptions of identity-relevant situational meanings and the set of self-meanings defining the character of an identity, one's identity standard. This model rests on perceptual control, that is, self-in-situation meanings match the identity standard. Thus, a woman compares her perceptions of others' appraisals of her behavior in a given situation (reflected appraisals) with her identity standard. If a discrepancy exists between her perceived self-meanings and the meanings contained in her identity standard, she is likely to be motivated to engage in behaviors that realign the perceived feedback with her identity standard. If no discrepancy exists, she will continue to engage in behaviors that maintain consistency between her self-perceptions and identity standard. For example, if a person has an identity standard which contains meanings consistent with being extremely feminine, she will act in an extremely feminine way. If, however, she gets feedback from others that implies she is only slightly feminine, she is likely to increase her level of feminine behavior in order to bring the perceived feedback in line with her feminine identity standard (Stets, 1995). Burke's model thus explains two processes that underlie the identity-behavior relationship across situations and over time: behavior to maintain a given set of identity meanings and behavior to counter any disturbances to those meanings.

The model assumes that individuals' behaviors reflect choices "made in situations in which alternative courses of action are available and reasonable to the person" (Stryker & Serpe, 1982, p. 205). In other words, the structure of the situation provides options for the behaviors to be enacted. Stryker (1989) recognizes, however, that all encounters have an objective structure defined in part by their social and cultural contexts, which limits behavioral possibilities independent of the identities of involved actors. Characteristics of the situation such as power differences between group members or institutional or organizational expectations for behavior may constrain identity-based behaviors. For example, power differences between a student and a teacher may lead the student to refrain from displays of dominance behaviors congruent with a masculine identity. Similarly, organizational expectations that employees will defer to their superiors may limit expression of masculine behaviors; expectations that workers prioritize business over personal matters may reign in care-giving behaviors stemming from a feminine identity. In addition to limiting behavioral options, situational structure may also affect the costs of choosing behaviors inconsistent with situationally defined demands. Thus, ultimately, the structure of a situation as well as the assessments of it by participants interact with identities to produce behavior.

In effect, emphasis on the structure of the situation allows for the introduction of status-based expectations for behavior. Moreover, structural concerns highlight key constraints on identity based behaviors: the lack of opportunities to express identities and the cost of doing so.

The Puzzle: Examining Status and Identity Processes Together

To date, Stets and Burke (1996) and Stets (1997) provide the most comprehensive attempt to examine the joint effects of status and identity on behavior (see also Stryker & Burke, 2000). They investigate how differences in four status positions (gender, age, education, and occupation) and in two identities (gender and control) predict negative and positive socioemotional behavior in discussions between recently married partners. In their study, Stets and Burke (1996) conceptualize gender as both a status position and an identity. When gender represents a position in the social structure, focus rests on how expectations attached to different status positions (men vs. women) affect behavior in interaction. When gender stands for an identity, the emphasis is on the meaning of being male or female for individuals and how this self-meaning guides behavior in interaction. They argue that gender as status and gender as identity are simultaneously produced and maintained in interaction.

Stets and Burke (1996) and Stets (1997) utilize SCT and IT to predict the effects of status and identity on the expression of socioemotional behaviors, such as showing support for group members, using humor, and challenging or criticizing others, in discussions between recently married, heterosexual couples. The investigators instructed each couple to discuss an area of disagreement within their marriage until they reached a resolution. Drawing upon SCT, they hypothesize that husbands are more likely than wives to use negative socioemotional behavior in conversation, controlling for other status characteristics such as education and occupation on which the partners differ, because they are more likely to believe that they have the right to express negative behaviors as a form of control (Ridgeway & Johnson, 1990). Stets and Burke make no predictions about how status may affect positive socioemotional behaviors.

In contrast, based on IT, Stets and Burke predict that individuals with more masculine and high control identities are more likely than those with more feminine and low control identities to use negative behaviors in conversations and less likely to use positive behaviors. They base these predictions on cultural assumptions about the meanings of masculinity, femininity, and control, which contend that the meaning of being male is associated in part with dominance, competitiveness, and autonomy, whereas the meaning of being female is associated in part with submissiveness, cooperativeness, and affiliation. Indeed, consistent with Stets and Burke' claims, Drass (1986) found that men and women who have masculine gender identities are more likely to use a dominant speech style (i.e. to interrupt and overlap the speech of others). Thus people who see themselves as more masculine or more feminine should identify with these cultural meanings and should behave accordingly in interaction.

Similar to gender identity, control identity encompasses self-meanings pertaining to power and dominance over another person. A high control identity suggests that one is highly controlling of others while a low control identity asserts that one is less controlling of others. Prior research (Stets & Burke, 1994) reveals that high control identities are associated with self-views as dominant, competitive, and cold, and low control identities are associated with self-views as submissive, non-competitive, and warm. Gender and control differ, however, in that gender is a role identity, whereas control is a person identity. Person identities are independent of the social structures unlike role identities such as gender. As a result, individuals may have more freedom to negotiate the meaning of person identity standards over time and place.

Stets and Burke find support for their identity-based predictions, but not for their status-based predictions. Husbands are *less likely* than wives to express negative socioemotional behavior in interaction. Wives are more likely to complain, criticize, and use negative relationship talk. Also, the more masculine and controlling either the wife or the husband's identity, the more likely that each will use negative speech acts and display negative affect. The more feminine and less controlling either the wife or the husband's identity, the more likely each will use positive social behaviors in interaction.

In a follow-up study, Stets (1997) finds additional support for IT. The lower status member of marital dyads (women, the younger partner, the less educated partner, and the partner with lower occupational status) engages in more negative socioemotional behavior than the higher status member. In addition, individuals with more masculine identities use more negative behavior than do individuals with more feminine identities. Overall, the effects for control identity are stronger than those for gender identity. Those with a high control identity frequently criticize and challenge their spouses, often disagree with their spouses, and rarely agree with their spouses. These findings suggest that status processes do not operate in *marital interaction* in ways proposed by SCT.

Stets and Burke note two explanations for their results. First, they acknowledge that their task situation falls outside the scope conditions of SCT.[6] The married couples' discussions are more personally relevant (i.e. disagreements in their marriage) than in traditional task groups. Second, the likelihood of identity affecting behavior is determined, in part, by whether or not individuals receive the opportunity to act in identity-consistent ways. Stets argues that marital interaction provides such an opportunity: "interaction in marriage may be viewed as a culturally appropriate place for expressing negative feelings without fear of rejection because trust and commitment are greater in marriage than in other interactions" (1997, p. 191). Thus, for example, partners with masculine identities have the opportunity to express negative behavior (thus acting in an identity-consistent manner) when disagreements arise. Such opportunity, however, is dependent on the context in which interaction occurs. Stets suggests that work settings may provide little opportunity to act in identity consistent ways or to challenge views of who one is. By raising the issue of opportunity, Stet's work echoes Stryker's (1989) emphasis that the structure of the situation provides the basis for opportunities to act in identity-consistent ways and the costs associated with such behaviors (Johnson et al., 2001).

Stets and Burke (1996) and Stets (1997) take initial steps in understanding the joint effects of status and identity on behavior. Here, my colleagues and I begin to tease out the puzzle of how status and identity work together in groups, by offering one process to explain under what conditions status and identity-based behaviors will occur. Although both status and identity are produced and maintained in interaction, we argue that the weight each plays in interaction depends upon the structure of the situation. We argue that the legitimacy of an authority and a task group's status structure affects the opportunities for identity-based behavior and costs associated with pursuing such actions (Johnson et al., 2001).

The Analysis: How Legitimacy Affects Costs and Opportunities

The Situation

Similar to the first section, the scope conditions are that members are task focused and collectively oriented. An additional scope condition is that identities must be ones that could be consistent or inconsistent with status.[7] Also, the present analysis can apply to situations in which members diverge on other common status characteristics (e.g. seniority, job experience, education) that operate in organizations (Cohen & Zhou, 1991).

We also assume the following in our analysis. First, we assume that gender identity (masculine or feminine) affects task-oriented behaviors such as participation, opinions, influence attempts, and directive/deferential behavior. Following in the tradition of much of the literature on status and identity (Drass, 1986; Stets, 1995, 1997; Stets & Burke, 1996), we chose to focus on gender identity in contrast to other types of identity (e.g. control). Moreover, our assumption extends emphasis by Stets and Burke (1996) and Stets (1997) on gender identity and socioemotional behavior. As noted above, Stets and Burke argue that masculinity corresponds to notions of power and dominance leading to links between masculinity and negative social behaviors. Femininity is associated with powerlessness and submissiveness, leading to links between femininity and positive social behaviors. In certain situations, however, powerful behaviors may not be construed as negative. The extension to task-oriented behaviors eliminates the evaluation of masculine or feminine behaviors as negative or positive. Here we suggest that individuals with masculine gender identities (and high control identities) will act more powerfully and dominantly in their task-oriented behaviors than individuals with feminine gender identities (and low control identities). Indeed prior research shows that actors with masculine identities demonstrate higher levels of initiation, leadership behavior, and dominance than those with feminine identities (Karakowsky & Siegel, 1999; Korabik, 1982; Seibert & Gruenfeld, 1992). Thus our gender identity/behavior assumption, specifies that: (1) actors with masculine identities will have higher rates of participation, influence, and use of task/directive behaviors suggesting power and/or dominance; and (2) individuals with feminine identities will have higher rates of deferential behaviors, which typify powerlessness and submissiveness (Johnson et al., 2001).

Second, we assume that gender identity and status position are consistent when superiors have masculine identities and subordinates have feminine identities. Such consistency ensures that status and identity prescribe similar behaviors. For example, individuals with masculine identities who also occupy a high status position should have high rates of participation, directive behavior, and influence. These individuals are acting according to expectations associated with their status position as well as their own gender-based self views. Individuals' identities, however, are often inconsistent with their status position. For example, superiors with feminine identities and subordinates with masculine identities have identities inconsistent with their status position. Inconsistency, thus, results in gender identity prescribing behaviors that are in conflict with those for status position.

Third, given our focus on the dynamics of behavior in task-oriented groups, we assume that the interaction of superiors and subordinates is interdependent. That is, the behavior of a superior is likely to constrain or open the range of responses of subordinates. For example, when a superior acts in a directive way, subordinates are less likely to do so. Conversely, if a superior is hesitant or appears to lack confidence in his or her influence, subordinates are likely to take advantage of the hesitation by acting in a more directive manner.

The Legitimacy Effect

Imagine a situation, similar to the one described in the first section, involving a three-person formal task group, consisting of a superior and two subordinates, charged with a task from an external authority. As before, we presume that formal position acts as a status characteristic (Johnson & Lupo, 2000; Willer et al., 1997). Superiors possess the highly valued state and subordinates possess the less valued state. Thus, in this situation, superiors should be more directive and influential and should participate more than subordinates.

Also, as discussed in the first section, formal position is the object of legitimation (Ridgeway, 1989). Expectations for both the diffuse status characteristic (formal position) and the specific characteristic (managerial skill) favor the superior for the valued position. As a consequence, the superior is likely to be more directive and influential than the subordinate, and subordinates are likely to engage in more deferential behaviors than individuals in the superior position (Berger et al., 1998; Ridgeway & Berger, 1986).

In contrast, IT suggests that individuals with more masculine identities should be more directive and influential and should participate more than individuals with more feminine identities. Members with feminine identities are more likely to be deferential than members with masculine gender identities.

Given the above theories, when members come together to work on a task for the first time, status and identity may operate simultaneously to affect members' behavior. The consistency or inconsistency between status and identity, however, influences the pattern of behavior that emerges. When members' status and identity are consistent (e.g. the superior has a masculine identity and the subordinates have feminine identities), then the superior clearly will be more directive and influential and the subordinates will be more deferential in interaction because their status and identity prescribe similar behaviors. When members' status and identity are inconsistent (e.g. the superior has a feminine identity and the subordinates have masculine identities), then the amount of inequality between directive and deferential behavior and influence should be lower compared to the status/identity consistent situations. Here, status and identity prescribe conflicting behaviors. Therefore, we offer the following prediction:

Prediction 1. The amount of inequality in behavior between the superior and the subordinates will be greater in consistent status/identity conditions than in inconsistent status/identity conditions.

Prediction 1 suggests a general pattern of behavior resulting from the consistency or inconsistency between status position and identity. That pattern, however, is independent of other contextual factors that may enhance or diminish the expression of behavior based on status or on identity. Here we examine the impact of one such contextual factor – legitimacy of the group leader – on the enactment of behaviors stemming either from status position or identity. We focus on situations in which status and identity are inconsistent in order to more clearly separate the effects of status from identity.

Similar to the first section, imagine that the superior is either authorized or deauthorized after work on an initial task. We argue that whether the superior is legitimated or delegitimated will affect the stability of the status order and the likelihood that the superior or subordinates will enact identity-based behaviors on a subsequent task (Johnson et al., 2001). Legitimation shapes both the opportunity to behave in identity-consistent ways as well as the costs of doing so. And, given the interactive nature of the situation, we must consider the opportunities and costs for subordinates as well as superiors.

Opportunities refer to a combination of circumstances that allow individuals to behave in ways consistent with their gender identities. In task groups, these opportunities would allow those with masculine identities to act in directive ways and to exert influence and those with feminine identities to act in more deferential ways. Costs refer to expenditures or losses experienced by individuals in the process of interaction. Such losses may occur or may be anticipated to occur when superiors or peers invoke sanctions on other group members, such as the expression of criticism or negative affect, an increased refusal to yield to influence, or conjuring the label "deviant" (Wagner, 1988). In effect, such sanctions represent non-material costs involving the loss of esteem, respect, status, etc. What is the impact of combinations of opportunities and costs for the superior and subordinates in groups?

Generally, legitimation of the superior reinforces expectations for performance and the effectiveness of status-based behaviors. Moreover, positive evaluation of the superior increases comprehensiveness of the formal status structure by activating outcome referential beliefs that reinforce the expectations that the superior occupy the most valued position. In addition, legitimation enhances the *certainty* that the superior is the right and proper person for the superior position. By exacerbating differences between the superior and subordinates and their expectations for status-based behaviors, legitimation constrains the opportunity for superiors and subordinates alike to deviate from status-based behavior. Accompanying the decreased opportunities for identity-based behavior are increases in costs associated with acting in a manner consistent with one's gender identity. If group members engage in behaviors either higher (e.g. subordinates acting in a masculine way) or lower (e.g. superiors acting in a feminine way) than that expected by their rank, they violate status-based expectations and may be subject to sanctions from others (Ridgeway & Berger, 1986; Wagner, 1988). Insofar as legitimation decreases opportunities for identity-based behavior and increases the costs of such behavior, group members are even less likely to engage in behaviors consistent with their identities yet inconsistent with their status position on subsequent tasks than they were on an initial task (Johnson et al., 2001).

In contrast, delegitimation of the superior undermines performance and status-based expectations for behavior. An explicit, negative evaluation of a superior's performance from an external authority (Berger et al., 1998) fails to activate outcome referential beliefs consistent with those based on formal position. Moreover, such an evaluation may induce doubt or *uncertainty* the initial ranking of performance expectations (Ridgeway, 1989) and thereby undermine normative prescriptions of who should have higher status on the subsequent tasks (Berger et al., 1998). As a result of the loosening of normative prescriptions, both superiors and subordinates are likely to perceive more opportunity for engaging in identity-based behaviors.

And, indeed, for subordinates, these opportunities allow for the enhancement of status.

Whether group members take advantage of the opportunities to express their gender identities, however, is likely to depend upon the costs of doing so. To the extent that delegitimation of the superior relaxes the behavioral expectations associated with the status order, individuals are less likely to encounter sanctions for deviating from status-based behavior. As a consequence, costs associated with enacting identity-based behavior decrease. These costs are likely to be lower for subordinates, whose position is already of less value, than for superiors who may cling to their valued status position. Moreover, for subordinates, the benefits of acting in a manner consistent with a masculine identity for themselves as well as for the success of the work group may exceed costs associated with deviating from status-based behavior whereas for superiors, costs of acting in a feminine way may exceed the benefits of doing so. Essentially, delegitimation inspires perceptions that status-based behaviors are ineffective (i.e. result in a negative evaluation), that the status order is uncertain, and that, for subordinates, acting in status-inconsistent ways may ensure task success. Thus, although delegitimation increases the opportunities for identity-based behavior and decreases the costs of such behavior for both the superior and subordinates, it is likely that subordinates are more likely to express masculine identities than superiors are likely to invoke feminine identities (Johnson et al., 2001).

The above discussion of the effects of legitimacy on the likelihood of enacting status-based or identity-based behaviors provides the basis for the following predictions:

Prediction 2. Given inconsistency between members' status and identity, the likelihood of members' enactment of their status position will increase under conditions of legitimation and decrease under conditions of delegitimation.

Prediction 3. Given inconsistency between members' status and identity, the likelihood of members' enactment of their identity will increase under conditions of delegitimation and decrease under conditions of legitimation.

These predictions could be tested in several ways. We could examine whether legitimated superiors with feminine gender identities are more likely to act based on their status position than their gender identity (e.g. be more directive), compared to delegitimated superiors with feminine gender identities. Also, we could see whether subordinates with masculine identities with legitimated superiors are more likely to act based on their status position (e.g. be more deferential), than similar subordinates with delegitimated superiors. We could also test whether superiors with feminine gender identities will engage in more deferential behaviors than superiors with masculine gender identities in delegitimated than legitimated conditions. Or will subordinates with masculine gender identities be more directive, participate more and be more influential than subordinates with feminine identities in delegitimated than legitimated conditions? Finally, we could see if, under conditions of delegitimation, subordinates with masculine identities are more likely to act based on their identities than are superiors with feminine identities.

Other status characteristics and identities are also likely to affect behavior in similar ways. For example, group members with high seniority and low control identity are more likely to act based on their status position than their identity when their seniority status is legitimated. Likewise, legitimation of the seniority status is likely to lead group members with low seniority and high control identity to more likely act upon their status position than their identity. In contrast, delegitimation of seniority is likely to increase behavioral expressions of control identity.

CONCLUSION

In this paper, I show how a consideration of legitimacy processes helps us tease out two puzzles found in the status literature: (1) under what conditions might the contrast between the sex composition of a work group and the sex composition of an organization's authority structure trigger the salience of gender status?; and (2) under what conditions will status position compared to identity be more likely to stimulate behavior, and vice versa?

In addressing the first puzzle, and modifying Ridgeway's extension of SCT, I argue that the contrast between the sex composition of the authority structure and sex composition of a work group will make gender status salient when an evaluation from an external authority figure creates some inconsistency and uncertainty in the current status structure of the group. I show how the delegitimation of a superior is one such process that produces this inconsistency and uncertainty. As a result of delegitimation, women superiors in male-dominated organizations who are delegitimated are more likely to face a disadvantage in interaction with their subordinates than their counterparts in female-run organizations (Johnson & Lupo, 2000). Empirical tests are underway to test the implications of our uncertainty/contrast argument. Future research should examine under what conditions the social composition of an organization's authority structure may trigger the salience of other status characteristics besides gender. For example, we know from Jackson et al.'s (1995) study that the racial composition of the organization affects minority perceptions of competence and well-being.

To address the second puzzle, I show how the legitimacy of the superior is a key factor affecting the expression of identity-based behavior of superiors and subordinates in group interaction. Specifically, the legitimation of the superior and the status order reduce the likelihood that group members will pursue status-inconsistent, identity behaviors. Delegitimation, however, increases opportunities for acting in identity consistent ways and reduces the costs for doing so, thus enhancing the probability of identity-based behaviors, especially among subordinates (Johnson et al., 2001).

Empirical studies testing the predictions are underway to complement this theoretical work on status and identity behaviors in task groups. Although both status and identity processes are simultaneously created and maintained in interaction, the processes are not mutually exclusive. It is the underlying balance of opportunities and costs that inevitably determines behaviors of group members and the richness of social interaction more generally. To more clearly understand the impact of each, theory and research on these processes should focus on the conditions facilitating or attenuating the likelihood that identity and/or status will most likely influence actors behaviors. For example, in addition to legitimacy, the distribution of power in a group may affect the opportunity for identity-based behaviors in groups. Power dependence theory (Emerson, 1962, 1972) argues that exchange dynamics in structured role relationships (such as between superiors and subordinates) are affected by the power each actor holds in the relationship. Research suggests that actors use information about the value and the availability of outcomes to infer their own and other's power (Bacharach & Lawler, 1976, 1980; Ford & Johnson, 1998; Hegtvedt, 1988). Using this theory, we could examine how the distribution of power in a group may also affect the opportunities and costs for identity-based behavior. For example, higher power subordinates may engage in more identity-based behavior than lower power subordinates.

It is my colleagues' and my hope that analyses presented in this paper that consider how legitimacy processes may affect interaction in work groups within organizations provide important insight into the dynamics of work situations, especially those in which minority and female authorities strive to ward off the threat of delegitimation.

NOTES

1. Several researchers argue that this contradiction is an artifact of Bales' IPA coding scheme (Aries, 1996; Bales, 1950, 1972; Carli, 1991). Studies finding gender differences in task behavior classified as socioemotional all speech acts that contain any social

element. For example, an opinion (a task behavior) accompanied by a compliment was coded as socioemotional behavior. Studies that find no gender differences in task behavior coded this example as both a task behavior and a socioemotional behavior (Ridgeway & Smith-Lovin, 1999).

2. In addition, research in informal groups suggests several key consequences of the legitimation of the status order. First, the extent to which group members perceive positions in a status order as legitimate affects the types of behaviors in which high status members may successfully engage (Ridgeway, 1982). High status members in legitimated structures engage more effectively in directive and domineering behaviors than those in less legitimated structures (Ridgeway et al., 1994). Thus, legitimacy is critical for atypical leaders such as women or minorities to successfully engage in directive, leader-like behaviors (Erickson & Wiley, 1976; Fennell et al., 1978). In addition, legitimacy enhances individuals' perceptions that the high-ranking member is the right and proper person for the leadership position in their group. Lower status actors are less likely to challenge a high-ranking actor's right to task activity in legitimated structures compared to structures that lack legitimacy (Meeker & Weitzell-O'Neill, 1977).

3. Zelditch and Walker's (1984) and Walker and Zelditch's (1993) formulation of legitimacy in formal groups focuses on the explicit support of others to indicate legitimacy. Like Ridgeway and Berger, they assume that legitimacy is ". . . the process by which patterns of social action acquire a normative character" (Ridgeway & Walker, 1995, p. 282). In their theory actions, actors, positions, and systems of positions are all possible objects of legitimation in formal status orders in organizations (Walker & Zelditch, 1993). To the extent that a behavior is legitimate or valid, individuals are likely to feel obliged to act in a manner consistent with the rules – the norms – governing that behavior even if they personally disagree with them. Focusing on formal orders, Zelditch and Walker emphasize the collective nature of legitimacy, examining its sources in the support of superiors and/or subordinates within an organizational hierarchy. They argue that collective sources of support (i.e. authorization and endorsement) are more powerful in producing compliance than propriety (individual-level beliefs). When an entity is strongly authorized and endorsed, individuals are more likely to comply because they anticipate formal sanctions from superiors or informal sanctions from peers. Several studies provide evidence for this claim (Thomas et al., 1986; Walker et al., 1986). Even if a subordinate privately disagrees with a superior's action, he or she is more likely to comply with that action if the superior is authorized and endorsed (Evan & Zelditch, 1961; Johnson & Ford, 1996; Kanter, 1977; Ridgeway, 1989).

4. I thank Cecilia Ridgeway for ideas on the distinction between status position and personally embraced self identities.

5. The conditions under which a status becomes an identity are beyond the scope of this paper. Such conditions may be connected to the salience and commitment of an individual to a particular status (see Burke & Reitzes, 1991).

6. In addition to the inconsistency of the scope conditions with SCT, Stets and Burke also contend that a status process is operating in the married couples' interviews. Low status partners engage in negative behaviors in an attempt to counter others' low evaluations of them to maintain a positive view of themselves.

7. We are grateful to a colleague, who upon hearing a discussion of these ideas, pointed out that our argument applies to a narrow range of identities' only those that could be consistent or inconsistent with status.

REFERENCES

Anderson, L. R., & Blanchard, P. N. (1982). Sex differences in task and socio-emotional behavior. *Basic and Applied Social Psychology, 3*, 109–139.

Aries, E. (1996). *Men and women in interaction: Reconsidering the differences.* New York: Oxford University Press.

Bacharach, S. B., & Lawler, E. J. (1976). The perception of power. *Social Forces, 55*, 123–134.

Bacharach, S. B., & Lawler, E. J. (1980). *Power and politics in organizations: The social psychology of conflict, coalitions, and bargaining.* San Francisco: Jossey-Bass.

Bacharach, S. B., & Lawler, E. J. (1981). *Bargaining: Power, tactics and outcomes.* San Francisco: Jossey-Bass.

Bales, R. F. (1950). *Interaction process analysis: A method of small groups.* Cambridge, MA: Addison Wesley.

Bales, R. F. (1972). *Personality and interpersonal behavior.* New York: Holt, Rinehart and Winston.

Balkwell, J. W., & Berger, J. (1996). Gender, status, and behavior in task situations. *Social Psychology Quarterly, 59*, 273–283.

Berger, J. M., Fisek, H. F., Norman, R. Z. (1989). The evolution of status expectations: A theoretical extension. In: J. Berger & M. Zelditch, Jr. (Eds), *Sociological Theories in Progress: New Formulations* (pp. 100–130). San Francisco: Jossey-Bass.

Berger, J. M., Fisek, H. F., Norman, R. Z., & Zelditch, M., Jr. (1966). Status characteristics and expectation states. In: J. Berger, M. Zelditch, Jr. & B. Anderson (Eds), *Sociological Theories in Progress* (Vol. 1, pp. 47–73). Boston: Houghton Mifflin.

Berger, J., Fisek, M. H., Norman, R. Z., & Zelditch, M., Jr. (1977). *Status characteristics and social interaction: An expectation states approach.* New York: Elsevier.

Berger, J., Fisek, M. H., Ridgeway, C. L., & Norman, R. (1998). The legitimation and delegitimation of power and prestige orders. *American Sociological Review, 63*, 379–405.

Berger, J., Rosenholtz, S., & Zelditch, M., Jr. (1980). Status organizing processes. *Annual Review of Sociology, 6*, 479–508.

Berger, J., Wagner, D. G., & Zelditch, M., Jr. (1985). Expectation states theory: Review and assessment. In: J. Berger & M. Zelditch, Jr. (Eds), *Status, Rewards, and Influence: How Expectations Organize Behavior.* San Francisco: Jossey-Bass.

Berger, J., & Zelditch, M., Jr. (1998). *Status, power, and legitimacy.* London: Transaction.

Burke, P. J. (1991). Identity processes and social stress. *American Sociological Review, 56*, 836–849.

Burke, P. J., & Reitzes, D. C. (1991). An identity theory approach to commitment. *Social Psychology Quarterly, 54*, 280–286.

Burt, R. S. (1992). *Structural holes.* Cambridge, MA: Harvard University Press.

Carli, L. (1989). Gender differences in interaction style and influence. *Journal of Personality and Social Psychology, 56*, 565–576.

Carli, L. (1990). Gender, language, and influence. *Journal of Personality and Social Psychology, 59*, 556–941.

Carli, L. (1991). Gender, status, and influence. In: E. J. Lawler, B. Markovsky, C. L. Ridgeway & H. Walker (Eds), *Advances in Group Processes* (Vol. 8, pp. 89–113). Greenwich, CT: JAI Press.

Cohen, B. P., & Zhou, X. (1991). Status processes in enduring work groups. *American Sociological Review, 56*, 179–188.

Cohen, L. E., Broschak, J. P., & Haverman, H. A. (1999). And then there were more? The effect of organizational sex composition on hiring and promotion. *American Sociological Review, 63*, 711–727.

Dovidio, J. F., Brown, C. E., Heltman, K., Ellyson, S. L., & Keating, C. F. (1988). Power displays between women and men in discussions of gender-linked tasks: A mutichannel study. *Journal of Personality and Social Psychology, 55,* 580–587.

Drass, K. A. (1986). The effect of gender identity on conversation. *Social Psychology Quarterly, 49,* 294–301.

Emerson, R. M. (1962). Power dependence relations. *American Sociological Review, 27,* 31–40.

Emerson, R. M. (1972). Exchange theory, Part II: Exchange relations, exchange networks, and groups as exchange systems. In: J. Berger, M. Zelditch, Jr. & B. Anderson (Eds), *Sociological Theories in Progress* (pp. 58–87). Boston: Houghton Mifflin.

Erickson, A., & Wiley, M. G. (1976). Sex composition and leadership in small groups. *Sociometry, 39,* 183–194.

Evan, W., & Zelditch, M., Jr. (1961). A laboratory experiment on bureaucratic authority. *American Sociological Review, 26,* 883–893.

Fennell, M. L., Barchas, P. R., Cohen, E. G., McMahon, A. M., & Hildebrand, P. (1978). Alternative perspective on sex differences in organizational settings: The process of legitimation. *Sex Roles, 4,* 589–604.

Foschi, M., & Lapointe, V. (2002). On conditional hypotheses and gender as a status characteristic. *Social Psychology Quarterly, 65,* 146–162.

Ford, R., & Johnson, C. (1998). The perception of power: Dependence and legitimacy in conflict. *Social Psychology Quarterly, 61,* 16–32.

Gecas, V., & Burke, P. J. (1995). Self and identity. In: K. S. Cook, G. A. Fine & J. S. House (Eds), *Sociological Perspectives on Social Psychology* (pp. 41–67). Boston: Allyn and Bacon.

Hegtvedt, K. A. (1988). Social determinants of perception: Power, equity and status effects in an exchange situation. *Social Psychology Quarterly, 51,* 141–153.

Hegtvedt, K. A., & Johnson, C. (2000). Justice beyond the individual: A future with legitimation. *Social Psychology Quarterly, 63,* 298–311.

Ibarra, H. (1995). Paving an alternative route: Gender differences in managerial networks. *Social Psychology Quarterly, 60,* 91–102.

Ibarra, H. (1997). Race, opportunity, and diversity of social circles in managerial networks. *Academy of Management Journal, 38,* 673–703.

Jackson, P. B., Thoits, P. A., & Taylor, H. F. (1995). Composition of the workplace and psychological well-being: The effects of tokenism on America's black elite. *Social Forces, 74,* 543–557.

Johnson, C., Clay-Warner, J., & Funk, S. (1996). Effects of authority structures and gender on interaction in same-sex task groups. *Social Psychology Quarterly, 59,* 211–236.

Johnson, C., & Ford, R. (1996). Dependence power, legitimacy, and tactical choice. *Social Psychology Quarterly, 59,* 126–139.

Johnson, C., Ford, R., & Kaufman, J. (2000). Emotional reactions to conflict; do dependence and legitimacy matter? *Social Forces, 79,* 107–137.

Johnson, C., Funk, S., & Clay-Warner, J. (1998). Organizational contexts and conversation patterns. *Social Psychology Quarterly, 61,* 361–371.

Johnson, C., & Lupo, K. (2000). Legitimation and delegitimation in formal power and prestige orders (unpublished manuscript).

Johnson, C., Lupo, K., & Hegtvedt, K. A. (2001). Status and identity-based behaviors: What legitimacy got to do with their expression? (unpublished manuscript).

Kanter, R. (1977). *Men and women of the corporation.* New York, NY: Basic Books.

Karakowsky, L., & Siegel, J. P. (1999). The effects of proportional representation and gender orientation of the task on emergent leadership behavior in mixed-gender work groups. *Journal of Applied Psychology, 84,* 620–631.

Korabik, K. (1982). Sex-role orientation and leadership style. *International Journal of Women's Studies*, 5, 329–337.

Mead, G. H. (1934). *Mind, self, and society*. Chicago: University of Chicago Press.

Meeker, B. J., & Weitzell-O'Neill, P. A. (1977). Sex roles and interpersonal behavior in task oriented groups. *American Sociological Review*, 42, 91–105.

Piliavin, J. A., & Martin, R. R. (1978). The effects of the sex composition of groups on styles of social interaction. *Sex Roles*, 4, 281–296.

Reskin, B. F. (1993). Sex segregation in the workplace. *Annual Review of Sociology*, 19, 241–270.

Ridgeway, C. L. (1982). Status in groups: The importance of motivation. *American Sociological Review*, 47, 76–88.

Ridgeway, C. L. (1988). Gender differences in task groups: A status and legitimacy account. In: M. Webster, Jr. & M. Foschi (Eds), *Status Generalization: New Theory and Research* (pp. 188–206). Stanford: Stanford University Press.

Ridgeway, C. L. (1989). Understanding legitimation in informal status orders. In: J. Berger, M. Zelditch, Jr. & B. Anderson (Eds), *Sociological Theories in Progress: New Formulations* (pp. 131–159). London: Sage.

Ridgeway, C. L. (1997). Interaction and the conservation of gender inequality: Considering employment. *American Sociological Review*, 62, 218–235.

Ridgeway, C. L., & Berger, J. (1986). Expectations, legitimation and dominance in task groups. *American Sociological Review*, 51, 603–617.

Ridgeway, C.L., & Diekema, D. (1992). Are gender differences status differences? In: C. L. Ridgeway (Ed.), *Gender, Interaction, and Inequality*. New York: Springer-Verlag.

Ridgeway, C. L., Diekema, D., & Johnson, C. (1995). Legitimacy, compliance, and gender in peer groups. *Social Psychology Quarterly*, 58, 298–311.

Ridgeway, C. L., & Johnson, C. (1990). What is the relationship between socioemotional behavior and status in task groups? *American Journal of Sociology*, 95, 1189–1212.

Ridgeway, C. L., Johnson, C., & Diekema, D. (1994). External status, legitimacy, and compliance in male and female work groups. *Social Forces*, 72, 1051–1077.

Ridgeway, C.L., & Smith-Lovin, L. (1999). Gender and interaction. In: J. S. Chafetz (Ed.), *Handbook of the Sociology of Gender* (pp. 247–274). New York: Kluwer.

Ridgeway, C. L., & Walker, H. A. (1995). Status structures. In: K. S. Cook, G. Allen Fine & J. S. House (Eds), *Sociological Perspectives on Social Psychology* (pp. 281–310). Boston: Allyn and Bacon.

Seibert, S., & Gruenfeld, L. (1992). Masculinity, femininity, and behavior in groups. *Group Research*, 23, 95–112.

Shelly, R. K., & Munroe, P. T. (1999). Do women engage in less task behavior than men? *Sociological Perspectives*, 42, 746–762.

Spreitzer, G. M. (1996). Social structural characteristics of psychological empowerment. *Academy of Management Journal*, 39, 483–504.

Stets, J. E. (1995). Role identities and person identities: Gender identity, mastery identity, and controlling one's partner. *Sociological Perspectives*, 38, 129–150.

Stets, J. E. (1997). Status and identity in marital interaction. *Social Psychology Quarterly*, 185–217.

Stets, J. E., & Burke, P. J. (1994). Inconsistent self-views in the control-identity model. *Social Science Research*, 23, 236–262.

Stets, J. E., & Burke, P. J. (1996). Gender, control, and interaction. *Social Psychology Quarterly*, 59, 193–220.

Stryker, S. (1968). Identity salience and role performance: The relevance of symbolic interaction theory for family research. *Journal of Marriage and the Family*, 30, 558–564.

Stryker, S. (1980). *Symbolic interactionism: A social structural version.* Menlo Park: Benjamin/ Cummings.

Stryker, S. (1989). Further developments in identity theory: Singularity versus multiplicity of self. In: J. Berger, M. Zelditch, Jr. & B. Anderson (Eds), *Sociological Theories in Progress: New Formulations* (pp. 35–37). London: Sage.

Stryker, S., & Burke, P. J. (2000). The past, present, and future of an identity theory. *Social Psychology Quarterly, 63,* 284–297.

Stryker, S., & Serpe, R. T. (1982). Commitment, identity salience, and role behavior. In: W. Ickes & E. Knowles (Eds), *Personality, Roles, and Social Behavior* (pp. 199–218). New York: Springer-Verlag.

Swann, W. B., Pelham, B. W., & Krull, D. S. (1989). Agreeable fancy or disagreeable truth? Reconciling self-enhancement and self-verification. *Journal of Personality and Social Psychology, 52,* 881–889.

Thomas, G. M., Walker, H. A., & Zelditch, M., Jr. (1986). Legitimacy and collective action. *Social Forces, 65,* 378–404.

Wagner, D. G. (1988). Status violations: Toward an expectations status theory of the social control of status deviance. In: M. Webster, Jr. & M. Foschi (Eds), *Status Generalizations: New Theory and Practice* (pp. 110–122). Stanford, CA: Stanford University Press.

Wagner, D. G., & Berger, J. (1993). Status characteristics theory: The growth of a program. In: J. Berger & M. Zelditch, Jr. (Eds), *Theoretical Research Programs: Studies in the Growth of a Theory* (pp. 23–63). Stanford, CA: Stanford University Press.

Wagner, D. G., & Berger, J. (1997). Gender and interpersonal task behaviors: Status expectation accounts. *Sociological Perspectives, 40,* 1–32.

Walker, H. A., Thomas, G. M., & Zelditch, M., Jr. (1986). Legitimation, endorsement, and stability. *Social Forces, 64,* 620–643.

Walker, H. A., & Zelditch, M., Jr. (1993). Power, legitimacy, and the stability of authority: A theoretical research program. In: J. Berger & M. Zelditch, Jr. (Eds), *Theoretical Research Programs: Studies in the Growth of Theory* (pp. 364–381). Stanford, CA: Stanford University Press.

Webster, M., Jr., & Foschi, M. (1988). Status generalizations: New theory and practice. In: M. Webster, Jr. & M. Foschi (Eds). Stanford, CA: Stanford University Press.

Willer, D., Lovaglia, M. J., & Markovsky, B. (1997). Power and influence: A theoretical bridge. *Social Forces, 76,* 571–603.

Wood, W., & Karten, S. (1986). Sex differences in interaction style as a product of perceived sex differences in competence. *Journal of Personality and Social Psychology, 50,* 341–347.

Zelditch, M., Jr., & Floyd, A. S. (1998). Consensus, dissensus, and justification. In: J. Berger & M. Zelditch, Jr. (Eds), *Status, Power, and Legitimacy: Strategies and Theories* (pp. 339–368). New Brunswick, NJ: Transaction.

Zelditch, M., Jr., & Walker, H. A. (1984). Legitimacy and the stability of authority. *Advances in Group Processes, 1,* 1–27.

Zeditch, M., Jr., & Walker, H. A. (2000). The normative regulation of power. *Advances in Group Processes, 17,* 155–178.